W9-BJS-052

Kennedy and Diefenbaker

By the Same Author:

History on the Run, 1984
Times to Remember, 1986
Prime Time at Ten, 1987

Kennedy and Diefenbaker

Fear and Loathing
Across the Undefended Border

Knowlton Nash

Copyright © 1990 by Knowlton Nash

All rights reserved. The use of any part of this publication reproduced,
transmitted in any form or by any means, electronic, mechanical,
photocopying, recording, or otherwise, or stored in a retrieval system,
without the prior written consent of the publisher – or, in case of
photocopying or other reprographic copying, a licence from Canadian
Reprography Collective – is an infringement of the copyright law.

Canadian Cataloguing in Publication Data

Nash, Knowlton
Kennedy and Diefenbaker

Includes bibliographical references.
ISBN 0-7710-6705-4

1. Diefenbaker, John G., 1895-1979. 2. Kennedy, John F. (John
Fitzgerald), 1917-1963. 3. Canada – Foreign relations – United States. 4.
United States – Foreign relations – Canada. 5. Canada –Foreign relations –
1945 – . 6. United States – Foreign relations – 1961-1963. 7. Canada –
Politics and government – 1957-1963. 8. United States – Politics and
government – 1961-1963. I. Title.

FC615.N3 1990   327.71073   C90-094314-9
F1034.2.N3 1990

McClelland & Stewart Inc.
The Canadian Publishers
481 University Avenue
Toronto, Ontario
M5G 2E9

Printed and bound in Canada

Contents

LIBRARY OF CBS

To Fred and Francesca Parker,
who give me joy and hope and pride.

LIBRARY OF CBS

Foreword

In more than four decades of journalism, I have never known two more fascinating political leaders than John Kennedy and John Diefenbaker. Privately, Kennedy was exciting, enriching, and demanding, with a sardonic, often self-mocking wit. You came away from a conversation with him with a sense of fun and of being intellectually challenged and stretched. Privately, Diefenbaker was living history, an entrée to the past, filled with old political stories richly embroidered and lovingly told. You came away from a conversation with him with a vivid sense of Canada's political heroes and vagabonds, triumphs and scandals. Both loved gossip and wanted to hear about the private lives of journalists and fellow politicians. In private conversations with both of them, I always had a sense that Kennedy's thrusting competitiveness was rooted in fear of failure and Diefenbaker's indecisive dithering and resentments were born of fear of rejection.

As a journalist working in Washington from 1951 to 1969, I knew both men. I talked with John Kennedy often before his presidency and visited with John Diefenbaker in Ottawa. I followed both of them through tens of thousands of miles of electioneering, mainstreeting with Diefenbaker from Prince Albert, Saskatchewan, to Sydney, Nova Scotia, and buckling my seat belt on the *Caroline*, Kennedy's family Convair airplane, as we flew the campaign trails from Jacksonville, Florida, to Seattle, Washington.

Although I was an ardent admirer of Kennedy from the days

when I covered him – we talked almost daily at hearings of the Senate Labor Rackets Committee or in his office, and several times at his home during the late 1950s – I was always taken aback at his lack of knowledge and even interest in things Canadian. When I asked him during the 1960 campaign what he thought of Canada and Canadians, he offered, "They're nice." At the same time, I was equally startled by Diefenbaker's private, obsessive dislike of Americans in general and John Kennedy in particular. Perhaps Diefenbaker expressed those sentiments to me more often than to most others because of my base in the U.S. capital. When I would come up from Washington every few months and see him, often in the privacy of his little office behind the Speaker in the House of Commons or sometimes at a suite in the Marlborough Hotel in Prince Albert, he would want to hear behind-the-scenes stories of the Kennedys and then launch into his own wicked mimicry of Kennedy.

As a journalist, I've been lucky in knowing most of the players in the Kennedy–Diefenbaker saga: politicians, diplomats, cronies, and senior advisers, some as friends, some as acquaintances, and some as news sources. Many an off-the-record lunch, dinner, or evening was spent with them at the time, listening to their stories of mutual contempt between the president and the prime minister. I had been well aware of Diefenbaker's dislike of Kennedy, but not until I went back to the Americans with specific, probing questions for this book did I realize the intensity and depth of the American hostility towards John Diefenbaker. With the passing years, the caution they had displayed earlier had fallen away to reveal a much deeper and more damaging wound than I had realized at the time. And in talking with old colleagues, adversaries, and supporters of Diefenbaker, I now realize how the "Chief" basically feared Kennedy, as Kennedy loathed him.

In a sense it was a failure of mine as a journalist to recognize the depth of the antipathy, but I simply didn't pick up on the signs more than a quarter-century ago. Perhaps I was too preoccupied with the incandescent Kennedy presidency, so exhilarating, bursting with life and commitment and pure joy – reminiscent, in a way, of those first halcyon years of the United

Nations, when we felt we could change the world, heal the sick, stop war, wipe out poverty, and end illiteracy.

As a young reporter, I was lucky not only to spend some time with both Diefenbaker and Kennedy, but also to share an office in Washington at one point with a couple of journalistic giants: James M. Minifie, the quintessential CBC foreign correspondent, who became a friend and mentor; and Max Freedman, who became the most influential Washington journalist of the Kennedy years, a Winnipegger reporting for the Manchester *Guardian* and the Winnipeg *Free Press*. I knew Max was a confidant of John Kennedy, but I had no idea of the important role he was playing in shaping Kennedy's attitude towards John Diefenbaker and as a middleman between Kennedy and Mike Pearson. He would have liked to have been minister of external affairs in a Pearson government, but they couldn't work it out.

After nearly fifty years as a bachelor, Max married a millionaire widow in 1962. A few years later, he suffered a heart attack and gave up active journalism, and his marriage ended in divorce. Max, who knew everything about power and nothing about money, had no financial resources of his own and went back to Winnipeg, receiving about fifteen thousand dollars a year as an allowance from his ex-wife. He never wrote again and spent his last years in a fourteen-dollar-a-night Fort Garry hotel room, seldom going out except to see his mother or get a haircut. He died there at age sixty-five in 1980.

There are so many people I should thank for their help and encouragement. My particular gratitude, for his patience and expertise, goes to Basil Robinson, former under-secretary of state for external affairs, whose book *Diefenbaker's World: A Populist in Foreign Affairs* is the richest chronicle of Diefenbaker's international forays. Not only as a rewarding source – both when we were in Washington together, and during my research for this book – but also as a reader of the manuscript, he has given me invaluable advice and guidance. So, too, am I grateful for the time given to me so generously and so often by Bunny Pound, John Diefenbaker's secretary for three decades, who revered the "Chief" but was aware of his warts. Also indispensable were Rufus Smith and Willis Armstrong, the U.S. State Department officials on the front line of the Kennedy–Diefenbaker battles. Former secretary of state Dean Rusk and his deputy, George Ball, gave generously of their time and knowledge, as did McGeorge Bundy, Ted Sorensen, Walt Rostow, and J.K. Galbraith, all of the Kennedy White House years. On the Canadian side, I am especially grateful for the time and information provided by Charles Ritchie, Douglas Harkness, Pierre Sévigny, Alvin Hamilton, Ellen Fairclough, Dalton Camp, David Walker, and Keith Davey, who searched their memories of those chaotic days in Canada–U.S. relations. There are numerous others who have been extraordinarily helpful in compiling this book, most of whom are noted in the sources. Historian Jack Granatstein steered me to valuable material, including oral histories he had recorded; and I am grateful, for the time they took in reading the manuscript and the suggestions they provided, to my friend and colleague Peter Mansbridge and my friend Julius Mallin.

The archivists at the Kennedy Library in Boston, the Diefenbaker Library in Saskatoon, the National Archives in Ottawa, the Province of Manitoba Archives, York University in Toronto, and Princeton University were also helpful in steering me through the records, diaries, letters, clippings, and oral histories of the period.

Special thanks must go to my patient and talented editor Barbara Czarnecki, whose skills in tightening, structuring, and clarifying turned a too-long tale into a more digestible story of the greatest president–prime minister feud in our history.

And finally, but foremost, my undying gratitude as well as love goes to my wife, Lorraine Thomson, who can now get back the use of our dining-room table, which has been piled high for two years with papers, notes, and books.

Prologue

Ottawa, March 1962
"He's a hothead. He's a fool – too young, too brash, too inexperienced, and a boastful son of a bitch!" John George Diefenbaker, prime minister of Canada, sputtered as we talked about President John Fitzgerald Kennedy in his hideaway office on Parliament Hill.

"Mark my words, he'll get us all in trouble with his arrogance and presumptions."

Washington, July 1967
"My brother really hated John Diefenbaker. He thought him a contemptible old fool," Robert Kennedy growled at me from the swimming pool of his Hickory Hill home in the Virginia countryside just outside Washington.

"In fact, you know, my brother really hated only two men in all his presidency. One was Sukarno [dictator of Indonesia], and the other was Diefenbaker."

"Hatred" was the word for the feud between John Kennedy and John Diefenbaker. Never before in Canada–U.S. history has there been such a poisonous and dangerous personality clash as between President Kennedy and Prime Minister Diefenbaker.

The aging, suspicious prairie populist and the youthful, quick-witted Boston sophisticate were headed for trouble from the moment they met. Their differences were irreconcilable, their clash inevitable.

Their roots fed on profoundly different soil. Kennedy was tomorrow's young hero; Diefenbaker was yesterday's old warrior. Kennedy was a man of the sea, staring into the infinity of the waves; Diefenbaker was a man of the prairies, his eyes scanning a horizon of wheat. Kennedy was rooted in hard realism, with a confidence bordering on arrogance; Diefenbaker was rooted in Canadian nationalism, with a fantasy life spilling into paranoia. In McLuhan terms, Kennedy was cool, Diefenbaker was hot.

"Kennedy was everything Diefenbaker wasn't," long-time Diefenbaker aide Tommy Van Dusen says. "He was Sir Galahad on a white horse; rich, young, a silver spoon in his mouth. Diefenbaker always had an irresistible urge to put the guy in his place."

"Diefenbaker felt Kennedy was a spoiled boy to the manner born," says Diefenbaker's close friend David Walker. "He felt Kennedy high-hatted him, and the Chief was very sensitive on how people treated him."

Diefenbaker thought Kennedy was "pathologically ignorant" about Canada. It was true that JFK knew practically nothing about Canada and Canada–U.S. relations when he moved into the White House. Like most Americans, he thought Canadians were agreeable souls, "just like us." He may have shared Al Capone's awareness of Canada; the infamous gangster reportedly said, "I don't even know what street Canada is on." In many ways, Kennedy felt Canada was a child nation, sometimes to be chided and sometimes to be patted on the head, but who would agree, willingly or not, that Father knows best. Kennedy's under-secretary of state, George Ball, says, "For Kennedy, Canada was just a place of nice people where you went to hunt and fish."

But Kennedy's attitude towards the prime minister of these "nice people" was less benign.

"Kennedy regarded Diefenbaker as an old Tory – a mossback, a crusty political crustacean," says Kennedy friend and pollster Lou Harris.

Kennedy told friends Diefenbaker was a grandstanding, insincere, "sanctimonious, platitudinous old bore." In time, he came to think the Canadian prime minister was a liar, a blackmailer, and a betrayer.

Kennedy's stinging condemnation of Diefenbaker was echoed throughout the Kennedy administration. "He was an inferior form of politician who carried his piety too far," recalls George Ball. "He was a sanctimonious old bugger."

"He was unpolished, unsophisticated, unhelpful, and un-wanted," says economist John Kenneth Galbraith, an old friend of Kennedy and one of his ambassadors.

A critical difference between the two that would play a role in the 823 days of their feud was that Kennedy, the realist masquerading as a romantic, relished the decision-making of government but had been an indifferent performer in the U.S. Congress, while Diefenbaker, the messianic nationalist, revelled and triumphed in parliamentary debate but was weak and indecisive in governing.

Aside from their personal enmity, there were basic policy clashes between the two men. Kennedy and his government felt Diefenbaker too frequently gave succour to American enemies in Cuba, China, and the Soviet Union, refused to fulfil Canada's military obligations to NATO and NORAD, pinched pennies on foreign aid, and encouraged anti-Americanism in Canada.

"The Canadian Prime Minister . . . embraced anti-Ameri-canism both as a personal view and as a political tactic," says Kennedy's closest associate, Ted Sorensen.

Diefenbaker was indeed anti-American to the tips of his toes; he echoed the ancestral Canadian voices of fear and resentment of the United States. In public, he always denied being anti-American. "I am not anti-American," he would say repeatedly in speeches and interviews. "I am pro-Canadian. . . . A Cana-dian I was born. A Canadian I shall die." But privately, anti-Americanism burst from his soul, and often in the heat of an election campaign or in the privacy of his office, he would attack the Americans for being slow to come into the two world wars. "When some nations," he said in one speech, "start pointing out to us what we should do, let me tell you this: Canada was in both wars a long time before some other nations."

Diefenbaker's anti-Americanism slipped out in public even before he won the prime ministership when he denounced investment in Canada by American "pirates"; in 1956 he warned, "If the St. Laurent Government is re-elected, Canada will become a virtual forty-ninth state of the American Union."

Even though he established a good personal relationship with President Dwight Eisenhower, one of Diefenbaker's first acts as prime minister was to travel to the United States and attack the flow of American money into Canada, which he felt was Yankee financial imperialism threatening Canadian economic independence.

"You've got to stand up to those Americans," Diefenbaker would say privately. He told political aide Jim Johnston, "You can't stand up for Canada with a banana as a backbone."

"He never did care for Americans," says David Walker. "He looked on them as cocky bastards, inferior to the British and first-class Canadians, and far too opinionated, and he thought, 'T' hell with you bastards.' For Diefenbaker, Kennedy was the personification of all that."

Diefenbaker was saturated with a sense of Canadian moral superiority that drove American officials nuts and bewildered Kennedy. But the American president simply couldn't be bothered trying to understand the personal and nationalist sensitivities that obsessed John Diefenbaker. He figured it just wasn't worth it.

"Kennedy gave up on Diefenbaker," says McGeorge Bundy, who was Kennedy's national security adviser, the top White House foreign policy official. "He never gave up on anybody else – even de Gaulle, who gave us a lot of trouble. But he did on Diefenbaker."

Their feud became a fatal cancer on the Diefenbaker government, while for Kennedy it was a festering sore, irritating and infuriating.

The Canadian prime minister became convinced Kennedy was plotting to overthrow his government "like a banana republic"; Kennedy arranged a coup d'état, he charged, to push him out of his prime ministerial office. "He was out to destroy me!" Diefenbaker thundered against Kennedy after his defeat by Liberal leader Lester Pearson in the 1963 election. "That was his objective. One hundred per cent."

Diefenbaker claimed even in the heat of his battles with Kennedy that "I am one who forgives," a sentiment his Washington enemies and Ottawa adversaries would find unimaginably improbable since, in fact, he shared Kennedy's more brutally realistic political motto: "Never forgive; never forget."

Kennedy also followed another old Boston Irish political guideline: "Don't get mad; get even." In his legendary feud with Diefenbaker, the Canadian prime minister got mad, but Kennedy got even.

Their clash finally erupted in the most flagrant direct interference in Canadian politics ever undertaken by the Americans or, for that matter, by anyone else. A State Department press release accused Diefenbaker of being a liar, brutally assaulted the prime minister for his indecision about accepting U.S. nuclear warheads for Canada's military, and denounced him for misrepresenting U.S. policies.

Diefenbaker delightedly seized the accusation as final proof of Kennedy's plot to get rid of him and install the man Washington wanted, Mike Pearson, whom Washington admired as one of the reliable "old boys" of the rarefied world of high-level Allied diplomacy. Pearson knew baseball, knew the Washington pros, and had a style Kennedy liked.

"In a way, Diefenbaker was right, for it was true that we preferred Mike Pearson," Kennedy's secretary of state, Dean Rusk, comments. Kennedy sought to help Pearson in every way he could, so much so that both Pearson and Kennedy's own State Department were embarrassed and tried to stop him. "He was lucky he didn't get caught," says Willis Armstrong, a senior State Department official at the time. "It was very unadroit."

It all ended in triumph for Kennedy, however, with the fall of the Diefenbaker government a few days after the press release and its defeat at the polls in the ensuing April 1963 election. If the defeat of the Conservatives was not a deliberate coup d'état, as Diefenbaker maintained, it was at least an accidental one, for which the State Department press release provided the catalyst. Washington did not officially intend to get rid of Diefenbaker, but it certainly intended to publicly humiliate and wound him.

The Kennedy–Diefenbaker rhetorical firefight could have been simply a fascinating spectacle of human confrontation at the highest level, but since one man was president and the other prime minister, the repercussions of their animosity spread across the whole canvas of politics, officialdom, and bureaucracy. In some cases, normal Canada–U.S. relations simply collapsed under the heat in spite of valiant, quiet efforts by the civil service mandarins to keep things going. "A personality clash like this is a problem because we have so much business with each other," says Dean Rusk. "We had so many things to work out with Canada."

Kennedy was a lover of history, but he seemed utterly unaware of the centuries-old American yearning to annex Canada. In sharp contrast, not only did John Diefenbaker have soul-deep suspicions of the Americans and distaste for what he considered their blow-hard style, but his nationalistic attitudes were shaped by the centuries of American effort to make Canada part of the United States. His supreme hero was Sir John A. Macdonald, whose mantle Diefenbaker assumed. He became "Captain Canada," defending the nation against the rapacious Americans. He was David against Kennedy's Goliath.

But Diefenbaker could not put an end to the American hunger for Canadian territory, which began growing almost from the first significant European settlements on this continent, in Virginia in 1607 and in Quebec a year later. Down through almost four hundred years there have been skirmishes, even wars, between those sharing North America, fear and loathing, suspicion and contempt, all of which John Diefenbaker inhaled but Kennedy ignored. To understand the Kennedy-Diefenbaker feud, we must understand that history.

Chapter One

DRUMS ALONG THE BORDER

We were the original anti-Americans.

We feared them; we resented them; we disliked them. Much later we envied them, and then we began to like them.

Until well into this century, the notion that peace and harmony reigned along our 3,966.8 miles of undefended border (5,516.6 when Alaska is added in), so often eulogized by luncheon club speakers on both sides of the Forty-ninth Parallel, was in fact hogwash. The rude realities of our earlier relationships are reflected in the military strategy that Canadian forces stood ready to deploy into the 1930s: its central focus was on how to fight off an American invasion.

John Kennedy would have laughed at it. His national security adviser, McGeorge Bundy, did when he heard of it recently. So, too, did Kennedy's secretary of state, Dean Rusk, who chuckled, "Oh, good heavens!" But John Diefenbaker understood the history that prompted the Canadian army's two-hundred-page Defence Scheme No. 1.

"The main objective of the United States Force would undoubtedly be Montreal and on to Ottawa," Defence Scheme No. 1 warned. "The next important objective of the United States would be the occupation of the Ontario Peninsula, including the cities of Hamilton and Toronto."

The Canadian military commanders were warned to "contend every inch of ground in retiring from Windsor and Sarnia towards Stratford. Further retirement will necessitate the evacuation of the Niagara Peninsula. . . . Further retirement if forced upon you, should be made as slowly as possible, covering Toronto which should be covered as long as possible." Montreal, the Canadian commanders were told, should also be defended as long as possible. "If the tide of war turned against us in Ontario and Quebec, and Montreal, Ottawa and Quebec were captured," they were warned, "the Maritime Area would be the only place where the Empire could land forces to retrieve the disaster."

The scheme warned, however, that the Americans would probably try to capture Saint John, New Brunswick, and take control of the Bay of Fundy.

The other objectives that the American forces were expected to move against were Winnipeg, Vancouver Island, and south-western British Columbia, including Vancouver and New West-minster. The scheme instructed that if Winnipeg fell, Canadian troops should retreat west and northwest into Saskatchewan and it added, "It is possible that the troops of British Columbia and Alberta may be forced back to the neighborhood of Edmonton."

But the Canadian army had an audacious counterplan to beat the Americans: "Pacific Command. A limited offensive into the State of Washington, Oregon, Idaho and Montana with the object of capturing and holding Spokane and Seattle in Washington, Portland in Oregon, Great Falls, Helena and Butte in Montana. . . .

"Prairie Command . . . should converge toward Fargo in North Dakota . . . and then continue a general advance in the direction of Minneapolis and St. Paul. The occupation of Minneapolis and St. Paul would cut most of the lines leading to Duluth. . . .

"Great Lakes Command . . . will, generally speaking, remain on the defensive, but rapid and well-organized raids should be made across the Niagara Frontier, the St. Clair Frontier, the Detroit Frontier and the St. Mary's Frontier, with sufficient troops to establish bridgeheads. . . .

"Quebec Command . . . will take the offensive on both sides of the Adirondack Mountains with a view of converging . . . in the vicinity of Albany, N.Y. . . .

"Maritime Command . . . will make an offensive into the State of Maine. . . . "

These Canadian army directives of just sixty years ago were prepared by Colonel James Sutherland ("Buster") Brown, the determined-looking, moustached director of military operations and intelligence from 1920 to 1927. Brown was a distinguished soldier, outspoken and strongly anti-American, who believed it essential that Canada prepare to combat an American invasion. He was not some military rogue elephant, for his planning had the full support of his superior officers, including the chief of the general staff, Major-General H.C. Thacker, as well as the deputy chief of staff, General A.G.L. McNaughton, who had warned of the "consistently imperialistic [U.S. policy] aimed at the hegemony of the Americas." Lieutenant-Colonel H.D.G. Crerar, who would later become a commanding general in World War II, supported Buster Brown's planning to counter an American invasion and agreed that the situation was not hopeless. The deputy minister of defence was aware of the planning to counter a U.S. invasion, so it is hard to imagine that his minister was not also aware of Defence Scheme No. 1. Brown was supported, too, by a future Canadian minister of defence, George Pearkes, who was then on the general staff. "It was a fantastic, desperate plan, but it just might have worked," Pearkes said.

None of the senior officers thought war with the U.S. was imminent, but they thought it prudent to prepare for one. All Canadian military district commanders were given the orders Brown prepared, and he frequently wrote to them about preparations to repel the invading Americans. When some complained they didn't have enough maps, Brown told them to get maps of the U.S. from the Motor League. His military plan remained official military strategy of Canada until May 31, 1931.

Brown followed up his planning with several espionage trips into the United States, mapping bridges, highways, mountain passes, rail junctions, and rivers, and noting the importance of capturing strategic points. "The capture of Albany would . . . block all communications in northern and Western New York and to a certain extent into Vermont," he noted after one such spy mission.

In 1931, however, McNaughton became chief of the general staff and decided that planning against an American invasion was senseless. He ordered that Defence Scheme No. 1 be burned. Canada thus gave up planning to beat off the Americans. But, unknown to Ottawa, the United States continued to plan for an invasion of Canada until nearly the beginning of World War II.

Defence Scheme No. 1 was drafted against a background of a couple of centuries of American invasions and threats of annexation that assaulted Canada. Even before there was a United States of America and a nation called Canada, there had been harsh words, raids, and even war between the northern and southern halves of North America.

A Virginia militiaman named George Washington led his soldiers against his northern neighbours in the 1750s. By the time of the American Revolution, the Founding Fathers of the United States believed Canadians would leap at the chance to be the fourteenth colony to join the new American nation. The Continental Congress, meeting in Philadelphia, sent troops to free Canadians from their British oppressors, attacking Quebec and Nova Scotia.

In the Articles of Confederation being worked out in Philadelphia, the Founding Fathers issued an invitation to Canada to join, saying, "Canada . . . acceding to the confederation joining in the measure of the United States, shall be admitted into and entitled to all the advantage of union."

The Founding Fathers were dumbfounded when Canadians both resisted the American invaders and rejected the invitation to join the new confederation. It was the first of a never-ending stream of flawed American assumptions about Canada that afflicted every American president, with the single exception of Franklin Roosevelt. But this inexplicable behaviour by their northern cousins did not dampen American hunger for Canada. "The unanimous voice of the continent is that Canada must be ours," cried John Adams, a future president, in 1776.

What they could not get by invasion or invitation, the Americans then tried to get by negotiation; in the peace talks in Paris after the revolution, American delegate Benjamin Franklin demanded that the British surrender all of Canada to the new American state. That, too, failed.

One result of the peace settlement, which would deeply influence the future Canadian attitude towards the United States, was that almost a hundred thousand United Empire Loyalists who had opposed the American Revolution fled to Canada. Their trek across the border was the greatest mass movement ever experienced in North America, solidifying a sense of Canadianism, immeasurably and lastingly strengthening anti-U.S. sentiment in Canada, and creating a sense of Canadian identity. Thus the American Revolution of 1776 was the cradle for the birth of two nations.

The first of the endless fishing disputes between Canada and the U.S. erupted a few years later. John Adams threatened that unless the Americans were given fishing rights off Canada's Atlantic coast, the U.S. might well go to war "and conquer from them the island of Newfoundland itself and Nova Scotia, too." A compromise was reached to avoid war, but it remained a dispute that has echoed noisily down through the centuries to the present day.

Raids and skirmishes across the Canadian border underlined the continuing American appetite for Canada, leading into the War of 1812. In another miscalculation about Canada, the Americans thought it would be an easy victory.

"The acquisition of Canada this year . . . will be a mere matter of marching," said a former president, Thomas Jefferson. "A military promenade," said a future president, Andrew Jackson. "A pleasing prospect."

It wasn't. Yet again, the Americans misunderstood their northern neighbours. Canadians fought back and, thanks to American military incompetence and the heroism of General Isaac Brock, the invading U.S. forces were driven back across the border. The Rush–Bagot Treaty demilitarizing the Great Lakes was a lasting result of the war. But as the years went by, slogans such as "Fifty-four Forty or Fight" and "Manifest Destiny" still fed a U.S. territorial hunger, and for many Americans the very existence of Canada was an affront to the idealism and the spirit of 1776.

President James K. Polk also echoed the cries of the sloganeers in demanding annexation to the United States of all Pacific coast territory north to Alaska. His words led to more noise than action, however. As the United States moved into the second half of the nineteenth century, it was preoccupied with the bitter dispute between North and South that led to the American Civil War.

Even that bloody war of brother against brother had its impact on Canada–U.S. relations. Most Canadians, as well as the British, favoured the South, more because of our dislike of the aggressiveness of the North than out of any admiration for the racial policies of the South. John A. Macdonald felt a Southern triumph would free Canada from the threat of U.S. invasion because the South was opposed to the Northern appetite for Canadian territory. "All the nicest and bravest men belong to the South," was the diary comment of Lady Monck, wife of the governor general.

More insulting to Washington than our sympathy for the South was the fact that Southern Confederate raiders operated out of Canada. At one point they attacked Vermont, robbing local banks of $200,000, killing one man, and wounding another before fleeing back into Canada. Northern newspapers were aflame with demands that Canada be invaded once the South was beaten.

Even Abraham Lincoln was alarmed at reports of Confederate forces being organized in Canada; he warned in his annual message to the country about "insecurity of life and property in the region adjacent to the Canadian border." The last thing Lincoln wrote before his assassination was a note about problems with Canada, which he penned at 8:30 P.M., just before going to Ford's Theatre.

After the Civil War ended in Northern triumph in 1865, Americans turned revengeful eyes north. One immediate target was a Canada–U.S. reciprocity trade deal that had been negotiated in 1854 during a pause in the stormy relations between the two countries. Washington abruptly cancelled the deal in 1866. One year later, President Andrew Johnson pointedly did not send a telegram to Ottawa to mark the birth of the Canadian nation in 1867, as Canada achieved by evolution what the Americans had done by revolution.

The Fathers of Canadian Confederation had learned a lesson from the Civil War. They designed a constitution with a strong central government and weak provinces. The American

Founding Fathers had done the opposite, and Canadian leaders felt that the American system had led inevitably to conflict and finally to the Civil War. Another profound Canada–U.S. difference was evident in the founding documents of the two countries: in contrast to the U.S. cry for "life, liberty and the pursuit of happiness," saluting the individual, the Canadian objective was to protect society as a whole with "peace, order and good government."

President Andrew Johnson still echoed the American dream of a United States of North America: "Comprehensive national policy would seem to sanction the acquisition and incorporation into our federal union, of the several adjacent continental and insular communities."

Secretary of State William Seward agreed, saying, "I know that nature designed that this whole continent, not merely these thirty-six states, shall be sooner or later, within the magic circle of the American Union."

President Ulysses S. Grant, who succeeded Johnson, shared Johnson's appetite for Canadian territory and wanted Britain to cede Canada to the United States. So, too, did his secretary of state, Hamilton Fish, who urged Grant to propose formally that Canada hold a plebiscite on annexation. He was supremely confident Canadians would vote yes. Grant examined the idea but dismissed it as desirable but hopeless.

President Grant, however, privately acquiesced in the activities of the hysterically anti-British Fenian brotherhood, an Irish-American group whose raiders invaded Canada at various border points with a battle cry of "On to Canada." President Johnson had allowed the first raids and talked of the possibility of recognizing a "Fenian Republic of Canada." The attacks were a burlesque failure and many of the Fenian raiders were arrested both in Canada and later in the United States.

More serious a threat to Canada–U.S. relations was the continuing fish war between the two countries. Angered at Canada's efforts to protect its fishing waters against American boats that Ottawa considered invaders, President Grant said he was ready to "take Canada and wipe out her commerce."

"The colonial authority known as the Dominion of Canada . . . this semi-independent but irresponsible agent, has exercised its delegated powers in an unfriendly way," Grant said in frustration over the fishing dispute. "I am tired of all this arrogance and assumption."

In the end, Canada was forced by the British, as part of the settlement of U.S. claims on Britain for its support of the South, to hand over extensive fishing rights to the Americans for $5.5 million. It was an incredible bargain for the richest fishing area in the world.

A colleague of Macdonald who attended the Washington fish negotiations with him was Justice Minister John Thompson, a future Canadian prime minister, who thought the Americans were simply not to be trusted. "These Yankee politicians are the lowest race of thieves in existence," he said in a letter to his wife. Macdonald agreed, speaking of "the faithlessness of the American Government" and adding in a note to the governor general, "There is no fair dealing to be expected from them." Macdonald's and Thompson's sentiments would be echoed by John Diefenbaker three-quarters of a century later.

Macdonald felt the British had sold out Canada to the avaricious Americans not only in fisheries, but in timber and boundary disputes as well. He had hoped to develop a free trade deal with the Americans, but when they refused he launched his policy of Canadian nationalism, building a protected Canadian economy and uniting the nation with steel rails in his National Dream. These nationalist actions led Grant to condemn him as "vexatious," "unfriendly," "unneighborly," and "irresponsible." Macdonald's legendary battles against Grant and his successors would provide a role model for John Diefenbaker.

Throughout the second half of the nineteenth century, the American army had detailed plans for the invasion of Canada, which concentrated on the capture of Winnipeg, destruction of the Welland Canal, seizure of the bridges at Niagara Falls, and blowing up the CPR route to the west. The American army estimated it could take over Canada in ten days at a minimum and two hundred days at a maximum. The *Canadian Military Gazette* reported in January 1896 that "loud-mouthed apostles of unreasoning spread-eaglism were threatening the conquest of Canada." Articles in newspapers such as the New York *World* talked about "the Future Great Republic," and the *U.S. Army and Navy Journal* carried a cartoon in 1887 with the following dialogue:

> Uncle Sam: "Oh Miss Canada, glad we met. I am thinking of annexing you."
>
> Miss Canada: "Oh! You are, you baldheaded, toothless old bachelor. I'll fight you first."
>
> Uncle Sam: "I was only joking. I wouldn't think of annexing you."
>
> Miss Canada: "Oh! You, you (boo hoo), mean thing you."

By the 1890s, many Washington officials still felt that despite their occasionally belligerent eruptions, Canadians in their hearts wanted to join the United States. U.S. Secretary of State James G. Blaine said, "Canada is like an apple on a tree just beyond reach. We may strive to grasp it, but the bough recedes from our hold just in proportion to our efforts to catch it. Let it alone, and in due course it will fall into our hands."

In New York City a powerful pressure group was established in the 1890s to urge Canada's political union with the United States. The National Continental Union League lobbied hard for that union, headed by such influential leaders as Teddy Roosevelt and business tycoons John Jacob Astor, Jay Gould, and Andrew Carnegie, who said that absorption of Canada by the United States would "add enormously to the power, influence and prestige of North America."

Americans of the time felt Liberal leader Wilfrid Laurier might be more responsive to their efforts than Macdonald and his Conservatives, and American money flowed into Laurier's political coffers for the election of 1891. Macdonald accused Laurier and the Liberals of "looking to Washington." Effectively demonstrating a tactic that John Diefenbaker would copy seventy years later, Macdonald warned against Canada becoming "Yankee-fied" and said, "We worked the loyalty cry for all it was worth and it carried the country."

After Laurier finally won the prime ministership in 1896, he ran into a major confrontation with the Americans on the Alaska boundary. The U.S. demanded ownership of the Alaska Panhandle, some of which Ottawa claimed as Canadian territory and as a necessary outlet to the sea for Canada's North. But Laurier faced Teddy Roosevelt's "big stick" and his anything but soft words. Roosevelt accused Canadians of "bumptious truculence," ordered the War Department to send troops to Alaska, and warned, "Let the fight come if it must. I don't care whether our sea coast cities are bombarded or not, we would take Canada." Roosevelt seemed to view Canada as San Juan Hill. He claimed western Canada "should lie wholly within our limits."

In response to American demands, Laurier said, "I am not to be either bulldozed or bamboozled by them." Canadian military authorities talked of "flying columns" being sent across the border to forestall a U.S. invasion. But when a British-American-Canadian commission was established to decide the Alaska boundary dispute, the British sided with the Americans against Canadian interests in what Ottawa regarded as the same kind of British betrayal that Macdonald had faced three decades earlier over fisheries.

Senator Henry Cabot Lodge, a rabid annexationist and influential U.S. political figure, called Canadians "a collection of bumptious provincial bullies" and "perfectly stupid." Laurier responded diplomatically to the American complaints, saying, "Personally, I like the Americans. . . . I would like them much more if they were not so intensely selfish and grasping." Governor General Lord Minto wrote to his brother, "There is general dislike of the Yankees here and I do not wonder at it. . . . What the Canadian sees and hears is constant Yankee bluff and swagger and that eventually he means to possess Canada for himself."

With all the high-level rhetoric, both Canadian and American military planners were busily studying a U.S. invasion of Canada. American Brigadier-General Leonard Wood developed a new invasion plan, and other schemes were examined at the U.S. War College. The British imperial general staff decided that Canada could not successfully invade the U.S., and that its forces would have to retreat into the North.

Laurier eventually swallowed his anxieties about the Americans, however, and on January 21, 1911, he signed a free trade deal with the United States. Liberal Prime Minister Alexander Mackenzie had made a deal with the American administration in 1874, but it was rejected by the U.S. Senate. Now, in 1911, it was back once again, but this time the Americans were enthusiastically pushing it, while Canadian voters were uneasy about being linked so closely with the Americans.

The Speaker of the U.S. House of Representatives, Champ Clark, declared he wanted free trade with Canada "because I hope to see the day when the American flag will float over every square foot of the British North American possessions clear to the North Pole." In the U.S. Senate there was similar sentiment, as reflected in the comment of Senator P.J. McCumber: "Canadian annexation is the logical conclusion of reciprocity with Canada."

President William Howard Taft regarded the free trade deal as "the most important measure of my Administration." He exalted its virtues by saying it would "make Canada only an adjunct of the United States. . . . It would transfer all their important business to Chicago and New York." Later, however, alarmed that Canadian fears of annexation might kill the trade deal, he declared, "The talk of annexation is bosh."

Not only Canadians were concerned about the implications of free trade with the United States. Rudyard Kipling warned, "It is her soul that Canada risks." In the end, "Canada's soul" won out as Canadian voters rejected the deal, threw out the Laurier government with the cry of "No truck or trade with the Yankees," and brought in Conservative Robert L. Borden as a prime minister who supported "Canadianism" and opposed "continentalism."

After 1911 the American territorial hunger for Canada diminished, at least in public comment. William Lyon Mackenzie King, then working for the Rockefellers, introduced the idea of the "undefended border" when he talked at an international meeting in 1914 of "this unfortified line running between the two great countries." While he was speaking, however, the American military staff was still making invasion plans, and the Canadians and British were planning how to ward off such an attack. The British wondered if they could reinforce Halifax quickly enough in the event of a U.S. assault. There were Canadian fears, too, that the U.S. could push into the prairies and cut Canada in two within the first day or two of an invasion, and then roll over the rest of the prairies within a week. Even with Canada fighting in World War I, U.S. planners were drawing maps for an invasion of Canada.

But by the 1920s, President Warren Harding could say publicly, "The ancient bugaboo of the United States scheming to annex Canada disappeared from all our minds years ago." It may have disappeared from Harding's mind, but not from Canadian military minds, as Defence Scheme No. 1 attests, nor from the mind of the American military, which had resumed its contingency planning of a possible invasion of Canada. U.S. plans for a naval assault in the Great Lakes and seizure of the St. Lawrence River were drawn up, and wide-ranging espionage in Canada was carried out to assess Canadian field batteries and air potential. Canadians were "unmilitary in character . . . but courageous, vigorous and . . . excellent soldiers when trained," one U.S. report noted. A U.S. scheme, called "Army Plan Red," noted that after a successful invasion, "The policy will be to prepare the Provinces and Territories . . . to become States and Territories . . . upon the declaration of peace. The Dominion Government will be abolished." American military officials were concerned, however, that Canada might bomb Boston, New York, Philadelphia, Baltimore, and Washington and would try to counter-attack in some border areas.

The Canadian public was not, of course, privy to the details of the American plans, which received approval all the way up to cabinet level, but there was speculation about U.S. invasion anyway. *Saturday Night* noted that the conventional wisdom was that Canadian forces would retreat into the North and the imperial navy would have to keep supply lines open to Hudson Bay. Looking ahead to annexation, *Saturday Night* commented, "The invaders could hardly avoid an eventual appeal to the referendum; but by delaying the vote and continuing their occupation as long as possible, and by insisting upon a separate decision from each province or from even smaller subdivisions, they could probably manipulate even the referendum so as to break off several essential fragments from the present national whole, leaving Canada a collection of isolated and economically helpless communities."

The American military invasion plan was current in 1923 when President Harding paid the first official visit to Canada by an American president. Never before had a U.S. president ventured across the border, except for Chester Arthur, who accidentally strayed into Canadian waters in 1882 while fishing in the Thousand Islands area of the St. Lawrence River. Harding's successor, Calvin Coolidge, earned his "Silent Cal" nickname with an impressive silence about almost everything, including Canada, except to ask once if it snowed in Ottawa and, on another occasion, if Toronto was near a lake.

The election of Herbert Hoover brought to the presidency a man who wanted badly to make a deal with Canada to build the St. Lawrence Seaway, something Hoover, an engineer, had dreamed about since the early 1920s. He thought it would enormously benefit the economy of the American midwest, but he found the government of Prime Minister R.B. Bennett cool to the idea. Bennett was less than eager to be associated with Hoover as Hoover's name became synonymous with the Depression. On his one and only prime ministerial trip to Washington during Hoover's presidency – a one-day visit – he refused the request of news photographers to have his picture taken with Hoover.

But in the spring of 1933, Bennett was back in Washington and eager to have his picture taken with the popular, newly elected American president, Franklin Roosevelt. Two years later Bennett lost the election to Mackenzie King; thus ended, for the time being, more than two centuries of truculent Canada–U.S. relations. Franklin Roosevelt and Mackenzie King ushered in a "good neighbour" policy that spawned Rotarian talk of the "undefended border" and lasted a quarter-century until blasted apart by the Kennedy–Diefenbaker feud. King was blissfully unaware, as Roosevelt likely was, too, of the U.S. military invasion planning.

Just one day after Mackenzie King became prime minister in 1935, he asked the U.S. embassy in Ottawa to arrange a meeting with Roosevelt, saying he particularly wanted to talk about liberalizing trade between the two countries. Two weeks later, King was being toasted at a White House dinner, where Roosevelt called him "an old friend." Roosevelt later claimed he and King had known each other "almost since we were boys." This was Rooseveltian hyperbole, for prior to their White House dinner, they had met only once; that was during World War I, when King was given an honorary degree by

Harvard University, where FDR was a member of the Board of Overseers.

Both men, though, were Harvard graduates, King having attended a few years before Roosevelt, and both combined a social conscience with political genius. At their first White House meeting, King gave the president a copy of the pioneering labour relations and social policy book he had written in 1918, *Industry and Humanity*, and Roosevelt surprised him by saying he already had a copy. He asked King to autograph it. King was in seventh heaven.

They were an odd couple. While FDR jauntily called him "Mackenzie," King never could bring himself to address Roosevelt other than as "Mr. President." King was a lonely bachelor with a mystic belief in fortune-telling, rattling tables, and talking to the dead, while Roosevelt was a rich, eastern-establishment sophisticate with a roving eye and a dutiful wife. Roosevelt knew King was no drinking companion, but they both were ruthless realists in politics; Roosevelt trusted King's judgement and shared secrets and strategies with him.

Over the next decade, they met more often than any other president and prime minister and reached a high point in Canada–U.S. relations that has never been equalled. Even so, the U.S. Army War College was still studying the possibility of invading Canada, although Army Plan Red was declared obsolete in 1937. But as political relations warmed between Ottawa and Washington, and King and Roosevelt spoke of joint defence efforts against any external enemy, the American invasion planning eventually petered out, more than seven years after Canada had abandoned Defence Scheme No. 1.

King and Roosevelt both had roots in each other's countries. The year after he was born, in 1882, FDR's parents bought a big rambling cottage on Campobello Island in New Brunswick. Young Roosevelt summered there amid its old-fashioned porches, hammocks, and spacious grounds. There, in 1921, he was stricken with polio while swimming in the cold waters of the Bay of Fundy.

King spent much time in the United States in his early years. His labour relations skills were put to work for John D. Rockefeller, who was particularly impressed with his efforts to resolve problems at Rockefeller's Colorado mining operations.

Indeed, the American tycoon later underwrote King's entire future career, enabling King to be free of financial worry – a relationship that would produce immediate scandal today.

Roosevelt became the first president to meet a prime minister in Canada when he came to Quebec City in 1936, and on that trip he marked another first that would echo into the Kennedy–Diefenbaker era. Roosevelt promised to defend Canada if Canada were attacked, and over the next five years that pledge hardened into specific commitments in Canada–U.S. defence co-operation.

King relished and embellished his role as a "bridge" between London and Washington, but he did sit in on several summit meetings of Roosevelt and Churchill in Quebec and Washington. After the 1943 Quebec summit conference, Roosevelt travelled to Ottawa to become the first American president to visit the Canadian capital.

King met Roosevelt in Washington for the last time one month before Roosevelt died in 1945. FDR's successor, Harry Truman, went into the presidency knowing practically nothing about Canada, except that he thought the War of 1812 was "the silliest damn war we ever had."

In a memorandum dictated to his daughter Margaret, Truman said, "Canada is alright. It's fine, but I believe that one of the reasons Canada has been able to grow is that they have a good neighbor south of them. I think we've contributed far more to Canada's growth and welfare than Britain has. There isn't any doubt about that because western Canada was mostly settled by people from the United States and if the situation hadn't developed that Canada's government is along the same lines as our own, we would probably have annexed the whole west end of Canada."

As president, Truman had a doubtful reputation among Canadian officials. Lord Athlone, governor general of Canada, told King that Truman was "a crook." King himself thought Truman was a lowbrow who was probably not up to the job of being president.

Truman, however, thought better of the Canadian prime minister. "An honest man," Truman wrote to his mother. "He has a very disarming smile, very deep dimple in his right cheek when he smiles. Eyes kindly and sympathetic yet strong."

But King feared the new American president did not fully understand the significance of the atom bomb and the dawning nuclear age. And the old Canadian fears of American territorial acquisitiveness returned. "The long range policy of the Americans," he told his cabinet, "[is] to absorb Canada. They [will] seek to get this hemisphere as completely as one as possible."

Those fears, however, abated temporarily as King made another effort to get a free trade agreement with the United States. His negotiators (including a very young Simon Reisman, who four decades later would finally succeed in achieving a free trade agreement that both governments approved) secretly reached a deal with the U.S. administration. But King, remembering the political fallout of 1911, got cold feet at the last minute and, fearing the Conservative opposition would crucify him for selling out Canada, cancelled the whole deal before it became public.

But if King was still suspicious of Washington, the Americans were becoming leery of Canada. A State Department memo to Truman in 1945 said Canada "is naturally inclined to resent any situations in which Canada is taken for granted or overlooked entirely." Vincent Massey said King once told him, "Canadians were looked upon by Americans as a lot of Eskimos."

John Diefenbaker echoed King's concerns. His sensitivity developed to the extent that he objected to any references to the American flag on Canadian broadcasts. "Reference to the Stars and Stripes and United States institutions on a program going out over Canadian CBC stations is something that I feel should not be permitted," he told the House of Commons in 1951. "There should be an agreement with United States corporations," he added, "that in their international advertising nothing shall be said indicative of the United States system of government being preferable to our own."

Also in 1951, External Affairs Minister Lester Pearson publicly signalled a new, less intimate Canada–U.S. relationship with a speech in which he declared, "The days of relatively easy and automatic relations with our neighbour are, I think, over." Those days had been relatively few, lasting only for the decade of the King–Roosevelt relationship.

"We are not willing to be merely an echo of somebody else's

voice," Pearson said. "It would help if the United States took more notice of what we do and indeed of what we say." On another occasion he exhibited Canada's long-held frustration over the pushy ways of U.S. diplomacy, saying, "We are not going to be pushed around by them," a sentiment John Diefenbaker would later echo in spades.

But in response to the Canadian complaints about not being consulted at times, an enraged U.S. Secretary of State Dean Acheson snorted to Pearson, in a memo on one difficult issue, "If you think that after the agonies of consultation we have gone through here [in Washington] to get agreement on this matter, that we are going to start all over again with our NATO Allies, especially you moralistic, interfering Canadians, then you're crazy."

In a letter to a friend, Acheson, whose parents were Canadian, described Canadians as "a tribal society, naive, terribly serious about the wrong things and not at all aware of their real problems. . . . Their best move would be to ask us to take them over; and our best move would be to say 'No.' "

King's successor, Louis St. Laurent, met Truman only twice and he, too, worried about Canada being taken for granted. He carried those worries into his somewhat formal and distant relations with President Dwight Eisenhower. Both were late-blooming politicians and reigned as chairmen of the board rather than ruling as chief executives of their countries; and neither man was steeped in knowledge about the other's nation. After a White House meeting with the golf-loving president on a pressing Canada–U.S. matter, Mike Pearson was stunned with Eisenhower's absence of awareness of the issue under discussion. "You'd think his caddy would have mentioned it to him," Pearson muttered.

The friendly Rooseveltian vibrations in Canada faded even further because of the arrogant, bullying style of Eisenhower's secretary of state, John Foster Dulles, and his penchant for going to the brink of war to win his Cold War diplomatic points with the Soviet Union. In domestic affairs, the vicious, soul-destroying smears of McCarthyism and the murderous agitation against blacks by white supremacists fed both the indignation of Canadians and our sense of moral superiority. But through smiles and charm, Eisenhower won the hearts of

Canadians and Americans alike who, in spite of the mess around him, cheerily said, "I like Ike!"

And no foreign leader "liked Ike" more than the sudden political tornado that blew in off the prairies in the greatest upset in Canadian political history, throwing out the arthritic Liberals of Louis St. Laurent and installing the "One Canada" evangelism of John Diefenbaker.

Chapter Two

IKE AND JOHN

In a sense, the Americans propelled John Diefenbaker into power.

As the Conservatives' foreign affairs critic, Diefenbaker had been warning for years about the danger of American money flowing into Canada to dominate Canadian industry. In mid-May 1956, the Liberal government of Louis St. Laurent handed him its head on a platter when it introduced legislation to have the Canadian government lend $80 million to the U.S.-controlled Trans-Canada Pipe Lines Ltd., to build a pipeline from Alberta to Winnipeg in order to export natural gas to the United States.

The loan was the key to a deal with high-flying Texas tycoons who for half a dozen years had been wheeling and dealing with the so-called "minister of everything," C.D. Howe, minister of defence production, minister of trade and commerce, and all-powerful in the St. Laurent government. The autocratic Howe demanded that the loan go through quickly so the pipeline could be finished before the next federal election, and he induced the government to impose closure to limit debate on the measure.

George Drew, whose leadership of the Conservative party was getting shaky, Diefenbaker, and other Tories seized on the arrogance of Howe and the Liberals to begin the most raucous episode in the House of Commons in this century, the infamous "Pipeline Debate." Their fire-storm of accusations concentrated on both the Liberals' imperious behaviour and the American financiers.

John Diefenbaker shouted about the Liberals' "brutalitarian tactics" and "executive absolutism," but he had equally poisonous contempt for the buccaneering Texas tycoons – "those Texas millionaires; those pampered pets" – especially Clint Murchison, C.D. Howe's friend and the central Trans-Canada Pipe Lines financier, whom Diefenbaker called a "pirate" who was "financin' by finaglin'." He accused the government of "playing around with . . . these adventurers from Texas and New York, trading away Canada's national resources at the expense of the Canadian people." The deal, Diefenbaker said, would make Canada "a virtual economic forty-ninth state."

The fact that Howe was originally an American and had close friends at senior corporate levels in the U.S. led to his personal vilification. But after a mob scene debate, the pipeline loan was smashed through Parliament by a powerful Liberal majority, and the government of Louis St. Laurent had its way – for a while.

Six months later, the Liberals seemed to have recovered from the parliamentary uproar and appeared headed for another cakewalk election victory. The Gallup poll reported Liberal support at 48.2 per cent and support for the Conservatives at 31.4 per cent. This time, though, the good, grey seventy-five-year-old "Uncle Louis" St. Laurent would confront a new face leading the Conservatives – John Diefenbaker, the temperamental loner who had captured the Tory leadership when the exhausted George Drew resigned shortly after the Pipeline Debate. In the spring of 1957, the election campaign was a dramatic contrast between the mesmerizing emotionalism of Diefenbaker and the stuporific world-weariness of the St. Laurent Liberals.

With eyes flaming, arms flailing and shoulders and jowls aquiver, Diefenbaker travelled the nation, fervently crying out for "One Canada!" and exultantly proclaiming, "I have come here with a vision of our nation's destiny."

It was a "Canada first" vision expounded with visceral nationalism. "I have but one love, Canada. One purpose, its greatness," he would say. Canadians hadn't heard such a magnetic spellbinder since the heyday of Sir John A. Macdonald.

Indeed, he likened himself to Sir John, saying that while

Macdonald's vision was east to west, his vision was north to south. In speeches early in the 1957 campaign, he described his plans for Canada's North as "the New Frontier policy." "The New Frontier" was a slogan he got from a key economic adviser at the time, Merril Menzies. "John Kennedy borrowed it in 1960," Diefenbaker would later grumble, "without attribution, and used it to great advantage." It was no advantage to Diefenbaker, however, failing to catch on as it later did for Kennedy, and Dief abandoned it as a campaign phrase after using it a couple of times.

Captured by his emotional evocation of Canadian nationalism and social justice, and sick to death of the insolent haughtiness of the Liberals, 6.6 million Canadians turned out at the polls on a sultry June 10, 1957, to stupefy political pundits by throwing out the Liberals. The Tories won a minority government with 112 seats – the Liberals had 105 – and Diefenbaker became Canada's thirteenth prime minister. The last-minute opinion polls had forecast a Liberal victory; most experts, dramatically miscalculating how fed up Canadians were with the Liberals, expected the Liberal majority would be reduced, but certainly not obliterated.

Maclean's magazine was so confident of the St. Laurent government being returned to office that its editors had printed ahead of time for their June 22 issue an editorial beginning, "For better or for worse, we Canadians have once more elected one of the most powerful governments ever created by the free will of a free electorate." Diefenbaker delightedly compared the editorial to the famous banner headline in the Chicago *Tribune*, printed before the results were final in the 1948 U.S. election: "DEWEY DEFEATS TRUMAN." For years, says Diefenbaker's secretary, Bunny Pound, he kept a framed copy of the editorial over his bedstead at his prime ministerial residence.

For the sixty-one-year-old Diefenbaker, it was a boyhood dream come true, a realization of his forecast as a child that he would be "Premier of Canada one day." After poring over a ninety-eight-cent encyclopedia (bought from Britnell's bookstore in Toronto), and reading about leading American politicians who had got their start as lawyers, he had decided, at age ten, that he too had to be a lawyer before he could be prime minister. He would regale associates and reporters with the story that as a fifteen-year-old newspaper boy he met Prime Minister Laurier at the Saskatoon railway station and "exchanged ideas on affairs of state."

Born in Ontario but brought up on a prairie farm in north Saskatchewan, John Diefenbaker was nourished on public affairs by his father, a schoolteacher, and got lessons in determination from his demanding, pushy mother, whom he idealized. She had wanted him to be a minister of the church. As prime minister, Diefenbaker wrote to her almost daily to tell her what he was doing. "She was a regular bitch . . . a real tough, bossy baby," says Bunny Pound, who felt her boss learned some of his more vexatious idiosyncrasies from his stern-faced mother.

She was a central influence on his life. A future Diefenbaker cabinet minister, Alvin Hamilton, describes how Diefenbaker would come back to Saskatoon from Ottawa early in his career as an MP and stay at his mother's home. Hamilton, a Diefenbaker protégé, would go over to the house, and usually he'd find the future prime minister "lying down, putting his head in his mother's lap, and she'd be stroking it as if he were a six-year-old kid. . . . She was a very strong Scot, determined her son was going to make good if she tore the whole world to do it. She kept on insisting that he had to be prime minister. His mother trained him and drilled him: 'You always must think and act like a prime minister.' "

At university, Dief was associate editor of the student newspaper and the star of the debating team. He was fascinated by Parliament; he read every Hansard from 1867 on and his memory was prodigious. A training accident in England cut short his World War I military career; a second lieutenant in the 19th Battalion Saskatoon Fusiliers, he was invalided home in 1917.

The same year Diefenbaker came back to Canada from the war, a blue-eyed boy was born at home in Brookline, Massachusetts, named John Fitzgerald Kennedy. If Diefenbaker's mother was the central influence on his life, it was Kennedy's short-tempered, opinionated father who dominated him. Like Diefenbaker, Kennedy as a youngster was fascinated by history, especially English political history, but while Kennedy was born to riches, the Diefenbaker family was forever on the border of poverty.

Graduating with a law degree from the University of Saskatchewan, Diefenbaker honed his oratorical skills in small-town courtrooms, gaining a province-wide reputation as the flamboyant champion of the little guy and a fierce advocate of civil rights. Of the twenty-six men he defended on murder charges, only two went to the hangman.

But his victories in the courtroom weren't matched by his ventures in politics. From 1925 to 1938, he lost every election he ran in, standing for mayor of Prince Albert, the provincial legislature, and the House of Commons. In this, his political career was sharply different from that of John Kennedy, who never lost an election. Diefenbaker's luck changed, however, and, having been chosen almost by accident as the Conservative candidate in Lake Centre, Saskatchewan, he astonished even his own supporters by squeaking to victory in 1940 while Tories in the rest of the country were slaughtered, electing a total of only thirty-nine members.

The same year Diefenbaker was making his first impact on the national scene as a newly elected forty-four-year-old MP, the twenty-three-year-old John Kennedy was similarly making his first national appearance with the publication of his best-seller (forty thousand copies sold) *Why England Slept*, about appeasement and democracy (polished by a family friend, Arthur Krock of the New York *Times*).

As Europe was aflame with Hitler's army on the march, Kennedy found his first love by joining the U.S. navy, and Diefenbaker found his political paradise in the House of Commons. With his ardent advocacy of social justice and his gaudy oratory, Diefenbaker quickly became popular with the public, but he was not trusted by the Conservative party hierarchy, some of whom labelled him "the Bolshevist from the west."

Within two years of his arrival in Ottawa, his driving ambition led him to run for the party leadership in 1942. One opponent who was to become an intimate colleague of Diefenbaker, and who, as minister for external affairs, would play a pivotal role in the Kennedy–Diefenbaker hostilities, was Howard Green, a Vancouver MP. Both Green and Diefenbaker lost to John Bracken, the premier of Manitoba, an early Red Tory who was responsible for the word "Progressive" being added to the name of the party.

Diefenbaker came in third, but his leadership craving inten-sified, astonishingly so for a man who had won his first election only two years earlier. As he manoeuvred to take over his party the next time the leadership was open, his future nemesis, Lieutenant (jg) John Kennedy, became a genuine South Pacific war hero in PT Boat 109, saving the lives of most of his crew after their torpedo boat was sliced in half by a Japanese de-stroyer in the Solomon Islands. His always troublesome back was badly damaged, and after his rescue, he was hospitalized for months.

John Bracken was thrashed by the Liberals in the 1945 election, but Diefenbaker was comfortably re-elected, the only Conservative to win in Saskatchewan. When Bracken resigned, Diefenbaker was a leading contender to succeed him. But the last man the Tory old guard wanted as leader was the renegade from the west, so they manipulated the leadership convention in favour of "the man from Bay Street," Ontario Premier George Drew, who personified the eastern-establishment stuffed shirts and appalled Diefenbaker.

While Diefenbaker was battling "them" in the Establish-ment, Kennedy got out of the navy after the war and, thanks to his father's friends, got a job as a special correspondent for the Hearst newspapers, reporting on the British election in 1945. Earlier in the year he had covered the founding of the United Nations in San Francisco. While Kennedy sat at the press table, John Diefenbaker was sitting in the centre of the hall as an adviser to the Conservative member of Canada's delegation. Other participants in the Kennedy–Diefenbaker drama that would unfold nearly two decades later who were also in that San Francisco meeting hall included Lester Pearson, Charles Ritchie, future ambassador to Kennedy's Washington, and Norman Robertson from the External Affairs Department.

Kennedy made a decision in the summer of that year that would put his career on a track parallel to Diefenbaker's, resolving to run for Congress from a Boston district. The legacy of his grandparents ensured that Boston Irish political history coursed through his veins. Ironically, in social concerns, speaking style, and zesty love of the game of politics, Kennedy's grandfather John ("Honey Fitz") Fitzgerald bore a striking resemblance to John Diefenbaker, who also displayed a flamboyance and a preoccupation with "the common people." John Kennedy won his congressional seat in the 1946 election in a landslide to begin his Washington career.

In Ottawa, Diefenbaker chafed under Drew's leadership, especially after an abysmal Tory showing in the 1949 election; the party won only forty-one seats. But Diefenbaker himself rolled up a huge majority in winning his seat as, again, the only Conservative elected in Saskatchewan.

Diefenbaker had visited Philadelphia for the 1948 Republican presidential convention, which chose as the GOP candidate New York Governor Thomas Dewey, considered a shoo-in to beat Truman. But Diefenbaker, as a man scorned by the political establishment, admired Harry Truman's "give 'em hell" common touch and his barnstorming campaign style. Dewey, on the other hand, was a product of the eastern élite, whom Diefenbaker hated. Identifying himself with Truman and against "them" as he would throughout his life, Diefenbaker said, "Dewey was above the people. He was removed from the average American. He was a New Yorker who saw things from the point of view of New York."

Four years later, Diefenbaker was back at another Republican convention, this time in Chicago, but now discouraged about his own political future and contemplating becoming a corporate lawyer. He was inspired by the convention, however, especially by the two candidates who were vying for the presidential nomination: General Dwight Eisenhower, who was loved by the delegates, and right-wing Ohio Senator Robert Taft, who was respected by the delegates. "Taft had always been the embodiment of what I would like to be, namely a person who, regardless of the ups and downs and uncertainties of political life, had strong principles and stood by them," Diefenbaker said years later.

In his heart of hearts, John Diefenbaker envisaged himself as a man combining the intellectual fibre of Taft and the style of Truman. But he reluctantly considered leaving politics at this point. He was discouraged with his party's treatment of him as an outsider, even though he was popular in public; and his Lake Centre riding had been gerrymandered out from under him and no longer existed. "I think I'm through politics," he told friends at the time. But he was persuaded by those same friends to run in Prince Albert in the 1953 election. It was a traditional Liberal riding, which a Conservative hadn't won in about forty years. Dumbfounding almost everyone, Diefenbaker won, and for the third time he was the only Conservative elected from Saskatchewan while the party itself was once again pounded at the polls by the all-powerful Liberals.

Meanwhile, the man Diefenbaker saw nominated by the Republicans at their Chicago convention had sailed into the presidency on a tide of adoring Americans. Everywhere Eisenhower campaigned, people shouted their thanks to him for leading the Allies to victory in World War II. They trusted him without hesitation and felt reassured by his integrity and cheered by his wide grin. But bucking the Republican sweep, just as Diefenbaker had bucked the Liberal sweep, was John F. Kennedy, who was elected as a Democratic senator from Massachusetts.

Both men had their eyes on bigger things. But for Diefenbaker, the party establishment had one more humiliation in store: in the fall of 1953 he was denied the post of deputy house leader, as George Drew picked a more reliable, right-wing political élitist, Earl Rowe. This public snub rankled, but Diefenbaker's bitterness lessened temporarily as his personal life changed. In December 1953 he married a childhood friend, Olive Palmer, daughter of a stern Baptist minister. She became a rock of support and comfort amid Diefenbaker's political tumult. His first wife, Edna Brower, had died in 1951.

As Diefenbaker's and Kennedy's political lives began to parallel, so too did their personal lives; three months before John and Olive were married, Jack Kennedy and Jackie Bouvier were married in the high society wedding of the year in the United States. Both newlywed couples honeymooned in Mexico, with the Diefenbakers in Mexico City and the Kennedys in Acapulco.

With Olive now at his side, Diefenbaker channelled his fury at the latest insults from the party establishment into vivid attacks upon the steamrolling arrogance of the Liberal government, particularly C.D. Howe, who once boasted to Parliament, "Who would stop us!" In three years, the Pipeline Debate and John Diefenbaker would stop them.

When Drew resigned as party leader in 1956, Diefenbaker got another chance at the top job. Again the party old guard tried to hijack the leadership convention with a "Stop John" movement. A Quebec party official, acting as a spokesman, came to Diefenbaker's hotel suite in Montreal demanding Diefenbaker stay out of the race. But Diefenbaker reportedly told him, "You get out of here, you baboon face, or I'll throw you out that window!"

The old guard, however, had lost its power and could find no strong alternative to the popular Diefenbaker, who offered fresh ideas and a fresh face. But Diefenbaker carried some historical baggage, too, echoing Sir John A.'s suspicions and dislike of the Americans. At the time of the leadership race Pierre Sévigny, a future Diefenbaker cabinet minister, was president of the Canadian Club of Montreal. Sévigny admired Diefenbaker, encouraged him to run for the leadership, and offered to get some money for his campaign from his wife's rich American relatives. "I'll never take money from the Americans," Diefenbaker shouted. "I'll never be subservient or in debt to them." Later in the 1957 campaign, Sévigny again offered to raise money in support of Diefenbaker from his American friends and relatives. "I'll never take five cents from the Americans!" Diefenbaker shouted in red-faced anger.

"You're not going to take the money yourself," Sévigny replied. "We can get it without conditions."

"No, no, no!" said Diefenbaker and the conversation ended.

Diefenbaker swept the convention on the first ballot but the Liberals still thought he would be easy pickings. The new Conservative leader thought differently. "We will be the next government," he told his party. "We have an appointment with destiny."

Three months before Diefenbaker won the Conservative leadership, his future enemy, John Kennedy, had made a bid to run as Democrat Adlai Stevenson's vice-presidential candidate in the 1956 election. On a wave of popular enthusiasm, he had almost made it, an underdog "fighting sailor who wears the scars of battle," as Senator Lyndon Johnson said at the time. He had lost narrowly to Tennessee Senator Estes Kefauver; Kefauver and Stevenson went on to be annihilated by Eisenhower in the fall. But the real winner in the American election of 1956 was Kennedy, whose grace under pressure and refreshing, youthful chutzpah propelled him into the forefront of American political life. His gallant battle for the vice-presidential nomination was indelibly implanted in the American political mind.

On November 25, 1956, John Kennedy sat down with his father after a family Thanksgiving dinner at Hyannis Port on Cape Cod and decided to run for the American presidency in 1960. Old Joe Kennedy's Wall Street money was to be a powerful weapon for his son's White House race; he and his son were among the first to realize that in politics, power used to get you money, but now, money gets you power.

Both Diefenbaker and Kennedy were defying the odds in their quest for national leadership. Diefenbaker got there first in his astounding triumph over the Liberals in the federal election of June 10, 1957. It was a dreamy whirlwind of transformation for Diefenbaker, who was bedazzled by having the power he had so long sought and overwhelmed by the multitude of events, issues, and decisions before him. Five days after his swearing-in, Diefenbaker was in a suite at the Dorchester Hotel in London, attending the Commonwealth Prime Ministers Conference, visiting the Queen, and reading front-page headlines describing him as the "NEW STRONGMAN FOR THE COMMONWEALTH." Even Winston Churchill was quoted as saying Diefenbaker's election was "the most important event since the end of the war."

It was heady stuff for the one-time prairie sodbuster and political outcast, and he flew home to parade about the country all summer, opening events and making after-dinner speeches galore.

Diefenbaker opened his first session of Parliament as prime minister in October 1957, with the Queen presiding for the first time in Canadian history. Diefenbaker had thought of looking particularly splendid that day by wearing the prime minister's Windsor uniform, as Mackenzie King and R.B. Bennett had done on several formal occasions. A few days before the Queen arrived, he got out the old uniform and tried it on. But the pants were too short and the jacket too tight, and he couldn't do up the buttons. He stood in his room at home in front of a mirror, with Olive and Bunny Pound looking on. Pound says, "He was like a little boy, so thrilled to be prime minister." But, she adds, both she and Olive Diefenbaker "never laughed so hard" at the sight of John Diefenbaker trying to squeeze into the Windsor uniform. "If I don't breathe in it, it will be all right," he said. His wife and secretary talked him out of trying to wear it.

He was having the time of his life, but there were early signs of his administrative sloppiness, his indecisiveness, and what some called his "pig-headedness." He "would much rather talk than listen," one of his cabinet colleagues said, and Alvin Hamilton complains that he surrounded himself with sycophants. "He had to have it to keep going, to feed this ego. Diefenbaker had to have praise," Hamilton says. He also wanted recognition, even from his friends in private, that he was now the prime minister. "Don't call me John," he told old friends. "He prepared himself all his life to be prime minister," says Hamilton. "He even slept in the proper position in case he died."

His arbitrariness increased, too, with what Hamilton calls his "technique of the tantrum" resulting in "ranting, yelling, and screaming." Says Hamilton, "He scared the devil out of the lazy and the arrogant." "Oh, fantastic, the anger of that man!" says his old friend Senator David Walker.

Diefenbaker's slight deafness was a nuisance to him and he was impatient with details, preferring to deal in sweeping generalities. His organizational disorder became legendary. He stuffed secret documents, letters of state, invitations, and memos into his pockets, into the handiest drawer, on a nearby bookshelf, and in other improbable places. In his early days as prime minister he lost an important letter from President Eisenhower; he found it only after weeks of searching, on the floor under his bed. A mislaid letter from Winston Churchill was found under his mattress; a communication from Harold Macmillan was located behind a book in a bookcase. Uncashed cheques (he never cared about personal finances), secret reports, and all manner of important papers were secreted away about his home and office in chaotic disarray. Sometimes he'd put papers he wanted to keep in "the vault," a small safe in his office, so they wouldn't get into his files. "He'd stuff them all over the place," Bunny Pound says. "I think he just didn't want people to see them for some reason."

In spite of his managerial disorder, Diefenbaker was at work one way or another from the time he had his morning glass of milk, at about six o'clock, until nine or ten o'clock, when he'd slip under the covers of what he proudly proclaimed was the bed Sir John A. Macdonald had slept in. At the office by eight, he'd pore over his voluminous mail from the public (he was deeply impressed by what people wrote to him on issues of the day), government papers, and political memos. He would see visitors every fifteen or twenty minutes, sometimes refusing to see some who had appointments, sometimes gossiping forever with political cronies, totally upsetting his other appointments. His officials learned to seek decisions from him in the morning, for as the day wore on, his indecisiveness increased. He'd generally lunch at his desk alone – often a tomato juice and a peanut butter sandwich, sometimes a thermos of soup, piece of cheddar cheese, glass of milk, and an apple – and would regu-larly nap in his office, falling dead asleep almost instantly, "and waking up raring to go," says Bunny Pound. She'd put choco-late bars in his top drawer and he'd furtively nibble on them during the day in defiance of his wife's dietary admonitions. When the House was in session he'd happily leave his office for his first love – the floor of the House of Commons.

If Ottawa had been awestruck by Diefenbaker's victory over the Liberals, Washington was simply agog. There was immedi-ate apprehension at losing the comfortable familiarity of the Liberals to the unfamiliar prairie prophet. "We'll really be dealing with an unknown quantity," a State Department official told reporters. What was known, though, worried the Ameri-cans. They had heard strong undertones of anti-Americanism in the campaign, and they feared Diefenbaker might seek trade with China against the Eisenhower–Dulles policy, might seek to retaliate against them for dumping farm surpluses on world markets, might be more critical of American military policies, endangering continental defence as well as Cold War unity, and might seek to limit American investment in Canada.

The American ambassador, R. Douglas Stuart, had admin-istered a public spanking to Diefenbaker and George Drew a year earlier by commenting on "the problem of the alleged domination by U.S. capital of Canadian industry and national resources." Stuart said the criticism had too much emotion and too little logic, adding, "Some of those who raise it do not appear to be seeking a solution but rather the creation of an issue."

During the 1957 campaign, Diefenbaker had harped on the dangers of American investment in Canada, saying it was pouring into Canada at the rate of $3 million a day, giving the Americans too much control over Canada's economy. Other Conservatives had talked of "economic slavery," "economic colonialism," and an "alien stranglehold."

It was an effective political weapon, and in Diefenbaker's first speech in the United States as prime minister, in Dartmouth, New Hampshire, he warned against American investment. "Can a country have a meaningful independent existence in a situation where non-residents own an important part of that country's basic resources and industry?" he asked.

As far back as his first federal election campaign in 1926, when he ran as a sacrificial Conservative against Prime Minister Mackenzie King in Prince Albert, Diefenbaker had stated his philosophy: "I want to make Canada all Canadian and all British." Now, three decades later, he said, "I do not belong to those who see a Canada and the United States in a form of continental arrangement. That's something my forebears didn't come to Canada to witness. They came to Canada to build a Canada strong and independent." He denied, however, that this made him anti-U.S., and he told the New York *Times*, "I am not anti-American. But I am strongly pro-Canadian."

Aside from the erosion of sovereignty through American investment, Diefenbaker was also concerned about the trade deficit with the United States, which had risen from $5 billion in 1945 to $12 billion in 1957. He said the answer was to switch trade away from the United States and stop "placing our eggs all, almost all, in one basket." "If we failed to diversify our trade," he later wrote, "Canada would cease to belong to Canadians; we would have no destiny to fulfill."

What he wanted was to divert fifteen per cent of Canadian imports from the United States to the United Kingdom, a switch of some $600 million worth of imports. The British responded with a counter-proposal of free trade between

Canada and the United Kingdom, but Diefenbaker rejected it and nothing came of either it or his rash diversion idea.

While Diefenbaker was bemoaning the extent of trade with the United States, some U.S. officials were trying to expand it further with free trade between the two countries. Eisenhower's chairman of the Council on Foreign Economic Policy, Clarence Randall, was urging on Ike the "economic integration" of North America. But Randall was defeated by opposition at the State Department, whose officials warned in a memorandum that "Canadians are still very sensitive on the whole question of economic relations with the United States."

The political tumult of Diefenbaker's victory may have bewildered official Washington, but it had only a glimmer of impact on John Kennedy, who was preoccupied with positioning himself for his run at the U.S. presidency in 1960. He took time out, though, to receive an honorary degree at the University of New Brunswick in the fall of 1957. In a speech written for him by his aide Ted Sorensen, he noted Diefenbaker's recent election, saying, "Your prime minister, I believe, has done well to remind both countries of the issues and potential areas of conflict," and he talked of Diefenbaker's "new compass bearing" in foreign policy. He spoke as a continentalist, an approach Diefenbaker abhorred, and told the students in Fredericton, "Our defence perimeters have merged all the way to the Arctic. . . . Our natural resources should not be neatly compartmentalized nationally." Here was the beginning of fundamental differences between Kennedy and Diefenbaker, although the future U.S. president said the U.S. had no designs on Canada, talked of "phantom American colonialism," and said, "Canada can neither be an extension of the Cornish coastline nor is she a mere northern vestibule of the United States."

In 1957 Kennedy came to Canada twice, having never been north of the border before. The second trip was for a debate at the University of Toronto on whether the United States was an effective leader of the West. Kennedy took the affirmative and won by a two-to-one vote of the students.

"Presidential fever" had gripped him, and he felt 1960 would be his turn. He said to a friend, "The gold ring doesn't come around very often and when it does, you better be ready to grab it." He was trying to grab it by building links with big-city

Democratic party bosses, criss-crossing the country making speeches, and attending political tea parties and back-room bull sessions.

Kennedy had written a Pulitzer Prize–winning best-seller, *Profiles in Courage,* about his political heroes and their moral courage. He had been named to the prestigious Senate Foreign Relations Committee, a post he was given by Senate majority leader Lyndon Johnson, who had been pressured by Joe Kennedy. Johnson said he liked the idea of Kennedy's father being indebted to him.

While not a "Senate man," Kennedy gained political supporters with his extraordinary capacity to grow intellectually and an ability to create the illusion of intimacy with strangers, even though the Democratic party old guard called him "a young whippersnapper." The young, handsome, activist senator was God's gift to television and was followed by cameras and reporters who covered his every word and action. New York television critic Jack Gould called him "the most telegenic person in public life."

For both Kennedy and Diefenbaker, 1958 was a turning point. They made politics fun again, compared with the yawning régimes of Eisenhower and St. Laurent, and they scored dazzling political triumphs: Kennedy with a smashing re-election as Massachusetts senator that dramatically boosted his 1960 presidential chances, and Diefenbaker with the biggest landslide victory in the history of Canadian federal elections.

Once again Diefenbaker was on his political pilgrimage, starting his 1958 campaign in Winnipeg with a cry of "A new vision. A new hope. A new soul for Canada." With fire-spitting, thunderclapping oratory, "Dief the Chief" hurtled across the nation gushing out his infectious nationalistic fervour, his "faith in Canada's future . . . faith in her destiny," and denouncing the hapless Liberals, now led by former external affairs minister Lester Pearson. Diefenbaker, who always thought Pearson overrated and considered him a "Yankee-lover," felt Pearson was the quintessential example of the hated "them": the Establishment, intellectuals, financiers, the media, business tycoons, and civil service mandarins, all of whom he felt were out to destroy him. He had developed a particular dislike for all Rhodes Scholars like Pearson. "As a young man he had his heart set on being a Rhodes Scholar from Saskatoon," says Bunny Pound. "But someone else got it and he resented that all his life."

As a spokesman for the common man, Diefenbaker had an evangelical eloquence that touched the hearts of Canadians. They were also impressed by the hyperactive legislative action of the Diefenbaker government in its first months: it had raised old age pensions, provided more money for western farmers, expanded unemployment insurance, made more loans available for homebuyers, and cut taxes, among other actions. Diefenbaker was the hero of the hour as he swept back into power in 1958, winning 208 seats; the Liberals took 48, the CCF 8, and one was an independent.

The Diefenbaker government, however, was not viewed in quite the same heroic light by the American government. Washington officials were sharply disappointed at Pearson's election loss because they knew him from his years at External Affairs, liked him, and respected him, and they believed relations with Canada would be much better with Pearson at the helm than with Diefenbaker.

The U.S. ambassador to Canada in Diefenbaker's early prime ministership was Livingston Merchant, a tall, thin, handsome WASP with an investment banking background and the impeccable credentials of the Ivy League élite. Merchant, a genial, articulate member of the old-boy network of foreign policy movers and shakers, was an old friend of Mike Pearson and a very adroit diplomatic smoothie. His ancestors played important roles in the American Revolution, and his friends included influential columnist Walter Lippmann, the Rockefellers, the Grahams of the Washington *Post*, and Jock Whitney, publisher of the New York *Herald Tribune*. In short, Merchant was everything Diefenbaker hated. It was a feeling that was reciprocated, for Merchant found Diefenbaker was "crude" and "a different breed of cat," and very unlike the sophisticated European diplomats he had been dealing with in his previous State Department jobs. He warned the State Department that the Diefenbaker rhetoric on Canada–U.S. relations would be "higher pitched, shriller . . . than we have been accustomed to."

Merchant had arrived in Ottawa in 1956 in the midst of the Pipeline Debate crisis. He immediately recognized the wisdom of a comment by Secretary of State John Foster Dulles, who had remarked on Merchant's appointment to Canada, "I don't think his post will be quite as soft as he may have thought." The new ambassador had been plunged immediately into the rising anti-American rhetoric coming out of the Pipeline Debate and Conservative fears about U.S. policies. He told a reporter after travelling to nine of the ten provinces, "I detect . . . a steadily growing criticism of certain policies of the United States government." He more bluntly and confidentially told the State Department, "The last year has seen the development of a strident, almost truculent nationalism."

In a series of public speeches during the first year of the new Diefenbaker government, Merchant followed the controversial example of his predecessor, Ambassador Stuart. Disputing Diefenbaker's criticism of U.S. trade and investment policies, he said, "If it is a problem . . . [it is of] Canada's own creation."

Diefenbaker was apprehensive not only about American trade and investment policies, but also about Washington's attitude towards the North. Washington considered Canada's North a critical piece of real estate in the sabre-rattling of the Cold War. It was the age of the bomber threat, and the U.S. wanted the earliest possible advance warning of approaching Soviet bombers flying over the Arctic towards American targets. Under an agreement made by the preceding Liberal government, Ottawa provided the land and the Pentagon provided the $500 million in hardware and manpower to build DEW (distant early warning) radar stations across Canada's northland. With so much investment and the U.S. military's assumption that they would be in charge, the Americans viewed the Canadian North almost as a colonial possession, flying American flags and insisting on U.S. approval before Canadians could travel in some areas.

"I put an end to that!" Diefenbaker said. More than three decades later, the memory of American arrogance in the North still rankles Alvin Hamilton, who says, "Those Americans didn't own the North. We did." He remembers one of the first things he did when he became minister of northern affairs in 1957 was to visit a radar station run by a U.S. colonel on the DEW Line. He says, "The colonel came running out and told me, 'You can't land here!' I said, 'I can and I did. I'm the minister of northern affairs. I'm in charge now and I run all this. You don't.' I was shocked to see an American flag flying over the base, but no Canadian flag. I told him, 'You get that flag down or I'll pull it down. You are not in Georgia here. You are in Canada and every square inch of this soil is Canada's. Take that thing down and put up a Canadian flag, and if you also put up an American flag make sure the Canadian flag is higher!' " The colonel took it down.

Years later, Kennedy's secretary of state, Dean Rusk, would agree with Hamilton's and Diefenbaker's views on ownership of the North. "I had great sympathy for the Canadian position," he says. "The U.S. took too theoretical a position on the North, and the Northwest Passage is by no stretch of the imagination an international waterway." By early 1959, most of the American air force officers were gone from the DEW Line, as Hamilton and others in the cabinet pushed to "Canadianize" it.

Diefenbaker was assembling a lengthy list of complaints about the Americans aside from investment, trade, and the North. The list included American dumping at subsidized, bargain-basement prices of surplus farm goods, which damaged Canadian commercial markets; growing protectionism in Washington; and the Cold War brinksmanship of John Foster Dulles, whom Diefenbaker distrusted and disliked, despite surface civility between the two. "Dulles made him feel uncomfortable," says Basil Robinson, Diefenbaker's key foreign policy adviser and later under-secretary of state for external affairs. Dulles had a lordly contempt for most non-Americans, was rudely insensitive to other people's feelings, and felt Canadians generally had an "inferiority complex." But he knew Canada was "a very important piece of real estate to be humoured along."

In turn, Washington feared Canada was too trusting of Moscow, too eager to trade with Cuba and China, and too suspicious of Washington. The Pentagon especially resented Ottawa's talk of "nuclearnuts" in Washington. Echoing thoughts that the State Department was too diplomatic to say publicly, Senator Wayne Morse, a maverick from Oregon, said, "We're not particularly appreciative of getting kicked in the teeth by Canada. . . . I think they have been guilty of gross injustice against the U.S. in a lot of their propaganda."

In May 1958, Ambassador Merchant told the Senate Foreign Relations Committee of "a change of climate" in Canada–U.S. relations and warned of "the strongly nationalistic attitude of the Conservatives." Merchant pleaded for more American recognition of Canada's economic concerns about the U.S. and a limit to what Canada's External Affairs Department called "opportunities for irritation."

"Any implication, however friendly and well meant, that Canada is sort of a forty-ninth state infuriates Canadians," Merchant warned.

In spite of the escalating Canada–U.S. friction, one major joint project dramatically advertised the kind of mutual economic benefit that could come from co-operation rather than confrontation. The St. Lawrence Seaway had been a political hot potato since the 1920s, when Herbert Hoover had dreamt of it. Hoover ran into reluctance in Ottawa; two or three decades later Ottawa ran into hesitation in Washington. Nowhere was there more U.S. resistance to the seaway than on the east coast, where American port cities feared losing jobs and business. With the seaway, ships would sail through to Chicago instead of unloading in Boston, New York, and Baltimore. Pushed by Ottawa, Eisenhower battled opposition in the Congress, especially from the Massachusetts congressional delegation. For twenty years, every senator and congressman from Massachusetts had voted no. In his 1952 campaign for the Senate, John Kennedy had opposed it. But two years later he was looking to broader horizons. Rejecting the advice of most of his political supporters, especially the Boston longshoremen who had been faithful backers, and endangering his political base, Kennedy took the guidance of his aide Ted Sorensen and voted yes. Walking over to the Senate from his office with Sorensen before speaking on the issue, Kennedy said he had had little sleep for worrying about his decision. He told the Senate that national interest demanded the seaway, adding that in spite of traditional New England opposition to it, "I am unable to accept such a narrow view of my function as United States senator."

He was accused by the Boston *Post* of "ruining New England" and warned not to march in the annual St. Patrick's Day Parade lest he be pelted with tomatoes. He walked in the parade without incident, and his action was a critical breakthrough in the final passage of the seaway legislation.

On a June day seven years later, John Diefenbaker stood on a platform with Queen Elizabeth and President Dwight Eisenhower for the formal opening of the St. Lawrence Seaway, which had cost a billion dollars. For Diefenbaker, the only sour note was that protocol demanded the Queen and President Eisenhower, as heads of state, be placed in the front row at the ceremony while he, as head of government but not of state, was placed in the second row. He got his revenge later that night by refusing to have booze served at a cocktail party for two hundred people at Montreal's Queen Elizabeth Hotel, in spite of protests from distressed protocol officials. Old friends said Diefenbaker had begun limiting his drinking as a young lawyer in Wakaw, Saskatchewan, when he drove his car off the road after a night of alcohol and poker.

Diefenbaker had waited an unusually long time before filling a vacancy in the ambassadorial post in Washington – four months – leading some U.S. officials to wonder if he was "spanking" Washington, deliberately keeping the ambassadorial job unfilled to show his independence. When he finally filled the post, it was a traditionalist appointment: the patrician Ottawa mandarin Arnold Heeney. A clergyman's son, Rhodes Scholar, and lawyer, the fifty-six-year-old Heeney had been Mackenzie King's private secretary in 1938, clerk of the Privy Council for nearly a decade, under-secretary of state for external affairs, and ambassador to NATO. He also had been ambassador to the U.S. from 1953 to 1957, so he had extensive first-hand knowledge of the American scene. Heeney was, however, distressed at Ottawa's anti-Americanism, which "dogged my diplomatic footsteps" and which he blamed on the "excess of general election oratory."

While combustible material lay all around for a major and bitter Canada–U.S. clash in these years, it never happened, thanks to President Dwight Eisenhower.

"Ike had Diefenbaker figured out right from day one," recalls Basil Robinson, the prime minister's foreign policy aide. "He was not condescending and he appreciated Diefenbaker's capabilities. . . . Ike was better at sizing up people than Kennedy." Moreover, Eisenhower was a genuine hero to Diefenbaker, who admired his military and political triumphs without any jealousy. "Diefenbaker had an enormous respect for people who had been war leaders and Eisenhower had proven his mettle," Robinson says.

What Eisenhower had, and Kennedy never would have, was patience with the Canadian prime minister's idiosyncrasies and sensitivity to his political style, an attitude that Ike had learned was essential for international harmony when he was the Allied wartime military leader in Europe and later commander of NATO. "Eisenhower could charm a statue," says Pierre Sévigny, who recalls Diefenbaker saying at the time, "This fellow Eisenhower is an American, but he's not so bad."

Eisenhower, like Diefenbaker, was more comfortable talking in generalities, unlike Kennedy, who often sought to zero in on details. And both Eisenhower and Diefenbaker shared a penchant for procrastination in decision-making, another sharp difference with Kennedy. In fact, Eisenhower was nicknamed by irreverent associates "the Great Hesitator" while Diefenbaker became to many colleagues "Old Tomorrow," a label also given to Sir John A. Macdonald.

Beyond that, "Ike" and "John," as they called each other, were close to the same age (when they first met, Ike was sixty-seven and Diefenbaker sixty-two), had known World War I and the Depression, had similar humble, western farm family backgrounds, and worshipped their mothers. They both had simple eating habits, enjoyed middlebrow television viewing, had similar moral values, and, most important, loved to fish. "Fishing," the prime minister said, "is the only time you can forget everything." Diefenbaker liked being alone with Ike, and on one trip to Ottawa Ike and John went off alone to fish in a small rowboat at Harrington Lake. Eisenhower showed Diefenbaker a new spinning plug that was his favourite, and it immediately became Dief's favourite.

"Diefenbaker was trusting of Ike," says Robinson, something he was of very few and certainly never of John Kennedy. "Eisenhower was a great man. . . . I like Ike," Diefenbaker said later.

Diefenbaker's emotions about U.S. investment in Canada, U.S. trade restrictions, and the hawkishness of John Foster Dulles and the Pentagon were often calmed down by Ike.

"Subservience is not an essential in the cooperation of Canada and the United States," Diefenbaker later wrote. "I might add that President Eisenhower and I were from our first meeting on an 'Ike and John' basis and that we were as close as the nearest telephone." In the Eisenhower years, Diefenbaker later commented, "Canada was not treated as a forty-ninth state composed of Mounted Police, eskimos and summer vacationers."

An example of Eisenhower's solicitude with Diefenbaker was a letter he sent the prime minister just before leaving Washington for a presidential world tour in 1959. Starting off as "Dear John," he explained where he was going and why, adding, "You and I have found from experience that there is no substitute for personal contact in furthering understanding and good will. . . . I leave Thursday evening . . . but if you would want to suggest anything to me before departure, I would, as always, welcome a phone call from you."

Diefenbaker succumbed readily to the combination of Eisenhower charm, flattery, and considerateness and to his own hero-worship of the American president. So much so that while bilateral issues continued to boil and differences sharpened between the two countries on specific issues, Diefenbaker spoke out in broad general support of Eisenhower and his policies. At meetings of NATO and the United Nations he took much the same line as Eisenhower on foreign policy. As Basil Robinson has noted, "He wanted to be seen as a loyal supporter of Eisenhower, the leader of the Western nations."

Eisenhower and Diefenbaker first met as president and prime minister in October 1957, when Diefenbaker accompanied the Queen to Washington after she had opened his first session of Parliament as prime minister. They met again two months later at a NATO meeting in Paris and would get together seven times over their years in office. Even with her husband's enthusiasm for Eisenhower, Olive's dislike for Americans remained; just before Eisenhower made his first visit to Ottawa, she told friends, "I hope they're better than those abominable people from the Roosevelt era."

When he came to Ottawa in July 1958, Eisenhower made an especially tough speech in Parliament to what he called "our sturdy northern neighbours," rejecting Canadian complaints about American investment, protectionist trade actions, and "fire-sale" farm surplus disposals, and directly attacking Diefenbaker's idea of shifting trade away from the United States to any other country to ease a trade deficit; he called it an "artificial redirection," to the applause of the Liberal opposition. It was a much more muscular speech than John Kennedy would give before Parliament three years later, but instead of being enraged, as he was with JFK, Diefenbaker simply smiled benignly and took good old Ike fishing. His objective was not so much to deal with issues as it was to forge a strong personal bond with Eisenhower.

In spite of the glowing personal relations between the two leaders, Washington was getting increasingly irritated at Diefenbaker's procrastination on key questions of defence policy. The focus was on whether Canada would arm its forces with nuclear weapons. It was an issue that would nag with Eisenhower and explode with Kennedy. The drumbeats of American impatience at Diefenbaker's hesitancy were muted, however, when the prime minister was greeted on a June 1960 Washington visit by brass bands, cabinet secretaries, and a state dinner. When Eisenhower raised the defence issues that were distressing his officials and prodded the prime minister to make some decisions, Diefenbaker didn't feel threatened or pressured. Nor did he even feel upset when Eisenhower raised the touchy question of when Canada would join the Organization of American States. When John Kennedy asked the same question one year later, Diefenbaker resented it, but when Eisenhower raised it, the prime minister purred that he was thinking about it. Even Eisenhower's references in a White House dinner party toast to Diefenbaker as representing "the great Republic of Canada" didn't mar the joy of the occasion for the prime minister, although Eisenhower's ignorance of Canada's constitutional structure shocked other Canadians at the dinner.

Diefenbaker and Eisenhower met alone much of the time, but had a handful of advisers on occasion. The atmosphere was friendly and casual, with "Ike brimming over with goodwill and intermittent profanity and seeming anxious to avoid any sharp differences," noted Basil Robinson in his book *Diefenbaker's World*. Earlier Eisenhower had told his new secretary of state, Christian Herter (who had taken on the job after Dulles died of cancer), that he wanted to have Diefenbaker visit the White House because, he said in a somewhat puzzled tone, "somewhere" he had heard "that our relationships with Canada were deteriorating."

When the White House meeting ended, Diefenbaker told Eisenhower, "The relations of Canada and the United States have reached a new height of friendliness, cordiality, and true co-operation that has never before been attained so far as I know." His personal relations with Eisenhower may have reached that "new height," but to those at the working levels in Washington, it was close to laughable hyperbole.

Diefenbaker's mail reinforced his own hesitancy on such things as Canadian acquisition of U.S. nuclear warheads. In a comment to Basil Robinson that summer of 1960, he said, "I have a number of letters critical of any action being taken regarding the storage of nuclear weapons and a number are strongly opposed to any defence alliance with the United States." His mail also fed his fundamental anti-Americanism, and in two long conversations with his ambassador to Washington a month after his visit with Eisenhower, he told Arnold Heeney that there was "an avalanche of anti-Americanism" in the nation. Sitting at his desk in his East Block office, the prime minister read Heeney excerpts from a pile of "highly emotional, abusive letters" denouncing the United States and urging a neutralist stance for Canada in world affairs.

Diefenbaker said the reaction stemmed from the impression that the U.S. was "pushing other people around"; distrust of the U.S. military; economic aggression by the U.S.; and resentment at lack of coverage of Canada by the U.S. media since American reporters in Canada were "second rate." Diefenbaker said the attacks on the United States had reached unprecedented proportions, but while the prime minister was quoting the letters, many of the sentiments expressed were undoubtedly his, too. It "all pointed," Heeney quoted Diefenbaker as saying, "to an accumulation of resentments and criticism of the United States which would, he repeated, burst in an 'avalanche' of unprecedented proportions. . . . Anti-Americanism . . . was sweeping across the country from one end to another."

"I had no idea that anti-Americanism had reached such a level in Canada," Heeney wrote in his diary. "He kept coming back to the new and violent sweep of anti-Americanism throughout Canada. . . . It had been a pretty shattering interview." With his tiny, almost indecipherable handwriting, Heeney wrote in blue ink, "In his judgement anti-American sentiment was now worse than at any time in his lifetime or mine."

Diefenbaker had not wanted to sully his relationship with Eisenhower by talking about this, but he wanted Heeney to make the president aware of the Canadian mood. "He was anxious," Heeney wrote, "that there should be nothing done during the remainder of the Eisenhower administration to exacerbate the situation."

Heeney talked to his old friend Livingston Merchant, who was now back in Washington as under-secretary of state for political affairs. He, in turn, talked to Secretary of State Herter, and a meeting was arranged between External Affairs Minister Howard Green, Herter, Merchant, and Heeney for that fall during a United Nations conference they were to attend. At the meeting in Herter's Waldorf-Astoria Hotel room, the secretary of state expressed deep concern at the anti-Americanism reflected by the prime minister and, Heeney noted in his diary, "The Secretary added, not with his usual degree of mildness, I thought, that he hoped that the tendency of Canadian political parties to compete in these anti-American attitudes would not develop and could be checked. He [implied] pretty directly that such a development could not but lead to serious consequence in our joint affairs." Green said that some Canadians felt the Pentagon was, as Heeney quoted him, "courting . . . disaster by provocative actions and words." After the meeting, Green told Heeney he liked Herter. "Completely the opposite of what Canadians expect an American to be!" he smiled.

While rising Ottawa–Washington tensions were moderated for the moment that summer by Eisenhower's charm and skill in handling Diefenbaker, John Kennedy was on his way to replace Ike in the White House. In mid-July in Los Angeles, he won the Democratic nomination. In August, it was a coronation for his Republican rival, Vice-President Richard Nixon, at the GOP convention in Chicago.

Of the two, Diefenbaker clearly preferred Nixon. "I'd be very worried if Kennedy became president," he told Pierre Sévigny. Although he knew he would never develop the friendship he had had with Eisenhower, he felt Nixon would provide a safer continuity in bilateral relations and might be rhetorically vigorous but pragmatically cautious in Cold War actions. "He's a predictable quantity," Diefenbaker said. He had developed a deep dislike for Kennedy based on his fear that Kennedy would be too "activist" and "too rash" in world affairs. Kennedy's foreign policy views were more hawkish than Diefenbaker's, and his record on civil rights and social justice was much less bold than the Canadian prime minister's. On a personal level, Diefenbaker worried about Kennedy's popularity in Canada and its effect on his own popularity. He had no use for the glamorous life-style of Jack and the other Kennedys, with their zesty testing of all the limits. Diefenbaker found all this personally threatening and politically dangerous in a tense world. "That pup!" he'd say scornfully, or sometimes he'd use Eisenhower's phrase, "That boy!"

"I just don't trust the Kennedys," Diefenbaker told cabinet associates. "His father was anti-British. He's a buccaneer." Says Gowan Guest, who was Diefenbaker's executive assistant at the time, "Clearly he would have voted for Nixon if given the chance."

Diefenbaker met Eisenhower in New York at a United Nations meeting in late September of 1960, in the midst of the presidential campaign. Diefenbaker told the president that the Kennedy–Nixon debates were a terrible mistake. "Such a debate should never take place," Diefenbaker told the president. The first debate, which did more than any one campaign effort to make Kennedy president, had been on television the night before Dief and Ike met. "I told him that the rest of the debates should be cancelled," the prime minister later said. "The debate would give Kennedy the publicity he lacked."

But Eisenhower disagreed, saying Nixon could handle himself in the debates because of his detailed knowledge of domestic and international affairs. Diefenbaker felt if his advice had been accepted, Nixon would have won the election, and in his memoirs he wrote that if Nixon had won, "I do know that the course of Canada–United States relations would have been a happier one."

On November 8, seventy million Americans went to the polls to elect John Fitzgerald Kennedy as the thirty-fifth president

of the United States. Kennedy won with only 118,000 votes
more than Nixon, a scant margin that Diefenbaker hoped might
constrain some of his adventurousness once he took office in
January 1961. Diefenbaker also couldn't help chortling over
Kennedy's razor-thin win, compared with his own landslide
triumph three years earlier.

But he still worried about Kennedy and told Basil Robinson
that he feared Kennedy's activism "might prove dangerous."
Reflecting on Diefenbaker's fears about Kennedy at this point,
Robinson says, "There was a new phenomenon on the political
scene. . . . He worried about how it would affect him."
Diefenbaker's cabinet colleague Pierre Sévigny sought to reassure him by telling him, "The man is young and full of energy
and a change is needed. He may be good."

"We'll see," replied Diefenbaker.

Meanwhile, the prime minister returned to his theme of
rampant anti-Americanism among Canadians. In mid-November he told Heeney, as he had in August, that it was sweeping
the nation. In unwarranted optimism, Heeney hoped things
might get better with Kennedy. "Why not an improvement in
Canadian–American relations?" he asked himself in his diary.
He was soon to find out why not.

Kennedy, it quickly became clear, would not match Eisenhower in his solicitude towards Diefenbaker, as demonstrated
by his slow response to a congratulatory message Diefenbaker
sent him on his election. A couple of weeks after sending it, the
prime minister had received no reply from Kennedy and was
miffed. "Not a bloody word!" he complained. Ottawa asked
the Kennedy people to reply and they finally did on November
23, but it was too late for the prime minister, for whom these
things meant a lot. It left an indelible stain and was a foretaste
of their coming rancour.

There was to be one final dance in the Eisenhower–Diefenbaker ball. The prime minister travelled to Washington just
three days before Kennedy was inaugurated, in response to an
invitation from Eisenhower to join him at the White House in
a formal ceremony signing the Columbia River Treaty. The
arrangement on joint control over power from the Columbia
was at last agreed to, after excruciating three-way negotiations
among Canada, the United States, and British Columbia.

Diefenbaker leapt at the invitation for one last grand public ceremony with the world leader he revered above all others.

As they lunched, gossiped, and went through the formal ceremonies, it was a nostalgic, bittersweet moment for Diefenbaker, who knew things would never be the same again in his relations with the occupant of the White House. In three days' time, John Kennedy, not Dwight Eisenhower, would be sitting there, and Diefenbaker sensed he was losing a trusting and understanding friend with whom he could share easy conversation and unthreatening discussion of problems, and to whom he could turn when crises resisted resolution at lower levels. Ike had been a safe harbour in a perilous world. Shortly after Eisenhower left the White House, Diefenbaker wrote to him, "The many evidences of your friendship to me will always be amongst the happiest of my memories. I felt that we were friends."

Back in Ottawa after the Columbia River Treaty signing and still bathing in the Eisenhower aura, Diefenbaker sharpened his apprehension about the incoming president. He "has formed an irrational prejudice against Kennedy . . . which could be a serious portent," Basil Robinson wrote in his diary. The prime minister, Robinson said, "seems to be almost relishing the more pessimistic omens."

One of those omens came from an encounter between Ambassador Heeney and Kennedy's incoming secretary of state, Dean Rusk. Rusk had questioned Heeney about why the U.S. should have "a special relationship" with Canada and worried that it might arouse "suspicion or resentment" among other allies. Rusk was persuaded, however, that for geographic and historical reasons a "special relationship" was justified. But much worse in Diefenbaker's eyes was Rusk's telling Heeney that he knew Canada well because he had been on several fishing trips to Canada with his son. Diefenbaker was infuriated, saying it showed that when Americans thought of Canada they thought only of hunting and fishing. "Is that all he thinks we're good for?" Diefenbaker growled.

Clearly, the storm signals were up.

Chapter Three

CROSSING THE
NEW FRONTIER

"Good morning!" President John F. Kennedy said to his news conference on February 8, 1961.

"I have several announcements. One, I would like to announce that I have invited the prime minister of Canada, the Right Honourable John G. Diefenbawker, to make a brief visit to Washington on Monday, February 20th, for discussion of matters of mutual interest to our two countries."

Diefen*bawker*!

Kennedy had committed the cardinal sin of publicly mispronouncing the name of the prime minister, who was notoriously thin-skinned about such things. Kennedy's press secretary, Pierre Salinger, blandly assured enquiring Canadian reporters that it came out as "Diefenbawker" only because of the president's New England accent. That, however, was a White House white lie.

The day before his announcement of the visit, Kennedy had called Secretary of State Dean Rusk about Diefenbaker's name. "How do you pronounce it?" he asked. "I want to be absolutely right."

"I'll call you back, Mr. President," said Rusk. He immediately called his assistant secretary of state for European affairs, Foy Kohler, who, like Diefenbaker, was of German descent. "It's Deef-en-bawker," said Kohler.

"It's Deef-en-bawker," Rusk called back to the president.

When Kennedy was told he'd mispronounced the prime minister's name, "he was furious with me," Rusk remembers.

Kennedy recovered his humour, however, and two days after seeing Diefenbaker he made a joke of his mispronunciation with Australian Prime Minister Arthur Menzies, who was also visiting the White House. He told Menzies, "When I saw Prime Minister Diefenbaker the other day, I called him 'Mr. Studebaker.' " Both Menzies and Kennedy would repeat the anecdote with relish as time went by and as they both grew to heartily dislike Diefenbaker.

Diefenbaker was so deeply affronted by Kennedy's mispronunciation of his name that, according to Pierre Sévigny, associate minister of defence at the time, he "asked the cabinet if we should lodge an official protest.

"We all thought it would be ridiculous if we made a scene about this, but he carried on with it. He ridiculed Kennedy, speaking of him as 'this man who can't even pronounce my name correctly.' " Eventually, Sévigny and his cabinet colleague Gordon Churchill calmed the prime minister down and no protest was filed. But Diefenbaker nursed his grievance, remembering his private tortures as a youngster, when he was not accepted by schoolmates because of his German-sounding name. A Conservative women's group once urged him to change his name. As Peter Newman reported in his book *Renegade in Power*, Diefenbaker refused, saying, "It's 'Dief' as in 'Chief,' followed by 'en' and then 'baker.' "

ABC-TV News referred to the Canadian prime minister as "Diefenbacon," the Washington *Post* called him "Diffenbaker," and United Press called him "Fiffenbaker." Even the American ambassador to Canada always called him "Diefenbacker."

Diefenbaker had insisted that he see the new American president before Menzies so that he could be the first Commonwealth leader to meet Kennedy in the White House. He wouldn't be the first foreign leader, since that honour went to the Danish prime minister, who had lunch with Kennedy on February 14. But he would be the second. He wanted only a couple of hours of informal conversation with the president before going to the Commonwealth prime ministers' meeting in London in March. Besides having everyone knocking on his door, Kennedy was beset with more dangerous problems: the Congo was aflame; the United Nations was under assault from the Soviets, who wanted a "troika," a three-man leadership instead of a single secretary general; tensions were rising in Berlin; and Soviet leader Nikita Khrushchev's belligerence was becoming more worrisome.

"Canada was the last thing on our minds. . . . Diefenbaker was certainly not a high priority," says Kennedy's national security adviser, McGeorge Bundy. Canadian Ambassador Heeney, however, cashed in on his contacts at the State Department; thanks to his friendship with Livingston Merchant, who had become the number two official in the State Department, an appointment with Kennedy was arranged. "I am particularly glad he's coming," Kennedy told reporters. "It's most important that harmonious relations exist between two old friends; therefore I am glad to have this chance to visit with the prime minister."

Kennedy began preparing for Diefenbaker's visit three days beforehand, soaking up details in a report from Rusk, who, in his first sentence, reminded him it was Diefenbaker, not -baw-ker. The memorandum gave Kennedy the most intensive crash course on Canadian affairs he had ever had; it covered defence issues, trade, U.S. surplus disposals, oil, China, Cuba, and Canadian attitudes on everything from Laos to the Congo. Kennedy also got advice from business friends, including the chairman of Olin Mathieson Chemical Corp. of New York, Thomas Nichols, who wrote him: "Today, long submerged problems threaten to overtake us and . . . are forcing our relations with Canada into a serious decline. . . . We must reset our course."

Rusk said Canada's and Diefenbaker's "introspection and nationalism" were the biggest problem in Canada–U.S. relations. Living next door to a giant, Rusk said, "has long engendered a Canadian inferiority complex which is reflected in a sensitivity to any real or fancied slight to Canadian sovereignty." He said Canadians fear being engulfed by the American culture and economy, but still feel entitled to a special relationship with the United States. He told Kennedy that in the 1957 and 1958 election campaigns, Diefenbaker's Conservatives "made strong nationalistic appeals which were called 'Canadianism' but often had anti-American overtones."

Rusk lamented Diefenbaker's "general indecisiveness," which he said had led to his falling popularity, and he feared that the prime minister might intensify his nationalistic fervour. "The Government's tendency to procrastinate and its defensive reaction to criticism of Canada's defense position," Rusk's memorandum advised Kennedy, "has tended to confuse the public and helped spawn some neutralist and semi-pacifist groups. . . . Should this general situation continue over a long period, a drift toward a kind of unconscious neutralism could develop with a concomitant loosening of defense ties with the United States. . . . Loss or diminution of U.S. use of Canadian air space and real estate and the contributions of the Canadian military, particularly the RCAF and Royal Canadian Navy, would be intolerable in time of crisis." Rusk warned Kennedy of Diefenbaker's preoccupation with Canadian sovereignty, say-ing, "Our defense arrangements have to be conducted with meticulous regard for Canadian sensitivities."

The most crucial feature of the "defense arrangements" of which Rusk wrote was the use of Canadian real estate to protect the American Strategic Air Command bases in the United States and the northeast industrial heartland of the U.S. SAC was the Western world's principal instrument of nuclear retaliation against a Soviet attack, and Washington felt Canada's full par-ticipation in the air defence of it was crucial. When the Cold War intensified in the mid-1950s, Ottawa and Washington had agreed on the Distant Early Warning (DEW) Line across Canada's Arctic and other radar installations across Canada that would provide at least three hours' warning of the approach of attacking Soviet bombers. Washington, however, wanted to go beyond a warning to a capacity to shoot down as many of the attackers as possible, as far north as possible. That meant, Washington said, placing nuclear anti-aircraft missiles in Can-ada, providing nuclear weapons for RCAF interceptors, and integrating the USAF and the RCAF in North American air defence.

It was a long way from Army Plan Red and Defence Scheme No. 1. Even after the preposterous preparations for invasion and counter-attack had faded in the Thirties, there had been no serious planning about joint North American defence. The most significant regular military contact between the two nations had been an annual hockey game between West Point and the Royal Military College at Kingston.

Franklin Roosevelt had sent out the first signal to change continental defence plans dramatically. In 1936, in response to a reporter's question, Roosevelt said the United States would defend Canada if Japan were to attack British Columbia. A year later, Prime Minister Mackenzie King and Roosevelt discussed having Canadian and American military officials meet to consider North American defence problems. In January 1938, the Canadian and U.S. chiefs of staff met in Washington, and later that year in a speech at Queen's University in Kingston, Roosevelt made a further commitment: "I give to you the assurance that the people of the United States will not stand idly by if domination of Canadian soil is threatened by any other empire."

Just two days later, King spoke in Woodbridge, Ontario, declaring, "We, too, have our obligations as a good, friendly neighbour, and one of these is to see that . . . enemy forces shall not be able to pursue their way either by land, sea or air to the United States across Canadian territory." Although King did not know it, he was offering the rationale for NORAD a generation later.

With the start of World War II, King and Roosevelt grew more concerned about North American defence. In 1940 at Ogdensburg, New York, they set up the Permanent Joint Board on Defence, whose responsibility was to "consider in the broad sense the defence of the north half of the Western Hemisphere." At the time, Conservative leader Arthur Meighen vigorously attacked the deal as a betrayal of Canada's history.

The King–Roosevelt Hyde Park Agreement on defence production came a year after Ogdensburg. During the war, Canada–U.S. co-operation in North American defence included many measures: U.S. troops undertook cold-weather training in Manitoba; Canadians took parachute training in Georgia; joint exercises were held in Saskatchewan, Alberta, and British Columbia; and the two countries built a highway to Alaska, a series of airfields called the Northwest Staging Route, weather stations in the Arctic, an oil pipeline from the Mackenzie River to the Pacific, and an oil refinery at Whitehorse. Tens of thousands of Americans came to Canada in all these projects, many assuming a domination that rankled Canadian authorities and led to talk of "U.S. occupation."

King was worried, too, and in October 1945 he wrote, "If the Americans feel security required it [they] would take peaceful possession of part of Canada with a welcome of the people of BC, Alta. and Saskatchewan." He said he "felt perfectly sure" western Canadians would look to the United States for their security if they became alarmed, not to Ottawa or Britain.

When King visited President Truman in 1946, Truman urged that a permanent U.S. Air Force bomber base be located at Goose Bay, Labrador. He was also concerned about the need for closer co-operation in North American air defence. Ottawa was uneasy about such co-operation in the North for fear of offending the Soviets; Mike Pearson, then under-secretary of state for external affairs, wrote in the October 1946 *Foreign Affairs* that Canada did not "relish the necessity of digging or having dug for her, any Maginot Line in her Arctic ice."

A year later, Ottawa and Washington agreed on continuing defence co-operation and noted in a joint statement that "all cooperative arrangements will be without impairment of the control of either country over all activities in the territory." It was a statement Diefenbaker, Howard Green, and Alvin Hamilton would refer to later to express their distress when Americans seemed to assume sovereignty at the radar bases in the Arctic. Even at the time, Green was unhappy about the presence of American forces in Canada's North; he warned that if war came between the U.S. and the Soviet Union, Canada, as a neighbour of both nations, would be the main battlefield. In a House of Commons debate about U.S. troops in Canada, the MP from Yukon, George Black, alleged that U.S. military phone operators in the North were answering callers with "The American Army of Occupation speaking."

"We are surrendering some of the sovereignty of Canada," Regina MP J.O. Probe told the House. Temiscouata (Que.) MP Jean François Pouliot warned of Canada being "Yankeefied." "All the Americans will have to do will be to stick nine more stars on their flag and that will finish it," said Skeena (B.C.) MP H.G. Archibald. "Either that or we can create one with a bald-headed eagle carrying a wet muskrat in its claws and that would be our national flag."

By 1950 the threat of Soviet nuclear attack by bomber on North America was a technological reality. The fear was that Soviet planes would come down the "air corridor" over the North Pole and head south over Baffin Island and Hudson Bay and into the U.S. Early in 1952, a group of U.S. scientists urged that a warning system be built, and the two nations began constructing a line of radar stations running along both sides of the Canada–U.S. border. Later that year, another group of scientists called together by the Pentagon concluded that such a border-hugging radar line would not give enough notice of impending air attack; they advised building radar lines in Canada's Far North to provide a three- to six-hour air raid warning. It was the first significant move to use Canadian territory to protect the U.S. in the Cold War.

In August 1953 the Soviets conducted a successful hydrogen bomb test, prompting President Eisenhower to accept the Pentagon's recommendations. With U.S. money, experimental radar stations were set up. A year later, Ottawa and Washington agreed to build two additional warning lines: the DEW Line stretching across Canada's Arctic, and the Mid-Canada Line across the middle of Canada. The Americans provided most of the money while Canada provided the geography. Public sensitivity about protecting Canadian sovereignty led Prime Minister St. Laurent to assure Canadians that the U.S. continental defence operations in the North would have "full respect for the sovereignty of the country in which they are carried out." Even so, Canadians found they frequently had to get clearance from a U.S. office in Paramus, New Jersey, before travelling to parts of the North. Even Mervyn Hardie, the Liberal member of Parliament for Mackenzie River, had to get permission to visit some of his constituents.

Ralph Allen, editor of *Maclean's* magazine, wrote at the time, "We have delegated the effective working control of at least 10% of our land area to the United States Air Force. . . . How much independence have we really lost? . . . How much more will be lost as our comfortable acceptance of the presence here of U.S. military commanders, U.S. military troops and U.S. military installations becomes as naturally ingrained as our acceptance of U.S. business capital and U.S. television, books and movies?"

In 1953, U.S. General Omar Bradley publicly advocated creation of a joint continental command with Canada. In 1955, the chairman of the U.S. House Armed Services Committee, Sterling Cole, raised the idea of a Canada–U.S. continental defence pact, but Defense Secretary Charles Wilson was uneasy about the idea. He told a Congressional hearing, "Our Canadian friends . . . are a little fussy about their big southern neighbors. . . . They don't want us to think we're running their country."

The idea of much closer North American defence co-operation was being promoted with increasing vigour, however, by both the RCAF and the U.S. Air Force. Canadian Air Marshal Roy Slemon said a joint command was "inevitable."

Not all Canadian military experts were equally enthusiastic. In 1956, Major-General W.H.S. Macklin, the former adjutant general who had earlier talked of "nuclearnuts" in Washington, spoke out in opposition. "Canada has permitted the United States Air Force a degree of interference in our national sovereignty greater than any Canadian Government would have conceded to Great Britain within my lifetime," he said to the Couchiching public affairs conference.

In spite of such concerns, a new Canada–U.S. military study group was established to examine what Slemon said was "inevitable." It recommended "establishment of a joint headquarters to provide for the operational control of the air defence of Canada and the United States."

The chiefs of staff of both nations approved the report, and so did U.S. Defense Secretary Wilson, reversing his earlier reluctance. The Americans now wanted to move quickly. Canadian Defence Minister Ralph Campney, in February 1957, recommended to the Liberal cabinet approval of what would become NORAD, with an American as commander and a Canadian as deputy commander. But some Liberals feared that such a joint defence arrangement might stir up Conservative charges of "selling out" to the Americans. In addition, Lester Pearson, minister for external affairs at the time, wanted changes in the agreement to provide more intensive Canada–U.S. consultations on defence policies, particularly at the political level. He later said the agreement would not have been approved as it stood by the Liberal government, had it been put to a cabinet vote at that time.

Campney, however, told Washington there was no disagreement on the substance of establishing NORAD and that the Liberal government would likely approve it right after the election, now scheduled for June. But there was to be no Liberal government after the June 1957 election.

Canada's military was nervous that the Conservative election victory might delay NORAD and sought to have the Liberals rush it through in their last days before the official Diefenbaker take-over, but the Liberals refused. It was an issue that was quickly thrust onto the table for the new administration. "Unfortunately, I am afraid we stampeded the incoming government with the NORAD Agreement," General Charles Foulkes, the chairman of the chiefs of staff, would later say. There was a rush to get the agreement approved because the Americans had already okayed it and Diefenbaker wanted to be able to tell U.S. Secretary of State John Foster Dulles that it was approved when Dulles came to Ottawa at the end of July on his first visit with the new prime minister. Foulkes was under almost daily pressure from the Pentagon, and his immediate target was Diefenbaker's first minister of defence, General George Pearkes.

Diefenbaker described Pearkes as "a soldier's soldier and a gentleman's gentleman." But a different view of Pearkes comes from a Diefenbaker crony, Senator David Walker, who says of Pearkes, "One of the most inefficient ministers we ever had. . . . Oh God, he was hopeless." Pearkes, however, was also a long-time friend of Diefenbaker, having nominated him for the Conservative party leadership in 1948. Pearkes was quickly convinced to agree to NORAD by his old comrade-in-arms General Foulkes, who, he said, "certainly gave me the impression that it was all tied up by the Liberal government, that promises had been made that it be signed immediately after the election."

Pearkes, in turn, quickly persuaded the new prime minister, with little or no real examination of the NORAD deal. The two had discussed it while flying to London together a few days after the election to attend the Commonwealth Prime Ministers

Conference. When they got back to Ottawa, Foulkes prepared a draft memorandum for Pearkes to present to the cabinet; Diefenbaker gave it immediate endorsement. As Foulkes remembered it, "Pearkes came back about an hour after and walked into my office, threw it onto my desk, and said, 'There it is, approved.' I was stunned." There was no consultation with other cabinet members or senior advisers, although the cabinet did get a brief explanation a few days later. It was item number 32 on the cabinet agenda for July 31, and discussion was confined to a brief statement by the prime minister that the appointment of a Canadian as deputy commander of NORAD gave Canada "a proper measure of responsibility in any decisions that might have to be taken to defend North America against an attack."

"Everything had been done and agreed upon by the St. Laurent Administration," Diefenbaker later said. "I saw NORAD as an extension of NATO." His comment was ingenuous and politically expedient, however, because the St. Laurent government had not approved NORAD and likely would have sought changes, especially on increased Ottawa–Washington political consultation. Nonetheless Diefenbaker was enraged at General Foulkes's comment that he "stampeded" the government into agreeing to NORAD. "I can never understand why General Foulkes . . . should have boasted in connection with NORAD that he bamboozled the St. Laurent and Diefenbaker Governments into accepting it. . . . That admission is proof positive that under the St. Laurent Administration there was a domination of Canada's policies by the United States military authorities."

On August 1, 1957, a joint public announcement was made by Defence Minister Pearkes and U.S. Defense Secretary Wilson: "A further step has been taken in the integration of the air defence forces of Canada and the United States. . . . An integrated headquarters will be set up in Colorado Springs and joint plans and procedures will be worked out in peacetime, ready for immediate use in case of emergency."

U.S. Air Force General Earle Partridge was named the first commander of NORAD; the first deputy commander was Canadian Air Marshal Roy Slemon, an ardent advocate of USAF–RCAF integration for North American defence. Slemon had served in the Canadian air force since 1923. NORAD would quickly become a multibillion-dollar system, consisting of 170,000 personnel at 400 bases. The U.S. would pay the bulk of the cost.

The key question for Canada, which Diefenbaker failed to address sufficiently in rushing into NORAD, was the degree of consultation between Ottawa and Washington that would take place before NORAD swung into action in an emergency. His failure to be firm at the outset would cause him months of political embarrassment at the time and would return to haunt him during the Cuban Missile Crisis, when Kennedy did not, in fact, consult him.

In an interview shortly after his appointment, General Partridge was asked about permission to use nuclear weapons. He responded, "The president has given his approval to use, without reference to anybody, any weapon at our disposal if there is a hostile aircraft in the system." This rang political alarm bells in Ottawa, and when Diefenbaker went to Washington in mid-October he raised the questions of consultation and civilian control over NORAD with President Eisenhower. The Pentagon was reluctant to agree to any heavy emphasis on consultation, which it thought might hamper quick reaction to an attack, but eventually it acquiesced. Diefenbaker reported to his cabinet that the president had confirmed civilian control over NORAD and that the NORAD commander would act only after talking to the president and prime minister or their representatives. "Mr. Diefenbaker said there was no limit to Mr. Eisenhower's congeniality and friendliness," a cabinet summary adds.

The prime minister did recognize that in emergencies time for consultation would be limited. "These consultations naturally will be intensified in times of emergency," he said. "It cannot be overlooked that the advantages of surprise lie with the aggressor. . . . To that end, we believe every precaution must be taken to ensure that the Canadian Government is consulted concerning circumstances which could conceivably lead to this country being committed to war." When the agreement was finally formalized in May 1958, it stated that there would be "the fullest possible consultation between the two governments on all matters affecting the joint defence of North America."

Like NORAD, the sensitive problem of the Avro Arrow was waiting for John Diefenbaker when he beat the Liberals and assumed the prime ministership. It began in 1953 when the Canadian chief of air staff proposed building six hundred supersonic, all-weather fighter planes for the RCAF and USAF to meet the Soviet bomber threat against North America. A year later, the St. Laurent government decided to go ahead with eleven prototypes. Development costs skyrocketed, however, and in late 1955, the government limited development of the CF-105, known as the Avro Arrow, until the design could be proved out by test flights. With rising costs and problems finding a suitable missile for the plane, the number of proto-types was cut to eight. The delta-winged jet was regarded as the world's most advanced fighter. By now, however, there was alarm in the Liberal cabinet at the costs involved and at the failure to elicit a sale to the United States to help pay for the plane. It "gives me the shudders," Defence Production Minis-ter C.D. Howe said. By the spring of 1957, he and many other cabinet ministers were ready to cancel the Arrow after the June election – but the decision would fall to the Tories.

There was a successful test of the Arrow airframe in August 1957 and by the fall, pushed by the chiefs of staff and the aviation industry, Diefenbaker agreed to continue development of the Arrow and continue to try to sell it to the Americans. The Russians, meanwhile, had launched their first interconti-nental missile, and in October, Sputnik went up, signalling the arrival of the space age and the missile era. Both events would profoundly affect Diefenbaker's political future.

The Arrow had its first full flight late in March 1958. The original cost had been estimated at $1.5 to $2 million per plane, but now costs were heading towards $12.5 million apiece, and there were still no foreign sales in sight. In Washington, Cana-dian Ambassador Norman Robertson kept getting refusals when he asked the Pentagon. Defence Minister Pearkes himself came to Washington in August and was left in no doubt the Americans were not going to buy the plane. Diefenbaker told several cabinet colleagues, "There go the Americans again. You can't trust them." That same month, the Canadian chiefs of staff faced the inevitable and reluctantly recommended that the Arrow be cancelled.

A month later, the prime minister announced that because the bomber threat was decreasing as we entered the missile era, Canada would not need as many interceptor planes. Therefore, he said, Canada would install the much cheaper U.S. Bomarc anti-bomber missiles and postpone the decision to begin production of the Arrow. The cabinet had basically decided to cancel the Arrow, but the prime minister felt it would be less politically damaging to do it in two phases. On February 20, 1959, Diefenbaker took the second bite, announcing the Arrow cancellation and stirring a lasting political upheaval. Fourteen thousand A.V. Roe Canada Ltd. employees in Toronto were immediately thrown out of their jobs, and almost as many in associated companies were also let go. "The Arrow has been overtaken by events," the prime minister said, reiterating that the bomber threat was lessening and so it would be wasteful to spend so much on the Arrow. "The threat against which the CF-105 could be effective has not proved to be as serious as was forecast," he told Parliament. "There is no purpose in manufacturing horse collars when horses no longer exist," he said a few weeks later.

Instead of the Arrow, Diefenbaker announced Canada would place two squadrons of the U.S. Bomarc-B missiles at bases in North Bay, Ontario, and La Macaza, Quebec. Earlier Pearkes had also considered putting Bomarc bases in the Maritimes and near Vancouver, but he had discarded the idea. There would be twenty-eight missiles per base, each with a range of four hundred miles. The Americans agreed to pay for the Bomarcs so Canada would pay only for support costs. It was a small price financially but, in time, the political cost would be enormous because of Diefenbaker's apparent commitment in his announcement to acquire U.S. nuclear warheads for the Bomarcs.

"The full potential of these defensive weapons is achieved only when they are armed with nuclear warheads," he told the House. "The Government is therefore examining with the United States Government questions connected with the acquisition of nuclear warheads for Bomarc and other defensive weapons for use by the Canadian forces in Canada and the storage of warheads in Canada. . . . We are confident that we shall be able to reach formal agreement with the United States." The "other defensive weapons" to which Diefenbaker referred were the American MB-1 air-to-air nuclear missiles for RCAF interceptors.

The cabinet was aware that in taking the nuclear-tipped U.S. Bomarc weapon, Canada ran the danger of falling under greater U.S. military control in North American air defence. The nuclear warhead question was discussed at numerous cabinet meetings in 1958 and 1959 with the underlying assumption that Canada would acquire the warheads for use by Canadian forces both in NORAD and in NATO. The summary of a February 23, 1959, cabinet meeting notes, "It should be remembered that maintaining freedom from U.S. control was a continuous struggle. It might appear that the present decision is a retrograde step. But there would be other opportunities to assert Canadian sovereignty and independence."

Douglas Harkness, who became defence minister the following year, later noted in a lengthy personal memo, "The decision to acquire weapons systems designed to use nuclear ammunition was a decision to enter the nuclear weapons field. I am not sure that the majority of members of the Cabinet realized this and certainly I think few of them realized what the implications were." As defence minister when the decision was taken, George Pearkes realized what they were, and cabinet summaries note that he informed his colleagues, "The missile could be fitted with an atomic warhead and the U.S. would probably supply heads on the same basis . . . as they made atomic weapons available to the United Kingdom."

At a December 9, 1958, cabinet meeting, the ministers had agreed with the American proposal of a "two-key," joint-control approach. A summary of the meeting noted that under this system, while only the American president could release the weapon, "in effect there had to be both U.S. and Canadian consent to their firing and no such weapons could be stored in Canada without consent of the Canadian Government. There could not be much more control than that."

Even opposition leader Mike Pearson agreed with Diefenbaker's apparent commitment to accept nuclear warheads, saying to the House, "With regard to the nuclear warheads of Bomarc missiles and defensive weapons of that kind, it seems to me it would be quite insupportable . . . to have Canadian air squadrons without them, and United States squadrons on the same airfield with them." He would later change his mind on this issue, and then change it back again at the height of the Kennedy–Diefenbaker confrontation.

But Diefenbaker had leapt out of the Arrow frying pan into the Bomarc fire; the missile was dogged by testing failures and attacked as being too costly. Members of Congress complained that Canada was getting "a free ride" on North American defence. Powerful Louisiana Democratic Senator Allen Ellender said the United States was spending billions on continental defence while Canada "does not furnish a nickel. We're just a bunch of suckers!"

Under heavy Congressional pressure, the U.S. Air Force cut back the number of its planned Bomarc bases and probably would have killed the Bomarc altogether if not for Canadian pressure to have two Bomarc bases in Canada as a replacement for the cancelled Arrow. Senator Warren Magnuson of Washington said the Diefenbaker government might collapse if the Bomarc were cancelled. The U.S. secretary of defence also noted the Canadian pressure for Bomarc, telling Eisenhower, "If we were to go out of the Bomarc business [I don't] think we could live with the Canadians who had just recently after long joint discussions, adopted it in preference to interceptors for their air defense." President Eisenhower promised the prime minister he would fight hard to save the Bomarc.

It was the beginning of a tragicomedy that saw the Diefenbaker government desperately pushing the Americans to provide Canada with Bomarc-B missiles to ease the political and defence problems of the Arrow cancellation but, in the end, refusing to take the necessary nuclear warheads for the Bomarcs. That made them headless and useless, endangering North American defence and leading to the white-hot clash between Kennedy and Diefenbaker and eventually to the prime minister's political collapse.

Diefenbaker also seemed committed to accepting the storage of defensive nuclear missiles for U.S. Air Force planes at Goose

Bay, Labrador, and at the U.S. base at Harmon Field, Newfoundland. In addition the U.S. wanted storage of high-yield nuclear bombs at Goose Bay for SAC, and storage at the U.S. navy base at Argentia, Newfoundland, of anti-submarine nuclear weapons. The cabinet approved in principle the storage of defensive nuclear warheads at Goose Bay and Harmon Field in September 1959 and added that there should be "some form of joint responsibility for the storage, removal and use of these weapons." The cabinet added, "The Canadian Government is prepared to permit the storage of nuclear air to air defence weapons in Canada in accordance with the conditions set out in the attached annex." The key condition was shared responsibility for use, something Washington indicated it was prepared to accept.

The government seemed similarly committed to acquiring nuclear warheads for the Canadian Brigade and the Canadian Air Division of the NATO forces in Europe. "In December 1957 at the heads of government meeting in Paris, the Diefenbaker government agreed, without reservation, to adopt nuclear strategy for the NATO forces in Europe," General Foulkes later said. Defence Minister Pearkes agreed. "We accepted the nuclear role in NATO," he said. "It was adopted by the meeting at which Diefenbaker was present." Later the government also agreed to a strike reconnaissance role for Canada's NATO air division, involving the use of a small atomic bomb, and to a nuclear warhead role for the Honest John artillery of the Canadian Brigade in NATO. "It is Government policy," Pearkes said, "that Canadian troops should be armed as efficiently and effectively as are troops with which they are cooperating."

In these early months of the nuclear débâcle, the Conservatives' position on control and use of the warheads seemed unequivocal. Diefenbaker told the House of Commons in February of 1959, "Believing that the spread of nuclear weapons at the independent disposal of individual nations should be limited, we consider that it is expedient that ownership and custody of the nuclear warheads [in Canada] should remain with the United States."

In cabinet, it was agreed that, as cabinet summaries note, "ownership of the weapons would remain with the United States and hence the cost could be expected to be borne by the

United States at least until the time came to use the warheads. . . . It should be said that they would be used in and over Canada only with the agreement of Canadian authorities. . . . The alternative to not coming to some agreement with the United States regarding nuclear weapons was that Canadian forces would not be equipped with the best weapons available."

In any case, U.S. law required that all U.S. nuclear warheads, no matter where located, remain under U.S. ownership and custody. But the Americans had developed the "two-key" joint-control system with the British and other European allies. Under this system, the president says yes to the use of nuclear weapons and the host country then decides whether to actually fire the weapon. Diefenbaker seemed agreeable to that system.

At a 1958 meeting, the Canada–U.S. Ministerial Committee on Defence had already had detailed discussion of Canada getting nuclear weapons. Pearkes had said at the time, "It was agreed by the meeting that there seemed to be no difference of principle between Canadian and U.S. views on the matter of control to be exercised over the use of nuclear weapons." As General Foulkes, chairman of the Canadian chiefs of staff at the time, said later, "We put forward a proposal in which the United States would supply nuclear weapons for Canada. . . . Nothing was signed, but a draft agreement was made up at the time."

The Diefenbaker Government proceeded to buy $500 million worth of planes and weapons that were designed for nuclear roles and was clearly marching towards the acquisition of U.S. nuclear warheads. But death intervened. Sidney Smith, Diefenbaker's first minister for external affairs, an old colleague and friend of Diefenbaker (whom he described as "the Happy Warrior"), died suddenly of a heart attack in March 1959. He had struggled with his portfolio, disappointing many who had thought he would be an ideal foreign minister. He had had less impact than expected on the prime minister, and on the question of Canada's nuclear role he had mostly acquiesced in the desires of his Department of Defence colleagues, although with some reluctance.

Diefenbaker assumed the external affairs portfolio himself for three months while he searched for a successor to Smith. His first thought was to choose Finance Minister Donald Fleming, who wanted the job. But there were problems in the

Department of Finance, and Diefenbaker felt Fleming should stay there to resolve them. In one of the great "if onlys" of Canadian history, if only Fleming had been named as external affairs minister, the clash between Diefenbaker and Kennedy would probably have been less ferocious and the dangerous collapse of Canada–U.S. relations might never have happened; Fleming's attitude towards defence and towards the United States was in sharp contrast to that of the man who was chosen.

Diefenbaker astonished diplomats and political observers by naming Howard Green, an old British Columbia political warhorse and long-time friend of Diefenbaker who had been serving as minister of public works. Green, at age sixty-three, had practically no experience in foreign affairs, had not been overseas since serving as a lieutenant in the 54th Kootenay Battalion in the trenches of World War I, and had never been to Washington. "He'd never been anywhere!" said cabinet colleague Douglas Harkness. "A very odd appointment." Even Green was astonished by his appointment when Diefenbaker called him into his office one morning.

"Well, you're it," said Diefenbaker.

"What do you mean?" responded Green.

"Well, you're going to be secretary of state for external affairs."

"I am, am I?" said Green.

That night Green called his mother to tell her the news. She said, "Howard, I won't stand for it. You can't do it. It's too hard work." Green said she later changed her mind.

In what would prove a mystifying challenge for his more sophisticated counterparts in other countries, the bespectacled, white-haired Green didn't drink or smoke and didn't know how to drive a car. He seemed a gentle soul, but he had a hidden tough side, as was noted by C.D. Howe, who said of Green, "He wanders through the halls of Parliament with a bible in one hand and a stiletto in the other." Even Green's colleagues agreed with this assessment. Immigration Minister R.A. Bell once noted, "Howard Green is a very delightful fellow, but a very good hater," and Ellen Fairclough, another cabinet colleague, once told Green, "Howard, you know, the trouble is, you never know whether to kiss you or kill you."

Green's power as external affairs minister came from having the same pro-British, anti-American sentiments as Diefenbaker, from his reverence for the prime minister and Diefenbaker's total trust in him, and from his quiet but mulish tenacity in pursuing what would become, in the words of historian Peyton Lyon, his "magnificent obsession" of disarmament. "Canada's main role in the world is to keep the big boys from rocking the boat," Green said.

He was the only cabinet minister who could walk into Diefenbaker's office without knocking. "Howard was steady as a rock compared to all the other twirps," says Bunny Pound. "He was the only one who wasn't afraid of Diefenbaker. A really decent, honest, open guy with a good head."

On an early trip to London as external affairs minister he asked to borrow the spacious Canada House office of the number two Canadian diplomat in London, George Ignatieff. He also asked for three cups of tea and "if possible, some biscuits." Ignatieff assumed it was a high-level, private VIP conference on world affairs, and was startled later to find Green was meeting with two elderly ladies to thank them for nursing him back to health after he'd been wounded in World War I.

The tall, soft-spoken Green had a human sensitivity that sometimes puzzled the Americans. He once drove Livingston Merchant almost to tears of frustration when Merchant was urgently pressing him on the nuclear weapons question. As they drove into Ottawa from a meeting at nearby Montebello, Quebec, Merchant pressured Green about warheads, but the only thing Green would talk about was a Walpole Island Indian who had stolen an outboard motor and had been arrested by U.S. police on Canadian territory. To Green at that moment, the infringement of the Indian's rights was far more important a question than anything else – and besides, the incident provided an excuse to forestall any talk with Merchant about warheads.

Looking back on his role at External Affairs, Green later said, "Quite early in the game, it became very apparent to me that the main problem for Canada was the danger of nuclear war. . . . If there is a nuclear war, Canada probably would be the main battleground. I think that would be the end of

Canada. This is where we had to put our stress. So that was what we did."

He combined an instinctive revulsion at any Canadian nuclear involvement with a kind of Woodrow Wilson idealism, frequently berating his colleagues with his disarmament fixation. "My, but Howard does get worked up," sighed George Pearkes to Canadian Press reporter Dave McIntosh after a phone call from Green.

Privately assessing the new foreign minister in his diary, Canadian Ambassador to the U.S. Arnold Heeney commented, "Green, the most pleasant of good, simple men, is an innocent abroad and what is more, obstinate and underneath, inclined to a sort of pacific-isolationism." At another point Heeney noted, "Howard Green . . . was sadly miscast. . . . He allowed himself to drift into the role of one who would have peace at almost any price."

"Green simply astonished us," admits Rufus Smith, a long-time Canadian expert in the State Department who would later head the Canadian desk at State and become the American minister in Ottawa. Rusk found Green "sanctimonious" and "self-righteous" and wrote in his memo to Kennedy that Green "has exhibited . . . a naive and almost parochial approach to some international problems which was first attributed to his inexperience but which is now believed to be part of his basic personality."

While Dean Rusk and Livingston Merchant were baffled by Green and often frustrated, they never doubted his genuine honesty, as they did with Diefenbaker. Nor did they feel any personal animus in their relations with Green. "To the Americans, Howard Green was the embodiment of the principle of nuclear rejection," says former Canadian ambassador to Washington Charles Ritchie. "Diefenbaker was not. Diefenbaker was viewed as wily, erratic, and politics-driven."

American officials joked about Green's innocent nature. They liked to tell the story of Congo leader Patrice Lumumba's visit to Ottawa. After a meeting, Lumumba asked Green to send "a girl" around to his Château Laurier hotel suite. Green, thinking Lumumba wanted to dictate correspondence, dispatched one of his secretaries. The aghast and unwilling secretary fled when

Lumumba's purpose was revealed. But Lumumba's urges were professionally satisfied the next night thanks to arrangements made by External Affairs; the department carefully entered the cost of the service in its books as "flowers."

But Green's single-mindedness on disarmament was no joking matter for the Americans, particularly since his influence on Diefenbaker was reinforced by his deputy minister, Norman Robertson, a mandarin's mandarin and a monochrome Machiavelli. Robertson had been clerk of the Privy Council, high commissioner in London, and ambassador to the United States. His philosophical alignment with Green on disarmament was strengthened by the fact that they were both British Columbians and their families had known each other for years. Green had studied with Robertson's father at university. Sometimes they would spend weekends together at Robertson's farm in Wakefield, Quebec, outside Ottawa.

They were, in truth, an odd couple: Robertson the chain-smoking, sophisticated, intellectual élitist, and Green the idealistic, parochial "everyman." Both, however, were rock-solid stubborn in their zeal about disarmament, and together they turned Diefenbaker and the government of Canada upside down on nuclear arms. Robertson's hands shaped the delaying tactics on Canadian acquisition of nuclear weapons, but in his impeccable mandarin style, his fingerprints were nowhere to be seen. As the hidden architect of much of the Diefenbaker–Green nuclear policies, he provided an intellectual respectability because of his wide-ranging mind, moral fibre, and determination bordering on obsession.

"If it hadn't been for Green and Robertson, we wouldn't have had the mess over nuclear warheads," says Willis Armstrong, former U.S. minister in Ottawa and senior State Department official. "If Diefenbaker had been a stronger character, he would have overruled Green. He didn't have the guts to settle the differences in his own cabinet."

"A great brooding man of intelligence and depth," as Robertson is described by historian J.L. Granatstein, he provided the intellectual reinforcement for Green's emotional commitment to disarmament. With deep sighs, Robertson would meditate at length on the future of Canada, so much so, a State

Department note said, that "his preoccupation with Canada's future in five or ten years makes it difficult to get him to think more practically about the decisions of today."

The Americans had been respectful of Robertson's intellect but nervous about his philosophy for a couple of years. The State Department regarded him as the grey eminence behind Green and Diefenbaker; a department memorandum said he "is prone to seek solutions that emphasize that Canada should not blindly follow the lead of the United States. It is possible that the growing tendency evident during the past year or so within the Canadian Government to take a 'softer' line toward the Soviet bloc . . . is due in part to Robertson." This was another aspect of the philosophical alignment between Green and Robertson: Green had always taken a "softer" approach to the Soviet Union. He had favoured having Khrushchev visit Canada in late 1959 as a way of showing that Canada was not a "crushed satellite" of the Americans, and he had told Eisenhower's secretary of state, Christian Herter, that Canadians "were not nearly so worried about the Russians" as the Americans were. The State Department also noted that "Robertson appears to have reservations in regard to close defense arrangements Canada has with the United States and, therefore, tends generally to resist any U.S. extension of joint defense facilities in Canada."

In his diary, Ambassador Heeney noted the potent combination of Green and Robertson, saying, "[Green's] own attitude and prejudices in a curious way combined with Norman Robertson's cosmic anxieties particularly in our defence relationships . . . to produce a negative force of great importance."

In June 1959, two days before Green became external affairs minister, Robertson had clipped out an article from the British magazine *The Spectator* that argued for unilateral nuclear disarmament and a strengthening of conventional arms. Author Christopher Hollis argued that the hydrogen bomb had changed everything and that a nuclear war would destroy civilization. Great nations would gain rather than lose power if they eliminated nuclear weapons, Hollis said. Robertson's antinuclear position was hardening, and he sent the article to Diefenbaker, saying he wanted the prime minister to know that he, Robertson, shared those views.

At the same time, however, Robertson still felt Canada had committed itself to accept nuclear warheads. In a memorandum to his new external affairs minister, Robertson said, "Although we plan to equip Canadian forces with modern weapons, we consider it expedient that the ownership and custody . . . should remain with the United States. . . . We are . . . on the threshold of equipping Canadian forces with nuclear weapons." But Robertson was about to change his attitude from one of acceptance to one of forestalling, as he became increasingly haunted by the spectre of nuclear war.

Diefenbaker didn't like Robertson but respected his advice, especially if it coincided with his own views. "Diefenbaker didn't like anyone with a reputation for brains," says Bunny Pound. "He knew Norman Robertson was well regarded, but he had no way of communicating with him. He felt abashed." Besides, Diefenbaker nursed an old grudge against Robertson stemming from a request Diefenbaker had made in 1945 when he was going to San Francisco for the founding conference of the United Nations. As the adviser to the Conservative member of the Canadian delegation, he thought he should have the prestige of a diplomatic passport. Prime Minister Mackenzie King thought otherwise and instructed Robertson to send a letter to Diefenbaker refusing the request. It was a slight Diefenbaker never forgot, nor did he forget Norman Robertson's signature at the bottom of the letter of rejection.

Diefenbaker read the article sent to him by Robertson, though, and was also reading his mail, which reflected growing concern with the lack of progress on disarmament and opposition to Canadian acquisition of nuclear arms.

Green had always been uneasy about U.S. military activities in Canada, especially in the North, and as he and Robertson went over the nuclear issue, he became increasingly apprehensive. He crossed the line from unease to rejection of Pentagon thinking in the late summer of 1959. The U.S. Air Force, working with the RCAF, had planned a training exercise over Canada for September. Operation Sky Hawk had been planned for six months and had already cost millions of dollars; U.S. officials had gone to Ottawa for extensive discussions about it with NORAD officials, Canadian military and transport personnel, and the ministers of defence and transport. The intent was to see how vulnerable North American defence was to Soviet electronic jamming. There had been no Canadian objections until Green heard about it and complained to the prime minister. "Totally inappropriate and provocative now," Green said, and Diefenbaker was outraged that he hadn't been personally informed earlier. Ottawa told Washington to cancel the exercise because it would disrupt civilian air traffic for several hours over Canada and might anger Khrushchev.

Urgent telegrams flew back and forth, the American ambassador personally pleaded with Diefenbaker to change his mind, and Ambassador Heeney was summoned twice to the State Department to hear American "shock" and "gravest concern." The Americans said, "The Canadian attitude in this matter might cause a serious cleavage in U.S.-Canadian relations and might tend to weaken NATO." But Diefenbaker and Green were adamant, because they felt that Sky Hawk would send out the wrong kind of message to disarmament negotiators. Diefenbaker also said the test would have put Canada "on the tail of the United States." Even a letter from his friend Eisenhower could not dissuade Diefenbaker. In fury, the Americans cancelled the air defence test; but later, with Canadian concurrence this time, they planned another one for the next year.

A few weeks after the Sky Hawk contretemps, Green attended the United Nations General Assembly meeting for the first time as external affairs minister and simply fell in love with the UN atmosphere and with his vision of Canada leading the world to disarmament. To the distress of Washington, he proclaimed in a UN speech on that first visit, "The Canadian people are unanimous in their wish to see an end to nuclear testing," and he launched his disarmament crusade.

At this point, Green and Diefenbaker differed on the prospects for disarmament. At a mid-November 1959 cabinet meeting, Diefenbaker said, according to the summary, "As far as disarmament is concerned, despite all the talk he could see little chance for progress." A few minutes later, however, the summary recorded Green's optimistic attitude: "Prospects for disarmament . . . at the moment, he felt to be quite good."

At that meeting Diefenbaker and most of the cabinet, with the exception of Green, indicated they were still intent on an agreement with the U.S. on nuclear warheads in Canada.

Ministers reporting to the meeting on a session of the Canada–U.S. Ministerial Committee on Defence said they "had pointed out that the Canadian Government had agreed to the storage of nuclear weapons of a defensive nature for the U.S. forces, but that details of the arrangement had yet to be worked out." The summary also notes, "The domestic political consequences would be severe if it became known that Canada was unwilling to do what was reasonable with the U.S. for the defence of North America." It was a prescient comment whose warning would be fulfilled three years later with the Cuban Missile Crisis, which spelled the beginning of the end for John Diefenbaker's prime ministership.

A critical new player came onto the stage when Douglas Harkness succeeded George Pearkes as defence minister in October 1960. He was even more deeply committed than Pearkes to acquiring nuclear warheads for Canadian forces both in North America and in NATO. When he took office, Harkness discussed with Diefenbaker the link between disarmament and warheads; he later wrote, in a private paper, "[Diefenbaker] agreed that the chances of a meaningful disarmament were remote and that we must secure the nuclear ammunition for the weapons we had ordered."

In short order Harkness became a powerful adversary of Howard Green on the nuclear issue. But it was an unequal match, in part because Green was a long-time Diefenbaker political ally, and Harkness had been a George Drew supporter and was never close to Diefenbaker. To counter Harkness, Robertson sought to reinforce Green's arguments within the cabinet, advising him, "At a time when Western Governments generally and Canada in particular, have been urging in the United Nations that every effort should be made to get disarmament discussions going again . . . it would be inconsistent and hypocritical for us at the same time to adopt policies which can only have the effect of compounding the nuclear problem."

With Robertson's "cosmic anxieties" and his concerns that nuclear weapons would lead to "global suicide," and with Howard Green's passionate and increasingly obsessive commitment to disarmament, the stage was set for a confrontation within the cabinet and a collision with Washington.

In November 1960, the Canadian delegation to a NATO

parliamentary conference had indicated that Canada's NATO brigade should have nuclear weapons by 1961, pushing the Harkness line. The government dodged questions on the issue in the House as Diefenbaker's private doubts about the political prudence of siting nuclear warheads in Canada became serious. He was deeply affected not only by the anti-nuclear mail he was getting but also by the noisy agitation of the influential anti-bomb group the Voice of Women, by the impact in Canada of Stanley Kramer's anti-nuclear-war movie *On the Beach*, and by the influential book *Peacemaker or Powder-Monkey* by CBC Washington correspondent James M. Minifie, who argued passionately for a neutralist Canadian foreign policy. Diefenbaker concluded that it was more politically beneficial to be pro-disarmament than to be pro-nuclear. But at the same time, he did not want to be seen to be shirking North American and NATO defence responsibilities. Thus began his indecision on the issue as he sought to placate both sides.

In a speech to the Canadian Club of Ottawa in late November, Diefenbaker said, "No decision will be required [on accepting warheads] while progress toward disarmament continues. . . . We shall not in any event consider nuclear weapons until, as a sovereign nation, we have equality in control – joint control." He also told Heeney at this time that he was deferring a decision on acquisition of nuclear warheads. "Ultimately," Heeney quoted him as saying, "Canadian forces would have to be armed with nuclear weapons but there must be satisfactory arrangements for joint control of use." Heeney knew Washington was agreeable to such "joint control" and wrote in his diary, "U.S.A. were totally mystified as to our position." He also noted his own embarrassment in dealing with American authorities who "had thought we were agreed." Heeney himself felt there was a Canadian commitment.

The Pentagon was particularly furious at Diefenbaker's delay in making a decision to acquire nuclear warheads for Bomarc. They dismissed his arguments about the link to disarmament. "It couldn't possibly accelerate the arms race since the Bomarc could only be used to shoot down enemy planes that were already over Canadian territory," a Pentagon official said. "Besides, the Bomarc range is only four hundred miles, so it's no threat to the Soviet Union itself."

But Diefenbaker was clearly leaning away from what the Canadian military, most of the government's senior advisers, NATO, and Washington believed to be a Canadian commitment to accept nuclear warheads for Bomarc, for storage at U.S. bases in Canada in Labrador and Newfoundland, and for the Canadian forces in Europe. Diefenbaker added confusion to complexity on the issue when, two weeks after giving his Ottawa speech, he had the cabinet lay down a broad policy framework for negotiations with the United States on acquisition of nuclear weapons. Discussions with the U.S. "concerning arrangements for the essential acquisition of nuclear weapons or warheads for use by the Canadian forces . . . may proceed as soon as they can be usefully undertaken with the acceptance of joint control to be a basic principle," said the cabinet directive. The Americans took heart from this statement, knowing "joint control" was agreeable to them through the "two-key" mutual veto arrangement. They were also heartened by a reminder in cabinet papers that "Canadian Ministers should recognize that the government has agreed, at the meeting in December 1957 and at other times, and is morally bound, to supply Canadian forces under NATO Command equipped and ready to use nuclear weapons if and when they are necessary."

Recognizing the juggling act that Diefenbaker was playing, Robertson and Green adopted the tactics of "delay, delay, delay" obstructionism so that there could be a façade of full co-operation with the United States on continental defence and in NATO, but a reality of no nuclear weapons – at least not yet. "Howard took a very stubborn position," says Harkness, who adds that Green began insisting on detailed examination of every facet of a deal with the Americans with the objective of delay.

Green also began trying to outflank Harkness at the United Nations by committing Canada to an anti-nuclear role. Towards the end of 1960, Ireland proposed a resolution requesting those nations without nuclear weapons not to acquire them. The Diefenbaker cabinet had decided to abstain from voting on the resolution, but under a threat of resignation from the tenacious Green, the cabinet reversed itself and Canada voted for it. The Irish resolution was used thereafter by Green as an argument that Canadian acceptance of nuclear weapons would be a violation of this UN pledge.

Diefenbaker flew down to Washington on the morning of February 20, 1961, full of apprehension and glad he was having only a short meeting with President Kennedy and not a long, detailed one. "As we were flying down he got himself up for it," says Basil Robinson, who went with him as his foreign policy adviser. "He was nervous, but the fact that it was a brief meeting made it easier for him." He may have sensed that he was not, in fact, the White House's favourite Canadian guest. From the very start of their relationship with Diefenbaker, both Kennedy and Rusk wished Lester Pearson had been prime minister instead of Diefenbaker. That was especially true of Rusk and his State Department associates, who had worked with Pearson when he was Canada's external affairs minister. "We'd been spoiled by a long association with Mike Pearson," Rusk says. "He was as comfortable as an old shoe."

Diefenbaker still nursed hurt feelings about Kennedy's mis-pronunciation of his name and the president's tardiness in responding to his congratulatory message. But with his worries about military pressure on defence policies, Diefenbaker had been encouraged by an early move by Kennedy to "muzzle" hot-headed Pentagon generals and admirals who had been speaking out for a tougher Cold War posture for the United States. It was an echo of Diefenbaker's own public condemnation a few months earlier of "those in positions of military responsibility who indulge themselves in the dangerous course of rocket rattling." Officials hoped the two leaders' shared unease with "rocket rattling" would help offset some of the prime minister's galloping distaste for the glamorous, activist Kennedy style, and his apprehension about "that boy."

Diefenbaker was also unsettled by the image of Kennedy's Washington with all the hot-eyed, brainy, thrusting New Frontiersmen, bursting with ideas and eager for action. There was around Kennedy a crackling electricity and, even when he was sitting still, a sense of motion forcibly restrained. Kennedy viewed the presidency as the highest of all adventures; barely suppressing his excitement, he told friends, "The pay is good and I can walk to work." For John Diefenbaker, it was all so unlike the reassuringly comfy calm of Eisenhower's Washington. And he still felt hurt that Kennedy had never mentioned Canada in the entire election campaign and, worse still, had

made no reference to Canada in his inaugural address. Diefenbaker petulantly noted that Nehru, Churchill, and de Gaulle
had been mentioned in the campaign, but not himself.

Diefenbaker had not taken time to study his briefing papers
for the visit until the last minute before leaving Ottawa. As he
flew over the snow-covered fields and mountains of New York
state and Pennsylvania en route to the American capital, he read
his papers and listened to Howard Green emphasize the importance of avoiding any commitments to Kennedy about accepting U.S. nuclear warheads. That, Green said, would destroy
Canada's influence at the United Nations in promoting disarmament.

After a two-and-a-quarter-hour flight, Diefenbaker stepped
off his plane at 11:25 A.M. into the spring-like weather to be
met by Angier Biddle Duke, the U.S. chief of protocol, Merchant, Heeney, and an honour guard. He was then whisked off
to the White House, where Kennedy and Rusk met him just
before noon for the first of their only three meetings. He had
met Kennedy a few years before, but it had been only a
handshake at a Washington reception. Unlike the "Ike and
John" friendship he'd had for three and a half years, it was now
"Mr. President" and "Mr. Prime Minister" and would remain
so throughout their tumultuous two-and-a-half-year relationship. Tall, trim, and youthful, Kennedy shook hands with
Diefenbaker, his grey-blue eyes dancing and a smile crinkling
the fading traces of a Palm Beach tan on his face. Kennedy was
half the tough, pragmatic, sometimes bawdy Boston Irish
politician, and half the graceful, stylish intellectual. It was a
combination that baffled and distressed the prime minister.

A month ago, Diefenbaker had been standing here on the
thick grey-green presidential carpet with Ike. Now he saw the
president's Oval Office transformed from a staid, formal place
of business into what was clearly a navy man's working space.
There were ship models, naval paintings, and a collection of
whale's teeth scattered along the curved walls and shelves, and
a massive, richly carved presidential desk made from the timbers
of a famous British frigate, HMS *Resolute*. The ship had been
wrecked in 1854 in the Arctic while searching for the explorer
Sir John Franklin, who had been looking for the Northwest
Passage. The *Resolute* had been found by an American whaler

and presented to Queen Victoria. In 1878 the ship was broken up and Queen Victoria had a desk made from the timbers. She gave it to President Rutherford Hayes, and it languished in a White House storage area for more than half a century until found by Jackie Kennedy, who gave it to her delighted husband.

Kennedy ushered Diefenbaker over to a sofa by the fireplace, and he sat in his white-padded rocking chair. Neither had much capacity for small talk so they quickly got down to business, with a general review of world troubles including Laos, the Congo, Soviet pressures on the UN organization, and NATO. There was general agreement on these issues. Then Diefenbaker launched into bread-and-butter bilateral questions, talking about the $1-billion-a-year trade imbalance with the U.S. and his worries about American investment in Canada. Kennedy and Rusk listened politely, but the president was unfamiliar with the issues and bored by their recitation, while Rusk didn't take Diefenbaker's concerns all that seriously. Years later he would say he felt Diefenbaker's fears about American investment engulfing Canada were psychological, not real. "I said to them, 'All right, we'll stop it,'" he says. "The Canadians said, 'Oh no! Don't do that! It'll hurt our tax base, our dollar, our development.' I came to the conclusion that Canadians wanted American investments but, at the same time, wanted to complain about them, too."

To Diefenbaker's concerns, Kennedy responded sympathetically, in one instance offering a solution to a problem on Canadian trade with China, which was being hindered by U.S. regulations barring American companies from involvement in China trade. Imperial Oil of Canada, because it was a U.S. subsidiary, was being prevented from providing bunker oil for ships transporting Canadian wheat to China. During the lunch break in their meeting, Kennedy asked his aide Fred Dutton to check out what could be done; later he said that if Canada would "quietly ask" Imperial Oil to provide the oil, then the U.S. regulations would not be applied. That was done and the oil was provided. The problem was solved much more smoothly than a similar problem had been earlier: the Americans had objected to Chinese shrimp imported by Canada being transported by truck from Vancouver to eastern Canada through the United States. Having the Chinese shrimp travel on U.S. roads endangered American security, Washington said. Diefenbaker had had to intervene before the U.S. would allow the shrimp to continue on their nefarious way.

Kennedy was significantly less adamant about China than Eisenhower had been. Although he maintained opposition to diplomatic recognition of China, he felt it was "just a matter of time" before the People's Republic became a member of the United Nations.

There was less agreement on Cuba, however. Unknown to Diefenbaker, Kennedy's CIA was plotting the Bay of Pigs invasion, and the president was in a hawkish mood about Castro. Kennedy was distressed, as Eisenhower and his administration had been, about Canadian trade with Cuba. Diefenbaker responded that Canadian trade was minimal and, in fact, worth less than the medical supplies and other similar goods still traded by the United States with Cuba. Diefenbaker said Kennedy should have no fear of Canada allowing circumvention of the American trade embargo by trans-shipment of U.S. goods through Canada to Cuba. "The position of my government was continually misinterpreted and misrepresented in the United States," Diefenbaker would later say, adding that Canada had a long tradition of doing business with Cuba and that "it became rather tiresome repeating over and over that . . . our motives in trading with Cuba were not simply economic opportunism."

The central focus of the Kennedy–Diefenbaker talks was the question of Canadian acceptance of nuclear warheads. Diefenbaker said there was sharp opposition to nuclear weapons in Canada but, portraying himself as a strong ally, he said Canada would not play merely a "birdwatching" role in continental defence. Canada, he said, would "not accept a policy which will lay upon the United States a responsibility which we should carry ourselves." He added that it was unacceptable for Canada to have only limited participation in NORAD because that, he said, would make Canada less, not more, independent. The prime minister spoke in similar terms on nuclear warheads for Canada's NATO forces, as well as on the question of storage of nuclear warheads at American bases located in Canada. Kennedy took from this a Diefenbaker commitment to acquire nuclear weapons. But then Diefenbaker added that the decision on warhead acquisition would be tied in not only to progress on disarmament and Canadian "control" of the warheads, but also to U.S. co-operation in a deal for defence production-sharing, by which he meant increased American purchases of Canadian defence equipment.

All this "confused the hell" out of Kennedy, according to one aide, but the president suggested Canada could have a joint-control arrangement for the warheads, similar to the arrangement the British had. Rusk had assured him that Washington found the two-key scheme acceptable. The Americans drew from Diefenbaker's comments the sense that although there was opposition in Canada to accepting the warheads and there was no written agreement between Ottawa and Washington, nevertheless Diefenbaker personally favoured acceptance and Canada would, in the end, acquire nuclear weapons.

Diefenbaker said later, "We reached agreement on the question of the conditions under which nuclear warheads for Canadian forces in Canada and Europe would be stockpiled." Only the "details," he said, needed to be worked out. He felt Kennedy had agreed that arrangements for accepting warheads would be made and be ready for implementation "when conditions made it necessary." But he never spelled out exactly what he meant by those "conditions," although his words later suggested he meant when the Soviet bombers were over the Pole and on their way to North American targets.

A few days after the meeting, R.B. Bryce, clerk of the Privy Council, sent a note to Harkness saying: "Mr. Diefenbaker said he had stated that negotiations should continue regarding such [nuclear] storage at Harmon Field and Goose Bay, but that Canada would insist upon joint custody and control and joint authority over use. The President had seemed to raise no objection. Regarding the submarine base at Argentia, Mr. Diefenbaker said he had stated that Canada would require joint custody, but that use should be determined by NATO. He had further stated that so long as serious disarmament negotiations continued Canada did not propose to determine whether or not to accept nuclear weapons for the Bomarc bases or for the Canadian interceptors; but that if such weapons were accepted by Canada, this country would require joint custody and joint control. . . . Negotiations for the necessary agreements should now continue on the basis of a 'package deal', no one agreement being signed before the others had been worked out. There would be no hold up if war should occur. The President had asked whether the same sort of 'two key' arrangement as the United Kingdom had would be satisfactory and Mr. Diefenbaker had said it would."

The different interpretations in Washington and Ottawa on the nuclear question led to conflicting newspaper headlines. The Toronto *Globe and Mail* reported, after a briefing by Canadian and American officials, that Diefenbaker had said the Canadian government intended to proceed with acquisition of nuclear warheads. Diefenbaker was quoted as saying, "We don't intend to be neutralist regardless of the opinion expressed by some people . . . simply to take on the responsibility of bird watchers." The next day, Diefenbaker denied that he had indicated that he would take the warheads. "Totally unfounded," he said of the report.

Diefenbaker had linked acceptance of the warheads to progress on disarmament because of the preoccupations of Howard Green. Kennedy knew of Green's obsession on disarmament, which was born in part out of his memory of the horrors of World War I. When the Oval Office meeting ended and Green had gone into an anteroom to get his coat, Kennedy suddenly came up to him. Green said, "President Kennedy appeared right beside me and he whispered in my ear, 'I want you to know, Mr. Green, that I'm going to do all I can on the question of disarmament.' "

Kennedy and Rusk were aware of the cabinet divisions in Canada on nuclear warheads, but they anticipated that the view of Defence Minister Harkness and the Canadian military would in the end prevail. Harkness had at first accepted Diefenbaker's delay on acquisition of the warheads because the planes, cannons, and Bomarc missiles that would use them had not yet been delivered. But within three or four months of his appointment, Harkness began to push Diefenbaker. "I went to Diefenbaker," he says, "and said that we should now go ahead and negotiate with the U.S. for securing these nuclear warheads . . . and he agreed that we would have to do it." He quoted Diefenbaker as saying, "We are going to sign them all right, don't worry about that. We'll complete the agreements, but we don't need to do it right now, and let's not get any great disturbance with Howard over it."

Harkness pressured Diefenbaker in public as well. Just days before the Kennedy–Diefenbaker meeting, Harkness had pleaded in Parliament for Canadian military reserve officers to go out and fight the Ban-the-Bomb groups who, he said, were damaging Canada's military effectiveness in order "to undermine the will of the Canadian people to resist aggression." In a Montreal speech, he said, "In the modern world, if you're going to be efficiently armed, there seems no question that you've got to have nuclear arms," and in a sideswipe at his colleague Green, Harkness noted, "We should invite jeers rather than cheers if we attempted to play India's game with Canada's hand."

As the White House conversations proceeded over a working lunch, Kennedy became increasingly uneasy about Diefenbaker, sensing – as Rusk had advised him – that the prime minister's talk of disarmament and his whole attitude towards foreign policy in general and the United States in particular were essentially driven by domestic political considerations. Kennedy managed to get a rise out of Diefenbaker by playing on those domestic concerns, however, when he said lightly, "Would I be right in thinking that the United States is not unhelpful to you for political purposes in Canada?" "That would be a not inaccurate conclusion," Diefenbaker smiled, in a rare instance of appreciation of Kennedy's sharp, mocking humour. Heeney wasn't so sanguine about the use of anti-Americanism by Canadian politicians, confiding to his diary, "I continue to shudder at the partisan capital that can be made at home with any anti-U.S. sentiment no matter how cheap."

At that point in their relationship, Kennedy was more high-spirited than mean-spirited about Diefenbaker's anti-Americanism, much as President Teddy Roosevelt had been six decades earlier when he commented, "Canadians like to indulge themselves as a harmless luxury in a feeling of hostility to the United States. . . . The average Canadian likes to feel patriotic by jeering at the man across the border."

Kennedy noted Diefenbaker's reputation as a fisherman and pointed to a stuffed sailfish on the wall of the White House "Fish Room" across the corridor from his office, asking, "Have you ever caught anything better?" Kennedy had caught the sailfish on his honeymoon in Acapulco. The prime minister gleefully responded that he had just been in Jamaica, where he had caught a 140-pound, eight-and-a-half-foot marlin. It was something of which he was inordinately proud, the biggest fish he had ever caught. But Kennedy teased him about it. "You didn't catch it," Diefenbaker remembered Kennedy saying. Diefenbaker replied that yes, he had indeed pulled it in, and it had taken three hours and ten minutes to do it. "Well, that stuck in his craw," Diefenbaker later said.

When he got back to Ottawa, Diefenbaker made arrangements to have the marlin mounted on his office wall. "That bloody marlin was always staring at you," Diefenbaker aide Tommy Van Dusen says. "When [Kennedy] visited Canada," Diefenbaker later said, "one of the first things he said to me was, 'Where's your marlin?' When he saw it, he said, 'That is big.' And then he added something revealing: 'You know, I spent $50,000 trying to catch a fish like that.' . . . My catch did not cost me anything." It was a little triumph over Kennedy that Diefenbaker savoured all his life.

Diefenbaker recalled that Kennedy said to him as they began talking in the White House, "Just imagine, here I am, president of the United States. . . . How am I doing?" It was a question Kennedy had earlier asked a reporter, who had responded, "Great"; Kennedy's reply to that was, "You have to kiss a lot of people's asses." In a less scatological conversation, Diefenbaker quoted himself as responding, "So far as I could tell, everything seemed to be going well with his new administration, but I told him I could not understand why he would appoint his brother Robert attorney general. He was not a practising lawyer and would know nothing about it." According to Diefenbaker, Kennedy came back with, "Can you tell me how he could learn law faster?" The prime minister had hit on a sensitive point, for Kennedy was well aware of scepticism about the appointment.

Diefenbaker was not only critical of Kennedy's brother Robert, he was also vicious about Kennedy's father. Alvin Hamilton recalls Diefenbaker saying that he had told the president that Joe Kennedy "had betrayed the British with his support of the Nazis during the war"; Diefenbaker said he spoke of "the disgrace that your father brought." Whether or not Diefenbaker actually said that to Kennedy, it undoubtedly was what he believed and further sharpened his conflict with the American president.

As he glanced about the light green walls of the Oval Office, Diefenbaker was struck by paintings depicting American naval victories over the British in the War of 1812. "It's as if the Americans won every damn war," he would later mutter to Tommy Van Dusen.

Diefenbaker told Kennedy how the British frigate *Shannon* had captured the U.S. frigate *Chesapeake* and taken it to Halifax in 1813.

"If I had that picture I would put it up," Kennedy said.

"I'll show you," Diefenbaker responded, and when he got back to Canada he ordered the national librarian, Dr. Kaye Lamb, to comb the art galleries of Britain and the United States to find a picture depicting the capture of the U.S. frigate. Lamb finally found a print in New York showing British sailors bloodily overwhelming the Yankees, but Diefenbaker's special assistant, John Fisher, thought the whole idea was a bad one. "Don't send that to Kennedy, sir," Fisher said. "What are you trying to prove by sending down something a hundred years after the event?"

"Oh, we must teach him some history. History must be taught," Diefenbaker responded with what Fisher called "devilish eyes."

In the end, Kennedy never saw the picture, and he continued to regard the War of 1812 as an American triumph.

Towards the end of his Oval Office visit, Diefenbaker glanced out the French doors at the sun-splashed flower garden behind the presidential office. He had never walked around the White House, he remarked, and Kennedy quickly said, "Let's go!" He knew the reporters and photographers waiting outside would gratify the prime minister with politically useful pictures and stories of their stroll about the White House grounds. So, smiling and chatting, and followed by the expected journalistic mob (mostly Canadians), the president led Diefenbaker along the grass and pathways up to Diefenbaker's car, which was waiting to drive him to the airport.

Another smile, another handshake, and after two and three-quarter hours of conversation and lunch, they parted. Diefenbaker happily and briefly met reporters ("Every source of disagreement has been removed after discussion," he said) and jumped into his car. "He had a much more optimistic picture of what the relationship might be than what he feared when he went down," recalls Basil Robinson. He couldn't keep still, and on the flight back to Ottawa he decided to go straight to the House of Commons and speak about his success with Kennedy. He strode up and down the aisle of the plane, dictating comments he wanted in his speech to describe the meeting. "Put in 'exhilarating,' " he said. Diefenbaker was especially pleased that Kennedy had accepted his invitation to come to Ottawa in the spring.

There was a far different reaction at the White House about the meeting. "Kennedy thought the Canadian insincere and did not like or trust him," presidential aide and historian Arthur Schlesinger says. That first meeting, he adds, "had not proved a success." Unimpressed and suspicious of Diefenbaker's motives, Kennedy laughed when he later heard Diefenbaker had described the visit as "exhilarating."

But most of all, Kennedy was simply bored by Diefenbaker. "I don't want to see that boring son of a bitch again," Kennedy told his brother Robert. Charles Bartlett, a journalist and long-time friend, said, "You could kick him. You could rob him. But you must never bore him."

The American media didn't think much of the Kennedy–Diefenbaker meeting either. While it was front-page news in Canadian newspapers, the New York *Times* had a brief story on page 20 the next day.

But to Diefenbaker, the meeting was an enormous success. Landing in a cold and clear Ottawa just at sunset, he rushed to the House of Commons and interrupted a debate to tell the House, "To me, this was a revealing and exhilarating experience. The President of the United States has the kind of personality that leaves upon one the impression of a person dedicated to peace, to raising economic standards in all countries and achievement in his day of disarmament of all nations of the world. . . . There is no problem which we cannot surmount."

But that night, Diefenbaker's "triumph" in Washington was

put aside as the prime minister was told that his eighty-six-year-old mother had died that day. It was an ill omen, and he would later associate seeing Kennedy with the death of his mother, who had goaded him to the political summit and to whom he had been devoted.

While Diefenbaker was publicly basking in the seeming success of his meeting with Kennedy, he was privately returning to his old suspicions and distaste for the new American president. When British Prime Minister Harold Macmillan came to Ottawa in early April en route home from his first meeting with Kennedy, Diefenbaker was eager to gossip about Kennedy. Macmillan said he was much impressed with the New Frontier and found Kennedy more "flexible" and "sensitive" to world problems than the Eisenhower administration had been. Diefenbaker pouted at this positive assessment, so much so that Macmillan's senior advisers remarked on it to External Affairs officials, and Basil Robinson noted in his diary, "Macmillan scarcely concealed his irritation at P.M.'s negative position." The incident reinforced Macmillan's growing distaste for Diefenbaker, which had started a year earlier at the Commonwealth Prime Ministers Conference in London dealing with South Africa. At that time, Macmillan had confided to his diary that he felt Diefenbaker was "woolly," "very disappointing," and "deaf, ignorant and little more than a 'tub thumper.' He never forgets party politics and talks of little else."

As Diefenbaker readied himself for the spring 1961 visit to Ottawa of President Kennedy, he knew the conversations with Kennedy would be more detailed and difficult than those of the February meeting. He turned to George Ignatieff, who had recently been named assistant under-secretary of state for external affairs, for advice on a rationale for his hesitation on acquiring nuclear warheads. "I tried to make him understand," Ignatieff said, "that by committing Canada to an integrated North American defence system, he had accepted a subordinate role in a strategy based almost entirely on the nuclear deterrent."

Diefenbaker told Ignatieff that he'd been misled by the

military into believing the Bomarc-B anti-aircraft missile could use conventional weapons – a claim that flies in the face of all evidence. An earlier version of Bomarc, the Bomarc-A, was capable of using conventional warheads, but Diefenbaker had deliberately committed Canada to the nuclear-only Bomarc-B. "The day he approved NORAD," Ignatieff said, "he embarked on a course which led to the acceptance of nuclear weapons."

Ignatieff, although a diplomatic realist, was also an indefatigable champion of disarmament, and he sought to provide Diefenbaker with a formula that he could use with Kennedy in articulating the near-incomprehensibility of Canada's official position on warheads. The urbane diplomat proposed that the prime minister say he would accept warheads on two conditions: first, if there were joint control in their use – a joint control of Diefenbaker's particular definition; and second, only if an all-out effort at disarmament were launched first and if, at the end, it was determined that there could be no progress. That formula would buy Diefenbaker some time and it might well wash politically in Canada, even if it wouldn't in Washington. "Making clear-cut decisions was not part of Diefenbaker's nature," Ignatieff later remarked.

The prime minister was worried that Kennedy would come on strong on the nuclear issue, which was attracting growing public attention. Two weeks before the Ottawa meeting, newspapers reported the critical remarks of Lieutenant-General Robert M. Lee, vice-commander of the U.S. Air Defense Command, who said the two Canadian Bomarc squadrons were useless without nuclear warheads. But shortly before the trip Kennedy was politically weakened by the disastrous Bay of Pigs invasion of Cuba, and Diefenbaker hoped the humiliation of that grotesque miscalculation might inhibit some of Kennedy's activist tendencies.

Almost since New Year's Day 1959, when Fidel Castro had seized power, Washington and Ottawa had been in conflict about Cuba. Eisenhower told Diefenbaker that Cuba was a Soviet outpost in the Caribbean, exporting revolutionary Communism into Latin America. When the Americans began economic retaliation against Cuba, they sought Canadian support. But with a firmness that surprised the Americans, Diefenbaker,

Green, and other ministers rejected a "get tough with Cuba" approach. Diefenbaker was certainly anti-Communist, but he knew there was domestic political value in opposing the increasingly harsh American policy towards Castro. He also felt that policy might drive Castro more quickly into the outstretched arms of Khrushchev. "It was also a fact that we had no serious grounds of complaint in our bilateral relations with Cuba," Diefenbaker said later in his memoirs. "I would have been hard-pressed to find any justification for yielding to American demands for an embargo against Cuba."

The American trade embargo against Cuba had gone into effect in October 1960 in the heat of the American presidential election campaign, but Diefenbaker said Canada would continue to trade with Cuba. Castro promptly announced that a high-level eleven-man trade mission would go to Ottawa to expand trade with Canada. With excessive enthusiasm, Trade Minister George Hees zestfully talked of $150 million a year in trade with Cuba (which would have been a ten-fold increase) and exulted to reporters, "You can't do business with better businessmen anywhere. They're wonderful customers!" It was a sentiment that did not go down well in Washington in the midst of their preparations for an invasion of Cuba. Canadian trade with Cuba did increase from $13 million to over $30 million in 1961, but quickly fell back to about $10 million a year.

During the presidential election campaign, John Kennedy was even tougher in his attacks on Castro than the Eisenhower administration or his opponent Richard Nixon. At the time he knew nothing of the CIA plans for the Bay of Pigs invasion, the genesis of which had first been secretly proposed by Nixon in the spring of 1959. But Kennedy's angry campaign oratory on Cuba encouraged the invasion planners and worried Diefenbaker and Green.

With Kennedy's presidential victory the Ottawa–Washington division on Cuba grew deeper. Just how much deeper, Arnold Heeney found out a few weeks after the Kennedy–Diefenbaker White House meeting, when he chatted informally with Dean Rusk at a Gridiron Club dinner in Washington, normally a relaxing gathering of Washington VIPs and journalists. Heeney was New York *Times* reporter James ("Scotty") Reston's guest and sat next to Rusk. The secretary of state told Heeney he expected Canada to stop shipment of mill and refinery parts to Cuba, but the Canadian ambassador doubted Canada would do that; Heeney suggested the U.S. trade embargo would only push Castro closer to the Soviets. "Rusk got quite hot in his response," Heeney noted in his diary. "The U.S. were simply not going to have a Communist base established in Cuba . . . and wd. do whatever had to be done to prevent it, including if necessary sending in troops. . . . U.S. policy was not going to be altered because Canada didn't like it."

There was anger in the U.S. Congress, too, at Canada's continuing trade with Cuba, with accusations that Canada was operating a "fast buck" policy of doing business. "It saddens me," said Oregon Senator Wayne Morse, "that Canada continues to trade with Communist Cuba, continues to send into Cuba spare parts necessary for the rebuilding of the industrial power of Cuba and the strengthening of the military might of Cuba, knowing full well there can be but one result of the trade . . . weakening the cause of freedom throughout Latin America."

A longshoremen's union official in New York condemned Canada for sending "tens of millions of dollars worth of vital equipment" to Cuba. *U.S. News and World Report* ran a series of articles on Canadian trade with Cuba, entitling one of them, "How Canada Helps Keep Castro Going." The Canadian embassy in Washington was picketed by anti-Castro Cubans, and there were threats against Canadian trade offices elsewhere in the United States.

On April 17, 1961, fifteen hundred CIA-trained Cuban exiles splashed ashore at the Bay of Pigs on the south coast of Cuba. Everything went wrong almost instantly: the terrain was different from what had been expected; Castro had advance intelligence hints; the U.S. air support was cut back; and, more significantly, there was no parallel uprising in support of the invaders in Cuba itself. It was, in short, a catastrophe, and within three days most of the invaders had been killed or captured.

A short time after the invasion, Howard Green was in Oslo

at a NATO meeting, where he told Dean Rusk that any further American intervention in Cuba would stir up "a hornets' nest" in Latin America and the United Nations. Green then left Oslo for a conference in Geneva; en route he mused to reporters that Canada might act as a "mediator" between Havana and Washington. He was particularly scornful of the American invasion of Cuba and the U.S. attitude in general towards Castro, and in a speech at Geneva he warned, "The more Cuba is pushed, the greater will become her reliance on the Soviet bloc."

His comments came on the weekend before Kennedy was expected in Ottawa. Washington officials were aghast and hurt, and Kennedy was furious. He angrily ordered Rusk to talk to Green, who he said showed "a distressing lack of awareness of the facts" in the Cuban situation. When Rusk met Green again in Geneva, he told him "an offer of mediation is not helpful" and virtually accused the Canadian external affairs minister of "neutralism." Ambassador Heeney was called in to the State Department so the Americans could express their "unhappiness." Heeney privately felt Green had been, at best, indiscreet. He was uneasy going to a Washington dinner party the same night that newspaper reports of Green's comments had been carried in Washington, and he reported being "set upon" by Kennedy officials, especially Arthur Schlesinger, who at the time was a key Kennedy adviser on Latin America. Schlesinger asked "with unrestrained sarcasm," as Heeney described it, whether Canada had now "put Castro and Kennedy on the same footing."

In the House of Commons Diefenbaker praised Green, but when he met Kennedy in Ottawa a few days later, Diefenbaker told Kennedy that Green had not been expressing his government's policy. "I made it clear to the president that the Canadian government has no intention of acting as a mediator between the U.S. and Cuba," he said later.

Diefenbaker, too, had been simmering as Kennedy's visit approached. The cause of his distemper, however, was not Cuba, nuclear warheads, or American investment in Canada. It was the U.S. Secret Service. "They want to put men with guns up all over the place! They're not going to shove me around!" the prime minister exclaimed to his secretary, Bunny Pound.

Basil Robinson has written, "Nothing so irritated the Prime

Minister as having to accept the presence of American security personnel. That the RCMP was not trusted to look after the President, even in the Canadian Parliament, caused Diefenbaker such waves of indignation and anger it must have affected his concentration on his briefing papers and his attitude towards the visit as a whole."

If Canadian officials were fussing about arrangements for the presidential visit to Ottawa, the U.S. embassy was almost berserk with a myriad of big and little problems, ranging from helping to draft the president's address to Parliament to finding out what kind of pillows the Kennedys would sleep on.

"What kind of pillows have you got?" the minister of the American embassy, Willis Armstrong, demanded of the officer in charge of arrangements at Government House, where the Kennedys would be staying.

"Goose feathers and down," the officer responded.

"They won't do," said the American minister. "The president sleeps only on shredded Dacron." A search was launched for two shredded Dacron pillows, which were found just in the nick of time in Armstrong's own bedroom and rushed over to Government House.

And in spite of the Canada–U.S. problems about trade with Cuba, another urgent request to the embassy was for Cuban cigars, which were banned from the United States. U.S. embassy official Rufus Smith remembers being told, "You've got them in Canada and Kennedy loves them. Get them!"

Kennedy's drinking tastes were also a matter of urgent concern, and instructions went out from the White House that the embassy must make sure the president had a ready supply of daiquiris and Bloody Marys available. There were precise instructions on how Kennedy liked them, and he liked them very strong: "Daiquiris – two parts Bacardi Silver Label Superior Rum; one part lemon, one tablespoon sugar; Bloody Marys – two parts Smirnoff Vodka; one part tomato juice; one dash of Worcestershire Sauce and a dash of salt and pepper."

Another rush was to get pictures of the president and Mrs. Kennedy to be given as a gift to their hosts, Governor General Georges Vanier and Madame Pauline Vanier. The pictures got there on time, but the silver frames with the presidential seal had to be sent later.

At his office, the prime minister hastened to make sure his marlin was back from the taxidermist and mounted on his wall so Kennedy could see it. Diefenbaker also wanted a rocking chair for Kennedy's use and borrowed one upholstered in green chintz from a friend in the Ottawa Valley. Late on the night before their meeting in his office, Diefenbaker called Basil Robinson to make sure the rocking chair was in place. It was, and Diefenbaker went to bed relieved.

Chapter Four

BIENVENUE AU CANADA

"Monsieur le Président, en vous souhaitant la bienvenue en français, Son Excellence vous a tenu un langage que je voudrais faire le mien. J'ajoute simplement: soyez les bienvenues au Canada."

In his excruciating French – mangling pronunciation, confounding Quebeckers, and stunning Jackie Kennedy, who spoke French fluently – John Diefenbaker welcomed the president and Mrs. Kennedy on their late-afternoon arrival in Ottawa on May 16, 1961. Switching to English with evident relief, the prime minister continued, "I welcome you as a great American. . . . "

"I am somewhat encouraged to say a few words in French from having had a chance to listen to the prime minister," Kennedy jokingly responded. ("He enjoyed needling Diefenbaker on his French," says White House aide Ted Sorensen.)

Kennedy had been coached by Jackie on the hour-and-a-half flight from Washington. Tugging at the lapel of his grey business suit, he plunged on in French that was, if anything, worse than that of the prime minister. "Ce voyage est le premier que j'ai fait . . . ," he began, as his aides grimaced and the fifty-six American correspondents travelling with him quietly chortled. He wasn't the first American president to manhandle the French language in Canada: Harry Truman's French had been incomprehensible, and Eisenhower spoke of "my execrable French."

Diefenbaker listened to Kennedy's awkward one-sentence linguistic effort with some grim satisfaction, for he was seething at Kennedy for poking fun at him for his own French, about which he was highly sensitive. First, Kennedy had doubted that he'd caught the marlin, and now he was ridiculing his French – and the roar of laughter from the welcoming crowd at Kennedy's jibe was particularly irksome. John Diefenbaker was not a man to appreciate Kennedy's teasing, and he turned Kennedy's bantering into personal torment. A further agony for Diefenbaker was that Kennedy once again mispronounced the prime minister's name as "Diefenbawker," compounding his earlier faux pas and, in Diefenbaker's mind, twisting the knife a little more.

Diefenbaker's welcome to Kennedy may have been personally soured, but Ottawa's welcome was stunningly joyous. Leaving the red-coated RCMP guard at the airport, the Kennedys, the Diefenbakers, and Governor General Georges Vanier and his wife, Pauline, took off on a sunny nine-mile drive into the city, along the banks of the Rideau Canal, past thousands of blooming tulips and daffodils and hundreds of Stars and Stripes and Red Ensigns snapping in the brisk northerly breeze. In downtown Ottawa more than fifty thousand people cheered the incandescent Kennedys – more, observers said, than were there for the Queen and Prince Philip on a recent visit. Police complained of the biggest traffic jam in city history, and front-page newspaper headlines later cried, "ENTHUSIASM ASTOUNDS OTTAWA" and "KENNEDY WAS A SMASH HIT."

Diefenbaker managed to smile ruefully as he told reporters, "I hope he doesn't come across the border and run against me." Although he was glad to share in the attention given to the state visit, Diefenbaker had not wanted the ceremonies to be too elaborate. "He was not willing to put on any kind of show for an American," says Bunny Pound.

If Kennedy was cocky and contemptuous of Diefenbaker, Diefenbaker was cranky and petty about Kennedy. He would scornfully tell Bunny Pound, "Kennedy's not all he's cracked up to be," caustically comparing JFK's Palm Beach mansion with "my little home on the prairies." When Pound once said she "felt sorry for Jackie," he snapped, "What do you feel sorry for her for? Buying all that china and playing classical music? That's not what the people want. They want the Beatles!"

It was Kennedy's first trip outside the United States as president, and he had told the airport welcoming crowd of two thousand VIPs, "It is fitting that I should come here to Canada, the oldest of our neighbors and the closest of our friends." In a prophetic comment, he added that sometimes the two countries "indulged ourselves in the luxury of criticizing the shortcomings of each other, forgetting how important it is that a strong and intimate understanding should exist between the United States and Canada."

The jubilant Canadian reception buoyed Kennedy. That morning in Washington, he had seen Soviet Ambassador Mikhail Menshikov and agreed to meet Nikita Khrushchev in Vienna in early June. He was apprehensive about the Vienna summit, and there were other worries on his mind, too. Commenting later on Kennedy's arrival in Ottawa, Diefenbaker said, "He was obviously still agitated by the humiliation of the Bay of Pigs fiasco."

His agitation didn't show, however, in one of the first events of his visit, as he enthusiastically grabbed a silver-handled shovel for the ceremonial planting of a couple of small red oak trees on the grounds of Government House, where he and Jackie would be staying with Governor General and Madame Vanier. Forgetting to bend his knees, he stood erect and shovelled a dozen spadefuls of black soil. A sharp pain stabbed his lower back, but he grimly smiled for the photographers and then handed the shovel to Diefenbaker. "I wonder if this is symbolic," he quipped, but he knew he had badly damaged his back again. As the pain grew acute, it became agonizingly reminiscent of his old back injury from World War II. The shovelling had destroyed years of restorative exercises, and it nagged Kennedy for two years, "something like having a steady toothache," said his press secretary, Pierre Salinger. For two years he got shots to ease the pain from his back doctor, and he couldn't pick up his children without wincing. He wasn't able to play golf again until the summer of 1963, and the incident made him forever leery of tree-planting ceremonies and reminded him unpleasantly of Diefenbaker. The president's pollster, Lou

Harris, recalls Kennedy telling him later, "The bastard insisted that I get a shovel and dig. It was one of the most painful episodes I've ever had."

When he was told that Diefenbaker had said the tree-planting was exhilarating, Kennedy responded to an associate, "If that was an exhilarating experience, I never want to be laid again!"

The tree-planting finished, Kennedy downed a daiquiri as he dressed for a candle-lit white-tie dinner. Invited to Government House were 112 of the high and mighty of Ottawa, who munched roast spring lamb and sampled three different wines. Protocol had put Kennedy between the governor general and Madame Vanier, thereby minimizing dinner chit-chat with Diefenbaker, whom he was finding increasingly boring. Jackie, however, was enjoying herself, animatedly speaking French with Madame Vanier and showing off her Oleg Cassini heavy white silk evening gown, all to the displeasure of Olive Diefenbaker. After dinner the president, his back throbbing, joked, gossiped, and smiled as he greeted five hundred more guests at a reception before getting to an aching sleep on his crushed Dacron pillows at midnight.

Just before nine the next morning, Kennedy met with his recently reappointed ambassador to Canada, Livingston Merchant, to review the upcoming day and meet U.S. embassy staff. No senior American official knew more about Canada than Merchant, nor did any U.S. authority have greater insight into the workings of the mind of John Diefenbaker. Merchant had been ambassador to Canada from 1956 to 1958; since that time, he had been under-secretary of state for political affairs. He felt somewhat uncomfortable with the Kennedy New Frontier in Washington and had asked Kennedy for a foreign posting, preferring to be ambassador to London or to NATO, although those jobs would be "contingent on increased allowances." "Ottawa," he said, "was my third choice."

London and NATO were reserved for others. Although initially reluctant to send him back to Ottawa, Secretary of State Rusk told him, "Well, why not Canada. It'll be handy to have you nearby." So on the same day Kennedy told his news conference that "Diefenbawker" was coming to Washington for a February visit, he announced that the fifty-seven-year-old Merchant would once again be the U.S. ambassador to Ottawa.

As he laid out the day's agenda for Kennedy, Merchant spoke of his own unease with Diefenbaker; the prime minister, he said, was quite unlike Mike Pearson, whose diplomatic skills he had admired for years. Still, he had hopes the Kennedy–Diefenbaker meetings that day would go well. Kennedy also had been briefed for the meetings by State Department officials, who had told him he had "stirred the imagination of many Canadians. This particular time, therefore, affords the United States a superb opportunity to advance our objectives with the Canadian public and Government because even those who resist American influence in Canada are now impressed by the new Administration and their criticism is muted."

The State Department remained optimistic on the nuclear issue, hoping Diefenbaker would agree at least to allow storage of nuclear warheads at U.S. bases in Newfoundland. In a memo to the president, the State Department reported, "Prime Minister Diefenbaker indicated during his visit to Washington on Feb. 20, 1961 the Canadian Government's willingness to proceed with negotiations on the text of an agreement for the storage of U.S. nuclear weapons at U.S. leased bases in Newfoundland. The United States is eager to renew negotiations. A custody and control agreement similar to that in effect with the United Kingdom would seem satisfactory." But Rusk, in a separate memo to the president, warned Kennedy that the stumbling block might prove to be Diefenbaker himself: "Since becoming Prime Minister . . . he has demonstrated a disappointing indecisiveness on important issues, such as the defense program, as well as a lack of political courage and undue sensitivity to public opinion."

However, Ambassador Merchant had met with the prime minister a week before the Kennedy visit and had found Diefenbaker in a positive mood. In a telegram to the State Department, Merchant quoted Diefenbaker as saying that Canadian opposition to nuclear weapons was coming from more than just "Communists and bums"; he said the External Affairs Department was "riddled with wishful thinkers who believe Soviets would be propitiated and disarmament prospects improved if only Canada did nothing to provoke Soviet Union such as accepting nuclear armaments." In his telegram, Merchant said, "This, he said, was ridiculous but views strongly and widely held. Diefenbaker went on to say that Cabinet must reach decision on this matter before much longer. Intimation was clear his sympathies lie with us. . . . I am certain we have a strong ally in the Prime Minister as well as Harkness." Diefenbaker told Merchant he would take up the question of nuclear acquisition with the cabinet within the next few days, and in the meantime, he warned Merchant not to say anything of their conversation to officials in External Affairs because that might run the risk of the matter "being flattened before it even got off the ground." This was a heartening conversation for Merchant because a month and a half earlier – on March 20 – he had been told by Howard Green that Canada would not accept nuclear warheads at home or in NATO; he also knew that Rufus Smith, one of his key embassy officials, was hearing that the nuclear answer likely would be no, because of the tough attitude of Green and Robertson.

Merchant and Kennedy conferred for half an hour; then Kennedy headed for downtown Ottawa, where under brilliant sunshine in the clear blue spring sky, he and the prime minister laid a wreath at the War Memorial just off Parliament Hill. With the Peace Tower carillon pealing out a welcome, they walked past thousands of applauding tourists and civil servants to the East Block of Parliament Hill, where Diefenbaker's principal prime ministerial office was located. Kennedy, noticing photographers, bounded up the stairs to the second floor, in spite of his back pain, and was greeted by grinning secretaries standing in the hallway. Kennedy eyed them appreciatively as he strode along, flirting with them in his boyish magnetism. He was so unlike John Diefenbaker, who had a courtly style with women. It was quite possible to envisage John Kennedy going to bed with Marilyn Monroe, but the idea of John Diefenbaker and Marilyn Monroe in bed together was preposterous. Equally beyond imagination was the possibility of Kennedy having the same intimacy with Diefenbaker as he had with Harold Macmillan. Kennedy felt able to say to Macmillan in a discussion about women, "I wonder how it is with you, Harold. If I don't have a woman for three days, I get a terrible headache." It was not a question he would ask Diefenbaker. "If Diefenbaker ever found a woman in his bedroom," says Ellen Fairclough, "he'd scream for help."

"Mr. Diefenbaker always took his hat off in the elevator if a woman was present and was always courteous," says Bunny Pound, who had been his secretary since 1952. "Whenever a cabinet minister or somebody was going to tell an off-colour joke and I was present, Mr. Diefenbaker would interrupt and say, 'Miss Pound, would you step out for a moment.' "

Diefenbaker was the old generation and Kennedy the new, and as he walked along the corridor towards the prime minister's office, "all the secretaries lined the walls, smiling and clapping their hearts out for Kennedy," says Pound. She sensed, though, that the prime minister was envious of the enthusiasm of his own staff for Kennedy.

Welcoming Kennedy into his office, Diefenbaker proudly pointed to the blue marlin he had now mounted on his office wall, and also to a painting of a victorious British warship in the War of 1812.

Diefenbaker sat behind his big desk to the side of a marble fireplace; Kennedy was to his right in the rocking chair, near the windows that looked out on the grass of Parliament Hill. There was, as usual, little small talk, and they immediately got down to business. Even with a light Florida tan, Kennedy seemed tired, probably because of his aching back, but with a habitual brush at the sleeve of his dark blue suit, he said he was "ready to go," and the president and the prime minister began what would be their longest and most substantive discussion. Flowing from this meeting would be recrimination, denunciation, allegation, and, on Kennedy's part, a sense of betrayal.

The president began talking quietly, knowledgeably, and convincingly in a business-like *tour d'horizon* of world problems from the Congo to Cuba, from Europe and the Common Market to Southeast Asia and Vietnam.

On Cuba, Kennedy "ruefully raised the Bay of Pigs and acknowledged it was a terrible gaffe," recalls Basil Robinson. The president said he had learned some lessons at the Bay of Pigs and stated in answer to a question from Diefenbaker that the U.S. planned no more military action in Cuba unless there was a serious provocation. In any event, he promised, "We would talk with you before doing anything."

Kennedy was preoccupied with Latin America, having just launched his Alliance for Progress development scheme, and he was hoping to get Canadian support; specifically, he wanted Canada to join the Organization of American States (OAS). Back in the early 1900s, when it was called the Pan American Union, the United States had wanted Canada to join; but later the Americans decided that was a bad idea. By the mid-1930s, they had changed their mind again.

Franklin Roosevelt made a strong plea to Mackenzie King in the early 1940s for a larger Canadian role below the Rio Grande to help "in the struggle between the forces of totalitarianism and the forces of democracy being waged in Latin America." Canada, however, was reluctant to get involved in an area with which it had relatively little contact and feared that membership in the inter-American organization would weaken Canada's Commonwealth links. There was also an element of smug superiority among Canadian decision-makers, who disdained what they considered to be the "banana republic" emotionalism of Latin nations. Thus Canada swung between amiable ignorance and callous indifference about Latin America. It was an attitude that was reversed only in late 1989 when Brian Mulroney finally brought Canada into OAS.

When Diefenbaker won the prime ministership, his first external affairs minister, Sidney Smith, became attracted to the idea of Canada joining the OAS after a fête-filled tour of Latin America. "A nice idea," he said in March 1959. Howard Green was also in favour of it. "Personally," he said later, "I would have liked to see Canada join the Organization of American States but I couldn't get that through the cabinet."

Diefenbaker himself flirted with joining OAS after a trip to Mexico in the spring of 1960, when he discussed the idea with the Mexican president and foreign minister. They urged Canadian membership, as did most other Latin nations. Diefenbaker told President Eisenhower that he was now "prepared to consider . . . this question."

In preparation for the day Canada would become a member, a big, ornate mahogany and red leather chair, marked with Canada's name and coat of arms, had been made in 1910. It had been sitting in readiness for decades in the dusty basement storage room at OAS headquarters in Washington, three blocks from the White House. In one OAS committee room, in anticipation of Canadian membership, a mural was put up three-quarters of a century ago depicting Samuel de Champlain, the father of New France, greeting a group of Huron and Algonquin Indians on the banks of the St. Lawrence River.

Now, sitting in his office, listening to Kennedy, the prime minister remained impassive even though he had changed his mind on OAS and had already indicated privately to U.S. embassy officials that he was not interested just then. "We're further from joining OAS now than a year ago," Diefenbaker said to Kennedy.

The president said Canada could use its influence to help stabilize Latin America, which he called "more dangerous than any other place in the world." Diefenbaker said OAS membership could harm Canadian relations with the U.S. if Canada happened to disagree with some U.S. Latin American policy; or, on the other hand, Canada might be viewed as subservient to Washington if it supported U.S. policies. Kennedy again pressed, and again Diefenbaker said no. Later he described what had happened:

"My arguments did not impress him. Having decided that he wanted Canada (he pronounced it 'Canader') as a member of the O.A.S., he wanted it done right now. I was not about to have Canada bullied into any course of action. This was the first of a number of occasions in which I had to explain to President Kennedy that Canada was not Massachusetts or even Boston."

Besides resenting Kennedy's pressure, Diefenbaker had developed a degree of contempt for many Latin leaders. He later told a television interviewer, "I didn't want to see Canada dragged into wars in which she could have no possible interest. . . . I saw no reason why she should become a vessel in danger of being smashed to pieces because of the activities of petty leaders and petty dictators in petty countries." "Besides," Diefenbaker told Bunny Pound, "we can't because we're too busy building our own country. We haven't got time to help build them up."

The answer to Kennedy's OAS plea was a clear and emphatic refusal, but with blind determination and not a little arrogance, Kennedy would raise it again in a speech to Parliament that afternoon, and yet again at breakfast with Diefenbaker the next day. The best Kennedy got in the end was a promise from Diefenbaker to consider the possibility of sending an observer to the next OAS meeting, but he also was told flatly that Canada would not consider membership.

Kennedy also tried to get a yes on increasing Canadian foreign aid to Third World nations to about one per cent of the gross national product. Diefenbaker had refused to do this in preparing his 1961–62 budget, and he later said, "The Canadian people would not look favourably on a Government that appeared to be more concerned over economic conditions abroad than those at home." So, again, the prime minister said no.

Diefenbaker felt Kennedy's motives on foreign aid were primarily spurred by selfish U.S. interests. "He was consumed with the belief that when the United States gave assistance to any country, that country must realize that it must bow to its will. He seemed surprised when I told him that Canada and the United States were the only two nations on earth that had never accepted anything in assistance for which they had not paid. Kennedy saw the United States striding the world like a colossus."

With two strikes against him, Kennedy finally got support from Diefenbaker on the growing crisis in Berlin. "When I see Khrushchev I will make it clear that we won't give way on our rights over Berlin," Kennedy said, to the nodding agreement of the prime minister. There also was agreement on the general U.S. attitude towards China, which the prime minister saw as a continuation of the Eisenhower policies, although Kennedy was less uneasy about Canadian trade with China than the Eisenhower administration had been.

Kennedy sought Canadian support on Vietnam and noted he was considering sending a hundred more U.S. soldiers to that country as military advisers. He felt Canadian support as a member of the International Control Commission was vital, but Basil Robinson recounts, "Again, the prime minister was cautiously negative." Diefenbaker avoided any specific comment on additional U.S. soldiers going to Vietnam, although American officials took from his comments that Diefenbaker would generally support the United States in Indo-China.

Aside from Latin America, the most sensitive issue raised between the two leaders was the question of nuclear warheads for the Canadian military. Kennedy "took an unexpectedly hard line" on this point, Diefenbaker said. Confounding Merchant's earlier optimism, the prime minister was still stalling. He wouldn't say yes and he wouldn't say no, but at different times he implied each.

Douglas Harkness, knowing the strength of the pressures on Diefenbaker to say no to a nuclear role, had hoped that during Kennedy's visit Diefenbaker would be persuaded to finally say yes. He was encouraged by the absence of his nemesis, Howard Green, who was at a conference in Geneva and would not be sitting in on the Ottawa meetings. A week before the Kennedy–Diefenbaker meeting, Harkness had written to Diefenbaker reviewing the warhead issue and noting that the first approval by cabinet for negotiations with the Americans on acquisition of nuclear warheads had been in October 1958. He said the cabinet had approved a draft agreement that provided for joint control over use, and that at a meeting of the Canada–U.S. Ministerial Committee on Defence in mid-July 1960, the two sides had agreed in principle. Harkness urged the prime minister to come to a deal with Kennedy at their meeting. But Diefenbaker, as indicated by his earlier conversation with Ignatieff, was even more hesitant than his cabinet realized.

The answer the president got from Diefenbaker at their meeting, as recorded by Merchant in his personal notes of the conversation, was that it was "politically impossible today in Canada to have nuclear warheads on Bomarcs . . . [but I] will speak over Canada this summer and fall to try to change public opinion."

At another point in the conversation, Diefenbaker specifically said he himself supported nuclear weapons for Canadian forces. "Personally, he felt there was a need for Canada to be equipped with nuclear weapons," Basil Robinson has written. "But it was necessary to have the support of the House of Commons and he could not be sure of that." Merchant's notes of the meeting quoted Diefenbaker as saying he needed time to educate the public "with the hopeful result that it would be politically feasible."

Diefenbaker also said, however, that the Canadian government opposed any "extension" of nuclear power and that view was powerfully held by many professors and clergy in Canada, and by the Voice of Women. He said that he couldn't accept nuclear warheads right now, but that if they were installed in Canada they would have to be under joint control, something Kennedy had already indicated he would accept.

When Kennedy asked what objection the anti-war groups had to nuclear warheads, Diefenbaker said the argument was a ridiculous concept that everything would be fine if Canada had no provocative weapons at all. The prime minister then said even some professors at Kennedy's alma mater, Harvard, took an anti-war attitude. Kennedy was stung by this sally and said those Harvard professors were not representative of university opinion. Diefenbaker, in turn, was stung when Kennedy added that the anti-nuclear attitudes noted in Canada by the prime minister, if supported by the government, could lead Canada into Cold War neutralism. As he said this, Merchant scribbled in red ink in his small notepad and underlined the word "neutralism."

Kennedy and his colleagues felt it was critical to have Canada "on side" in continental defence because, aside from the need for protection against attack, if Kennedy couldn't get his closest neighbour's support, how could he get other nations to support him? He looked earnestly at Diefenbaker and reiterated, "It's really important."

Diefenbaker replied, "Well, there's a lot of opposition. But I'll see if I can turn public opinion around in the next few weeks."

As this part of the conversation ended, the president and the Americans with him were convinced that despite a certain degree of circumlocution, Diefenbaker had pledged to launch a speaking campaign for acquisition of nuclear warheads and that within a few weeks he would be able to accept them.

"Certainly Diefenbaker did promise to turn public opinion on warheads around," says Willis Armstrong, the American minister to Ottawa at the time.

The nuclear question, however, was tied in to a "swap" defence production-sharing deal with the United States, which was raised next in the Kennedy–Diefenbaker conversation. The deal, an outgrowth of the 1941 Hyde Park Agreement between Roosevelt and King, had been percolating since 1958, and this time Diefenbaker talked about it with a president who had learned the details. In one discussion with President Eisenhower, Diefenbaker had been "stunned" to discover Eisenhower had forgotten all about the deal and said he had never heard of it, even though it had been discussed at some length previously. It was still in debate when Kennedy and Diefenbaker discussed it in Ottawa. The deal had changed over the past couple of years, but as the two leaders discussed it in the prime minister's office, it involved the U.S. providing sixty-six F-101B interceptor aircraft for the RCAF NORAD squadrons, which would be armed with nuclear weapons and be based in Canada; the U.S. buying from Canada F-104G interceptor planes to be provided to NATO partners; and Canada assuming the cost of the Pinetree radar installations in Canada, which were being paid for at the time by the United States.

The sticking point for Diefenbaker in the swap deal, of course, was nuclear weapons for the RCAF F-101Bs. Kennedy said the nuclear warheads for the interceptors would have to be stored at Canadian bases so they would be immediately available in time of crisis. Besides, he said, it would be hard for him to justify spending so much American money in Canada to buy interceptors for NATO use if there weren't a net gain in North American defence capability, which could only come through nuclear weapons for the F-101Bs.

Diefenbaker refused. He asked if the interceptors could simply be armed with conventional weapons, but also be made capable of using nuclear weapons, which could be stored in the United States and shipped to Canada in an emergency. Kennedy looked puzzled by Diefenbaker's comments, and the swap deal remained unresolved at their meeting because of this issue. Even so, Kennedy was hopeful that Diefenbaker would fulfil his pledge to turn around public opinion and accept the warheads. To encourage him, less than a week after the Ottawa meeting, Kennedy overrode objections in Congress and at the Pentagon and agreed to complete the swap deal without the requirement of the F-101Bs having nuclear arms stored at Canadian bases. In a sense, it was a final payment to Canada for the cancellation of the Arrow, which had been due to American refusal to buy the plane. Diefenbaker had won his immediate point, and now he had won a fat order for Canadian airplane factories, which would produce politically valuable jobs and profits.

But for Kennedy, the swap deal was simply bait to get the

Canadian prime minister on side on the nuclear question in the long run. Diefenbaker, no mean political poker-player himself, knew that, and he knew he had given Kennedy a promise to turn around the nuclear critics. That sense of obligation to the president nagged at him.

After two and a half hours of intense discussion, Diefenbaker was flagging and Kennedy's back was aching, and they concluded the only detailed discussion they would ever have. In his notes of the meeting, Ambassador Merchant summed it up:

> J.D.
> Firm on Berlin.
> Firm on I.C.C. [International Control Commission]
> Weak on nuclear.
> Weak on DAG. [development assistance]
> Weak on O.A.S.

Although hopeful that Diefenbaker would agree within a few weeks on warhead acquisition, Kennedy was disappointed in their conversation. Diefenbaker had been negative on the things that had really mattered to Kennedy and had waffled on others. "Kennedy felt Diefenbaker was not straight with him," Willis Armstrong says. "He promised things that never happened."

"He felt he had not had a very co-operative response in the meeting from Diefenbaker," says Robinson. "Everything went down from there. If only we had given some little sign, a positive response to something, even agreeing to send an observer to the OAS meeting. We were so negative."

With the conference over and Kennedy and his aides gone, Diefenbaker shut his office doors and sat alone, ruminating about the discussions and gazing about his office. Precisely what happened next remains a mystery, but it led, in time, to the most vicious name-calling ever recorded between a president and a prime minister, with Diefenbaker charging "arrogant pressure" by "the young son of a bitch," and Kennedy calling him a "blackmailer" and a "prick."

The cause of it all was a single sheet of vellum paper headed "Memorandum for the President" from "W.W. R.," the initials of Walt W. Rostow, the State Department policy planning director, who had sat in on the meeting. The subject was "What We Want from Ottawa Trip."

Rostow had been in charge of preparing Kennedy for the meeting, except for the nuclear warhead issue. Although his memo to Kennedy was a fairly normal briefing paper of the type usually provided to leaders for such meetings, Diefenbaker was outraged by it.

SECRET

May 16, 1961

What We Want from Ottawa Trip

1. To push the Canadians towards an increased commitment to the Alliance for Progress. Concretely, we would like them to have at least an observer at the July IA-ECOSOC [Inter-American Economic and Social Council].

2. To push them towards a decision to join the OAS.

3. To push them towards a larger contribution for the India consortium and for foreign aid generally. The figures are these: they have offered $36 million for India's Third Year Plan. We would like $70 million from them. Over-all their aid now comes to $69 million a year; if they did 1% of GNP the figure would be $360 million. Like the rest of us, they have their political problems with foreign aid, but we might be able to push them in the right direction.

4. We want their active support at Geneva and beyond for a more effective monitoring of the borders of Laos and Viet Nam.

Diefenbaker said in his memoirs, "The President apparently dropped it into my wastepaper basket at the end of our meeting," and, he said, it was found at the end of the day by his staff. At other times he said it was found crumpled on the floor, or beside the cushion on a sofa, or left on a table. He also said at various times that it was found by security people, by a secretary, Marion Wagner, or by his office assistant, Gilbert Champagne.

In truth, the paper was not crumpled, and Diefenbaker

probably found it himself. Champagne remembers going into the office a few minutes after the meeting and seeing him holding a piece of paper. Diefenbaker later that day told Champagne, "Oh, I found a piece of paper. It was all crumpled up and I opened it up to see what it was. He must have had it in his hand and it fell to the floor."

Diefenbaker gave the paper to Marion Wagner and told her to "put it in the vault." She showed it the next day to Basil Robinson, who was surprised and worried, and recommended that it be returned to the U.S. embassy at once. "It was theirs, although we might have made a copy," he says.

Two days later in a meeting with Robinson, Diefenbaker pulled out the paper, waved it in the air, and pointed to the language as evidence that the Americans thought Canada could be "pushed around." Robinson felt Diefenbaker regarded the paper "as a sort of trophy."

Robinson told Ambassador Heeney that he thought the paper had been left on the sofa in Diefenbaker's office, where Rostow had been sitting. Others think Kennedy himself probably dropped the paper inadvertently as he rose from his chair when the meeting ended. "He was always sloppy as hell!" says Willis Armstrong. "It was just a working piece of paper. There was shorthand language but nothing provocative." The memo had been given to Kennedy by Rostow only that morning. "It was really a benign thing," Rostow says. "I don't know why he made such a fuss about it." Rostow recalls Kennedy had taken the paper out of his coat pocket and held it in his hand when chatting with Diefenbaker, and at one point had even laid it on Diefenbaker's desk.

The lost paper wasn't the only security screw-up on the Ottawa visit of President Kennedy. Two members of the president's entourage had forgotten to bring along their formal clothes and had to rent black-tie suits from Classy Clothes Ltd. of Ottawa. When they returned the suits, an ex-army sergeant working for Classy Clothes found several pieces of paper marked SECRET stuck in a jacket inside pocket. He called the American embassy, saying, "We've got some papers here that look like classified documents, and they don't belong to us." Armstrong hustled two men over to pick up the documents and preserve American security.

The sergeant from Classy Clothes may have called the U.S. embassy, but nobody called from the prime minister's office. The Americans would remain ignorant of the presidential paper loss until a year later, when Diefenbaker would take his "trophy" out of the "vault" and threaten to use it in his escalating war with Kennedy.

While Diefenbaker stewed over the memo, Kennedy had gone back to Government House briefly. Then he and Jackie crossed the street to the prime minister's 24 Sussex Drive residence for lunch with John and Olive Diefenbaker. If Kennedy had found the morning conference with the prime minister frustrating, he found lunch tedious, although Jackie sought to ease the weary and wary atmosphere by talking about the weather and the Diefenbakers' "lovely home" and exclaiming over "the view of the river from the dining room table."

But even Jackie and Olive didn't get along, for they, too, had little in common. Jackie's whispery, little-girl voice grated on Olive, who felt it was affected. Bunny Pound notes, "Olive didn't like Jackie. She thought she was snippy." Diefenbaker's long-time friend Senator David Walker agrees, saying, "Olive just hated Jackie."

Olive's early life in the sparse parsonage of her rigid father was utterly unlike Jackie's early years of blue blood and old money. Her hard-drinking, philandering father was known as "Black Jack" Bouvier. Jackie's world was Vassar, the Sorbonne, and Manhattan high society, while Olive's was the University of Saskatchewan, high school teaching, and vocational guidance.

Both, however, reinforced their men: Jackie brought class to Kennedy and culturally enriched her husband, while Olive gave loyalty to Diefenbaker and provided an anchor of stability in her husband's sea of emotion. Jackie was an enhancing and elegant adornment for Kennedy, but Olive was a behind-the-scenes streetfighting defender of her husband. "She would rip you up and down if she thought that you were trying to take credit for anything she thought belonged to John," says Diefenbaker cabinet minister Alvin Hamilton. "One of those people who had a bitter outlook," says Bunny Pound.

There were complaints about Jackie being a spendthrift; Olive, on the other hand, was regarded as "mean" with money.

Jackie was uninvolved and even uninterested in affairs of state; Olive was forever "interfering," according to Diefenbaker associates.

After an hour and a half of stilted conversation at the 24 Sussex dining table, Kennedy went back to Government House to change and then on to Parliament, where he was to speak to a joint session of the Senate and the House of Commons. As his limousine pulled up in front of the Parliament Hill Centre Block, Kennedy's Secret Service guards leapt out of their cars, eyeing the crowds who had waited for two hours in the cool breeze to catch a glimpse of the president. Diefenbaker stood on the steps to greet him. Kennedy squinted in the sun, smiled, waved, and shook hands yet again with the prime minister with one hand while carrying a fedora in his other hand. He hated hats, but on some occasions when he knew he would be photographed, Kennedy carried one as a concession to the hatters' union, which had strongly supported him. But he rarely put the hat on.

Diefenbaker led the president inside, where he met the Speakers of the House and Senate and the leader of the opposition, Mike Pearson, whom he would see again later that evening at dinner. Then Kennedy was escorted into the House of Commons for his address. He was only the third American president to speak to Parliament, after Harry Truman and Dwight Eisenhower.

Kennedy nervously began with a sentence in French and then happily switched to English, poking fun at his narrow victory in the presidential election and saying how grateful he was for all those of Canadian descent who had voted for him in Massachusetts. He also poked fun at the Canadian Senate by noting "the lofty appearance of statesmanship on the faces of the members of the Senate who realize that they will never have to place their case before the public again."

Even John Diefenbaker chortled. But Diefenbaker's outward smile quickly became an inward frown as Kennedy launched into another plea for Canada to join the OAS, reiterating, this time in public and before Parliament, the same arguments Diefenbaker had rejected in private four hours earlier in his office.

"Your country and mine are partners in North American affairs," Kennedy said. "Can we not now become partners in inter-American affairs?"

To Diefenbaker, this was an arrogant and intolerable insult after he had already given a firm no to OAS membership, and he felt Kennedy was deliberately going over his head. It was, in fact, a stupid move on Kennedy's part because it seemed a naked pressure play and angered even some who favoured Canadian membership in OAS. Shudders went through External Affairs, and Howard Green later attacked "those who said we should have jumped through the hoop when the president of the United States made the suggestion."

American embassy official Rufus Smith was also shuddering, because he had written the words about Latin America. He had prepared a draft of the presidential speech and had been told to put in a plea for Canadian membership in OAS. He and Merchant argued against inclusion of the OAS pitch because they said Diefenbaker had already made it clear he would refuse and they felt a renewed plea in the speech would be considered offensive. However, Canadian ambassador Arnold Heeney had been asked about it in Washington, and he had advised Rostow that a reference to OAS would be all right; in fact, he encouraged it. As Smith listened to the president in Parliament, he realized unhappily "there was nothing of mine left in the speech except for the comment on OAS, which I didn't want in there in the first place."

Looking back a quarter of a century later, Kennedy's national security adviser, McGeorge Bundy, rues Kennedy's pitch on Latin America. "The Kennedy administration," he says, "should not have preached the Alliance for Progress to Canada as it did in the early 1960s. . . . It is still annoying to others when Americans assume that what is good for them has to be good for everyone else on the continent."

The rest of Kennedy's speech to Parliament was a non-controversial review of world affairs and a plea to strengthen relations between Canada and the U.S., which, he said, are "co-tenants of the same continent; heirs of the same legacy." In typically Ted Sorensen–polished language, Kennedy told the parliamentarians, "Geography has made us neighbors. History has made us friends. Economics has made us partners. And necessity has made us allies. Those whom nature hath so joined together, let no man put asunder."

Kennedy got a standing ovation, in sharp contrast to the half-hearted hand-claps Diefenbaker had gotten from a conference of U.S. governors a year earlier, where he had made similar comments about the "kinship" between Canada and the U.S., Luther Hodges, now Kennedy's commerce secretary, had been at the Diefenbaker speech, which, in fact, had been mortifying for the prime minister. "He was a serious-minded, rather arrogant type of person," said Hodges, "and he was furious when after about a third of his speech, which was of a serious, almost ponderous type, he was suddenly interrupted." The paging system of the hotel had not been turned off in the room, and as Diefenbaker spoke, it boomed out, "Call for Sargent Shriver!" "People tittered and Mr. Diefenbaker glared," said Hodges. Ten minutes later, the loudspeaker again reverberated with "Call for Sargent Shriver!" "It was worse and the crowd broke into laughter. Mr. Diefenbaker was livid with rage but finally finished his speech."

Diefenbaker was again livid after Kennedy's parliamentary speech, and even more so at a small dinner party at Ambassador Merchant's residence. That evening Kennedy, seemingly almost deliberately, insulted Diefenbaker by spending an extraordinary amount of time in animated conversation with Mike Pearson, the prime minister's mortal political enemy. Diefenbaker was deeply jealous of Pearson's popularity. "Everybody knows Pearson," he pouted to Bunny Pound. "Mr. Diefenbaker was never comfortable with himself and he envied Mr. Pearson's ease," she says. The prime minister constantly worried about Pearson's many friends throughout the senior civil service, and he feared leaks of his policy plans would get to Pearson through what he called "the Pearsonalities" in External Affairs. Diefenbaker told friends Pearson was a "pipsqueak," but he was everlastingly jealous of Pearson for winning the Nobel Peace Prize for his role in settling the Suez Crisis; he had refused to attend a bipartisan parliamentary dinner for Pearson in 1957, before Pearson flew to Oslo to receive the prize. On the day Pearson died, Diefenbaker privately told a reporter seeking a comment, "That man should never have won the Nobel Prize."

"That man" also had the black mark in Diefenbaker's eyes of being admired in Washington. In fact, he was arguably the best-known, best-liked Canadian in the world. He had been Washington's choice to be the first secretary general of the United Nations, but the Soviets had threatened a veto and Norway's Trygve Lie was chosen instead. The one-time University of Toronto history teacher had been a founder of NATO, ambassador to Washington, and a key participant in establishing some of the UN specialized agencies; he literally knew and was admired by everyone who was anyone in Washington and London. Like Kennedy, Pearson cultivated friends among influential journalists; he would often see New York *Times* correspondent Scotty Reston in New York or Washington. These contacts produced many favourable stories about him.

His only critics in Washington seemed to be FBI chief J. Edgar Hoover, Senator Joseph McCarthy, and their Communist-hunting allies. A publicity-seeking one-time Communist and confessed agent, Elizabeth Bentley, once told a congressional committee that when Pearson was at the embassy in Washington, he provided information to a Communist agent. The FBI developed a thick file on Pearson, and Diefenbaker was given some of the information, which he kept in the "vault" in his office. He would sometimes refer to it privately when especially angered at Pearson, although Washington dismissed the allegations and Bentley herself recanted later on. Now, Kennedy wished Pearson were prime minister instead of Diefenbaker.

A couple of years earlier, Kennedy had reviewed Pearson's book *Diplomacy in the Nuclear Age* for the *Saturday Review of Literature*. He wrote, "Mike Pearson has been the chief architect of the Canadian foreign service, probably unequalled by any nation. . . . He has been the central figure in the growth of the Atlantic Community and NATO, even while taking a leading role in the shaping of the United Nations. In diplomacy he has always been the guardian of good sense and has enjoyed the confidence of very many nations. . . . He has been a superb interlocutor between the realms of statesmanship and scholarship."

Pearson returned Kennedy's admiration, joking, "It seemed to me that anyone who valued my literary efforts must possess some special quality." He had hailed Kennedy's election in November, saying, "He represents a new generation which now is emerging as a powerful force in the direction of world affairs."

Pearson had tried to see Kennedy in January when both men were in New York, but Kennedy failed to return Pearson's extraordinarily persistent phone calls. Kennedy's excess of attention to Pearson at the embassy dinner may have been prompted in part by that failure. Just before coming to Ottawa, Kennedy had received a personal memorandum from a White House staff member saying, "Mr. Lester 'Mike' Pearson, the leader of the Liberal Opposition in Canada, tried very hard to reach you at the Carlyle Hotel [in New York]. He hoped very much to see you for a few minutes or at least talk to you on the phone. He'd apparently tried two or three times and was told that you would try to return his call that evening or early the next morning. He waited by the phone without receiving any message either directly or indirectly. . . . You might want to mention this oversight to him when you encounter him in Ottawa."

At cocktails and through the dinner Kennedy and Pearson chatted, gossiped, and laughed, sharing a sardonic humour that Diefenbaker never really understood. "That was the worst of all in the visit, when Kennedy spent what Diefenbaker thought was an excessive amount of time with Pearson at the embassy dinner," says Basil Robinson. "It was embarrassing. Even the U.S. guests were embarrassed."

There were only twenty guests at the dinner table in Merchant's twenty-five-room stone mansion, with the president sitting across from Pearson and beside Diefenbaker. Kennedy made it abundantly clear which man he preferred talking to, as they sliced into their filet mignon; his preference was especially obvious after the ladies withdrew, following the strawberry tart dessert, and the men stayed sipping their brandy and puffing cigars. Half a dozen others joined them at this point, but Kennedy still concentrated on Pearson. "We all saw it," says Willis Armstrong. "It was absolutely discourteous. But Kennedy was insensitive to Diefenbaker's feelings."

Merchant looked on but shrugged his shoulders in response to nervous enquiring glances, as if to say, Armstrong remembers, "I can't do anything about it."

Diefenbaker left the dinner early. Shortly afterwards, Mer-

The "Chief" and his idol, "Old Tomorrow." Sir John A. Macdonald's nineteenth-century nationalism inspired John Diefenbaker's own vision of the True North strong and free. *National Archives of Canada/PA-57939.*

Leaders in wartime service. John Diefenbaker (left) prepares to go overseas with the 19th Battalion Saskatoon Fusiliers, August 1916. *National Archives of Canada/C-24908.* John Kennedy's navy career in the South Pacific made him a World War II hero. *Photo No. PC-95 in the John F. Kennedy Library.*

The only Conservative member of Parliament elected from Saskatchewan in the 1945 election: Hon. John Diefenbaker. *National Archives of Canada/C-499.*

President Dwight D. Eisenhower meets Diefenbaker and External Affairs Minister Howard Green in New York in 1960. Green "simply astonished" the Americans with his naïveté and his "magnificent obsession" with disarmament. *National Archives of Canada/PA-122743.*

Defence Minister Douglas Harkness was at odds with Diefenbaker and Green over nuclear warheads from the day he was appointed until the issue forced his resignation in February 1963. *National Archives of Canada/PA-52510.*

A rare light moment in the Oval Office before getting down to business, February 1961. Standing: Secretary of State Dean Rusk, Canadian Ambassador Arnold Heeney, American Ambassador Livingston Merchant. Seated: Kennedy, Diefenbaker, Green. *Photo No. AR6363A in the John F. Kennedy Library.*

Heading for Norway to collect the Nobel Peace Prize in 1957, Lester Pearson (*right*) is accompanied by Norman Robertson, who was under-secretary of state for external affairs through most of the Diefenbaker years. Robertson's ''cosmic anxieties'' about nuclear weapons reinforced the Diefenbaker government's delaying tactics on warhead acquisition. *National Archives of Canada/PA-114541.*

The crowds that greeted the Kennedys in Ottawa in May 1961 were bigger than those that turned out for royalty. "I hope he doesn't come across the border and run against me," said the prime minister. *National Archives of Canada/PA-113480.* Governor General

Georges Vanier escorts the two leaders while the ladies follow behind. *National Archives of Canada/PA-121705.*

Jackie Kennedy does what is expected of a visiting First Lady; Olive Diefenbaker, who found Jackie ''snippy'' at best, plays the gracious hostess. *National Archives of Canada/PA-176447.*

President Kennedy addresses a joint session of Parliament during the May 1961 visit. Of the Canada – U.S. relationship, he said, ''Those whom nature hath so joined together, let no man put asunder.'' *National Archives of Canada/PA-176448.*

Diefenbaker, Kennedy, and British Prime Minister Harold Macmillan share a luncheon table unexpectedly in Nassau, December 1962. Said Kennedy, "There we sat like three whores at a christening." *Rt. Hon. J.G. Diefenbaker Centre/JGD-1454.*

"To be ambassador in a capital where relations between your own government and the government to which you are accredited are bad and getting worse, is always a tricky situation," Charles Ritchie mused when posted to Washington in 1962. *National Archives of Canada/PA-165050.*

At ease: Newly elected Prime Minister Pearson and Kennedy at Hyannis Port, May 1963. Their meeting, wrote Walter Lippmann, was like "a good scrubbing and a cool shower after a muddy brawl."
Photo No. ST-C159-11-63 in the John F. Kennedy Library.

chant whispered to Douglas Harkness that Kennedy wanted to see him privately, in the study. Kennedy asked the defence minister directly, "Are you going ahead and get those nuclear warheads?"

"Yes," said Harkness. "I'm doing everything possible. Diefenbaker is assuring me. I am sure that we will go ahead."

"Fine," said Kennedy.

Both his conversational intimacy with Pearson and his quick private word with Harkness reflected a New Frontier insensitivity that was not only a problem with Kennedy. On another occasion Secretary of State Rusk displayed the same trait. Going to Canada for a fishing holiday, he told Armstrong, "I'll go and see Pearson while I'm there. Maybe we can play some golf at Montebello."

"You can't do that!" Armstrong recalls remonstrating. "Mr. Green is the foreign minister."

"But I don't like Mr. Green," Rusk replied.

Kennedy didn't like Diefenbaker either, making it painfully evident at the dinner. The prime minister bitterly made another black mark next to the president's name in his bad books.

The next morning Kennedy and Diefenbaker had an eight o'clock breakfast at Government House. Kennedy made one last pitch to push the prime minister into action on nuclear warheads and OAS. Walt Rostow had given him a handwritten note the night before, saying that Diefenbaker might at least agree to having an official observer at the forthcoming OAS meeting in Montevideo. "This is what the best Canadian civil servants – who are all with us – suggest," Rostow said. Again, the president got a curt refusal on OAS membership, but the prime minister did say that the observer was a possibility – and indeed he advised Kennedy the next day that Canada would send someone to Montevideo. The president again offered Diefenbaker the "two-key" deal on joint control of nuclear weapons. Diefenbaker, however, equivocated, reiterating his political concerns on warheads.

After breakfast, the two leaders drove to the airport, where the Kennedys were serenaded by the RCMP Pipe Band playing "Will Ye No Come Back Again" as they boarded the presidential jet at 10:15 A.M. As soon as he'd bidden farewell, Diefenbaker got aboard his own jet to fly to Halifax, to get an honorary degree from Dalhousie University. Flying east, he was simmering with resentment at Kennedy's insensitivity towards him and what he considered the arrogant American attitude towards Canada. "Diefenbaker expected more respect from Kennedy, but he didn't get it," says Tommy Van Dusen.

The prime minister told Heeney that he deeply resented Kennedy's personal slights. Later, reflecting on the visit, Diefenbaker wrote in his memoirs, "[Kennedy] was activated by the belief that Canada owed so great a debt to the United States that nothing but continuing subservience could repay it. He could not believe it when I told him that in the First World War Canada's contribution in men killed in action had been larger than that of the United States, or that on a percentage basis, our casualties in the Second World War had been about equal to those of the United States."

"That callow young man!" Diefenbaker exploded to George Ignatieff. In his assessment of the Ottawa meeting, Diefenbaker later said, "By his own criteria, Kennedy's mission to Ottawa was a failure. We did not 'shape up'. We made no commitment on the Alliance for Progress. We were not about to join O.A.S. Our position on foreign aid did not change. On his fourth point, we were prepared to do all we could to make the International Control Commission in Viet Nam more effective. As things turned out, there was very little we could do." In fact, the only positive results of the meeting were the progress on defence production-sharing and Canada's agreement to send an observer to the OAS.

On another occasion he said of the visit, "I became increasingly aware that President Kennedy had no knowledge of Canada whatsoever." Diefenbaker began making fun in private of his New England accent, mimicking to colleagues Kennedy's pronunciations of words like "Way-ust" for West, "Ee-ust" for East, "des-payuh" for despair, "pow-aw" for power, "Moaner Leeser" for Mona Lisa. "The way Kennedy said 'Canader' annoyed Diefenbaker no end," says Alvin Hamilton.

In extraordinary contrast to the clearly dyspeptic reaction to Kennedy that he displayed to Ottawa colleagues, he wrote to his brother Elmer, "We get along very well together. The opinion I formed of him when I first met him – a brilliant intellect and a wide knowledge of world events – was not only borne out but intensified as a result of our discussions in the last two days."

The prime minister was more than a little jealous of the editorial hurrahs echoing across the nation's newspapers for Kennedy, typified by the conservative Toronto *Telegram*, which said, "Canada will never have a better offer of partnership on mutually satisfactory terms in the great enterprises of world politics that lie ahead than she received from President John F. Kennedy yesterday."

Diefenbaker's temper would not have improved had he seen a White House memorandum by Kennedy aide William Hartigan, who said, "We had a very fine reception from the Canadian people – just like American citizens coming out to greet their President."

Expressing a sentiment Diefenbaker shared, his friend David Walker says, "John Kennedy, who was a perfectly charming man, came up here as if he was coming up to one of his colonies. . . . He thought we were a bunch of backwoodsmen." "Kennedy felt we were just a bunch of small fry," says Ellen Fairclough. "He was a very arrogant man."

Arnold Heeney and his wife, Margaret, hitched a ride with Kennedy back to Washington, and Kennedy asked Heeney to sit beside him as he read through memorandums and cables, occasionally asking the Canadian ambassador's advice and treating him as a trusted confidant. He did not, however, reveal his private feelings about the Canadian prime minister, asking only how Heeney thought the meeting had gone and then quickly moving on to other matters. Jackie Kennedy, however, told Margaret Heeney that she "adored" the Vaniers. She made no comment on the Diefenbakers.

On arrival back in Washington about noon, Kennedy told reporters the Ottawa trip had been "extremely worthwhile" and that he was "very, very pleased" with his talks with Diefenbaker. That, however, is not what he told associates after helicoptering from the airport to the White House. He regaled them with comments that Diefenbaker was "boring," "insincere," "shallow," and "erratic." Kennedy's secretary, Evelyn Lincoln, says, "He looked almost exhausted, and even more surprising to me, acted somewhat cranky."

The trip "marred his buoyancy," says Arthur Schlesinger.

Ted Sorensen says more sharply, "He was simply pissed off with him. He was aggravated. Diefenbaker got under his skin."

On his return to Washington, Kennedy went straight to his office to face racial crises in the American South; busloads of Freedom Riders were being attacked by white supremacist mobs in Alabama. He also began planning his next foreign trip, which would take him to Paris to meet President de Gaulle and to Vienna for a fateful meeting with Nikita Khrushchev. His foreign policy focus was now on Europe, not on Canada.

In the process he rubbed more salt into the wounds in Diefenbaker's vanity by seeing Mike Pearson in Washington for an hour-long discussion on the forthcoming Khrushchev meeting. Pearson was in the American capital in late May for a luncheon speech at a conference of American mayors when the president found out, and "he asked me to have a talk with him" about East–West issues, Pearson said. Kennedy spoke to the same group the next day.

While Kennedy was making plans for Khrushchev, Diefenbaker was celebrating a deal with Mao Tse Tung. The Chinese grain crop had failed in 1959, failed again in 1960, and failed for a third straight year in 1961. The Canadian Wheat Board, spurred on by Agriculture Minister Alvin Hamilton, made a deal with China for the biggest grain deal in Canada's history: the Chinese bought 186 million bushels of wheat and 46 million bushels of barley for delivery by the end of 1963. The deal was worth upwards of $400 million and it was a political windfall for Diefenbaker, winning him everlasting gratitude from prairie farmers.

Many Americans, however, were decidedly unenthusiastic about Canada coming to China's rescue and making a fat profit as well. "This was regarded as heresy in Washington in 1961," Diefenbaker later said.

In June the U.S. Treasury Department, acting under regulations of the American Trading With the Enemy Act, threatened the Canadian grain shipments to China. The ships chartered by China to transport the grain needed special unloading equipment, suction devices called vacuators that could pump six hundred tons of grain a day. The shipowners ordered the equipment from the Dunbar-Kattle Co. in Batavia, Illinois. On June 2, the U.S. Treasury Department told the Illinois company that it was not U.S. policy to issue a licence allowing an export deal that involved trade with China. "It was all caused by some damn woman civil servant," says Hamilton, who'd been informed about the problem by the Shipping Federation of Canada. He couldn't understand it, because he had kept U.S. Agriculture Secretary Orville Freeman regularly informed of his negotiations with the Chinese.

On June 5, Diefenbaker got word that the necessary vacuators were being held up by the U.S. Treasury. They were actually in Vancouver and ready for use, but now the company was being ordered to bring the equipment back to the United States. According to the prime minister, he reached for the phone and called Kennedy. The conversation quickly degenerated into a shouting match, the prime minister told his colleagues. In telling the story, Diefenbaker would imitate Kennedy's New England accent and laugh as he recalled Kennedy saying, "You can't send the wheat. When I tell Canader to do something, I expect Canader to do it."

"I will not be talked to that way," Diefenbaker said he shouted back. "You're not going to stop Canada from carrying out our policies."

"We'll see to it that you won't get the grain loaders," Kennedy responded, according to the prime minister, and he said he snapped back, "If you stop this, I'll go on national TV and denounce you and the United States."

Nevertheless, on June 8, the grain unloaders were released by the U.S. Diefenbaker said, "That was the end of any friendly personal relationship between President Kennedy and myself."

In conversations and interviews thereafter, Diefenbaker cited this contretemps as a model of how to stand up to the Americans for Canadian rights.

The Kennedy–Diefenbaker phone conversation so vividly and so often told by Diefenbaker to his intimates was rooted more in his enriching, creative imagination, however, than in reality. He occasionally changed the locale of the conversation from the telephone to the president's office in February, four months before the incident actually occurred, and said the president had "thumped" the table. He once told Southam columnist Charles Lynch that Kennedy may have called him a son of a bitch.

Diefenbaker's telling off the president was more likely what he wished had happened, but it didn't. Bunny Pound says the prime minister was livid after talking to Kennedy. "I told him off," she remembers him saying. "I told him you're not going to push us around!" Although she did not overhear the conversation, Pound doubts her boss was quite as vigorous as he claimed. "It was just what he wanted to believe," she says. "But he was grumbling and growling about the conversation for years. . . . Most of the time on the phone to the president, he'd say, 'I'll think about that, Mr. President,' or 'Yes, Mr. President.'"

Kennedy was in Europe when the incident was unfolding, returning to Washington late on June 5. "No such conversation took place," says his under-secretary of state, George Ball. "It's absurd and preposterous. Kennedy was very careful in talking to other chiefs of government. He would always be at least tolerably polite and never try to threaten them."

"It would be quite out of character for Kennedy to talk that way in any event," says Willis Armstrong. "Diefenbaker had a quality for facile retrospection. . . . He had a flexible attitude to the truth."

Armstrong, in fact, was the man who unscrambled the vacuators problem. "External Affairs called me about it," Armstrong recalls. "And I said it was not U.S. government policy to object to the Canadian government wheat sale to China, and I'd see what I could do." He talked to Washington, urging an exemption to the U.S. rules to allow the American-made vacuators to be released. Meanwhile, Ambassador Heeney was making representations to the State Department. George Ball discussed the matter with Treasury Secretary Douglas Dillon on June 8. With Kennedy's blessing, the vacuators were released and the problem solved.

While privately castigating Kennedy, Diefenbaker publicly praised him in a statement in the House of Commons on the day after the issue was settled. He spoke of "the prompt and careful attention" the matter had received in Washington, adding, "This is further evidence of the relations between our countries whereby each country, without any derogation from its own sovereignty, endeavours by diplomatic means to accommodate the other. Such cooperation is an example to all the world." His comments were greeted with desk-thumping approval by the MPs.

Diefenbaker called Kennedy with his thanks, and he also sent his appreciation to Armstrong. Years later, when made aware of Diefenbaker's private feelings about the incident, Washington officials shook their heads in dismay and anger at what they considered the pure fantasy of the prime minister's fervid imagination. Even External Affairs Minister Howard Green agreed that Kennedy had been "helpful" in resolving the issue. But in Diefenbaker's mind it was a major confrontation for which he had to pay a price. "It is a fact that after I blocked President Kennedy's attempt to interfere with Canada's grain sales to Communist China in June, 1961," Diefenbaker later said, "his Administration went out of its way to cause difficulties for my government."

Kennedy, who had been in Paris meeting de Gaulle, in Vienna to see Khrushchev on June 3 and 4, and in London on June 5 to talk with Prime Minister Harold Macmillan, was preoccupied with Berlin, not vacuators. Khrushchev's Cold War rigidity, as displayed in Vienna, startled the president. "Kennedy was sobered and shaken by that experience," Dean Rusk says. Khrushchev said he would back East Germany's demands in Berlin "to the point of war." "Well then," Kennedy replied, "if that's the case, there will be war, Mr. Chairman. It's going to be a very cold winter."

The Soviet leader warned he would sign a peace treaty with East Germany by December 31, which would end Allied access rights to Berlin and end Western legal status in the city. He vowed to "eradicate this splinter from the heart of Europe."

The Soviets had tried twice before to force the West out of Berlin, in 1948 and 1958–59, but now that they had nuclear capability, the threat was much more serious. Kennedy had always believed that the most likely place where World War III might start was Berlin, and he warned of the danger of a fatal Soviet miscalculation. The American president, still smarting from his humiliation at the Bay of Pigs, declared that the West would never surrender its rights in Berlin. "West Berlin has now become the great testing place of Western courage," he told a national television audience on his return from Vienna. "We cannot and will not permit the Communists to drive us out of Berlin."

Privately, Kennedy told General Lucius Clay, his senior representative in Berlin, that Khrushchev had to see American muscle. "That son of a bitch won't pay any attention to words. He has to see you move," he said. So move Kennedy did. He sent more U.S. troops into West Berlin, dispatched Vice-President Lyndon Johnson to Berlin to "show the flag," called up the reserves, enlarged civil defence, asked Congress for an extra $3.25 billion for arms, and demanded a rapid strengthening of NATO forces.

Khrushchev responded with his own national television address, which was tough, belligerent, and inflexible. In mid-August the Berlin Wall went up. Pentagon and State Department officials were privately critical of some NATO nations, who they felt should have reacted more firmly in the Berlin Crisis, and Kennedy told a news conference, "We're going to meet our responsibilities and we're asking them to meet theirs." The Pentagon and Canadian defence officials felt that, at least in part, he had Canada in mind for its failure thus far to accept nuclear warheads in Europe or North America.

The dangerously escalating Cold War was now much on Diefenbaker's mind, and he grew increasingly nervous about what he considered Kennedy's inexperience and immaturity. He seemed almost to relish what he felt was Kennedy's less than strong performance at the Vienna summit; later he wrote of how Kennedy "was bitterly offended by the fact that Khrushchev continually referred to him as 'the boy,'" a characterization that Diefenbaker himself used privately to describe Kennedy. His public speeches, however, were strongly supportive and brought applause from the White House and the American media. "A wise speech," said the Cincinnati *Enquirer* of one Diefenbaker address, and the Miami *Herald* said of Diefenbaker, "A spokesman for our best friend in the world, neighbor Canada, is quite right."

Diefenbaker now began to feel it was his duty in this crisis to increase Canadian military preparedness, including accepting nuclear warheads. Seeing the danger of the Berlin flashpoint, hearing Kennedy's plea for a strengthening of NATO, and listening to Defence Minister Harkness, Diefenbaker finally approached a decision to accept the warheads for our NATO forces as well as for the Bomarcs and North American interceptors and for nuclear storage on U.S. bases in Canada. He knew the political appeal of saying no to nuclear weapons, but, as Basil Robinson has noted, "He did not want to be accused of hindering the United States in its global defence responsibilities or of depriving Canadian forces of modern equipment."

Besides, Diefenbaker knew he had told Kennedy at their May meeting in Ottawa that he personally favoured the warheads; he knew he had promised he would speak out to try to change public opinion to favour warhead acquisition, and he had not lived up to that promise. Meanwhile, in Washington, the Berlin Crisis intensified Kennedy's frustration at Diefenbaker's unfulfilled promise. "Diefenbaker was waffling, but in waffling he was supporting Green," says Willis Armstrong. "Kennedy didn't regard Diefenbaker as a trustworthy gentleman." Rufus Smith puts a sharper edge on Kennedy's mood, saying Kennedy felt "betrayed" by the prime minister's "utter lack of effort" to speak out publicly for the warheads.

On August 3, President Kennedy reminded Diefenbaker of his promise. In a letter to the prime minister, Kennedy wrote of the need for military preparedness because of the Berlin Crisis, and he urged Diefenbaker to fulfil his commitment to acquire nuclear warheads for North American defence. Kennedy did not want to go into a nuclear confrontation with Khrushchev with a gaping hole in North American defence, laying bare the whole northeastern United States, because of Diefenbaker's reluctance to take on a nuclear role for the Canadian forces.

Diefenbaker replied a week later with a promise that he would consider the decisions necessary to start discussions with the Americans, looking towards an agreement. "On receipt of your message," he told Kennedy, "I sent word to our Minister of National Defence to ensure that final preparations were expedited for the negotiation of the agreements to which you referred." He said he would speak to Green and Harkness to get the process under way and would write again shortly to the president. Four days later, he made his first speech to begin fulfilling his commitment to Kennedy. Speaking to a meeting of the Weekly Newspaper Association in Halifax, he condemned those who urged Canadian withdrawal from a nuclearized NATO. They were, he said, "advocating a course that would be dangerous to survival of the forces of NATO should war begin and it would be dangerous for the survival of freedom itself. . . . Would you place in the hands of those who guard the portals of freedom nothing but bows and arrows?"

To his adviser Basil Robinson, he said, "I just do not understand those who do not want to accept them [nuclear warheads]." There were five cabinet meetings in the next ten days, all involving at least in part the Berlin Crisis and the implications for Canada. Diefenbaker wrote to his brother Elmer: "The world situation is terrible and people not knowing the situation are loud in their opposition to Canada having any nuclear defence. It is an ostrich-like philosophy which while adhered to by many sensible people, is most beneficial to the Communists."

If the Americans had seen that letter, they would have broken out the champagne. But before he could assert to the Americans the views he had revealed to Elmer, other events intruded.

On September 1, the Soviets resumed testing nuclear bombs; a few days later, Kennedy decided to resume testing, too. Diefenbaker was angry that Kennedy had not consulted him before making the decision, saying it was "preposterous" and that Kennedy had thrown away a propaganda advantage over Khrushchev. He told the House of Commons that Howard Green's hard work on world disarmament may have been damaged by the nuclear test resumption.

The absence of consultation on the U.S. test resumption (for which Kennedy later apologized to Diefenbaker), and the revival of Diefenbaker's apprehension at what he felt was the political danger in Canada accepting nuclear weapons, combined to lessen Diefenbaker's hitherto growing willingness to accede to Kennedy's August 3 request for Canadian acquisition of warheads. Even so, the prime minister warned the House of Commons on September 11 of "the terrible danger of a nuclear war," which, he said, "causes us to re-examine some of the principles of Canada's foreign policy." The *Globe and Mail* banner headline on September 12 read: "DIEFENBAKER HINTS NUCLEAR WEAPONS FOR ARMED FORCES."

Harkness, believing the Berlin Crisis was at last leading Canada into acquisition of the warheads, told the House of Commons the day after Diefenbaker spoke that it would be prudent for Canada to get nuclear warheads "now so that they will be available and our forces trained to use them." He said, "It is the policy of the government that our forces should not be required to face a potential enemy with inferior weapons." The commander-in-chief of NORAD, General Laurence Kuter, came to Ottawa and Toronto at this time and publicly spoke of the need for all NORAD forces to have nuclear warheads. Diefenbaker seemed on the verge of announcing his acceptance of nuclear warheads.

But almost as soon as the words flew out of Harkness's mouth suggesting a decision to acquire nuclear weapons, Diefenbaker began retreating to his hesitancy, listening again to Howard Green, who was warning about "Jeremiahs and crepe hangers" who talk of impending war. Suddenly Diefenbaker turned inflexible. The reason for the reversal seemed to be the public revelation of Kennedy's August 3 letter, which had been marked "SECRET." Diefenbaker was furious when a story about it appeared in *Newsweek* and on Canadian Press. To his mortification, it was front-page news across the country. The Montreal *Star* bannered "JFK PRESSES CANADA ON NUCLEAR WARHEADS." In reporting a behind-the-scenes Washington–Ottawa fight over warheads, the *Newsweek* story said, "A straight-from-the-shoulder letter sent by JFK to Prime Minister Diefenbaker now is expected to resolve the impasse." The fact that the Washington editor of *Newsweek* at the time was Ben Bradlee, a close friend of Kennedy's, may well explain the leak. Diefenbaker initially denied Kennedy had pressured him on North American defence and then said that in any case it was a personal letter "and personal letters are not revealed."

Diefenbaker ordered Arnold Heeney to protest to the White House, saying the public exposure of the letter would harm defence co-operation between the two countries. From the U.S. embassy, a furious Willis Armstrong cabled the State Department, "Press story . . . cannot fail to be quite disturbing to Prime Minister and others in Canadian Government who are seeking to arrive at decision we want and confirmation by White

House spokesman of Presidential letter to Prime Minister may be special factor in postponement or delay decision. . . . Totally unnecessary publicity resulting from conversations by U.S. Government officials with Canadian reporters in Washington. . . . Thus forecasts . . . of action within next week or two must be withdrawn."

Alarmed, Kennedy apologized for the leak and sent a message to Diefenbaker that he would be glad to make a public comment that might help the prime minister. Diefenbaker declined the offer, still infuriated that publicity given the Kennedy letter had exposed him to public awareness that the president was pressing him on nuclear warheads. He had planned a CBC broadcast for September 20, buttressing his Halifax speech. But now, he said, that was impossible.

"It seemed ironic," Basil Robinson has written, "that this should have occurred just at the stage when he was bracing himself to move against the anti-nuclear advice he was getting from Green."

Diefenbaker may well have been reversing his inclination towards acceptance of warheads in any event after pressure from Howard Green, but the embarrassing publicity about Kennedy's letter was the last straw. He turned his back on the Kennedy request and on Harkness and adopted instead a policy of deliberate vacillation, refusing to formally say no, but hinting at a maybe under certain conditions. That was fine for Green, who felt Diefenbaker's convoluted rhetoric of delay was as good as a flat no.

Green was now back on top in the nuclear debate in Ottawa, particularly when on September 25, President Kennedy unveiled a new disarmament plan at the United Nations, emphasizing that there should be no expansion of "the nuclear club." By that he meant no new independent nuclear offensive capability in other nations, but not any lessening of the need for NATO or NORAD nuclear defensive weapons systems. He simply didn't want any more nations to have the ability to start a nuclear war on their own, an ability that could not, by the wildest stretch of the imagination, be said to flow from Canada's acceptance under joint control of nuclear warheads for North American defence.

Diefenbaker, however, seized Kennedy's theme of no expansion of the nuclear club as the centrepiece for his rationale against Canadian acceptance at this time of nuclear warheads – although he granted that the Bomarcs should have nuclear capability in the event of war, and then, he said, Ottawa could decide whether to use them. He lavishly praised Kennedy's disarmament speech and told colleagues it represented a profound change in Kennedy's nuclear weapons strategy.

Kennedy had changed his mind on warhead acquisition by Canada, Diefenbaker maintained. "I considered that it effectively ended the prospect of joint control and with it the prospect of nuclear weapons in Canada, unless there was war," Diefenbaker later wrote. "I also considered that unless a satisfactory form of NATO control was worked out to govern the use of nuclear weapons, the arming of our Air Division and Brigade in Europe with other than conventional weapons would breach our commitment not to expand the 'Nuclear Family.' Only after war had started might nuclear warheads be moved to Canadian bases." In other words, he transformed Kennedy's speech into a welcome peg on which to hang his own reluctance and indecision. As Basil Robinson has noted, "For the Americans it must have been galling that Diefenbaker was giving to the President's words an interpretation exactly opposite to what was intended."

Diefenbaker felt his rationale for procrastination on nuclear warheads was strengthened when, in mid-October, the Berlin Crisis began cooling down. Khrushchev said the West was showing some understanding of the Berlin situation, and he no longer would insist on his December 31 deadline for a treaty with East Germany. The prime minister was also reinforced in his nuclear virginity by a seventy-two-hour anti-nuclear demonstration on Parliament Hill in October, at which he was handed a twenty-one-pound petition with 142,000 signatures.

Canada's enthusiasm for disarmament reached new heights at the UN. The Diefenbaker government welcomed resolutions to end nuclear testing, stop the spread of nuclear weapons, and otherwise advance disarmament. At one point Canada made sympathetic noises on a resolution to ban nuclear weapons altogether, a policy that would have set Canada totally apart from NATO policy. Only at the last minute did instructions come from Diefenbaker to vote against the resolution.

Canada did, however, vote for a Swedish resolution that the secretary general enquire into the possibility of non-nuclear countries refraining "from manufacturing or otherwise acquiring such [nuclear] weapons and to refuse to receive in future, nuclear weapons on their territories on behalf of any other country." The Canadian vote outraged Washington; furthermore, Diefenbaker cited it as prohibiting any Canadian decision on accepting nuclear warheads at least until the next election, which would come in mid-1962.

The prime minister felt he was on the side of the political angels with his nuclear policy. On December 1, however, came the first inkling that Diefenbaker might not be reading the public correctly. A poll by the Public Opinion News Service showed Canadians favoured nuclear acquisition by a two-to-one margin. Diefenbaker dismissed the poll. But he was careful about any public criticism of Kennedy, who he knew stirred powerful support among Canadians. Conservatives, in fact, tried to associate their party with Kennedy at times; for instance at the 1961 party annual meeting, Diefenbaker cabinet minister Léon Balcer told a cheering crowd, "Ninety per cent of the legislation planned by the Kennedy administration in the U.S. has been inspired by John Diefenbaker."

The ever-optimistic American ambassador, Livingston Merchant, came away from a November 27 meeting with the prime minister thinking there was still a chance that Canada would accept the nuclear warheads. In a report to President Kennedy, he said, "I do not share the apparent Canadian Government assessment that acquisition [of] nuclear weapons constitutes [an] issue on which it would encounter overwhelming opposition." Merchant urged Kennedy to send another letter to Diefenbaker, seeking a resumption of defence negotiations, which, Merchant admitted, had for months "been stalled on dead center."

But as the year ended, the warhead question remained unresolved. Harkness was down, Green was up, Kennedy was angry, and Diefenbaker was contentedly applying to nuclear warheads a variant of Mackenzie King's famous World War II phrase: "Not necessarily conscription, but conscription if necessary."

Chapter Five

UNRELIABLE ALLY

Canada can't be trusted.

That was increasingly Washington's attitude as 1962 dawned and the Americans watched Diefenbaker's deliberate but nervous sidestepping to maintain Canada's nuclear chastity. The Americans came to feel that we were not a reliable ally; our ability to influence the U.S. on world problems decreased sharply as they listened to us less. The Americans were certainly disinclined to listen to Ottawa on such issues as disarmament. Canada was simply no longer trusted on the question, and consultations became more perfunctory than substantive.

The Americans looking north to Ottawa found Diefenbaker's nuclear vacillation confusing and at times incomprehensible. The tensions and trials of 1962 would be characterized by muddled perception, disappointed expectation, and deteriorating communication with the prime minister.

Washington was galled, as were many NATO allies, by our loudly proclaimed moral pre-eminence on questions of nuclear weaponry, especially when Canada was making fat profits from sales of war matériel to the United States and even complaining about the termination of American contracts for Canadian uranium (valued at more than $1.37 billion from 1947 to 1962), which was used to make the American nuclear warheads. During World War II, Canada had been involved with the Americans in the Manhattan Project, which developed the atomic bomb. As historian James Eayrs has written in *Northern*

Approaches, "The maiming of Hiroshima and Nagasaki was a by-product of Canadian uranium." In the Cold War, it was American nuclear warheads made mainly from Canadian uranium that provided the Western deterrent and protected North America. Ironically, much of the uranium was mined at Elliot Lake, Ontario, in Mike Pearson's riding.

There was, indeed, a certain lack of moral logic to Canada's selling the raw material to make nuclear warheads with one hand and putting the other hand over our national heart in virtuous indignation at the idea of accepting the finished product for North American defence. Logic would have had Diefenbaker stop selling uranium for military purposes; but given the profits and the jobs, it was not a politically attractive option. In effect, we were behaving like the dope pedlar who sells the stuff but doesn't use it and publicly condemns those who do. Thus Diefenbaker and Green's moral majesty in refusing to accept nuclear weapons, or at least refusing to decide on acceptance, was deeply flawed.

Exacerbating Diefenbaker's nuclear waffling ("A running sore . . . a failure to deliver on a promise," Kennedy's national security adviser, McGeorge Bundy, calls it) was the painful reality that the defence systems Canada had ordered were now being put in place. Without nuclear warheads, the Bomarcs and the Voodoo interceptors for North American defence and the Honest John rockets for our NATO brigade would be hundreds of millions of dollars worth of empty cannons. The Voodoos carried conventional weapons, but the Bomarcs and Honest Johns were loaded with only sand. The F-104s to be used as our NATO strike reconnaissance aircraft, like the Bomarcs and Honest Johns, were designed for nuclear warheads and would be equally ineffective when delivered in the fall of 1962.

Seething with outrage, senior Canadian and U.S. military officers began speaking out publicly in carefully chosen words of warning, while privately they began a lobbying campaign. Journalists, business and labour leaders, educators, and other professionals were given tours of NORAD headquarters at Colorado Springs, Colorado, shown NORAD exercises, and persuasively massaged with pro-nuclear arguments. The NORAD commander, General Laurence Kuter, made speeches in Canada, as did his deputy, Air Marshal Slemon, trying subtly to shape public opinion to force Diefenbaker into acceptance.

A key player in this campaign was a senior RCAF officer with wide media contacts, Wing Commander Bill Lee, who extensively and effectively lobbied reporters and editors to plant stories designed to demonstrate the lunacy of Diefenbaker's nuclear policy. The highly popular and charming Lee ate and drank with reporters at the National Press Clubs in Ottawa and Washington and visited others at quiet lunches and dinners, expressing surprisingly open hostility to the government's policy. His effectiveness was a product of his zeal and his air of boyish innocence (he had been a church choir soloist), a quality he found profitable in his poker games with parliamentary reporters. He had a ready audience in the media and was instrumental in undermining Diefenbaker's policy among journalists. Lee eventually became executive assistant to Liberal Defence Minister Paul Hellyer; years later he was one of the most influential private lobbyists in Ottawa and, briefly, campaign manager for Liberal leader John Turner.

Lee, others in the RCAF, and the USAF brass worked together to sap public support for the prime minister in what Diefenbaker later called "a supra-governmental relationship between the Canadian military, in particular the Royal Canadian Air Force, and the Pentagon." At the time Diefenbaker's personal radar and contacts kept him aware of the campaign and intensified his distrust of the military. "Leading Canadians," he said, "were brainwashed with the necessity of Canada's acquiring nuclear weapons for its NORAD Forces." It was done, he said, "in order to soften what the United States was doing to Canada to put out Canada's government because it dared to believe that it had the right to determine the course that Canada would take. Never has there been anything in history to equal [it]."

He was absolutely right. "It was a flat-out campaign, because Diefenbaker was not living up to his commitment," says Lee. "Roy Slemon was going bananas down in Colorado Springs. We identified key journalists, business and labour people, and key Tory hitters, especially in Toronto, and some Liberals, too, and flew them out to NORAD. It was very effective. We'd have Slemon speak to them, and others. We wanted people with influence on members of the cabinet. All we wanted to do was to have Canada honour our commitment. In the end, the pressure paid off."

Lee's targets were not only Diefenbaker but also Howard Green and Norman Robertson, whose campaign against warheads Lee sought to discredit. "Those guys were good. It was hard to beat them," he says.

What Lee didn't want was to have the Americans big-footing it on the issue, which would play into Diefenbaker's anti-American hand. "The key was not to have the Americans take the lead," he says. Lee's U.S. Air Force colleagues were appalled by Diefenbaker; one senior Pentagon official asked Lee, "Where in hell did you get a man like that up there? He's one of the biggest nerds I've ever come across." Lee himself would visit Washington a couple of times a month to confer with authorities there and talk to the media, and he met informally from time to time in Ottawa with Charles (Chuck) Kisseljak of the U.S. embassy. Altogether, it was the most effective public relations campaign in Canadian military history.

It was Lee who orchestrated the campaign, but he had full support from his superiors. The RCAF Air Council, the senior body of the air force, had authorized Lee, as head of RCAF Public Relations, to carry out the campaign. Air Marshal Hugh Campbell talked to the chairman of the chiefs of staff, Air Marshal Frank Miller, who said simply, "You go ahead. Just don't tell me the details." As for the minister of defence, "Harkness knew of the effort, but he was not a party to it," Lee says.

Playing a supporting role, U.S. diplomats began briefing journalists to clarify what they called "misinformation and misinterpretation" propounded by the prime minister and the external affairs minister. In Ottawa, Ambassador Merchant held informal background briefings in the basement recreation room in Chuck Kisseljak's home. Parliament Hill reporters had sought the briefings, and the Americans were only too glad to provide them. "Backgrounders," as they are called in the media, are a normal way for government officials to disseminate information and the government's views without being quoted. At this time, it was a more regular practice in Washington than in Ottawa, and Merchant was a past master at it. Confident and candid, he provided reporters with the sense that they were getting the "inside story." There was an air of camaraderie in Kisseljak's basement as twenty or so journalists and U.S. officials would spend about two hours drinking beer, eating spaghetti, and listening to Merchant's earnest and smoothly articulated version of the warhead issue and other Canada–U.S. questions.

"It was a hard sell, but it was the presentation of a legitimate national concern on their part," says reporter Arch MacKenzie, who attended a briefing as Canadian Press Ottawa bureau chief. For the reporters, it was useful background information, buttressed by what they were hearing from the RCAF and NORAD, but it contrasted sharply with what Diefenbaker was saying. When Diefenbaker heard about the Merchant briefings a couple of years later, he accused the reporters of being "traitors" and "foreign agents," specifically attacking Southam columnist Charles Lynch during a television program. It was, he said, a "scandalous school" giving "secret lectures" to reporters who were "brainwashed by Lee on the Hill and Merchant at the embassy." "You were given briefings as to how the Canadian government could be attacked on the subject of nuclear weapons and the failure of the Canadian government to do that which the United States dictated," the prime minister blasted at Lynch.

Political support was slipping away from the prime minister. There was rising disapproval among business leaders, educators, and professionals, especially in the big cities. Washington was becoming increasingly outspoken. The Canadian media were jilting yesterday's hero, Diefenbaker, in favour of today's Lochinvar, Kennedy, and the American media were awakening to the Ottawa–Washington squabble.

"Anti-Americanism is an ugly reality in Canada today," American syndicated columnist Richard Starnes wrote. "The frank and friendly Canadians regard us as bristling and belligerent, smug and self-righteous," wrote columnist Sydney Harris. A long-time political ally of Kennedy's, Congressman Teno Roncalio of Wyoming, commented, "I never realized they resented us as much as they do. I didn't realize they felt we were a monstrous, mammoth obliteration of their own identity, and of their own arts, and of their own culture." Visiting Washington, Canadian writer Bruce Hutchison found, "Our national prestige has sunk to a new low."

But Howard Green felt just the opposite. He was encouraged by the enthusiastic applause he was getting from Third World countries and from the United Nations for his ardent pursuit of disarmament and determined rhetoric on the subject. Canada's reputation in the world, Green claimed, was never higher. He spoke of Canada's "destiny" to lead the world to disarmament and said, "Today, Canada stands as one of the leaders, perhaps the leading nation of the world, in efforts to bring about disarmament."

"Green had a great success at the United Nations," says Canada's UN ambassador at the time, Charles Ritchie. "He was competing with India for purity. But we more and more found we were distancing ourselves from the United States."

The first official visitor of 1962 to Ottawa was Edward Heath, later a British prime minister, who came in early January in his role as United Kingdom negotiator for British membership in the European Common Market. Diefenbaker was a hard sell for Heath because he maintained virulent opposition to British membership and demanded that the Commonwealth prime ministers discuss the whole question at their next meeting. Green claimed that Kennedy was pushing Britain into the Common Market.

Finance Minister Donald Fleming agreed, and when senior members of the Kennedy cabinet came to Ottawa two weeks after Heath, he warned them of Canadian opposition; like Diefenbaker, Fleming felt British membership in the Common Market would weaken Commonwealth links and injure Canadian trade with Britain. He suspected that Washington viewed British membership primarily as a way to get rid of British trade preferences for Commonwealth countries. Diefenbaker worried that if the U.K. "married" Europe, Canada would be forced into even closer relationships with the United States. Kennedy had shown enthusiasm for British Common Market membership when he spoke with the prime minister in Ottawa in May 1961, but Diefenbaker had given him no support.

Although the Common Market was on their minds, the American cabinet members were much more eager to discuss

President Kennedy's plans for a major trade initiative. Kennedy planned to propose that the industrialized nations cut all tariffs by as much as fifty per cent and cut some to zero. It was a politically daring move towards liberalization of trade, and the Kennedy cabinet members sought Canadian endorsement to help Kennedy get his proposals through an uneasy Congress. They felt sure of getting Canadian support because the proposals represented enormous potential to increase Canadian trade with the United States.

Fleming was enthusiastic about Kennedy's tariff-cutting plan. It had already been hailed by Canadian business; one study indicated that Canada could gain an extra $262 million a year in trade with the U.S. through the scheme. "Statesmanlike," Fleming said, as he indicated his support to the U.S. cabinet members. The Diefenbaker cabinet had also discussed the Kennedy proposal, and Fleming felt he had full support to endorse the trade scheme. After the first meeting with the Americans, however, Howard Green pulled Fleming aside to tell him not to support the Kennedy initiative.

Fleming was startled. "You're not running everything around here yet," he snapped at Green. But, in fact, Green was simply echoing Diefenbaker's attitude. When Fleming went to the prime minister's office after talking with Green, Diefenbaker told him, "Never would I support this. . . . No, don't express support for Kennedy's plan. Is that understood? We will not support it. That young pup is not going to push me around. He's got to learn his lesson!" Fleming went white as a sheet, muttered, "Yes, sir," and told Pierre Sévigny, who was with him when he saw Diefenbaker, that it was the greatest humiliation of his life. "He was close to tears," says Sévigny. "He told me, 'Why should I take that kind of treatment?'"

A chastened Fleming told the Americans that Canada would not support the Kennedy trade scheme. They were dumbfounded and "crestfallen," Fleming said. "I felt ashamed and humiliated. It sprung from Diefenbaker's growing personal dislike for President Kennedy." It was a "petty" act, the finance minister said. "We squandered an opportunity." He bemoaned the "poisoned and blighted" Kennedy–Diefenbaker relationship.

The prime minister, however, changed his mind and a week

later voiced support for the Kennedy plan, never explaining his reversal to Fleming. Privately, he didn't think Congress would approve it anyway. But after intensive debate, it was passed by Congress late in the year and led to the Kennedy Round of tariff reductions among the industrialized nations.

Diefenbaker's anger at the New Frontier was further fuelled early in 1962 by Under-Secretary of State George Ball. The prime minister said Ball, on a visit to Ottawa, was trying to push Canada into using its wheat exports to China as a diplomatic pressure point on the Chinese. He was trying, Diefenbaker told associates, to "turn our ploughshares into swords." Ball had warned the Canadian cabinet, the prime minister said, that there could be a general war in the Vietnam area, imperilling the whole of Southeast Asia as well as Australia and New Zealand, unless Hanoi and Peking were restrained. Ball's "unsavoury" idea, Diefenbaker said, was to have Canada tell the Chinese that unless they stopped encouraging the subversive activities of North Vietnam in the South, Canada would cut off wheat supplies.

A few weeks later Walt Rostow proposed that all NATO countries further restrict their trade with Cuba, and the prime minister angrily rejected that idea, too, saying such a proposal "could be interpreted as unwarranted intervention in Latin American affairs." Diefenbaker was also distressed when Washington pressured Canada to endorse an OAS condemnation of Cuba for spreading Communism in Latin America. The Americans, he said, had "a hell of a colossal nerve." Diefenbaker profoundly disagreed with the American approach of trying to isolate Cuba from the rest of the Western hemisphere. "We are not convinced that isolation is the best method of enabling the Cuban people eventually to free themselves," he tartly told a joint meeting of Canadian MPs and U.S. congressmen in Montreal.

"PM steamed up about the bad press Canada is getting in U.S. re trade with Cuba," Basil Robinson noted in his diary. "Blames Kennedy Administration, again without justice, and relates it all back to the Rostow memo which will be with JGD until he dies."

The New Orleans *Times-Picayune* had suggested "Canada's national anthem be changed to 'Red Sales in the Sunset.' "

Canadians were being called "scavengers" and "bone-pickers" on the floor of the House of Representatives, and New York Senator Kenneth Keating added to Diefenbaker's furies with sharp criticism of Canadian policy towards Cuba. The prime minister lashed back at Keating, and Robinson noted, "PM obviously thinks anti-American statements are good and timely and relished another opportunity."

"Kennedy," says Alvin Hamilton, "was always issuing threats to us – when the United States speaks, Canada jumps. He always wanted us to jump to it."

Diefenbaker did Kennedy one favour on Cuba, however. When the president asked the prime minister to appeal to the Cubans for clemency for the Bay of Pigs prisoners facing trial in Cuba, Diefenbaker did, and Kennedy sent him a note of thanks.

Fidel Castro listened to Diefenbaker because Ottawa had refused to give in to American pressures. The few Canadians travelling to Cuba were greeted as heroes for defying the Americans. Cuban newspapers reported extensively on Diefenbaker's quarrels with Kennedy. A Canadian correspondent travelling to the city of Camaguey was startled to see in his hotel lobby a huge picture of John Diefenbaker on the wall beside pictures of Castro, Marx, and Lenin. The hotel room clerk told him, "You must refuse the *bombas atomicas.* Your Mr. Diefenbaker is a great man. It's a shame the Americans are trying to throw him out of office. Mr. Diefenbaker, I think, is a lot like Fidel." That diplomatic "money in the bank" with Cuba paid off eight years later when Havana helped Canada in the FLQ October Crisis by allowing into Cuba the kidnappers of British Trade Minister James Cross.

On February 20, the prime minister sent a congratulatory note to the president on John Glenn's space trip around the globe. No answer came back from Kennedy, and Diefenbaker exclaimed repeatedly to Ambassador Heeney, "Not a bloody word!" It was the same language he had used to blast Kennedy's earlier delay in acknowledging Diefenbaker's congratulations on his presidential election victory. "The PM has manifested increasing suspicion and resentment," Heeney wrote in his diary.

Diefenbaker continued to search for a tolerable way to evade his commitments on the acquisition of nuclear warheads. In January he had received a background paper from External Affairs, growing out of conversations over the previous months between George Ignatieff, Norman Robertson, and Howard Green, that was intended to help him publicly justify his hesitancy. It suggested that warheads could be stored at U.S. military bases near the Canadian border and delivered quickly when needed to the Bomarcs and RCAF interceptors, which could be "positioned" in readiness. External Affairs told the prime minister that the time it would take to get the nuclear warheads to the Canadian Bomarcs and interceptors in the event of an emergency "may well be reduced to a matter of minutes, at most to perhaps an hour."

This new escape route – nuclear weapons for war but not for deterrence – was manna from heaven for Diefenbaker. He took his formula of carefully contrived ambiguities to Edmonton in late February, where he spoke to a conference of a thousand Alberta Conservatives. He felt comfortable with the rationale of this politics-driven formula, for he could now ensure Canadian sovereignty by demanding his version of joint control with the United States (without specifying what that was), which would appeal to Canadian nationalists; he could demand an all-out effort for disarmament, which would please the Ban-the-Bomb types; and in the meantime, he would seek to protect the safety of the nation by having nuclear warheads sitting at the border, ready to be rushed to Canada within an hour if war came. That, he thought, should appease those who worried about Canada's defence capability.

In speaking to the Alberta Conservatives the prime minister admitted the Bomarcs and interceptors would be more effective with nuclear warheads. At a news conference after the speech, he told reporters, "We have taken the precaution of building a weapons system to handle nuclear arms. . . . In the event that nuclear war was launched, nuclear weapons should be placed in the possession of Canadians." He said he had read a report saying that nuclear warheads could be made available "in half an hour or an hour."

The Americans were astonished. The Pentagon said it would take at least fifteen hours to transport nuclear warheads to

Canada. Besides that, the Americans said, there was no agreement with Canada on shipping the warheads to Canada in the event of war, a point that Diefenbaker eventually had to concede in the House of Commons. The prime minister, however, persisted in his statement that the warheads could be in place on Canadian weapons in plenty of time if war came.

At the same time, Diefenbaker seemed to realize he was on thin ice. When he came back to Ottawa, he asked his officials to flesh out an explanation of the time needed. Questions flew at him in the House of Commons. On his theme that "joint control is of the essence," he told Parliament, "So long as the law of the United States is as it is at present, joint control is impossible." But when he came back to his office after making this statement, he asked Robinson, "Did I go too far in saying that 'joint control' was impossible?"

In Washington, Kennedy muttered to a colleague, "That son of a bitch Diefenbaker." Secretary of State Dean Rusk took a more diplomatic course by issuing a statement, saying Canada could have "joint control" of the warheads that would be "fully consistent with national sovereignty" and that the U.S. was ready to negotiate.

Two years earlier, in July 1960, six months before Kennedy became president, Diefenbaker had appeared to accept the joint-control approach that other NATO countries had agreed to. "It is a well-known fact," he told the House then, "that United States law requires that the ownership of nuclear weapons must remain with the United States and that the use of such weapons requires Presidential authorization. . . . At the same time, as I have said before in the House, if and when nuclear weapons are acquired by the Canadian forces, these weapons will not be used except as the Canadian Government decides and in the manner approved by the Canadian Government. Those two elements together constitute joint control."

But after Kennedy's election Diefenbaker had altered his thinking. He argued for more Canadian control over the use of nuclear warheads while at the same time arguing against any expansion of the "nuclear club," two mutually incompatible positions. His nationalism was in combat with his desire for disarmament, a struggle that, combined with his perpetual reluctance to make any decision, led to his self-contradictions on the nuclear issue.

Diefenbaker supported his inaction on nuclear warhead acquisition by constant reference back to the Irish resolution on disarmament approved by the UN in 1960, which, among other things, urged states controlling nuclear weapons to refrain from relinquishing control of them to other states. He also cited the Swedish resolution endorsed by the UN at the end of 1961, setting up an eighteen-nation committee, of which Canada was a member, to further the cause of world disarmament. Diefenbaker declared in the House of Commons in late February, "We take the stand that in the interests of disarmament everything must be done to assure success if it can be attained, and that the nuclear family should not be increased so long as there is any possibility of disarmament among the nations of the world."

Howard Green took a leading role in these UN discussions. In a telegram to Green, attending disarmament discussions in Geneva, Diefenbaker said, "I am very proud of the superb contribution you have made to the cause of peace and disarmament." In a phone conversation, he also urged Green to stay on in Geneva as long as necessary. "You stay where you are," he said. "You follow the cocktail circuit over there. . . . They haven't run out of tomato juice yet."

The prime minister also seized on a comment of Kennedy's. The president had said he wanted to improve the conventional weapons capacity of the United States so that the U.S. would not always be faced with only the nuclear choice in crises. Diefenbaker said this indicated the Americans were shifting emphasis from nuclear to conventional weaponry, a statement Washington vigorously denied. "Deliberate misinterpretation," some in the Pentagon and State Department said.

This sequence of statements brought more damaging political questioning of Diefenbaker and more heartburn to Washington. Canadian Ambassador Arnold Heeney told colleagues that he was dismayed by the damage the prime minister was doing to Canada–U.S. relations.

Meanwhile, Mike Pearson was reviewing his own attitude on nuclear warhead acquisition. After his initial reaction in favour of acquisition in 1958, when Diefenbaker announced the

Bomarc program, Pearson had steadfastly rejected acceptance, thereby buttressing Diefenbaker although attacking the prime minister for not saying no unequivocally. Early in 1962, Pearson was still saying no to warheads for Canadian NORAD forces, but he felt they could be used by Canadian NATO forces if the warheads were under NATO control, not national control. And as 1962 progressed, Pearson began listening to other pro-nuclear arguments, especially from Liberal defence spokesman Paul Hellyer.

The NATO option was one that some of Diefenbaker's cabinet ministers and some officials in External Affairs thought might be an eventual compromise the prime minister could make. The CIA had advised Kennedy in a National Intelligence Estimate in the spring of 1961 that "Canadian leaders will probably continue to exploit 'Canadianism' with its anti-American overtones for internal political advantage," but the agency felt that with pressure from NATO, "the government probably would not refuse nuclear weapons for Canadian NATO forces in Europe."

But if Diefenbaker was considering a compromise, he was not admitting it. Looking to an election in the late spring, he told Donald Fleming, "The grass roots don't want nuclear weapons. The grass roots are against this." He showed Fleming some of what he said were thousands of anti-nuclear letters pouring into his office.

American Ambassador Livingston Merchant, making his own survey on a cross-country swing, saw the national mood differently. He felt Canadians supported Washington's view on nuclear warheads. He also found Kennedy's enormous popularity was helpful; in truth, in a straight Kennedy–Diefenbaker vote, Kennedy would have been an easy winner. After a three-week tour of western Canada, Merchant reported to the State Department, "The overwhelming majority of businessmen and other community leaders consider the possession of such weapons necessary and hence inevitable." Surveys during the year by Gallup and by the Canadian Peace Research Institute confirmed this view. Diefenbaker dismissed the evidence with the comment "Polls are for dogs," and continued to rely on his letters and his instinct.

Although only back in the job for a year, Merchant was weary of fighting with Diefenbaker and saddened at the deterioration of relations between Canada and the U.S. He had worked hard at cultivating relations among senior Canadian officials while defending the American position, but he could never get through to Diefenbaker. "Mr. Diefenbaker didn't like him," the prime minister's secretary, Bunny Pound, says. Merchant's senior embassy adviser, Rufus Smith, says, "I had a feeling that with Diefenbaker, Merchant didn't try as hard as he might have." Whatever the reason, the two men did not have an easy relationship. The whole experience had begun to affect Merchant's health, and at fifty-eight, with a yearly pension of $11,095 awaiting him after what he described as "twenty pressurized years" of high-level diplomacy, Merchant decided to retire. Rusk asked him whether his decision was "irreversible or discussable," and Merchant replied, "The former."

Before driving off into retirement in Washington, Merchant met the prime minister on March 8 to talk once again about nuclear warheads; he met him again a couple of months later to say goodbye. The first meeting was far more satisfactory than the second. Reporting to the State Department on the first one, he said Diefenbaker seemed once again to be moving towards acceptance of warheads, no matter what he was saying publicly. Merchant even quoted the prime minister as dismissing the significance of peace activists in Canada.

In Merchant's view, the prime minister was sending positive messages to Kennedy on warhead acquisition, just as he had done in August during the Berlin Crisis. He quoted Diefenbaker as saying confidentially that he would "proceed forthwith on negotiations looking at least to initializing texts as finally agreed." But just as he had abruptly changed his mind because he felt personally insulted by the leaking of Kennedy's August 3, 1961, letter to him, a similar incident changed the course of Diefenbaker's thinking again, and Merchant's hopes for bridging the chasm between the White House and 24 Sussex Drive were smashed.

President Kennedy was throwing a White House dinner party in late April for the Nobel Prize–winners of North America. Among those invited was Diefenbaker's political adversary Lester Pearson. Diefenbaker was particularly sensitive about Pearson at this time because he was about to call an election for June 18, a month and a half away.

The prime minister had been advised of the White House Nobel dinner invitation to Pearson and had not been pleased, for he was close to paranoia about the Kennedy–Pearson relationship. "Diefenbaker always feared Kennedy was in touch with Mike Pearson," says Charles Ritchie. When the election was called a few days after the invitation went out, the Americans were uneasy about Pearson's invitation becoming an election issue. However, they decided that it would be worse to withdraw it, and besides, they knew Kennedy liked Pearson and wanted him there.

Kennedy asked Pearson to come to the White House before dinner so they could chat. "I need your guidance and advice," he said. Pearson took the weekend off from his campaigning and met Kennedy in the study of the presidential living quarters upstairs at the White House. They conferred while Kennedy got dressed for dinner. Their conversation was interrupted three times by Kennedy's daughter, Caroline, who popped in and out of her father's study. The third time she stamped her foot and cried, "Come on, Daddy, quit working!"

The president and Canada's opposition leader spent forty minutes talking about Vietnam and how the U.S. could extricate itself, about nuclear testing, about British membership in the Common Market (which Pearson favoured), and about Kennedy's meeting with British Prime Minister Macmillan, who had just been in Washington and was now going on to Ottawa. Pearson maintained that the subject of Canadian politics did not come up. "We were very very correct," he said, adding that the meeting had been "very private and personal." It stretches credulity, however, given Kennedy's nature, to believe the president didn't make at least a joshing reference to the election. Pearson said later, "I did not expect . . . that my presence at the White House would be publicly interpreted by some Tories as United States intervention in our election and as proof of their suspicion that Kennedy was hoping Diefenbaker would be defeated."

In casual grandeur, the forty-nine Nobel Prize–winners sat down to dinner in the White House State Dining Room and the Blue Room with Kennedy, Jackie, Lyndon Johnson, and Robert Kennedy. One of the Nobel laureates, ardent Ban-the-Bomb activist Dr. Linus Pauling, came to dinner direct from a picket line in front of the White House protesting Kennedy's decision to resume nuclear testing.

In typical Kennedy style, the president told the gathering, "Ladies and gentlemen, Mr. Lester Pearson informed me that a Canadian newspaperman said yesterday that this is the president's 'Easter egghead roll on the White House lawn.' I want to deny it . . . [but] I think this is the most extraordinary collection of talent, of human knowledge, that has ever been gathered together at the White House – with the possible exception of when Thomas Jefferson dined alone." It was generally regarded as one of the great events of the Kennedy White House years, but not so by John Diefenbaker, who sat scowling in Ottawa.

It was clear to reporters who chatted with Pearson after the dinner that Pearson and Kennedy shared much the same out-look on world affairs and thoroughly enjoyed each other's company. It was equally clear among Kennedy's associates that Kennedy did indeed hope that the coming election would see Mike Pearson as prime minister rather than John Diefenbaker.

Diefenbaker was now in "an ungoverned rant about how they [the Americans] were out to get him." Basil Robinson noted in his diary: "There is every sign that this will be an anti-American election."

Donald Fleming said, "He complained that Kennedy did not know Canada. He was anti-British like his father. He expected Canada to be subservient to the United States." Furthermore, said Fleming, Diefenbaker claimed Kennedy had "brainwashed" Pearson in a Kennedy–Pearson "plot" to overthrow him.

A few days later, when Harold Macmillan arrived in Ottawa fresh from meeting Kennedy in Washington, Diefenbaker con-tinued his ranting. He said the Americans wanted Britain in the Common Market as a way of ending Commonwealth trade preferences, and if that happened, it would throw Canada under the yoke of American economic domination. Robinson, who sat in on the Diefenbaker–Macmillan meeting, noted in his diary, "PM's performance full of overtones of anti-Americanism and thinly veiled threats to use it in the campaign."

Macmillan, however, had staked his political future on Britain's joining the Common Market, and he welcomed Kennedy's support. In this battle Macmillan's friend was Kennedy and Diefenbaker was his adversary. With his own admiration for Kennedy growing, Macmillan was beginning to give up on Diefenbaker; Kennedy already had.

Diefenbaker was still feeling insulted and humiliated by the Kennedy–Pearson meeting and by the unsympathetic hearing he'd had from Macmillan when Merchant called on him for a farewell visit. Unaware of Diefenbaker's paranoid mood, the ambassador was hopeful that Diefenbaker was at last coming "on side" on nuclear warheads. It was the worst shock of his career when the prime minister dramatically revealed the Rostow memorandum left behind at the Kennedy–Diefenbaker meeting one year earlier.

Those few Canadian officials who knew about the Rostow memorandum were shocked that the prime minister hadn't returned it at the time he found it. Arnold Heeney said he was "distressed" when Diefenbaker told him he would not hesitate to "use" the memo "when the proper time came." "I have rarely if ever been so disturbed by a conversation with the head of the Canadian Government," Heeney noted in his diary.

Nobody had told the Americans about the memo, however. As Merchant walked into the study of Diefenbaker's 24 Sussex Drive residence, the meeting began pleasantly enough, with Merchant saying this was his farewell call on the prime minister. But suddenly Diefenbaker launched into a sputtering anti-American diatribe, the likes of which Merchant had never heard. The prime minister exploded in rage over Kennedy's invitation to Pearson, and he disclosed his secret of the Rostow memorandum, calling it "an offensive document" and saying it was proof Kennedy was "arrogantly" trying to "push Canada around." In a head-shaking frenzy, he attacked Kennedy personally and charged that the president was trying to get rid of him and make Pearson prime minister.

Merchant was staggered by the intensity of Diefenbaker's stinging assault. The prime minister was practically out of his mind with rage, Merchant would later tell Kennedy. Merchant said the prime minister threatened to use the memo in his election campaign against Pearson, who he claimed was a

Kennedy stooge. The American ambassador told Diefenbaker he was astonished at the threat. The memo, he said, was a private presidential paper inadvertently left behind by the president of the United States, who had been a guest of the Canadian government; decency and diplomacy should have led the prime minister to return the document immediately. At that moment, however, Diefenbaker was interested in neither decency nor diplomacy, but revenge. Merchant said there could be tragic consequences for Canada–U.S. relations if the prime minister used the memo as he indicated he might, but Diefenbaker refused to withdraw his threat.

After an hour with Diefenbaker and still trembling with indignation, Merchant returned to the American embassy to have emergency meetings with his senior staff. "I never heard of this memo before, did any of you?" he asked them, shaking his head in wonderment. "What the hell should we do about it?" "None of us knew it was missing," embassy official Rufus Smith remembers.

Because of the incendiary nature of the insults to his president and the threats to use the memo publicly to attack Kennedy, Merchant was reluctant to make any report in writing at that point. So he phoned the State Department to ask Secretary of State Dean Rusk precisely what was in the memo and to discuss what to do. Rusk and Under-Secretary George Ball were dumbfounded. "Unforgivable," Rusk now says. "He should have returned it or burned it. It was a disguised attempt at blackmail by Diefenbaker."

The president's reaction was the strongest of all. "Jeezus Christ!" he exploded when he heard of it. Kennedy talked about "cutting his balls off" in an expletive-filled roar of vituperation; he called Diefenbaker "a prick," "a fucker," "a shit," and other salty characterizations. "The air was blue with his language," Rusk recalls with a rueful smile. Rusk, always the Southern gentleman, was uncomfortable with Kennedy's swearing.

The president lashed back at Diefenbaker's threat to use the memo in an anti-American campaign by saying, "Just let him try it!" Ted Sorensen notes that Kennedy was always at his sternest when threatened. "He was not a man who took threats passively," says Sorensen. "He was prepared to respond to Diefenbaker, although I'm not sure how, but he would have."

McGeorge Bundy, who also discussed the Diefenbaker threat with Kennedy, said it was "a shocking affair. . . . Kennedy's opinion of Diefenbaker went way down, especially when he saw such fraudulent use of a document."

When they calmed down, Kennedy, Bundy, Rusk, and Ball agreed that Merchant had to go back to the prime minister with the only response they felt he could give: that he had thought "long and seriously" about what the prime minister had said and that he could not report it to his government. To do so, Merchant should say, would mean that the president could never again have any dealings with the prime minister.

Merchant had the text cabled to him and, armed with his Washington instructions, went back to see Diefenbaker. As he went through his formally phrased warning to the prime minister, Merchant found Diefenbaker a changed man: charming, friendly, and calm. Diefenbaker now said he wouldn't use the Rostow memo as a weapon in the election campaign. But having said that, Diefenbaker ended the meeting by saying, to Merchant's astonishment, that in any event "as a friend" he would call Merchant in Washington forty-eight hours in advance if he decided to change his mind and use the memo. The ambassador was perplexed and shocked at what he called Diefenbaker's "bad taste." Meanwhile, Diefenbaker put the memo back in the "vault."

When he got back to Washington, Merchant went to the White House and saw the astounded president, who tapped his fingers and swung his foot in agitation, as he always did when he was angry. "That son of a bitch," he grimaced yet again, calling the affair "a species of blackmail" and wondering why Diefenbaker "didn't do what any normal, friendly government would do. Make a photostatic copy and return the original."

At that point, Kennedy swore he would never see or talk to Diefenbaker again. *Time* White House correspondent Hugh Sidey says Kennedy told him that Diefenbaker's attacks on him had become so personal that he finally decided he "could not safely deal with the man." Rusk confirms that Kennedy decided he would never see Diefenbaker again, and thereafter he kept formal communication to a frosty minimum. "Kennedy decided," Rusk says, "that relations between the two countries would be in better shape if the two left each other alone." "The president profoundly detested Diefenbaker," says the author of the controversial memo, Walt Rostow.

There was also a change of ambassadors on Canada's part that spring. In April Canada's new ambassador arrived in Washington to replace Arnold Heeney, who had returned to Ottawa for a new assignment. Diefenbaker had appointed the spare, sardonic, and insightful Charles Ritchie, a veteran diplomat educated at Oxford and Harvard. Ritchie knew he was heading into a diplomatic hornets' nest. "To be ambassador in a capital where relations between your own government and the government to which you are accredited are bad and getting worse, is always a tricky situation," he says.

In a private report to the president, the State Department had described Ritchie as having a "somewhat old world manner" with great "astuteness and cleverness." "He has wit, imagination, an agreeable nature," the State Department said, but added, "Ritchie occasionally appears somewhat absent minded" and it suggested he might have "too weak and inefficient a personality."

When he got to Washington, Ritchie quickly found a powerful anti-Diefenbaker atmosphere. "There could be no doubt in my mind, or in anyone else's, of the personal quality of the President's dislike of Mr. Diefenbaker, whom he regarded with supercilious aversion."

Ritchie sensed some of Kennedy's disdain for Diefenbaker as he met Kennedy for the first time in late May. Ritchie came to the White House Oval Office one day at noon to formally present his letter of credence, signed by the Queen. In the quaint formal language of diplomacy, the document said:

To the President of the United States of America.
Sendeth Greeting!
Our Good Friend!
Being desirous to maintain and without interruption the relations of friendship and good understanding which happily exist between Canada and the United States, We have made choice of Our Trusty and Well-beloved Charles Stewart Almon Ritchie, Esquire, to reside with You in the character of Ambassador Extraordinary and Plenipotentiary of Canada.

Kennedy's behaviour seemed to belie the Queen's communication about Canada-U.S. relations. He was "distinctly cool," Ritchie recalls, "deliberately creating a distance." There were long pauses in their twelve-minute conversation. During one pause, the Canadian ambassador felt a sudden alarm, which he described in his diary:

"The President half rose from the rocking chair in which he was sitting, stretched out his arms, and said 'Shoo, shoo.' For a moment I was frozen in my place. The thought passed through my mind that I might be the first Ambassador in history to be shooed out of the White House. I didn't see that behind the sofa on which I was sitting, coming through the French windows out of the garden, was his young daughter, the little girl Caroline, leading her pony. They hastily backed out of the window into the garden but my reaction will give some idea of the uncomfortable coolness of the atmosphere created."

That chill reflected not only Kennedy's detestation of Diefenbaker, but also his scorn for ambassadors in general and the State Department in particular. Diplomats were useful for providing facts, but would not take risks, he felt, and he had developed what he called a "shit list" of forty names of those in the State Department he wanted to get rid of. But none were fired. When asked by a friend how many on the "shit list" had left, Kennedy said, "Not one. Not a fucking one. . . . The bastards stay there forever." "A bowl full of jelly," he called the State Department. Sending an instruction to State was "like dropping it in a dead letter box," he said to a friend.

Ritchie agreed to the extent that he felt Secretary of State Dean Rusk was an implementer of policy, not an innovator. But he felt Rusk's Buddha-like face and shiny, pumpkin-shaped bald head might also harbour "a demure slyness like an unfrocked Abbé." Soon after Ritchie arrived in Washington, Rusk subjected him at a private dinner to a less than demure attack on Canadian government policies and the prime minister. Influential columnist Walter Lippmann, who was also there, said he'd never heard any ambassador assaulted with such intensity about his government.

Ritchie quickly found that the Kennedy–Diefenbaker feud had seeped through the whole American administration, delay-

ing, complicating, and hindering progress on a wide range of
Canada–U.S. issues beyond the nuclear warhead impasse.
American officials groaned when they saw a Canadian coming.
"Even if you were doing some rather minor piece of business,"
Ritchie says, "you were soon aware that a sort of signal had
gone out: 'Those Canadians, don't give them an inch on
anything.'

"There was a measure of contempt in their comments that I
found very distasteful, almost a class contempt," Ritchie says.

The poisonous Kennedy–Diefenbaker relationship affected
even the Canadian media in Washington. Officials in the U.S.
administration, down to relatively junior levels, were occasionally snippy with Canadian reporters. They all knew and were
affected by the feud at the summit. "Inevitably," admits Dean
Rusk, "it seeped down into the bureaucracy."

The Americans didn't like our defence policies; they didn't
like our trading with Cuba and China; they didn't like our delay
in ratifying the already signed Columbia River Treaty to share
power in the west; they didn't like our opposition to Britain's
application to join the Common Market; they didn't like our
flirtation with the unaligned world in disarmament discussions;
and above all, they didn't like John George Diefenbaker.

The prime minister thought all this made an ideal election issue.
He could wrap himself in Canadian nationalism, as Sir John A.
Macdonald had done successfully three-quarters of a century
before. He headed into the campaign for the June 18 election
as a man "they" were out to get.

"They" were not only the Americans, but also Bay Street,
the big-city slickers, the intellectuals, the Establishment, and
the media. Veteran Ottawa reporter Val Sears told his press
gallery colleagues when the election was called, "To work,
gentlemen, we have a government to overthrow," thereby
earning Diefenbaker's everlasting contempt and giving what
Diefenbaker declared was proof of the media's plot to destroy
him. He thereafter referred to Sears as "Mr. Snears."

In this election he would face questions about his leadership,
his indecisiveness, his pettiness, his economic mismanagement,

and his quarrels with Kennedy. The campaign was focused more on Diefenbaker's style of intuitive and situational hip-pocket government, and less on his earlier passionate emphasis on social justice, human rights, and nationalism.

It was Diefenbaker's misfortune that the election came in the midst of a financial crisis. There was a run on the Canadian dollar, and Canada's foreign exchange fund lost about $1 billion from January to the end of June 1962. Diefenbaker was forced to devalue the Canadian dollar, setting it at a rate of 92.5 cents to the U.S. dollar after it had floated between 95 cents and par or better for years. This gave the Liberals a potent political advantage, which they used effectively, tagging the shrunken dollar the "Diefenbuck," a symbol of government mismanagement. "The Diefenbuck really did us in," says Dalton Camp, who was in charge of advertising for the Tory campaign. "Diefenbaker wanted a simple explanation for the economic crisis, but there was no simple explanation. And he wanted to say the lower Canadian dollar was a good thing for Canada."

There had been criticism by Wall Street, too, of Diefenbaker's economic policies. A respected voice of the American financial community, *Barron's*, had warned that Diefenbaker was "playing with fire" with his "misguided economic and fiscal policy."

Always looking for villains, Diefenbaker blamed it all on Kennedy, believing the financial crisis to be an American plot to elect Pearson and the Liberals. Although he said nothing publicly at the time, he later wrote that the crisis had begun when the New York money market was "spooked" and "orchestrated for political reasons" by Kennedy. "Its object was to get rid of my government," he said.

There is no evidence for Diefenbaker's assertion that Kennedy deliberately started the financial crisis to undermine him. But there is ample evidence that Kennedy wanted Diefenbaker's defeat in the June 18 election. Although he did nothing directly to help the Liberals, he certainly helped indirectly.

Keith Davey, who ran the Liberal campaign, was in love with the style, verve, and political chutzpah of the American president. "Here was a young, attractive, exciting political leader who was also a man of action," Davey says. He knew Mike Pearson was different, but he sought to adopt much of the

Kennedy campaign architecture, and his bible was Teddy White's classic book on the political bricks and mortar of the 1960 U.S. presidential election campaign, *The Making of the President 1960.*

A key element in Kennedy's campaign had been strategic public opinion polling by Lou Harris, who had become the official Kennedy pollster and a good friend of the president. Harris knew little about Canada and less about Canadian politics; but Davey, seduced by the Kennedy aura around Harris, wanted to hire him. Veteran Liberal bigwig Robert Winters suggested the idea, and Harris came to Ottawa to have lunch with Davey and campaign chairman Walter Gordon in the Château Laurier Hotel Grill. They fell head over heels for Harris's consummate professionalism and his aggressive creativity. For his part, Harris found Pearson an extraordinarily attractive politician. "Very much like Adlai Stevenson," he says. "In some ways, Mike Pearson was too nice a guy. As noble a soul as you'll ever meet in politics. A dedicated, decent human being."

But there was danger in hiring Harris because he was well known as Kennedy's pollster, and any publicity about that would play right into Diefenbaker's hands. It was "likely to be interpreted by Mr. Diefenbaker and his party as a direct intervention by President Kennedy in Canadian politics," Gordon said later.

The answer was to keep the contract with Harris secret. Few even in the Liberal party knew of his work. "They were afraid someone would recognize me as Kennedy's poll-taker," Harris says. As a precaution, Harris used an assumed name while working for the Liberals. His mother's maiden name was Smith, so he was introduced to people and made plane and hotel reservations using the name Louis Smith. The closest call came when Davey and Harris met prominent and media-wise Conservative Frank McGee at the airport in Toronto. Davey said, "Hi Frank, I want you to meet Lou Smith," and McGee never realized it was the famous pollster Lou Harris.

Before agreeing to work for the Liberals, Harris had checked with Kennedy. Earlier, British Labour leader Harold Wilson had asked Harris to do some polling for him and Harris had discussed it with the president. "I don't trust Harold Wilson, and I'd hate to see you do anything that would harm my friend

Macmillan," Kennedy said, and he discouraged Harris from taking the assignment. Harris turned Wilson down. But when he saw Kennedy about polling for Mike Pearson, it was a different story. Kennedy had no objections at all. "You do what you want," Kennedy said. "I suppose Diefenbaker is going to beat Pearson, but good luck to you. I'm not certain you'll succeed."

In their conversation about whether he should work for Pearson, Harris found Kennedy shared his opinion of the Liberal leader. "Besides, he'd have been a hell of a second baseman," Kennedy mused at one point, recalling Pearson's encyclopedic baseball knowledge and the fact that he had once played semi-pro ball. "Maybe he might have won the pennant for the Red Sox."

So Harris went to work for the Liberals. He says, "It certainly wasn't at Kennedy's specific request, but rather with his acquiescence. Kennedy never stood in the way as he did with Wilson."

Harris hired a field force of five hundred women whose in-person polling produced in-depth research on every major campaign issue. His particular value to the Liberals was an ability to translate the polling results into campaign strategy; he said the party should concentrate on the economy and unemployment. "It was the first serious polling ever done in Canada, and we couldn't have achieved what we did without Harris," says Davey.

For party workers, Davey produced a "how to" book on campaigning, a red-bound, printed series of lectures that he called his "Campaign College" red book. He sent a copy to Kennedy, who, Davey says, "thought it was terrific. He said our book was better than anything they were doing at the time."

Harris was impressed with Diefenbaker as a campaigner and found he was running ahead of his party in popularity. "Diefenbaker had a gritty political quality that surprised me. He was a stemwinder," Harris says in grudging admiration.

Diefenbaker was a one-man show on the campaign trail, blasting the Liberals, concentrating on his nationalism, and playing an anti-American theme, although playing it more *sotto voce* than he felt. Several times in his campaign Diefenbaker said the Kennedy administration wanted his defeat because he

wouldn't "bow down to Washington." The U.S. embassy
protested, and officials feared the prime minister would use the
Rostow memorandum as he had threatened he might. Willis
Armstrong, who was at this time back in Washington at a senior
State Department post, says, "He would have done anything.
Actually, I always thought he was not fundamentally anti-Amer-
ican. It was more a political device. He would use whatever was
handy to stay in power."

In his "Follow John" campaign, he did stretch the credulity
of some as he sought to portray himself as a powerful world
statesman. "Oh, it's not easy for us, the Macmillans, the
Kennedys, the Adenauers, and the de Gaulles," he said at one
point.

On several campaign occasions he portrayed himself as the
cause of Nikita Khrushchev's famous shoe-banging at the
United Nations in 1960. At an ethnic rally in Montreal he
sought to identify himself with the world's oppressed, saying,
"I told Mr. Khrushchev, 'Give the Ukrainians the vote', and
then he got mad and that's when he took off his shoe, you
remember." On another occasion, emphasizing the need for
better treatment of minorities, he said, "It wasn't long after I
finished this speech that in his rage, [Khrushchev] pounded his
desk after removing his shoes to have the necessary missile to
convey his views." At yet another campaign rally, Diefenbaker
said, "I stopped. I waited. Khrushchev showed his annoyance.
There was hatred in his eye."

In fact, Khrushchev wasn't even in the UN Assembly Hall
when Diefenbaker spoke; the Soviet Union's chief UN delegate,
Valerian Zorin, was the senior Soviet representative in the
assembly at the time. Indeed, the shoe-banging incident occurred at the General Assembly in October 1960 during an
address by the Philippine delegate, more than two weeks after
Diefenbaker had spoken there. The speech Diefenbaker gave at
the UN was one of his best, but it was buried on page 16 of the
New York *Times*, and his subsequent embroidery of it on the
campaign trail diminished its lustre.

As the campaign progressed, it was clear that Harris had been
right in advising the Liberals to emphasize bread-and-butter
economic issues. The nuclear warhead question did not play a
significant role for the voters, especially since the Liberal

platform also urged a non-nuclear defence role for Canada and, in fact, talked about getting Canada out of NORAD entirely. Thus the nuclear issue was neutralized as a political weapon, even though the Liberals attacked the Tory government for wasting money by buying nuclear-capable weapons while rejecting the nuclear warheads themselves.

As the campaign ended, Diefenbaker reiterated his traditional "please everybody" stance by saying, "To the mothers and wives we have given the assurance that Canada will not join the family of nuclear nations, but at the same time [we will] discharge our responsibility for the security of Canada by assuring that if war should come – which God forbid – Canadian armed forces will be in a position to defend with the best defences available."

Kennedy remained publicly aloof from the campaign, but Khrushchev did not. Four days before the vote, Moscow warned Canada against accepting nuclear warheads. In a diplomatic note, the Soviets said, "If measures on location of nuclear weapons on Canadian territory have been taken on the part of Canada, the U.S.S.R. Government would be forced to draw out of it a proper conclusion with the aim of guaranteeing the security of the Soviet Union."

Howard Green returned the note to the Soviet embassy in Ottawa, saying "it constituted interference in Canadian affairs." The Conservatives used the incident publicly as proof that Diefenbaker would stand up to the Communists.

Diefenbaker said that Khrushchev had earlier accused Canada of being a tool of the American nuclear war machine. Given his sensitivity about the U.S. military presence in Canada's North, the accusation was one that Diefenbaker was particularly eager to deny: "He contended that Canada was simply a puppet being pushed around by the United States and that our northern areas were being used as jumping-off places for the United States in potential aggression against the U.S.S.R. . . . I said, 'There's no such thing.'"

The Liberals began the campaign substantially ahead in the public opinion polls; they had forty-three per cent, compared with thirty-eight per cent for the Tories, in the last pre-election Gallup poll. But they dropped steadily, and Harris kept warning the Liberals that Pearson was trailing his party in support while

Diefenbaker was leading his. "Emphasize the team," was Harris's advice. Pearson's first words when Davey and Harris would arrive on his Ottawa doorstep on their regular polling reviews would invariably be, "Lou, how bad am I this month?"

But by the end of the campaign, it was Diefenbaker who was exhausted, nervous, and despondent. "He looked and sounded like a beaten man," says Pierre Sévigny.

Seven and a quarter million voters went to the polls and returned Diefenbaker to office with a minority government. His Conservatives won 116 seats to 100 for the Liberals, 19 for the NDP, and 30 for Social Credit. It was a stunning and humiliating loss of 92 seats, compared with his 1958 triumph, but still enough to squeeze through.

But Diefenbaker now faced the horrendous economic crisis, which Pearson was glad was not his. On election night, Pearson had telephoned his mother to tell her he was losing the election and was not going to be prime minister. She said she had noticed all the talk about the economy and said soothingly, "Perhaps it's just as well that you haven't been asked to take on the prime minister's job at this time because you were never very good in arithmetic."

Diefenbaker was forced to offer the country some nasty economic medicine. He imposed a surcharge on imports, cut duty exemptions for tourists, reduced government spending by $250 million, raised the bank rate, and announced he was borrowing about $1 billion: $300 million from the International Monetary Fund, $100 million from the Bank of England, $250 million from the United States Federal Reserve System, and $400 million from the Export-Import Bank of Washington. The Winnipeg *Free Press* editorialized that Diefenbaker had gone hat in hand to his two major adversaries like "an underdeveloped Asian state in need of charity. And that aid, let us never forget, came from two countries most damaged by Canada's tariff increases and most viciously attacked by the Canadian Government."

As the crisis eased, the Americans hoped Diefenbaker would be grateful for the financial help they had given in the dollar crisis. Some thought it might provide useful leverage to encourage Diefenbaker to change his nuclear warheads stand. They saw no such change and were outraged when Diefenbaker later made the accusation that the crisis had been caused by Kennedy. After the 1962 election, Diefenbaker was unshakeable in his conviction that Kennedy was out to destroy him. "It's now very clear," he said later, "that it was part and parcel of the beginning of actions by President Kennedy and his associates to get rid of the Conservative Party of Canada."

Diefenbaker now wallowed in a swamp of miseries, beset, he felt, by a horde of malignant enemies, deeply wounded by his election pummelling, shamed by having to ask for help in Washington and London to ease his financial crisis and always obsessed with Kennedy, Kennedy, Kennedy. And personal blows battered his fragile psyche, sending him into a tailspin that verged on an emotional breakdown. He collapsed like a pierced balloon.

He lost his two best friends and closest political advisers. Senator William Brunt was killed in a car crash as he drove home from Ottawa to Hanover, Ontario. "I was shattered," Diefenbaker said. "He was my confidant in every political matter, a tower of strength." Brunt had been with Diefenbaker in Prince Albert on the night of the election. In the last conversation they had, Diefenbaker said he wanted Brunt to be Speaker of the Senate.

His other close friend was Toronto MP David Walker, whom Diefenbaker nicknamed "Big Boy." Like Brunt, Walker had been a Diefenbaker supporter ever since his run at the party leadership in 1942. Walker had managed Diefenbaker's 1948 leadership campaign against George Drew. He had been defeated in the June election and had gone back to his Toronto law practice.

Diefenbaker felt he had no one left he could trust. "It was shocking, the effect on him," says Walker. "He was so tired and so exhausted after that campaign. I don't think he knew how to get out of bed in the morning. His mind wasn't working at all and he was very, very upset and melancholy."

Two weeks after Brunt's death, Diefenbaker broke his ankle when he fell into a gopher hole as he stepped off the flagstone terrace at the prime ministerial summer retreat at Harrington Lake in the Gatineau Hills, north of Ottawa. It healed poorly and pained agonizingly, and he stayed flat on his back in bed in his second-floor bedroom at 24 Sussex Drive for much of the next five weeks, with an occasional spell on a lounge chair in his garden. According to cabinet colleagues, his doctors even feared amputation might be necessary. Blood vessels behind his knee burst, and there was swelling and a large area of dis-colouration. He was a nervous wreck; irritable, indecisive, yet still wanting to run everything.

"There was a real change in him," says Bunny Pound. "He wanted to stay away from everybody, and he didn't want to have any trouble brought to him. He wanted to just sit there in his bed and rumble. He lost all his effervescence. It came back now and then, but never the same way. . . . I thought possibly he realized that he had bitten off more than he could chew."

"You just couldn't make contact with him," recalls Dalton Camp. "He often went to bed when he was in trouble."

Pierre Sévigny says, "The man was suffering from nervous exhaustion, a nervous breakdown. In our first cabinet meeting after the election he seemed close to tears. He was scared and very tired. The cabinet should have had the courage to tell him to take three months off."

Diefenbaker's old friend and protégé Alvin Hamilton was even blunter. "He was completely off his rocker for three or four months! You have to admit it, he was unstable. He just seemed confused. . . . He thought Kennedy was trying to gun him down."

"I don't think anybody ever said anything or would say that it was mental illness, but certainly all of us in the autumn knew that he was subject to fits of depression and to a much greater emotional instability than had been the case previously," said R.A. Bell, citizenship and immigration minister. "His mind was so black and so sour."

Amid his pain and private furies, Diefenbaker agonized over re-shuffling his cabinet. It was nearly two months after the election before the new cabinet was appointed. The swearing-in took place at noon in Diefenbaker's living room at 24 Sussex. The prime minister stood awkwardly with his leg tightly wrapped in wide adhesive tape as his ankle continued swelling. The first meeting of the new cabinet took place in Diefenbaker's bedroom two hours later.

Finally, in a grim mood and hobbling on a cane, Diefenbaker went to a meeting of party officials at the Château Laurier in

Ottawa to review the election campaign. He was incensed that, for the first time, Eaton's had not contributed to the Conservative campaign. "I just want to tell you," he snapped, "that Olive has torn up her Eaton's shopping card." The implication was clear: their wives should do the same thing. "It was right out of Captain Queeg," says Dalton Camp. As they were leaving the meeting, one senior party official muttered to Camp and several other colleagues, "Gentlemen, we have a prime minister who is insane!"

Diefenbaker began talking about resignation and at one point told Gordon Churchill, his most ardent cabinet supporter, that he was seriously thinking of quitting by the end of the year. "He couldn't pull himself himself out of the depression and it was then that he got into the habit of threatening resignation," said R.A. Bell.

Diefenbaker had another loss in this summer of his disconsolateness when his foreign affairs adviser, Basil Robinson, left Ottawa to become the Canadian minister and number two man at the Canadian embassy in Washington. Robinson had served Diefenbaker loyally and well for five years, walking a minefield between the Prime Minister's Office and External Affairs. Incredibly, he had the trust of both Diefenbaker and External, but he looked forward to his Washington posting as a respite from political infighting. It would turn out to be anything but a respite, as he and Ambassador Charles Ritchie faced an increasingly hostile Washington environment.

Kennedy sent a not-so-subtle rebuke to Canada by waiting for more than four months before he appointed a replacement for Livingston Merchant. In July, he asked Erwin Griswold, dean of the Harvard Law School, to become ambassador to Canada, but Griswold declined. Three more names were suggested to Kennedy in late August. Finally, in mid-September, he named Louisiana-born W. Walton Butterworth, a big, egocentric bull in a china shop whose qualities seemed almost designed to infuriate Prime Minister Diefenbaker. Butterworth's senior official at the Ottawa embassy, Rufus Smith, says, "In some ways, he was a pompous ass. But a smart one. He could be haughty and had supreme confidence in his own abilities."

"He was a very intelligent, perceptive man," says Willis

Armstrong, "but he had a hell of a lot of difficulty understanding a guy like Diefenbaker. And he didn't have much use for Green."

Diefenbaker privately called him "old Butterballs" or "Butterfingers," and sometimes, caustically, "Big Boss"; he was always wary when they met. "Every time he came into my office, I thought to myself, 'Butch, what's your racket?'" he told colleagues. In time, Diefenbaker refused to attend social functions where Butterworth was present.

Gordon Churchill said of the new American ambassador, "Mr. Butterworth, as I understand it, was a hatchet man." Charles Ritchie calls Butterworth "a very amusing and likeable, but very overbearing and arrogant man."

Kennedy's ambassador thought Ottawa was "terribly provincial and the people there are terribly provincial." However, he felt the job was important and he was determined to woo or, if necessary, bludgeon Diefenbaker into accepting nuclear warheads.

Butterworth had been a third secretary at the U.S. embassy in Ottawa in 1932. He had served with Kennedy's father when Joe Kennedy was the American ambassador to Britain, where he had struck up an acquaintance with young Jack Kennedy. To Diefenbaker's chagrin, Butterworth was also a Rhodes Scholar, a Princeton graduate, a protégé of Dean Acheson, and an ardent advocate of British membership in the Common Market.

As the fall of 1962 arrived, it was the Common Market that preoccupied Diefenbaker. He shook off his pain and despair and flew to London, just before his sixty-seventh birthday, for a last-stand battle against Harold Macmillan and his plans for Britain to join the Common Market. His ankle still hurt, and he still needed a cane to walk, although he discarded it in public. But Diefenbaker was spoiling for a fight and resentful of Kennedy's support for Macmillan. "If Britain turned inward to Europe without protecting the interest of the Commonwealth, the Commonwealth might cease to exist," Diefenbaker said. He had told his cabinet that British entry into the Common Market might well mean the end of the Commonwealth by about 1970.

At the Commonwealth Prime Ministers Conference, Diefenbaker created a sensation with endless emotional assaults on Macmillan's Common Market plans. It was "a broadside attack," said Macmillan, and the British press characterized him as "shaky," "muddled," "badly briefed," and "highly emotional." "Macmillan had hoisted the flag of Europe," the London *Sunday Observer* said. "Diefenbaker was shooting it down. As he went on, the British became more and more anxious and more and more annoyed. Must he go on forever . . . ?"

At one private session of the prime ministers, Diefenbaker was quoted by British officials as warning of the political implications for Canada: "We have spent a hundred years resisting the magnetic pull of the United States. Now this will put us in danger of being sucked into their orbit." He warned that France would veto British Common Market membership in any event, and he spoke vaguely of alternative trade-expanding schemes, a kind of world common market. Australian Prime Minister Menzies said Diefenbaker's conclusions were "absurd," and Macmillan noted later that Menzies "resorted to his favourite sport of teasing Diefenbaker."

In fact, Macmillan encouraged Menzies in his dislike of Diefenbaker, and he recorded his own anger at the Canadian prime minister in his diary. He accused him of making a "false and vicious speech" in starting off the debate on the Common Market, and said Diefenbaker was "difficult" and "something of a mountebank. A very crooked man . . . so self-centred as to be a sort of caricature of Mr. Gladstone." As the conference progressed, Macmillan found a way to forestall Diefenbaker to some extent: "Diefenbaker's deafness helped and I was able to pass from one clause to another fairly rapidly."

The British launched an all-out assault against Diefenbaker, making him the target of a withering smear campaign through the British press. One London paper characterized the Canadian prime minister as "the rude country cousin who spoiled the family picnic." Others called him a "fuddy duddy," "Colonel Blimp," an "Empire sentimentalist."

Diefenbaker's opposition to U.K. Common Market membership drew significant support from other Commonwealth prime ministers, however, and complicated and delayed the British plans, thereby drawing the wrath of Macmillan and, in Washington, of John Kennedy. Howard Green was furious at the way the British had treated Diefenbaker, calling their criticism "utter nonsense." Green was all the more distressed because he, like Diefenbaker, had always been a strong sup-porter of the British. During the Suez Crisis of 1956, Green had angrily denounced the Liberal government's condemna-tion of the British and French attack and said, "It's high time that Canada had a government that won't knife Canada's best friends in the back." Now those best friends were knifing Diefenbaker and Green. The trump card of Canadian diplo-macy had always been the ability to talk persuasively to both the United States and Britain, as we had done in the Suez Crisis, but now that was being discarded. Diefenbaker had succeeded in alienating both London and Washington.

Washington also continued to be puzzled by Canada's nu-clear policies and so did, in private, Canada's ambassador to Washington. "Diefenbaker's policy was simply inexplicable, it didn't hang together," says Charles Ritchie. "And the Ameri-cans felt that if Canada wouldn't have nuclear arms, then that would encourage other allies not to have them either."

Diefenbaker's distress intensified when Kennedy introduced foreign exchange conservation measures because of a U.S. financial problem. Secretary of Defense Robert McNamara said that Canada had a $240-million defence trade surplus with the United States, and he warned there might have to be restric-tions on Canadian shipments to the U.S. He also said Canada should be spending $400 million to $500 million more on defence in NATO and NORAD. In addition to these pressures, Washington was pushing Diefenbaker to adopt long-term fiscal restraint programs as part of the conditions for the loans provided to Canada in July during the Canadian dollar crisis.

"Harassment," Diefenbaker muttered to colleagues. "What the Kennedy Administration actually wanted," he later wrote, "was the Canadian acceptance of nuclear weapons in NORAD and NATO. . . . We were to take the warheads because the President said we must."

The split within the cabinet over the issue of nuclear war-heads was becoming more evident as an increasingly frustrated Defence Minister Harkness lobbied privately for the warheads, saying that Canada was committed to them; that most Canadians approved; and that the Soviet bomber threat was still the main worry, not ICBMs.

But the prime minister continued to rely on his mail as reinforcement for his position. "John Diefenbaker now read every letter of his voluminous correspondence and started to refer to his famous mail in almost every conversation," says Diefenbaker's associate defence minister, Pierre Sévigny. "He seemed to feel that those who wrote represented the thinking of the average Canadian. His constant references to this letter or that letter made us nervous and became as annoying as the constant evocation of what Sir John A. had done or would have done on each particular occasion." Beyond that, his temper was getting shorter. "Mr. Diefenbaker felt that he could treat you like a schoolboy, and he did not brook any criticism," says Marcel Lambert, Speaker of the House at the time.

External Affairs Minister Howard Green's rejection of warhead acceptance and his enthusiasm for disarmament were now in the ascendant in Ottawa, as was vividly demonstrated in another spat with Kennedy over proposals for a nuclear test ban treaty.

Ever since he had made his disarmament proposals to the United Nations in the fall of 1961, the American president had been doggedly pursuing the possibility of a test ban. The stumbling block was verification. Khrushchev wanted little; Kennedy a lot. Diefenbaker and Green were more trusting of the Soviets than Kennedy was, and they were urging that even modest verification procedures would be all right if they led to Soviet agreement to a test ban. When he became external affairs minister, Green had advocated "the soft approach" to Moscow; he had said at one point, "The time has come for the West to accept Russian protestations of sincerity at face value." That was something Washington was not going to do.

Kennedy sent Diefenbaker a "Dear Prime Minister" letter in April 1962, saying, "For some time I have had an uneasy feeling that perhaps the positions of our two countries were becoming increasingly disparate on the nuclear test question." The president was concerned at signs that Canada was prepared to accept a test ban with little verification. "May I urge you most earnestly to join with us in opposing any such proposal,"

Kennedy said. "I fully understand the sincerity and good will of those who are attracted by such proposals. But, in fact, they do not serve peace among nations or understanding among men."

But in the fall, Diefenbaker announced that he was going to support a test ban even if it had only minimal verification, and he said he would endorse a UN resolution for such a test ban. Howard Green's pressure on Diefenbaker had been successful. "Howard got the peace bug," says Douglas Harkness. "Everything else was subordinated to it. . . . It was an absolute obsession."

Kennedy was furious. "To my distress," he began in an unusually harsh four-page letter to the prime minister, written on October 19, "I have learned that your government intends to support in the General Assembly this year a resolution . . . calling for an unverified moratorium on nuclear weapons tests. As I wrote to you on last April 13, I am convinced that there is no safety in such a proposal and it leads away from the only honest and workable road to arms limitation. . . .

"Should Canada cast its vote in favour of a moratorium this year, it will be tantamount to Canada's abandoning the Western position in Geneva on this issue. This will be seen by the Soviet Union as a successful breach of Western position. In this event, what hope can we hold for pressures on the Soviet Union to take the extremely reasonable step we have proposed?

"I can assure you most strongly, Mr. Prime Minister, that the United States will not agree to end tests unless we have reasonably adequate assurances that the Soviet Union will not carry out such tests.

"Mr. Prime Minister, I cannot overemphasize my concern in this matter. . . . I hope you will reconsider this decision to cast an affirmative vote for a resolution which can only damage, and damage seriously, the Western position on an essential issue of Western security."

Kennedy got support from Harkness, who also wrote to the prime minister: "I continue to believe very strongly that Canada should not vote in favour of the so-called neutral resolution." He told Green in a letter, "There would be grave risks to Western security in its acceptance."

Diefenbaker, however, was adamant and rejected the arguments of both Harkness and Kennedy. On October 30, he replied in a "Dear Mr. President" letter, saying, "I would state unequivocally that Canadian policy on this question involves no endorsement of an uncontrolled moratorium on nuclear testing. . . . I am fully aware, Mr. President, that there remains a risk that low yield underground tests can be carried out in secret. Such a risk should not be judged in isolation and should be weighed against the graver dangers that will continue to exist as long as an agreement is not reached and the tests go on. In the opinion of the Government of Canada, the resolution of the non-aligned nations represents a genuine effort to achieve a compromise position on the question of nuclear tests."

Kennedy swore in indignation at the "neutralism" of Diefenbaker. The State Department prepared a draft response for Kennedy to send Diefenbaker, but White House aide Carl Kaysen said to the president in a memo, "I recommend against the reply; why thank him for nothing?" No answer was sent to the prime minister. On November 6, the UN General Assembly passed the resolution, with Canada supporting it. The United States, the United Kingdom, and almost all other NATO countries abstained.

Kennedy was also upset about the surcharges on imports that Diefenbaker had imposed in the summer during the Canadian dollar crisis. In another letter to Diefenbaker at this time, Kennedy said, "I look forward to your being able to remove the remaining surcharges."

What was remarkable about this correspondence and contributed to Kennedy's short-tempered attitude was the timing: it was mid-October 1962. Kennedy's letters were dated October 18 and October 19, 1962, while he was in the midst of the world's closest call with nuclear war. This global crisis would lead to a defiant confrontation between Diefenbaker and Kennedy that imperilled North American defence and fatally weakened the Canadian prime minister.

Chapter Six

OUT OF CONTROL

Fidel Castro's brother Raúl arrived in Moscow on July 2, 1962. By the end of the visit, Moscow and Havana had agreed on the most audacious move of the Cold War. A few weeks later Castro's number two man, Che Guevara, came to Moscow for military discussions, and shipments of Soviet offensive nuclear weaponry began arriving in Cuba in early September.

Castro feared an American invasion, and Khrushchev wanted a trump card in negotiations with Kennedy over Berlin. For the Soviet leader, Cuba was a flanking move in the power politics of Europe.

It was a macabre dance of perilous miscalculation that could have destroyed most of civilization. Castro and Khrushchev thought they could put in the missiles in secret and then unveil them with a flourish, believing that when they did so the Americans would do nothing. At the same time the Americans never dreamed Castro and Khrushchev would install offensive weapons just ninety miles away from the United States and were staggered when they found out.

Through the late summer of 1962, while Diefenbaker hobbled about moodily with his broken ankle, forty-two Soviet offensive missiles, each designed to carry nuclear warheads twenty to thirty times more powerful than the Hiroshima bomb, were arriving in Cuba. When the presence of these missiles in Cuba was verified, Kennedy was incredulous at the reckless audacity of Khrushchev and Castro and at the realization that he was staring into the abyss of nuclear war. He had ten days, he was told, before the nuclear missiles would be ready for firing; if they were fired, eighty million Americans would die. That portentous deadline haunted all his thoughts and plans. It meant, among other things, that he would not risk any delays by advance consultation with allies, nor would he present the issue to the United Nations, until he had decided what to do.

Through an agonizing mid-October week, Kennedy and his advisers secretly debated the range of possible responses, from an invasion or air strike against Cuba to a naval blockade. The debate turned when the president's brother Robert, remembering Pearl Harbor, told a meeting, "I can't see letting my brother be a Tojo." With rivetting intensity he argued, "All our heritage and ideals would be repugnant to such a sneak military attack." With strong support from Defense Secretary Robert McNamara, this argument won the debate, and a majority of the president's advisers recommended a naval blockade of Cuba as a first move. The president agreed, saying, "Let's not push this guy [Khrushchev] into a situation from which he cannot get out."

"The president was as cool as a block of ice in looking at the alternatives," says Dean Rusk.

While Kennedy and his advisers were debating war, a long-planned meeting of international intelligence experts was going on at the British embassy, a couple of miles away. As the meeting progressed, it drew a diminishing number of CIA and other U.S. espionage representatives. Two Canadian intelligence officials attending the conference, including James McCardle, head of the Intelligence and Security Division for External Affairs, deduced, along with their fellow "spooks," that there was a crisis over Cuba. They passed their conclusions on to Ottawa. What they didn't know, however, was precisely what Kennedy was going to do.

At the White House, with secrecy crumbling, the president wanted to address the nation on October 21, a Sunday. The State Department, however, urgently asked for another day so there would be time to brief allies and prepare to meet the Organization for American States. Kennedy reluctantly agreed, and his speech was set for 7:00 P.M. Monday. As Ted Sorensen says, "He was . . . going ahead regardless of Allied reaction, though he wanted them to be informed."

British Prime Minister Macmillan, French President de Gaulle, German Chancellor Konrad Adenauer, and John Diefenbaker were singled out for special personal briefings. Former secretary of state Dean Acheson, who had served under Truman, would brief the European leaders, and former ambassador to Canada Livingston Merchant was called out of retirement to fly to Ottawa as a special presidential emissary. Merchant had been located at his alma mater, Princeton, where he was watching a Saturday football game.

Diefenbaker had spent that Saturday making speeches in Winnipeg, but he was back in Ottawa on Sunday and already aware there was a crisis with Cuba, although he did not know any details. By midday Sunday he knew that Merchant would fly to Ottawa on Monday.

Sunday afternoon, Kennedy went over the letters to be given to American allies, including the letter that Merchant was to carry to Ottawa. Diefenbaker was kept informed through Sunday night and Monday morning of all the latest intelligence, although the prime minister remained in the dark about exactly what Kennedy was going to do. One foreign leader who was aware, however, was Harold Macmillan. Kennedy, who had a deep admiration for Macmillan, spoke with him often during the crisis on a special secret phone line. Initially, Macmillan later said, "I had thought of advising him to seize Cuba and have done with it." But Macmillan endorsed Kennedy's blockade strategy. The president apologized to Macmillan about deciding on a course of action without consulting him in advance; it had been essential, he said, because of the need for security and speed. From now on, though, Kennedy said on Sunday night, he would keep in closest touch with the British prime minister. Macmillan said he fully understood and he pledged his total support.

Kennedy sought support not only from Macmillan and NATO countries; he wanted to use his speech to gain endorsement from western hemisphere nations also. As he worked with Sorensen on it, he inserted references to Canadian and Latin

American areas within the target range of the Soviet missiles in Cuba. Meanwhile, preparing for any eventuality, American missile crews were put on maximum alert; more troops moved into Florida; five army divisions were put on alert; 180 navy ships were deployed in the Caribbean; and the Strategic Air Command B-52 bomber force went on airborne alert, loaded with atomic bombs. All this, in the event the Cuban crisis suddenly escalated into World War III.

Monday dawned crisp and bright in Ottawa. By ten o'clock Douglas Harkness and Howard Green had been told that Merchant was flying to Ottawa with "an important message." Associate Defence Minister Pierre Sévigny says that later that morning, President Kennedy himself, still refusing to speak to Diefenbaker, called Green but could not reach him. He then called Harkness, but the defence minister was out of his office, so Sévigny took the call. At the time, Sévigny was at his desk, playing chess with his executive assistant. When his secretary told him, "The president of the United States is on the line," he looked up from the chessboard and said, "Is that a joke?" It wasn't, and when he picked up the phone, Kennedy said, "We haven't met, have we?"

"No, Mr. President," Sévigny replied.

"Well, there is something extremely important, Mr. Minister. Mr. Livingston Merchant is flying to Ottawa and he must meet immediately with your prime minister. Can you arrange things?"

"Of course, Mr. President, I shall carry that message," Sévigny replied. He immediately called the prime minister's office and was told by John Fisher, one of Diefenbaker's aides, that the meeting had already been arranged by Ivan White of the U.S. embassy for 5:15 P.M.

That morning, the prime minister and his wife were planting tulips in their garden at 24 Sussex, while in Washington, Kennedy briefed former presidents Hoover, Truman, and Eisenhower. In mid-afternoon, Kennedy met with Ugandan Prime Minister Milton Obote to discuss U.S. aid; and at five o'clock, he briefed key members of Congress about Cuba. They angered Kennedy by arguing for much tougher action than just a blockade.

While Kennedy was talking to the senators and congressmen, Merchant met Diefenbaker for the first time since their confrontation five months earlier over the Rostow memo. Harkness and Green were with the prime minister. Originally, Under-Secretary of State Norman Robertson, Privy Council Clerk R.B. Bryce, and the chairman of the chiefs of staff, Air Marshal Frank Miller, had been invited to the meeting, but Diefenbaker had insisted they not be present. Merchant brought two CIA officers with him to the meeting, along with two officials of the U.S. embassy.

The session in a small meeting room down the hall from Diefenbaker's East Block office began stiffly, with the prime minister extremely cool towards Merchant. Diefenbaker appeared to be "tired, harassed, and wrapped up in other things," Merchant later said. He added that the prime minister was "upset and annoyed" at not being consulted personally by Kennedy. With wounded pride, Diefenbaker made a particular point of noting he was being "informed" only two hours before Kennedy was to speak publicly.

Diefenbaker read Kennedy's "My Dear Prime Minister" letter, laying out the evidence of the presence of Soviet missiles in Cuba and revealing the American demand for their removal and the "initial" U.S. response of a blockade. "Nobody knows what the outcome will be," Merchant said. "If we have to fire on those Soviet vessels, it'll be really war. Then what will the Russians do?" Merchant said Kennedy wanted Canadian support at the United Nations and elsewhere. Diefenbaker pored carefully over the blown-up photographs of the missile sites that Merchant showed him. Dalton Camp, a key Conservative party official at the time, says Robert Kennedy later told him that Diefenbaker had demanded to see more blow-ups. "Bobby Kennedy told me," Camp says, "that when his brother heard that, he was just dumbfounded. That of all the nations in the world, the only one that gave him any trouble was Canada. The president was absolutely infuriated."

After looking at the photos, Diefenbaker listened as Merchant read the speech Kennedy would deliver at 7:00 P.M. Diefenbaker objected to one paragraph that he felt was an unnecessary personal attack on Soviet Foreign Minister Andrei

Gromyko. Merchant agreed and called Rusk in Washington, and the paragraph was taken out of the speech.

Green said little at the meeting, but Harkness asked if the president had considered tougher action than a blockade. "Well, have you considered landing troops in Cuba and taking over control of the missile sites and destroying them?" Harkness asked. "There would be less possibility of war if you concentrated efforts on Cuba instead of on Russian ships."

Merchant told Harkness that all options had been considered, including that one, and it was felt the blockade was the best first move. Despite his personal feelings, at the end of the meeting, Diefenbaker said he believed that in the circumstances, the president had no alternative but to take the action he planned, and that Canada would live up to its commitments under NATO and NORAD in the event of a missile attack from Cuba.

Merchant left to brief Robertson, Air Marshal Miller, and other Canadian officials, while Green, Harkness, and Diefenbaker stayed on to discuss what Canada's response should be. Merchant left feeling Diefenbaker was "on side" and that the Canadian government would issue a strongly supportive statement on Tuesday. He so advised Washington and flew back a contented man. Diefenbaker went home to have dinner and watch the president's televised address.

"Good evening, my fellow citizens," Kennedy said, as he began the most serious speech of his life. " . . . This sudden, clandestine decision to station strategic weapons for the first time outside Soviet soil is a deliberately provocative and unjustified change in the status quo which cannot be accepted by this country if our courage and our commitments are ever to be trusted again by either friend or foe."

Kennedy noted that the Soviet missiles not only could obliterate American cities but also could strike "most major cities in the western hemisphere as far north as Hudson Bay, Canada, and as far south as Lima, Peru." Later, Canadian reporters in Washington were pointedly told that this meant Toronto, Ottawa, Montreal, and other Canadian cities were directly endangered by the missiles in Cuba.

As he spoke, the Pentagon began assembling an invasion

force of more than 100 ships and 250,000 men; if an invasion became necessary, it estimated probable American casualties at 25,000. (It might well have been worse because the Americans had drastically underestimated the number of Soviet troops in Cuba – there were 40,000 of them at the time, along with 270,000 Cuban soldiers.) Preparing for the possibility of the crisis escalating into World War III, ICBMs, medium-range missiles, and Polaris submarines were put on alert, ready for action and pointing at their pre-selected Soviet targets. Strategic Air Command bombers loaded with atomic bombs circled in the air, ready for action if needed, and the U.S. North American Air Defense units were placed on an alert called Defcon (Defensive Condition) 3, which meant a full alert for "imminent danger." It was midway between Defcon 5, which meant normal, and Defcon 0, which meant a nuclear attack was under way. The Americans assumed Ottawa would automatically authorize putting the Canadian NORAD forces on Defcon 3 alert, but they were wrong.

Despite the supportive statement he had made to Merchant, the prime minister believed Kennedy had a hidden agenda. "Diefenbaker thought Kennedy was playing politics with Cuba – that he was grandstanding," says Diefenbaker's special assistant at the time, Dick Thrasher.

"I knew that President Kennedy was still smarting over the 1961 Bay of Pigs fiasco," Diefenbaker later said, "especially over charges that he had callously allowed the anti-Castro forces to be sacrificed by failing to provide the umbrella support from the air they had expected. I knew also that the President thought he had something to prove in his personal dealing with Khrushchev after their unpleasant Vienna meeting when Khrushchev had treated him like a child, referring to him as 'the boy.'

"I considered that he was perfectly capable of taking the world to the brink of thermonuclear destruction to prove himself the man for our times, a courageous champion of Western democracy."

Furthermore, "Canada certainly had the right to expect notice longer than two hours, if military measures were to be involved," Diefenbaker said. "It was obvious that Canada was not to be consulted but was expected to accept without question the course to be determined by the President."

Kennedy's national security adviser, McGeorge Bundy, today smiles with a trace of disdain at the idea of the president calling Diefenbaker for advance consultation. "Kennedy simply couldn't trust Diefenbaker," Bundy says. "If he had thought of calling him, his first likely reaction would have been, 'Oh my God, he'll only make trouble.' There was not a good track record."

In any event, Kennedy had made a decision that precluded advance consultation with any ally, with the sole exception of Macmillan. Besides, Dean Rusk says, "things were moving so fast in a crisis of that magnitude. . . . We did not want multilateral management of the Cuba crisis."

Diefenbaker, with his acutely sensitive personal radar, felt this rejection. "Diefenbaker felt Kennedy didn't trust him," says his former aide Tommy Van Dusen. "He was hurt, and he tried to slap Kennedy on the wrist." The prime minister was also furious about Kennedy's call to Sévigny. John Fisher warned Sévigny, "The Chief is very upset. He should have been called by the president himself, not you. We can expect some fireworks."

"He was right," said Sévigny. "Kennedy should have called Diefenbaker."

It is evident from memos, memoirs, recollections, and diaries that the personal animosity between Kennedy and Diefenbaker played a significant role in Ottawa's decisions – or lack of them – during the Cuban Missile Crisis; to a lesser extent, it was also a factor in Washington. As Robert Kennedy said, "The president hated Diefenbaker – had contempt for him."

While Diefenbaker fumed at Kennedy's lack of consultation with him, the Canadian ambassador to Washington, Charles Ritchie, more realistically says, "How could we really expect to be fully consulted when the world was so near to the precipice?" Diefenbaker's defence minister, Douglas Harkness, agrees. "Kennedy handled it well and decisively," he says. "He couldn't have consulted us under those circumstances."

A contrary view is held by Basil Robinson. "In view of the NORAD partnership," he says, "the president, or Rusk on his instructions, would have been wise to call the prime minister before the TV speech. . . . If he had been taken into the Americans' confidence, the prime minister might well have agreed to put the forces on alert much sooner than he did. It would have been psychologically important, a hand reaching out. But the Americans were afraid of what Diefenbaker would have done and said. They thought he couldn't be counted on." In the end, even the promise that Kennedy did give Diefenbaker – to stay in close contact as the crisis unfolded – was not kept.

After his address that Monday night, Kennedy told his secretary, Evelyn Lincoln, "Well, that's it, unless the son of a bitch [Khrushchev] fouls up." He went upstairs to his living quarters, read stories to Caroline, and then had dinner alone with Jackie.

In Ottawa, Liberal leader Mike Pearson phoned the prime minister immediately after Kennedy's speech and suggested Diefenbaker make a comment in the House of Commons, which was meeting that night. Diefenbaker agreed, although at the meeting with Merchant a couple of hours earlier, he had indicated he would not say anything until Tuesday. Howard Green and his External Affairs colleagues had prepared a memorandum for the prime minister earlier in the day, suggesting an approach Diefenbaker might take in any telephone conversation with Kennedy before the president made his address; Kennedy never phoned, and Diefenbaker did not read the memo until after he went home for dinner. Now Diefenbaker reached for the memo as a guide for what to say in the House. It was a damaging mistake.

Shortly after eight o'clock, the prime minister interrupted a House debate on the economy to make his comment on Kennedy's speech. He spoke of the gravity of the crisis and said, "What people all over this world want tonight, and will want, is a full and complete understanding of what is taking place in Cuba. . . . The only sure way that the world can secure the facts would be through an independent inspection." The prime minister proposed "an on-site inspection of Cuba [by] the eight nations comprising the unaligned members of the eighteen-nation disarmament committee." He added, "It will provide an objective answer to what is going on in Cuba."

The proposal for the on-site inspection by a UN team of neutrals had come from Under-Secretary of State Norman Robertson, but his intention had been for Diefenbaker to propose this idea privately by telephone to Kennedy before

Kennedy's address. When Diefenbaker said it publicly, Washington was astounded. Merchant heard of it as he landed back in the American capital and was angered and perplexed. He had told the president that Canada was "on side"; now the prime minister was casting doubt on the veracity of the president's evidence. Diefenbaker went farther with reporters after his statement in the House, telling them that if his proposal were implemented, "the truth will be revealed," and he told colleagues he wanted to "prevent any rash and hasty decision by the U.S."

Ellen Fairclough says the prime minister made the proposal "largely because Diefenbaker did not trust Kennedy. Kennedy had a sort of 'to hell with them' attitude with respect to Canada." R.A. Bell, another cabinet colleague, shared Diefenbaker's feeling that Kennedy was unreliable, calling the president "an irresponsible young man if there ever was one."

So far as Washington was concerned, the truth was in the photographic evidence that revealed the Soviet offensive missiles in Cuba. Merchant told colleagues the Diefenbaker comments "took the bloom off" Canadian support for the U.S. and "put a most unfortunate face" on Kennedy's statement. Willis Armstrong, the senior State Department official handling Canadian affairs at the time, puts it more bluntly, blaming Green and Robertson for much of Diefenbaker's attitude. "The two of them were enough to destroy any relations between the two countries, although personally, I liked Green," he says.

The Diefenbaker statement was particularly disappointing for Kennedy, who had hoped that Canada would be especially supportive as a neighbour and ally. Macmillan, Adenauer, and de Gaulle had given immediate and full support to Kennedy. De Gaulle said he didn't need to see the photographic evidence, adding that the president's word was good enough for him.

The only Western nation that expressed doubt and questioned Kennedy's evidence was Canada. Washington officials were privately incensed, but Rusk now says, "We felt Canada would eventually come on board." Rusk, however, was concerned that if Khrushchev had seen significant dissension, "he could have misjudged the entire situation."

Shortly after Kennedy's address, American officials issued a public statement on the support he was getting, ignoring

Diefenbaker's hesitancy and including specific reference to the Canadian support that Merchant thought Diefenbaker had given. That drew the prime minister's rage. "Kennedy took it upon himself to jump the gun and say this," Sévigny says. "Diefenbaker got mad and said, 'That young man has got to learn that he is not running the Canadian government. . . . What business has he got? There is no decision which has been made as yet. I am the one who is going to decide and I am the one who has to make the declaration. He is not the one.'"

All Diefenbaker's old fears of American imperiousness towards Canada and all his hatred for Kennedy flowed forth in a flood of acrimony. He was especially enraged when he learned that NORAD headquarters in Colorado Springs had notified Canadian defence officials that it assumed all Canada's NORAD forces would officially and immediately be placed on the heightened Defcon 3 alert. Since Kennedy had not consulted him beforehand, however, Diefenbaker was damned if he was going to agree automatically to a Defcon 3 alert, nuclear war crisis or not. For him, there was going to be no "Ready, aye, ready!" to Washington's gunboat diplomacy.

Immediately after Kennedy's speech, Air Marshal Miller, the chairman of the chiefs of staff, had gone to Defence Minister Douglas Harkness's office to ask him to get authorization of the heightened alert, which NORAD had assumed was only a formality. In fact, all NORAD forces, Canadian included, had been on the Defcon 3 alert from the moment the Americans went to that alert status. Nothing was said publicly at the time, but two and a half months later, NORAD issued a statement saying that the Canadian NORAD forces – five squadrons of F-101 jets and all other Canadian NORAD personnel – had gone on the Defcon 3 alert by the time Miller went to see Harkness.

Harkness was not aware of this, but he fully agreed with Miller's request, which would have given political approval to what NORAD had already done. "Well, you go ahead and do it," he told Miller. The chairman of the chiefs of staff frowned, however, and said, "You may not have the authority to declare Defcon 3." He said the War Book, which sets out procedures and authorizations in such situations, was at that very moment under review. "The old one had been cancelled and the new one hadn't been approved by the cabinet, so we didn't really have any policy to go by," Harkness says. Harkness then went to the prime minister to seek the authority. They met in the prime minister's hideaway office behind the Speaker at the House of Commons.

"No, we'd better hold off," said Diefenbaker.

"Why, Prime Minister?" asked Harkness.

"Oh no. No. We'd better wait," Diefenbaker insisted.

Later, Diefenbaker would write of this night, "We were not a satellite state at the beck and call of an imperial master." He certainly had the law on his side, since the NORAD Agreement specifically refers to consultation about changing alert status and notes that each government reserves the right to freedom of action. "The establishment of integrated air defence arrangements . . . increases the importance of the fullest possible consultation between the two governments on all matters affecting the joint defense of North America," the NORAD Agreement states.

A few minutes after Harkness began arguing for the increased alert, Howard Green came into Diefenbaker's office. To Harkness's surprise, he says, Green agreed with his request for the increased alert, but Diefenbaker, however, still said no. Propelled by his fury at Kennedy's failure to consult him, Diefenbaker raised a series of objections: Would the public be alarmed? Would it heighten the danger of war? How much support should Canada give the U.S.?

But there would be "hopeless confusion," Harkness argued, if Canadian airmen working side by side with U.S. airmen were not on the same alert status as their American colleagues. Diefenbaker insisted there had to be a cabinet discussion of the matter, which would be held the next day. The defence minister suggested the cabinet meet immediately on the matter, but again Diefenbaker said no. Disgusted, Harkness went back to his own office to confer with Canadian military leaders.

The military impracticability of the prime minister's refusal to authorize an increased defence alert was clear to the Canadian chiefs of staff and Harkness. In truth, when John Diefenbaker signed the NORAD Agreement, Canada lost most of its ability to act independently of the United States in a military crisis, no matter what the agreement said about advance consultation. The integration of the RCAF and USAF in

North American defence, in practical terms, forced Canada to go along with "Big Brother." The same realities governed the Canadian and U.S. navies, primarily in the Atlantic. Thus, when he came back to his office to meet his military advisers with the prime minister's refusal ringing in his ears, Harkness faced a dilemma: how to reconcile Diefenbaker's "no" with the practical necessity for a "yes."

"I decided I would put the troops on alert without making any announcement," Harkness says. "I ordered the navy to oil up and put out to sea, and the army and air force to go on alert. I told them we'll go ahead and do this anyway, but do it quietly." Now, both Canadian NORAD and Canadian regular forces were ready for war.

"Tomorrow," he told the military leaders, he would get formal authorization. The military leaders quickly left Harkness's office to put his orders into effect. "They were anxious to get going," he says. Reflecting on his actions that night, Harkness says, "I took all the steps that you would have taken or could take to meet the possible outbreak of war. But I didn't do it in an official way." The RCAF and the navy, in fact, went far beyond the defence minister's orders; as Diefenbaker went to bed much later than his usual bedtime that night, Canadian air and naval forces were already co-operating fully with their American counterparts.

Early Tuesday morning, Khrushchev sent a harsh private letter to Kennedy denouncing the planned blockade as "piracy." Kennedy answered within hours, restating his decision and reasons, adding, "I am concerned that we both show prudence and do nothing to allow events to make the situation more difficult to control than it is."

Three blocks away from the White House, the OAS was debating the American request for support; it unanimously adopted a resolution fully supporting the American action. At four o'clock, the United Nations Security Council began its debate, with the Soviets claiming the CIA had manufactured phoney evidence of the missile sites.

At six o'clock Kennedy agreed to put the blockade into effect at 10:00 A.M. Wednesday, giving orders to the navy to "disable, don't sink" any ship trying to break through the blockade. Meanwhile, the Soviet cargo ships were still heading for Cuba, undeterred by the U.S. threat, and Soviet submarines were beginning to move into the Caribbean. Kennedy was keeping minute-by-minute, hands-on control of the diplomatic and military manoeuvring, well aware, after the Bay of Pigs, that, as Ted Sorensen says, "the momentum of events and enthusiasts could take issues of peace and war out of his own hands."

Diefenbaker, in contrast, was fighting a losing battle for control of events in Ottawa that Tuesday. He began the day by dressing down his associate defence minister over Sévigny's conversation with Kennedy on Monday. At quarter past seven Sévigny came to 24 Sussex Drive to be greeted by a glowering Diefenbaker, who demanded, "What's this about you getting a call from Kennedy? You must never ever say anything about that! You love the Americans. Your wife loves the Americans."

Sévigny responded, "I won't take this from you." They argued for half an hour; with Olive's intervention, they calmed down, and Diefenbaker ended the argument by saying, "Well, you're a great fellow."

"He said that after giving me shit like you wouldn't believe," says Sévigny, and together they went to the nine o'clock cabinet meeting.

The cabinet was to discuss Canadian support for the U.S. in general and especially Washington's request for Canadian NORAD forces to go on the Defcon 3 alert. Most members of the cabinet began the meeting agreeing with both general support and Defcon 3, and they assumed the discussion would be short and smooth. It was anything but. In a quiet but emotional speech, Howard Green changed his position from the mildly supportive attitude Harkness had heard the night before. Now he urged a "go slow" on any support for the United States. "If we go along with the Americans now, we'll be their vassals forever," one cabinet minister quoted him as saying. Green also argued that Canada could have a moderating influence on Cuba if it did not automatically give total endorsement to the U.S. "We shouldn't get excited by this," Green said. "If the Americans want to go to war, let them go to war."

Diefenbaker agreed with Green, saying Canada would not "snap to attention" for the U.S. "He became totally irrational," says Sévigny. "He said Kennedy had succeeded in getting to some members of caucus and some ministers." After intense debate, according to Health and Welfare Minister J. Waldo Monteith, a majority of the cabinet swung over to backing Diefenbaker, so Harkness again lost his argument and the prime minister refused to authorize Defcon 3. "He and I finally came to fairly hot words, but he refused to agree to the alert, chiefly, I think, because of a pathological hatred of taking a hard decision," Harkness wrote in a memo ten months later.

An infuriated Harkness stomped back to his office and called in the chiefs of staff. The military men were outraged and clearly felt Diefenbaker had slid from indecision to irresponsibility. Failure to support the Americans in the crisis, they felt, was degrading, even traitorous. Harkness told them to proceed with the alert "but in as quiet and unobtrusive a way as possible." He said nothing to Diefenbaker about his instructions to the military.

In spite of the prime minister's inaction, the army went on full alert, on the basis of the Harkness orders; so did the RCAF. The NORAD forces were at Defcon 3, and Royal Canadian Navy ships were fuelled and armed. "There was no authorization," recalls Rear Admiral Jeffry V. Brock, vice-chief of naval staff at the time, but he ordered back Canadian ships that were visiting the U.K. and recalled men on shore leave. "I issued the orders, controlled the situation, and was quite happily prepared to place my head upon the chopping block in the event of serious political repercussions."

"We went to our war stations," Admiral Kenneth Dyer, the Atlantic maritime commander, later said. Dyer was in hourly contact from the start of the crisis with NATO Supreme Allied Command Atlantic Headquarters in Norfolk, Virginia. Canadian ships worked in full co-operation with the U.S. navy in setting up a surface, submarine, and air-sea barrier in the North Atlantic to track Soviet submarines and monitor Soviet fishing boats, which had sophisticated communications equipment aboard. At the time, the Soviets had 550 trawlers and supply ships off the eastern seaboard, which the Canadian navy said were "a potential menace in time of crisis." Navy Argus planes from Greenwood, Nova Scotia, and Summerside, Prince Edward Island, were loaded with charged and ready depth bombs and homing torpedoes and were out scouring the Atlantic in partnership with U.S. planes. Naval historian Commander

Tony German has written about this episode, "The Navy, with Maritime Air Command, honoured Canada's duty to stand by her North American ally without one scrap of paper, minute, or message, or one public announcement to give it direction or approval."

At the height of the crisis, the RCAF moved planes onto bases in the American South, ready for action. "We moved them without authority," says Wing Commander Bill Lee. "Maybe it was wrong, but we found good reason for some training exercises in Florida. If we'd asked for political permission we would have been turned down."

Given Diefenbaker's sharp instincts and wide-ranging contacts, however, he may well have suspected the Canadian military had gone on a heightened alert and just let it happen informally. "He had a big informal intelligence network," says his special assistant, Dick Thrasher. "He was always getting phone calls and information from people. He knew most everything that was going on."

Diefenbaker may have been aware of the situation, but he was not in control of it. Harkness had gone farther than Diefenbaker wanted or knew; the chiefs of staff had gone farther than Harkness himself realized; the deputies to the chiefs of staff had gone even farther; and the RCAF and RCN operational officers in charge of various commands had gone farther than anybody in Ottawa knew. But everybody in the military chain of command winked and nudged and went on a war footing, and said to hell with Diefenbaker's indecisiveness.

In his later comments on the crisis, Diefenbaker agreed that the Soviets had acted improperly in putting the offensive missiles into Cuba, but he gave a much more flattering portrait of Khrushchev than of Kennedy. "I saw Nikita Khrushchev as essentially a cautious man," the prime minister said. Khrushchev exercised "relative moderation" and "went out of his way to cultivate a moderate and reasonable image."

With this attitude, Diefenbaker was not in a happy frame of mind when Kennedy finally telephoned him Tuesday afternoon. It wasn't to consult, however, but to ask for Canadian support at the United Nations and for more co-operation on North American defence, including formal authorization to put the Canadian NORAD forces on the Defcon 3 alert. It was a bad-tempered conversation, probably the nastiest Diefenbaker ever had with Kennedy. The prime minister repeatedly raised his voice and even shouted a couple of times. "Diefenbaker was very agitated, very upset," says Bunny Pound, who took notes of his end of the conversation. Kennedy spoke at some length at the beginning, but Diefenbaker's responses were brief and sharp. "No, we can't possibly do that!" he told Kennedy at one point; he said at another, "Well, I will have to clear that with cabinet." He bitterly denounced the lack of advance consultation once again, asking Kennedy, "When were we consulted?" He quoted Kennedy as responding curtly, "You weren't."

At least twice in the conversation Kennedy requested that Diefenbaker authorize the Defcon 3 alert, but the prime minister answered with a question: "I asked him why he had not raised United States forces to a level of maximum alert," Diefenbaker said. "He said that this would cause international repercussions but that if Canada did so it would not have the same effect. . . . He thought that what he wanted Canada to do, we would do." Diefenbaker told Kennedy he did not think Khrushchev would go to war over Cuba, and besides, the prime minister felt, the Soviet missiles in Cuba did not alter the U.S. – U.S.S.R. balance of power "one iota."

Kennedy's request for support at the UN ran into a similar roadblock. "President Kennedy objected to my suggestion for a United Nations on-site inspection," the prime minister recalled. "It soon became obvious that while I wanted a UN solution to the Cuban missile problem he simply wanted UN approval for the course of action he was initiating."

After the conversation, Kennedy complained to aides about Diefenbaker's "negative rasping." Diefenbaker, when he hung up the phone, muttered to Bunny Pound, "He could have got in touch with me before."

"He felt terribly hurt and that hurt turned to anger," she says. "Dief was furious with Kennedy." He was also frightened at the possibility of war. "Kennedy wants his own way," he told Pound. "He wants the Russians out of there, and then they'll bomb us." She said she doubted that, but he replied, "Oh, you just don't know the trouble we're in." He worried about whether the cabinet would be able to get to the bomb shelter in nearby Arnprior, Ontario, before it was too late.

At a NATO meeting in Paris that day, Ambassador George Ignatieff recalled, he sat in silent distress as one Western ally after another declared whole-hearted support for Kennedy. "I have seldom felt more uncomfortable or isolated," he said.

When the House of Commons met that same Tuesday afternoon, the prime minister showed some sensitivity to growing public unease about the absence of strong Canadian support for Kennedy. He complained again to the House about the lack of advance consultation by Kennedy, but added, "I was not, of course, casting any doubts on the facts of the situation as outlined by the president of the United States." Furthermore, Diefenbaker said his proposal the previous night for a neutral UN on-site inspection was not designed "to compete with any proposal of the United States that might be placed before the United Nations, but rather to supplement it."

While the prime minister was softening his public criticism of Kennedy's actions, the Canadian embassy in Washington was also assuring the State Department that Diefenbaker did not in any way question the Americans' evidence. And on the UN proposal, Basil Robinson says, "We were authorized to say that the Prime Minister's proposal had been inspired by the thought that a neutral inspection under UN auspices would be a good way of demonstrating that the President had been justified in the measures he had decided to take." At the end of the day, Ottawa also told Washington that Soviet planes would be refused permission to fly over Canada, except under certain circumstances, and that Eastern European and Cuban planes would also be subject to special restrictions.

In Washington that night, Kennedy had a quiet dinner at the White House with his old friend the British ambassador, David Ormsby-Gore. They knew the eighteen Soviet dry-cargo ships and six Soviet submarines now with them were nearing the blockade line that the U.S. navy had drawn around Cuba. It was designed to be beyond the range of most MIG fighters based in Cuba. Ormsby-Gore suggested that Kennedy give Khrushchev more time to decide what to do by shortening the blockade line from 800 miles off Cuba to 500 miles. Kennedy agreed and telephoned Defense Secretary McNamara, telling him to shorten the line. It was done, although the navy objected.

Kennedy was worried about what would happen when U.S. sailors boarded the Soviet ships. He wondered if there would be fighting and where that escalation would lead. "What would you do then," he said, "if we go through all this effort and then find out there's baby food on it?" He decided to intercept only ships that were clearly carrying military equipment.

The British ambassador had another bit of advice for Kennedy. Why not make public some of the photographic evidence of the missile sites? Again, the president agreed; he sent for the photos, and he and Ormsby-Gore went through them, picking out the ones most vividly showing the missile sites. They were released the next day.

On Wednesday morning the Soviet ships were nearing the 500-mile blockade line. The moment of confrontation had arrived, the brink of nuclear holocaust. As President Kennedy met his advisers that morning, his brother Robert later recalled, "His hand went up to his face and covered his mouth. He opened and closed his fist. His face seemed drawn, his eyes pained, almost gray. We stared at each other across the table. . . . I felt we were on the edge of a precipice with no way off."

At 10:25 A.M., a messenger brought in a note saying, "Some of the Russian ships have stopped dead in the water." Fourteen of the Soviet vessels had stopped just short of the blockade line. A feeling of relief swept around the table. Kennedy quickly said the Soviet ships should not be interfered with and should be given every opportunity to turn around.

"We're eyeball to eyeball and I think the other fellow just blinked," said Dean Rusk. American diplomat Averell Harriman, who had dealt with Moscow since the days of Franklin Roosevelt, shared that view. He called White House aide Arthur Schlesinger and said everything Moscow was now saying indicated Khrushchev was desperately signalling a desire to make a deal. "We must give him an out," said Harriman, whose advice Kennedy was to follow.

While Soviet ships circled near the blockade line off Cuba, and Washington, Moscow, and the United Nations searched for a resolution of the nuclear confrontation, Diefenbaker called another cabinet meeting to discuss again the degree of support Canada should give the Americans. It was an acrimonious debate, with Harkness and three-quarters of the cabinet now demanding the increased NORAD alert. Again, however, Diefenbaker and Green vociferously opposed the move. "Kennedy is trying to push us into this thing and we shouldn't be pushed," the prime minister said. Harkness angrily charged that Canada was failing in its responsibilities by not going to the higher alert.

Diefenbaker then told the cabinet he'd been in touch with British Prime Minister Macmillan. Macmillan was worried about escalation of the crisis and had sent word to Diefenbaker through High Commissioner Lord Amory. Bunny Pound remembers the prime minister was anxious about the message and kept coming out of his office that Wednesday morning to ask whether Amory had arrived. Macmillan's message counselled the Canadian leader against any provocative action. Diefenbaker told his cabinet colleagues that going to Defcon 3 could be interpreted as provocative. Finance Minister George Nowlan remembered him quoting Macmillan as saying, "Whatever you do, don't do anything to encourage that hothead in Washington! Cool it! The more we make Kennedy provocative, the more difficult we make it for Khrushchev."

Diefenbaker had not talked directly to the British prime minister, and it seems improbable that Macmillan would use such language in a written message. In fact, Macmillan was strongly supportive of Kennedy throughout the crisis and later spoke of Kennedy's "calm wisdom" and "remarkable skill and energy" during the crisis. In contrast, he later scoffed at Diefenbaker's hesitancy, saying the Canadian prime minister was "the only faint heart." It is more likely that Macmillan's message to Diefenbaker spoke in general terms of the dangers of the crisis, and Diefenbaker massaged that generality to back up his personal disinclination to help Kennedy.

The cabinet meeting broke up with, again, no decision about putting Canada's NORAD forces on the heightened alert. "We were deliberately playing it cool," Green would later say. Once again, Harkness went back to his office, fuming in defeat. There he was told that the Soviets had intensified their military preparations and that the U.S. Strategic Air Command and some U.S. naval forces had now gone to the Defcon 2 alert level, which meant "immediate enemy attack expected." "The

Americans were indicating that very likely war would develop," he says.

Alarmed, Harkness raced back to the prime minister's office, confronted him with this new information, and demanded that he formally authorize the placement of Canadian NORAD forces on the same alert level as the American NORAD group, which was still at Defcon 3. Diefenbaker shook his head ruefully and said, "Oh well, all right, go ahead . . . go ahead."

"I never did tell him that I'd already done so," Harkness says with a bitter smile. But Diefenbaker told Harkness to keep the authorization secret until he himself announced it in the House of Commons the next day, Thursday.

Canadian support for the United States still seemed wobbly as the House of Commons met on Wednesday. Given the importance the government attached to the United Nations in the crisis: Howard Green was asked why he was not at the UN in New York. "My one interest in this present crisis," he said, "is to do the very best I can for Canada and for peace in the world, and I really don't need any prompting . . . as to what is my duty." In fact, Green believed he had to stay in Ottawa to reinforce the prime minister's reluctance to fully support Kennedy. That night, Green went on a CBC television interview program and inadvertently underlined the government's hesitancy in backing the United States.

"We're trying," he told interviewers Norman DePoe and Charles Lynch, "to keep the Canadian people and the people around Ottawa from getting all excited about this business and from panicking." In answer to insistent questions about the strength of Canadian support for the United States, Green dodged and ducked, and finally said, "We are friends of the United States and we're standing beside them."

In answer to questions about North American defence, he said NORAD was not involved in the crisis, "not at the moment." Pushed by Lynch on what specific action Canada was taking in the crisis, Green responded, "Well, we're not called on to do anything about those [Cuban] bases at the moment." The impression left by the interview was one of a reluctant government giving hesitant and tepid support to the Americans. There was considerable public and media criticism of Green's comments, but the prime minister thought Green had done well.

He called the television station where the interview had been held to congratulate Green immediately after the live program was aired. Two decades later, Green still insisted in an oral history interview that the Americans had never asked Canada to help out in the crisis: "Not really, no, no. . . . We weren't asked to supply naval vessels or anything of that kind."

But Diefenbaker began to have second thoughts as the criticism came in and as Mike Pearson publicly and solidly endorsed Kennedy's actions. The next day – Thursday – he announced that Canadian NORAD forces had gone to the Defcon 3 alert and noted a number of actions taken by Canada to support the United States. After discussion in cabinet Thursday morning he told the House of Commons, "We intend to support the United States and our allies in this situation. . . . The Government is seeking to find means by which this dangerous, threatening situation can be settled without recourse to arms. On the other hand, we recognize the fact that the free world as a whole cannot afford to permit its essential security to be endangered by offensive weapons mounted on bases adjacent to North America."

With this statement and with the formal authorization of Defcon 3, Canada was finally "on side" with the Americans. The delay, however, cost Diefenbaker dearly. In Washington it destroyed any remaining fragment of a Kennedy–Diefenbaker relationship and outraged officials in the Pentagon and State Department, who began yearning in earnest for Diefenbaker's political demise; and it profoundly undermined the prime minister's political support in Canada as a significantly increasing number of Canadians felt Diefenbaker had inexcusably dithered or worse in the Cuban Missile Crisis. While Diefenbaker seemed indecisive and petulant, Kennedy seemed heroic. Recollecting a conversation with the prime minister at this time, R.A. Bell said, "I do remember Diefenbaker . . . making some snide remarks as to what he could do to this young man if he really decided to."

"This young man," meanwhile, was responding to another letter from Khrushchev, mindful of Harriman's advice and facing the sharpening demands of his own warhawks for an invasion or air strike. The hawks included not only the military advisers but such civilians as Harry Truman's secretary of state,

Dean Acheson. George Ball recalls one tense meeting where
Kennedy heard pleas for an air strike or invasion of Cuba and
said, "Well, I'll take this discussion under consideration." Acheson replied with his usual pungent irreverence by saying, "It's
simple, Mr. President. Just make up your goddam mind!"

Kennedy listened to Acheson, the generals, and the admirals,
but he listened more to his brother, McNamara, and the British
ambassador. Ormsby-Gore played an extraordinary role for a
foreign official during the crisis, staying with Kennedy in the
White House Situation Room for hours, tracking Soviet ships
and insisting that Khrushchev be given time.

At six o'clock Friday evening a long, emotional letter arrived
from Khrushchev, protesting that he had no offensive inten-
tions in placing the missiles in Cuba, melodramatically pleading
for understanding, and proposing a deal: the missiles would be
withdrawn if Kennedy promised not to invade Cuba and ended
the blockade. The crisis seemed to be easing.

But everything changed again on Saturday morning. A
second letter came in from Khrushchev, more formally written
and demanding much tougher terms from the Americans –
tougher than they were prepared to give. Worse still, a U.S. U-2
spy plane was shot down by Soviet anti-aircraft gunners in
Cuba, killing the pilot. That outraged the Pentagon hard-liners,
who pushed more strongly for an attack on Cuba. Intensifying
the tension, another American U-2, on a mission out of Alaska,
strayed over Soviet territory and ran into Soviet fighters. It was
allowed to return to its Alaska base with no damage, other than
momentary heart failure at the White House.

Events were now rushing towards the nuclear precipice; the
Americans intensified planning for an air strike and invasion if
the blockade failed. The joint chiefs of staff reiterated their
demand for invasion by Sunday or Monday. The president said
there would be no invasion on Sunday; at this point Kennedy
estimated the chances of nuclear war as being "somewhere
between one out of three and even."

Late Saturday afternoon, Robert Kennedy came up with a
startlingly simple way to answer Khrushchev's latest bombastic
demand: don't answer it. Answer only the first, more concilia-
tory letter. The president leapt at the suggestion and sent off a
reply that evening, accepting the offer in the Soviet leader's first

letter. Robert Kennedy took a copy of the letter to Soviet Ambassador Anatoly Dobrynin and told him that unless the U.S. received Khrushchev's assurances of a deal quickly, the United States would take military action against Cuba no later than Tuesday.

In the next few hours the world came as close as it ever has to a nuclear holocaust. As officials went to bed in London, Moscow, Washington, and Ottawa, they wondered if World War III would arrive in the morning.

In Ottawa, the prime minister believed it was possible that, as he said later, "we would all be obliterated in a few days." The Canadian cabinet had discussed evacuating the government from the city, and George Nowlan worried if there would be enough liquor in the cabinet bomb shelter. He later recalled that R.B. Bryce, clerk of the Privy Council, who was in charge of arrangements for the bomb shelter, heard of his concern, went to the bank, and withdrew enough money from his personal account to buy an adequate supply of scotch, rye, and gin for the cabinet.

The teetotalling Howard Green didn't worry about that, but as the world stood still Saturday night, he thought it might be the last night of civilization. "I believed . . . that before morning Ottawa might be demolished as well as Montreal, Toronto and . . . Vancouver," he later told the House of Commons. He worked at his office that evening until five o'clock and then, he said, "My wife and I went up to Pink's Lake in the Gatineau Hills outside Ottawa and walked around [it]. . . . I thought there would be war before morning." Then they came back to their apartment and went to bed. "In the middle of the night," he said, "a transformer blew up outside the Roxborough Apartments. . . . [It] made an awful noise and I woke up and I thought, 'Oh, that's it. There's the first Russian bomb.'"

Douglas Harkness spent much of the night at National Defence headquarters, reading intelligence reports flowing in from Washington.

Just after nine o'clock Sunday morning in Ottawa and Washington, Moscow began broadcasting Khrushchev's reply to Kennedy's letter. The Soviet leader accepted the terms, and the crisis was over.

With President Kennedy hailed in Canada and the world over

as the hero of the hour, Diefenbaker now sought to portray himself as a staunch supporter of the president in the missile crisis. "At first, he wanted to avoid giving any idea that we were doing just what the Americans told us to," Harkness says. "Then he realized practically the entire population was in favour and that he'd better get on the bandwagon or be left behind." Within hours of the resolution of the crisis on Sunday, the prime minister told reporters that the happy ending "resulted from the high degree of unity, understanding, and co-operation among the Western allies. In this, the Canadian government has played its full part."

A few days later, he told a Toronto banquet, "There never was any question as to where Canada stood. . . . We supported the stand of the United States clearly and unequivocally." He made a general complaint about the lack of consultation: "It should be made clear that consultation is a prerequisite to joint and contemporaneous action." The first draft of the speech had praised "the firm action of President Kennedy," but in his blue ink scrawl, Diefenbaker had scratched out Kennedy's name and inserted "the United States."

The public, however, wasn't buying his claim of support for the Americans. The media weren't either; newspapers across the nation praised Kennedy and criticized Diefenbaker's limp-wristed support. *Maclean's* magazine condemned Diefenbaker for what it called his "coquettish indecision" during the crisis; the Regina *Leader Post* saluted Kennedy, saying, "The President won himself new status." A public opinion poll by the Canadian Peace Research Institute showed 79.3 per cent of Canadians backed Kennedy's action.

Two cabinet ministers, George Hees and Pierre Sévigny, said privately they were considering resigning. Sévigny complained of Diefenbaker's "vacillating attitude."

"The political consequences were disastrous," Sévigny says. "It augmented the prevailing opinion that John Diefenbaker was incapable of making up his mind and this permitted our enemies to claim in a loud voice that the care of the nation's affairs could no longer be entrusted to such a hesitant leader. Many Conservatives joined in this criticism. . . . We were now in deep trouble. . . . Few believed that Canada had played the part it should have during the desperate hours that preceded the enemy's withdrawal."

Dalton Camp feels Diefenbaker had lost his political antennae in his conflict with Kennedy. He says of the prime minister's behaviour in the Cuban Missile Crisis, "It was the largest wound inflicted on him. It was a disaster because, in the country's view, Diefenbaker was wobbling."

Other Conservatives, including party national vice-president George Hogan, were embarrassed by the prime minister's hesitation in the crisis. In a speech ten days after the crisis had ended, Hogan attacked "some Conservatives" for "emotional jingoism. . . . Any hint of anti-Americanism is not only silly but dangerous. . . . When the security of the North American continent is menaced by the threat of nuclear attack, that is the time to stand by the Americans, clearly, swiftly, unequivocally. There is no place for an attitude of quasi-neutralism when it comes to the defence of North America."

Diefenbaker was outraged at Hogan's comments. R.A. Bell described the prime minister at a cabinet meeting discussing the matter: "He became so incensed he lost his reason completely. . . . It was an absolutely ghastly scene." Diefenbaker then went into the House of Commons to answer questions about Hogan's comments; said Bell, "This man who was a raging lunatic ten minutes before was in total possession of himself."

Diefenbaker displayed a remarkable creative hindsight a few years later when he told reporters who queried him about a delay in Canada's NORAD alert authorization, "There was no delay on our part. There was, however, an extension of a day or so in order to prepare our defences to the end that our responsibilities in NORAD would be carried out." The prime minister offered another rationale for the delay in his memoirs: "Once we determined that there was no essential role for Canada in finding a United Nations solution to the Cuban crisis, we then authorized that our air defence squadrons be placed on the same alert level as their United States counterparts."

But as Bunny Pound says, "Going back, you just wonder how much his deep dislike of Kennedy was behind this." Heward Grafftey, then a Conservative MP, recalls Diefenbaker telling him, "I have no lessons to learn from that young whippersnapper."

"If it had been Eisenhower he was dealing with and not Kennedy, it would have been very different," says Harkness. "He just had an obsession about Kennedy."

The State Department tried to paint over the problems, swallowing hard and saying Canada's co-operation in the crisis had been "very satisfactory." The State Department, Pentagon, and White House may have felt it prudent to say that publicly, but privately they felt otherwise. In addition to the foot-dragging on public support for Kennedy and on the heightened NORAD alert, Pentagon officials told reporters that Canada had failed in other areas. They claimed the U.S. had made requests for 640 flights over Canada of U.S. bombers carrying nuclear weapons in the air alert, but Canada gave permission for only eight flights. Harkness, however, says no formal request for the other flights came to him. The Pentagon officials also said Canada refused to allow nuclear-armed USAF interceptors to move into Canada and refused to allow the U.S. to move nuclear warheads from Bangor, Maine, to U.S. bases at Harmon Field, Newfoundland, and Goose Bay, Labrador. While the Pentagon was incensed at Diefenbaker, it remained grateful to the Canadian military, especially the RCAF and the RCN, which had defied the prime minister's "go slow" directives.

The Canadian ambassador in Washington, Charles Ritchie, found himself trapped in the middle between Diefenbaker's mood and the American anger at the prime minister. "They are exasperated by our attitude," he wrote in his diary. "But so far they are holding their hand. It remains to be seen how long they will resist the temptation to bring pressure upon us of a kind that might bring about a change of government." The ambassador was brilliantly prescient: time was running out for John Diefenbaker, and American patience was wearing thin. American historian Henry Pachter says Diefenbaker's behaviour in the Cuban episode was "a slight for which Kennedy was to take revenge not long afterward."

The Defcon incident is important not only as a milestone in the Kennedy–Diefenbaker relationship, but as an example of the difficulty, if not impossibility, of Canada's political leadership controlling the Canadian military forces in an emergency if those forces are working side by side with their American counterparts in a joint defence system. In an emergency threatening global nuclear confrontation, chances are that the American inclination to consult in advance of decisions will be minimal, as it was in the Cuban Missile Crisis. The only effective approach would be for Washington and Ottawa to have a detailed agreement long beforehand.

For Harkness, the Cuban Missile Crisis underlined the need for Canada to accept nuclear arms for its Bomarcs, its air defence interceptors, and its NATO forces in Europe. For one thing, the crisis clearly destroyed the credibility of the prime minister's promise that when an emergency arose, Canadian forces would quickly obtain the American nuclear weapons necessary to the national defence. That promise had been the excuse he leaned on to continue his opposition to having nuclear warheads in place permanently. There had never been a greater emergency than the Saturday night of the Cuban crisis. And yet, not only did the military not have the nuclear warheads for the Bomarcs or the Voodoo interceptors, but the government refused to allow nuclear-armed U.S. planes to disperse into Canada and it refused, in almost all cases, to allow atom-bomb-loaded SAC bombers to fly over Canada. Even the Defcon 3 alert was largely useless, except for its symbolism and the easier working arrangements it allowed, since the Canadian Bomarcs were armed with sand and the interceptors with only conventional weapons.

To Harkness, the stark nakedness of Canada's defence position, as exposed by the crisis, made an agreement with the United States a stunningly real necessity. And now, Harkness had clearly demonstrable public support behind him; a survey by the Canadian Peace Research Institute showed about sixty per cent of Canadians supported a nuclear role for Canada. Polls by Gallup and Sam Lubell showed similar support.

Diefenbaker, however, still paid more attention to his mail than to the polls, and his mail said no to nuclear weapons. Shortly after the Cuban crisis, he met a delegation from the Royal Canadian Air Force Association. Diefenbaker pulled out some letters and said to the air force veterans, "The letters are running two or three to one against nuclear weapons. The people of Canada don't want them."

But Diefenbaker recognized the shift in the political climate. He later commented, "It is true the Cuban crisis brought a new urgency to the defence debate in Cabinet, in Parliament and in the country as a whole." Privately, he began to talk about getting nuclear weapons. On October 26, the Toronto *Telegram*, which had close links to Diefenbaker, bannered on its front page: "PM HINTS STRONGLY IT'S A-ARMS AT LAST."

"I became absolutely insistent that we had to start negotiations right away," Harkness says. The Cuban Missile Crisis, he says, "convinced nearly everybody in cabinet that we should go ahead and complete this agreement and secure this nuclear ammunition as soon as possible." He seemed to have got his way on October 30, when the cabinet unanimously agreed to re-open negotiations with Washington on a deal for nuclear weapons in Canada and for our NATO forces. But Diefenbaker and Howard Green had a couple of delaying tactics up their sleeves. They wanted a "package" of agreements on acceptance of nuclear weaponry for the Bomarcs and interceptors in North American defence and for our NATO forces. They also wanted in that package the agreements for storing defensive nuclear weapons on U.S. bases in Newfoundland and Labrador. "He . . . argued that the whole thing should be announced at one time and would not agree to immediate action for the European end of the business," Harkness said in his diary of the events. Green later said, "I wasn't worried much about NATO," although he criticized Canadian acceptance of an air strike role in Europe. "We should never have got into that position in the first place. It was crazy to do that," he told an oral history interviewer.

While Harkness was hopeful about the cabinet agreement for negotiations, Green and Diefenbaker knew that the talks would forestall any decision for a little longer. For Green, no decision meant no nuclear weapons; for Diefenbaker, no decision meant he did not have to choose one way or the other. "He kept assuring me we would get these nuclear weapons, it was just a matter of timing," Harkness says. "But I was getting suspicious. I'd put it on the cabinet agenda time after time to settle it, and he'd always leave it to the end and then say we'll have to deal with it the next time. Then it would be the same thing at the next one. It was very frustrating. He was a master of evasion and delay."

If Diefenbaker was frustrating for Harkness, Harkness was too pushy for Diefenbaker. "Dief was always a little on edge with Harkness," says Bunny Pound. "He was leery of him. After a while, I felt Harkness was saying to himself, 'What's the use of carrying on with this?'"

Diefenbaker's indecisiveness drove his colleagues and the Americans up the wall. "We could have coped, made other arrangements, if we'd had a definitive no on nuclear weapons," says senior State Department official Willis Armstrong, who calls Diefenbaker "a gutless wonder." "What drove us nuts was his wishy-washy indecision. Decide one way or the other, for God's sake, but decide!"

Armstrong's frustration was echoed at the White House, where Kennedy fumed. McGeorge Bundy says, "If he had said no from the beginning. . . . If he had said yes or no, we could have dealt with it. But he said neither."

"He could find a million excuses to continue with his beloved procrastination," says Sévigny. "He would insist on a detailed study of the matter and ask repeatedly for more opinions until everyone was thoroughly confused." It was paralysis by analysis and Diefenbaker himself admitted, "I took my time before deciding. Time is often the politician's best friend." He even began to talk of calling an election on the issue, but he got little support for the idea.

Diefenbaker's bargaining position at the start of the talks was, not surprisingly, confusing. As he later described it, his approach at the time was: "Canada had to achieve the maximum degree of political control over the use of the warheads and the means of delivery." That, however, suggested the possibility of sole, not joint, decision-making on the use of nuclear weapons, meaning an expansion of the nuclear club – which he had repeatedly said he feared. It would also be against U.S. law to hand over sole control to another country.

Furthermore, the prime minister and his cabinet told Washington they wanted to see nuclear warheads in Europe held in storage under NATO command; in North America, they wanted warheads to be held at bases in the U.S. for the Canadian

Bomarcs and interceptors, and moved north in an emergency when Ottawa requested. This proposal, called the "stand-by" arrangement, was one of Diefenbaker and Green's ploys to keep the talks moving at glacial speed.

Harkness doubted the stand-by arrangement was militarily practical, but he hoped it could be used as a discussion point to move the Canadian governments towards acquisition. The cabinet decided the negotiations should proceed "forthwith," with Harkness, Green, and Veterans Affairs Minister Gordon Churchill leading the Canadian side. The negotiating team seemed stacked against Harkness, since Green and Churchill were total Diefenbaker loyalists. The prime minister was especially concerned that there be no public discussion whatsoever about the negotiations with the Americans. He said Washington must be warned that any leak at all would terminate the negotiations.

Canadian diplomats had a tough job persuading the State Department and Pentagon that it would be worthwhile having talks on the basis of the Canadian proposals for NORAD, but as a basis for at least having talks at all, the Americans agreed. They knew the importance of Canadian geography and shared the sentiments of Melvin Conant, an influential U.S. authority on North American defence, who wrote at the time in his book *The Long Polar Watch*, "Today, Canada finds itself inextricably bound up with U.S. defense policy and actions and the United States is heavily dependent upon Canada for a large measure of its continental security. Without the closest cooperation of these two states it would be impossible to provide for the defense of North America."

The negotiations were not helped by a statement to the UN in November by Canadian disarmament official General E.L.M. Burns, who implied that Canada was not likely to accept nuclear weapons in the near future. It was a theme Green harped on repeatedly, saying, "I couldn't continue my efforts on disarmament if we brought nuclear warheads onto Canadian soil. . . . We would simply be branded as hypocrites."

Green also made clear his disdain for NORAD itself. He told the House of Commons a few weeks later that he had never visited NORAD headquarters and never would, and that he had never had a conference with any of the senior officers of NORAD and never would. At the height of the Cuban Missile Crisis, the NORAD deputy commander, Air Marshal Roy Slemon, had repeatedly telephoned Green, but the external affairs minister would never take the call.

On November 20 several American military and diplomatic officials, led by a U.S. Air Force general, came to Ottawa. They were especially eager to get an agreement for the new Canadian NATO Starfighters, which were now on base in Europe. Because they were not armed with nuclear weapons, NATO had been forced to reassign defence responsibilities away from the Canadian squadrons to other British, American, and German squadrons.

The American negotiators also brought to Ottawa Pentagon studies on the feasibility of storing warheads in the U.S., then rushing them to Canadian Bomarc and interceptor bases when war was imminent. To nobody's surprise, the studies showed the idea would not work. It would take more than three hours, the Pentagon said, to get the warheads onto Canadian bases, and the warning time for a Soviet bomber attack was only three hours. "It would have been too late," Harkness says.

The Canadians tried again. Norman Robertson and Howard Green had come up with a scheme to have stored in the U.S. a small "missing part" of the warheads, which could be flown to Canadian bases at the crucial time. The weapons could be made operational more quickly than if the complete warheads themselves were stored in the U.S. No one was sure exactly what part would be kept in the U.S.; Harkness thought it would be the firing mechanism. Others suggested the "power plug" on the Bomarc, the ejector rack cartridge on the interceptors, and the umbilical power cable of the MB-1 rocket. Whatever missing part might be considered, the notion was more "delaying tactics," Harkness says, by Green and Robertson. "I never thought it was a feasible proposition," he says.

The Americans began to think the Canadians simply weren't serious and reported their doubts to the Pentagon and State Department. They were close to giving up on the Diefenbaker government on this issue, but they did agree to study the missing-part idea, and after three days of meetings in Ottawa they went back to Washington. Ambassador Ritchie was as frustrated as Harkness and the Americans. "It was getting more and more impossible to make any sense of what was coming out of Ottawa," he said. "The government was falling apart."

Even in the prime minister's own office there was a sense of confusion. "He didn't know what to do," says Bunny Pound. "Harkness was pushing one way, Green pushing the other. The trouble was, he wouldn't come down on any side. He was not as tough as Mackenzie King on warring colleagues. King lopped off heads, Diefenbaker agonized and procrastinated."

For Harkness, there was one bright spot in the negotiations, however. The Americans felt there would be no problem in Europe. Canada could simply sign the standard agreement that other NATO members had signed to confirm a joint-control arrangement for nuclear weapons. Even Howard Green began to ease his objections to this approach, while maintaining his visceral and vociferous opposition to nuclear warheads on Canadian soil. The Canadian and American military officials were puzzled at his attitude, because Green was accepting nuclear weapons that could be used in offensive strikes in Europe, but rejecting nuclear weapons in Canada that could be used only for defensive purposes. For Green, however, the issue was exquisitely simple: Europe was far away and Canada was home, and with passionate conviction he refused to have nuclear warheads in his own back yard. He had the support of the prime minister, who viewed the question more in political terms; Diefenbaker felt he could sell the electorate on warheads in Europe but not at home, although the public opinion polls showed most Canadians would accept warheads in Canada.

On December 4, the Americans presented their detailed report on the feasibility of the missing-part approach. They said it would take between one hour and fifty-five minutes, and two hours and ten minutes to bring the missing part to Canada and install it. "The part would just be flown in from Sault Ste. Marie, Michigan, or some such place and it could be screwed in in a couple of hours," says Alvin Hamilton. "It sounded like a good idea."

"It seemed then that we had a workable solution at last," Diefenbaker later said. "The 'missing part' approach was reconcilable with all the stated policies of my government and quite capable of meeting the requirements of effective North American defence."

Not quite. There were serious reservations in Washington and among the Canadian military. On December 14, Green and Harkness met with Dean Rusk and Robert McNamara at the annual NATO meeting in Paris. Green and Harkness felt the missing-part idea was at least not being rejected at that time by the Americans. Not long after, however, McNamara called Harkness in Ottawa to say it wouldn't work. The idea, his military aides advised Ottawa, was too technically complicated and time-consuming. They suggested instead that the missing part be stored in Canada, under either American or Canadian control; it would still be separate from the weapons themselves but more quickly available than if it were stored in the U.S. That idea had no appeal whatever for Diefenbaker or Green. A "ludicrous counter-proposal," Diefenbaker said.

Diefenbaker also began hedging again on nuclear arms for the Canadian NATO forces, which the cabinet had agreed to on October 30. Harkness tried several times to get Diefenbaker to sign the papers authorizing the nuclear weapons, but each time Diefenbaker put him off. "No hurry," he'd say, adding that he didn't object to the idea but he wanted to sign the deals for both Europe and NORAD at the same time. That meant more delay and more stalling, and Harkness was getting close to the breaking point.

In Paris, George Ignatieff found himself embarrassed and derided at the annual NATO review. The conference was reviewing, among other things, Canada's failure thus far to equip its forces in Europe with nuclear weapons. Although a zealous disarmament supporter, Ambassador Ignatieff admitted to himself that Canada had reneged on its commitment to nuclear warheads for its NATO troops. As he faced the NATO review, he said, "I felt like a schoolboy whose examiners are confronting him with his failures."

Diefenbaker denied publicly that there was any pressure from Washington or anywhere else for Canada to acquire nuclear weapons, but the Americans were fed up. They began to look more closely at the increasingly divided cabinet and at Diefenbaker's deteriorating political support. Two things might happen, they thought: Diefenbaker could be overthrown by a palace coup – the Americans were fully aware of the increasing internal distress with Diefenbaker's leadership; or the

minority government itself might fall, leading to an election
that Mike Pearson might win. With either scenario, Kennedy's
nemesis would be gone. With these thoughts percolating
through some parts of Washington, the Americans became less
eager to make a deal with Diefenbaker. They thought they
might get a better one with somebody else, possibly within
months.

The man Washington really wanted as Canadian prime
minister was Mike Pearson. Even though Pearson's public
position was against acquisition of nuclear warheads for North
American defence, the Americans thought they could do
business with him, and at least get some definite decisions.
Pearson himself, moreover, was privately moving towards the
acceptance of nuclear warheads. The Cuban Missile Crisis had
dramatically affected his thinking. He felt the Canadian government had failed abjectly to fulfill its obligations to the
United States, and he began considering the possibility of
reversing his position.

He was also influenced by the Liberal defence critic, Paul
Hellyer, who returned to Ottawa in mid-November after a
ten-day trip to Europe; in Paris, he had atttended the NATO
parliamentarians' conference. Hellyer found low morale among
Canadian forces in Europe and frustration among the allies that
the Canadian NATO troops continued to be without nuclear
weaponry. Hellyer met privately for forty minutes with the
NATO commander, General Lauris Norstad, who urgently argued that Canadian NATO forces were failing to fulfill their
obligations by not putting nuclear warheads on the planes and
guns committed to European defence.

"The military people at SHAPE [Supreme Headquarters Allied Powers Europe] are very concerned about the indecision
of the Canadian government," Hellyer told Pearson on his
return to Ottawa, and he urged his leader to change his
position. He warned about two critical repercussions if Canada
did not meet its nuclear commitments. "If we do not fulfill our
commitment [to NATO], there will be intense pressure on us
to withdraw and turn the facilities over to others," he said.
"Our influence in NATO will be reduced to negligible. . . . If
we don't fulfill our agreements [on NORAD] the Americans are
almost certain to reduce or terminate their production-sharing

arrangements with us." Such a possibility always lurked in the back of Washington minds, but nothing official was ever said.

In a speech in Walkerton, Ontario, on December 18, Hellyer "flew a kite." He said, "I have come to the conclusion that . . . Canada should sign a bilateral agreement with the United States which will permit the supply of atomic weapons to Canadian forces as required." Hellyer sent Pearson a copy of the speech. The Liberal leader read it carefully and listened to other Liberals such as Judy LaMarsh, who also had been to the NATO parliamentarians meeting with Hellyer and who also felt Canada was failing in its commitment to NATO. They privately urged Pearson to support acquisition of nuclear warheads.

Pearson chided Hellyer for going public with his comments, which went beyond official party policy, but a Liberal change was clearly in the wind. Canadian military affairs writer John Gellner wrote Hellyer, endorsing his speech, and Hellyer sent a copy of his letter to Pearson. "Probably Gellner's opinion rated higher in his mind than mine," said Hellyer. Over the 1962 Christmas holidays, Pearson concluded he had to make a speech in January to announce a new position.

Meanwhile, John Diefenbaker was in Nassau to confer with British Prime Minister Macmillan and, as luck would have it, with Kennedy, too. Diefenbaker was delighted with the prospect of the meeting, feeling it would provide a badly needed boost to his political stock. At the same time, it would satisfy his personal need to feel he was part of the big time. Getting to Nassau, however, had taken some delicate diplomatic footwork, since neither Macmillan nor Kennedy wanted to see him. In an interview with his British biographer Alistair Horne, years later, Macmillan would say of Diefenbaker, "It might have been said of Diefenbaker what Disraeli so naughtily said of Gladstone – 'intoxicated by the exuberance of his own verbosity.' Poor old Diefenbaker."

In late November, Diefenbaker had heard that the British prime minister would fly to Nassau to meet the American president in mid-December. The year before, Macmillan and Kennedy had met in Bermuda just before Christmas, and Diefenbaker was deeply hurt that he had not been invited. "They could ask me to Bermuda," he had pouted to Bunny Pound. "He was very upset about not being part of the event," she says. "He was like a little boy being left out of a game of tag. . . . He was practically in tears at not being invited to meet them in Nassau. He felt they were treating him like a child."

But he was determined he would not be snubbed again. First, Diefenbaker asked Macmillan to come to Ottawa following his meeting with the president. The British prime minister said he would not have time to do that, but he suggested Diefenbaker might come to Nassau on December 21 after Kennedy had left, "if you could manage this." Diefenbaker could indeed manage this, and on the appointed day he took off in high spirits, leaving behind the icicles of Ottawa for the palm trees of the Bahamas. When he landed at about noon in seventy-five-degree weather, the sixty-man white-uniformed Bahamas Police Band played "O Canada" with a native beat as he was greeted by the Bahamian governor general, Sir Robert Stapleton. The plan had been for him to arrive a few hours after Kennedy had left, but the president was unexpectedly still in Nassau. Macmillan had tried to avoid having Kennedy meet Diefenbaker when he found things were running late. "Macmillan made an effort to delay Diefenbaker's flight down from Ottawa to Nassau," says the prime minister's special assistant, Dick Thrasher, "but Diefenbaker wouldn't do it."

Kennedy, who had not seen Diefenbaker for a year and a half and never wanted to see him again, was repelled by the idea of meeting him in Nassau and said he would not stay for lunch with him. Macmillan was aghast, for, although he did not relish the idea of lunching with the Canadian prime minister either, he felt it would be inexcusably offensive not to do so. "I persuaded him to remain for lunch," Macmillan said laconically. "This, under great pressure, he agreed to do." But Kennedy warned Macmillan, "Don't leave me alone with that man."

The Macmillan–Kennedy argument over lunching with Diefenbaker, say those who heard it, went like this:

Kennedy: "No, I won't. I have to go home and t' hell with him!"

Macmillan: "You can't do that. It's a definite slight. You can't do it. Besides, I've arranged lobsters and a very fine lunch."

Kennedy: "Hell, I can get all the lobsters I want in Hyannis Port without having to eat it with that guy."

Kennedy had a similar argument with his friend J.K. Galbraith, ambassador to India at the time, who attended the Nassau conference. Galbraith, a graduate of the Ontario Agricultural College at Guelph, was a native of Iona Station, Ontario. His father had been president of the Elgin County Liberals. Shortly before lunch, the president told Galbraith, whom Kennedy still regarded as a Canadian, "Your prime minister is coming down. You have to stay with me. I don't want to be alone with him."

"Not me!" said Galbraith, who promptly took a plane back to Washington. "Kennedy was always on edge with Diefenbaker," Galbraith says. "He talked of him as 'an old son of a bitch.' Diefenbaker had a real capacity for bruising people."

"Diefenbaker horned in on the meeting," Robert Kennedy said later, reflecting his brother's distress at the get-together.

The Diefenbaker–Kennedy feud was known among reporters. One of them asked the prime minister at a Nassau news conference, held under the palm trees at a hotel poolside, "Is it true that the president hates your guts?" Pausing only a moment, he told the reporters, "I've never known relations between individuals or countries to be other than the closest since I became prime minister."

Lunch was at the Lyford Cay home of former Montrealer Mrs. Robert Holt, where Macmillan was staying. Diefenbaker got there before Kennedy, and he and Macmillan greeted the president when Kennedy arrived. Diefenbaker smiled nervously, and his first words to Kennedy were, "Well, Mr. President, what are we going to do about the unemployment problem in North America?" Dick Thrasher, standing just to the side of the president and the prime minister, thought it was a very odd first thing to say. With some asperity, Kennedy responded, "Well, we solved ours by reducing taxes," and he walked up the path towards the house. "He seemed to be saying, 'That's your problem, don't bug me,' " says Thrasher.

The president and the two prime ministers had lunch sitting at a round, glass-topped table in the garden, dressed in heavy business suits under the warm sun. Kennedy sat between Macmillan and Diefenbaker, and their aides were off to the side.

"Kennedy loved to tell the story of that lunch," says Willis

Armstrong. "He'd laugh at the awkwardness of it." Using an old Boston Irish saying to describe the inappropriateness of the lunch, Kennedy would tell colleagues, "There we sat like three whores at a christening."

"It had a comic aspect. It was a sideshow, because Macmillan didn't really want to see him either," Armstrong says.

Diefenbaker had a different view. "In all, I thought it a useful conversation and pleasant enough. . . . I considered it the course of irresponsibility to allow any conflict of personality to encroach for long upon the practical matters that concerned our countries. I could only hope that President Kennedy would see American interests served by a like attitude."

As they dug into the lobster, Diefenbaker told the president he hoped they would soon have an opportunity to talk about North American defence issues, including "the provision of nuclear-armed missiles for Canada." He didn't go into details, but he was still thinking of the missing-part idea, even though the Americans had already rejected it. Kennedy didn't pursue the matter, and the lunch conversation turned to Canadian trade with China and Cuba. Diefenbaker thought that Washington might soon take action against U.S. parent companies for the trade, but Kennedy said he had no objection to non-strategic trade by Canada.

Throughout the lunch, Kennedy seemed fidgety, talking about radio, then about landing on the moon and other insubstantial things. Thrasher says, "There was no easy communication. I think he just wanted to get the hell out of there. There was a stiffness and a brusqueness about Kennedy."

Kennedy left after the two-hour outdoor lunch, walking across the lawn to the house next door where he was staying, the home of Canadian industrialist E.P. Taylor. Meanwhile, Macmillan walked Diefenbaker into the air-conditioned living room of his temporary home and briefed the Canadian prime minister on what he and the president had discussed. In spite of Macmillan's private antipathy towards Diefenbaker, especially after their Common Market arguments, Macmillan seemed cordial with his Canadian colleague in contrast to the strains of the lunch with Kennedy.

Macmillan told Diefenbaker of a U.K.–U.S. agreement to give India $120 million in military aid to meet a threat from

China. It was a delicate move because, given India's squabble with its neighbour Pakistan over Kashmir, Pakistan might be alarmed by the aid being sent to India. But Diefenbaker, in an absent-minded indiscretion at his news conference later that day, revealed the aid program before either India or Pakistan was informed. This surprised the Indians and Pakistanis and infuriated U.S. and U.K. officials, leaving them shaking their heads yet again over the antics of the Canadian prime minister. "It disturbed everybody," says Galbraith. "The Americans thought they had some right to announce it first since it was mostly their money."

Kennedy's main message to Macmillan at Nassau had been that the U.S. was cancelling the costly Skybolt missile, which Washington had promised to provide to the British. It was a victim of Defense Secretary McNamara's passion for cost-effectiveness, but Kennedy recognized that the cancellation gave Macmillan serious domestic political problems; the government would be embarrassed by appearing to be dependent on U.S. military hardware. Because he admired Macmillan, Kennedy sought ways to provide other defence weaponry to ease Macmillan's political difficulties.

"At Nassau, Kennedy was very concerned about Macmillan politically," says George Ball. "He wanted to make it less painful for Macmillan." Walt Rostow felt Macmillan went too far in his pleading for help, saying he was "like an Edwardian Shakespearean actor overplaying the drama of poor old Harold at the end of the road." Kennedy proposed and Macmillan accepted a plan for a NATO multilateral seaborne nuclear force using Polaris missiles – an idea that eased Macmillan's political problems but that had little Pentagon support and, in the end, faded from the scene.

When he arrived in Nassau Diefenbaker had seen a chance to mediate the differences between Macmillan and Kennedy. "Regardless of recent difficulties with the Kennedy Government," he later said, "I expected that I might be called upon to assume a modest role in providing friendly intervention." That was the last thing either Kennedy or Macmillan would have wanted and, in any event, they had settled their differences before Diefenbaker sat down to lunch.

At first, Diefenbaker said the Nassau Agreement on defence

systems discussed by Kennedy and Macmillan had no particular significance for Canada. "As I considered the Nassau Agreement, however," the prime minister later said, "it was increasingly obvious that the whole Western defence concept had been completely changed by what amounted to the announcement that the United States was now dependent upon Polaris weapons as their main deterrent. . . . If there was ever a reason to seriously re-examine every Canadian defence commitment, this was it."

To the Americans, and to Harkness, this interpretation was utter nonsense. But Diefenbaker saw the Nassau Agreement as a godsend because he could use it as a rationale for yet another delay in his decision on acquisition of nuclear warheads. He said there was now a real question as to whether the Canadian NATO forces needed nuclear weapons at all, and that the Bomarcs and North American defence interceptors also might not now need to be armed with nuclear warheads. He combined that thought with Kennedy's earlier comment on the need for a strengthening of conventional weapons (which Diefenbaker had interpreted to mean instead of, not in addition to, nuclear weapons) as a vindication for his hesitation on the nuclear decision. Diefenbaker also saw the Nassau Agreement as another example of Kennedy's intention to dictate the defence policies of other countries, in this case, Britain.

But American officials and, increasingly, Canadian officials, too, felt Diefenbaker's nuclear tactics were now being driven by personal resentment against Kennedy as well as his political instinct, rather than any intellectual rationale. In Washington, Charles Ritchie commented in his diary, "As to the Prime Minister, I doubted whether he had deep convictions on the nuclear issue, and thought him more influenced by his resentment at Canada's being taken for granted by the United States."

The prime minister stayed on in Nassau for a week and a half at the Lyford Cay home of wealthy and prominent Bahamas business leader Harold Christie. He spent the time fishing, sunning, swimming, and making a twenty-minute speech at the local Kiwanis Club, in which he once more criticized Kennedy's attitude in the Cuban Missile Crisis: "We were not consulted in advance." He also told the Nassau Kiwanians, "There was no delay on our part" in responding to the Cuban crisis. He wrote a letter of thanks to Macmillan for lunch, but did not write to Kennedy.

"He was having the time of his life on the beach," Bunny Pound says. "Mrs. Diefenbaker kept telling me, 'Bunny, don't let him go out too far.'" In his fishing endeavours he landed a thirty-pound shark, a barracuda, and a tuna.

Diefenbaker also participated in a traditional tree-planting ceremony in Nassau, throwing spadefuls of dirt on a *ficus benjamina* tree and joking about Kennedy's back problems from the Ottawa tree-planting. Kennedy had learned his tree-planting lessons in Ottawa, and when he was at a similar ceremony in Bermuda in December 1961, all he did was snip a ribbon hanging from a palm tree. "That's a very good way of doing it," he said. "Much better than in Canada." In Nassau, the president had planted a tree with a couple of gentle shovels of earth. "Mr. Diefenbaker laughed about it and went back years later to see if Kennedy's tree had died," says Pound. "He said a bit gleefully that it had."

Kennedy's tree was gone, but so were the ones planted by Macmillan and Diefenbaker. Nassau police reported that someone had stolen all three trees three weeks after the leaders had been in Nassau.

Nassau, however, was the last moment of glee for the prime minister. Now deeply tanned and relaxed, he headed back to a snowy Ottawa – and into a fire-storm showdown with President Kennedy.

Chapter Seven

WASHINGTON DROPS
A BOMB

The high-noon confrontation with John Kennedy began for John Diefenbaker on January 2, 1963, when the president gave an interview to Associated Press. In a cocky mood, Kennedy said he was going to take a stronger leadership role in the Western alliance "even at the risk of offending sensitive allies." It was one of the lessons he had learned from the Cuban Missile Crisis, he indicated.

For Diefenbaker, this was impetuous arrogance that could plunge the world into jeopardy. He was still boiling over the lack of advance consultation in the Cuban crisis, and he believed Kennedy had run roughshod over Macmillan at Nassau in killing the Skybolt missile, even though Macmillan had told him that he was very happy with his new deal with Kennedy for the Polaris missile and the multilateral nuclear force. To Diefenbaker, as he reflected on Kennedy's interview, a stronger grip on the Western alliance by Kennedy meant more unilateral American actions. "He wanted to control us," says Alvin Hamilton. "The whole American dream is to control all countries around the United States. And it was Kennedy's dream too."

Diefenbaker did not have to wait long to see what he felt was clear evidence of that. The next day, January 3, American General Lauris Norstad came calling in Ottawa on his farewell tour after seven years as commander of NATO. Given the pyrotechnical potential of the arguments over Canada's nuclear commitment to NATO and NORAD, the prime minister decided on minimum protocol for Norstad's courtesy call. He would not meet with the general, and Associate Defence Minister Pierre Sévigny was sent to the airport to greet him. In his five-hour visit to Ottawa, Norstad called on the governor general, had lunch with senior Canadian military officers, and then held a news conference. It had been organized by RCAF public relations director Bill Lee, who knew the nuclear war-head question would come up; Lee hoped Norstad's answers would help the air force's fight to get nuclear weaponry. "We knew absolutely full well what was going to happen," he says. "We didn't need to prompt any journalists."

Norstad was a man much admired by military and civilian leaders of NATO, with a reputation for honesty, skill, and diplomacy. Pearson knew him well and had "a great admiration for him," which in itself was enough to arouse the suspicions of John Diefenbaker.

In May 1959, Norstad had come to Ottawa to explain to the Diefenbaker cabinet exactly what was involved in Canada's commitment to a strike reconnaisance role in NATO. That role had included the use of nuclear weapons, as agreed in principle by Canada at a December 1958 meeting of the Canada–U.S. Ministerial Committee on Defence and formally accepted in July 1959 by the Diefenbaker government. Now, three and a half years later, as Norstad stood before the Ottawa reporters, the Canadian NATO squadrons remained without nuclear weapons and Canada was not fulfilling its promises of 1959. The first question came from Southam columnist Charles Lynch, who drove to the heart of the defence debate by asking bluntly, "General, do you consider that Canada has committed itself to provide its Starfighter squadrons in Europe with tactical nuclear weapons?"

Norstad replied, "My answer to that is yes. This has been a commitment that was made." At this point, Norstad looked over to the chairman of the chiefs of staff, Air Marshal Frank Miller, who said, "I think you're right on that; quite right." Norstad then went on, "We established a NATO requirement for a certain number of strike squadrons. This includes tactical atomic strike squadrons, and Canada committed some of its force to meet this NATO establishment requirement. And this we depend on."

Sévigny got increasingly nervous as he sat off to the side watching Norstad squirm through what he knew was a political minefield. "Norstad knew that he was in a hot seat and did his best to be evasive as possible," Sévigny says. "But he could fancy-skate to a point and no farther."

The tall, gaunt veteran USAF general was then asked, "Does it mean, sir, that if Canada does not accept nuclear weapons for these airplanes, that she is not actually fulfilling her NATO commitments?"

Norstad answered, "I believe that's right. . . . We are depending upon Canada to produce some of the tactical atomic strike force."

The thirty-five-minute news conference ended, and Norstad and Canadian military officers gathered for a final drink before the commander flew back to Washington. "I hope that my remarks will not cause you any inconvenience," Norstad smiled. Grinning sweetly, Sévigny said, "All is well." But he thought otherwise, and Miller said, "Yes, it's going to create a bit of flak."

"I'm terribly sorry," said Norstad. "I didn't come here to do that."

"We all knew that a political explosion was in the making. . . . I knew only too well that all hell would break loose," Sévigny says.

It did indeed. Coming on the heels of Diefenbaker's hesitancy in the Cuban Missile Crisis, Norstad's comments reverberated in the House of Commons, splashed across the country in newspaper headlines and television newcasts, and exposed the prime minister to more allegations of indecisiveness. The Winnipeg *Free Press* attacked the prime minister for having "reduced our defence policy to fiasco, poisoned our relations with the American people and humiliated the people of Canada. To such a record of pugnacity abroad and indecision at home, there is no parallel in Canadian experience."

Diefenbaker was almost apoplectic. He felt it was all a plot by John Kennedy to undermine his authority. "[Norstad's] visit to Ottawa could only have been made at the behest of President Kennedy," he later wrote. "His purpose was to establish a basis for Mr. Pearson's conversion to United States nuclear policy."

The habitually blunt Alvin Hamilton says, "Kennedy sent

Norstad to do this hatchet job on us. It was American imperialism of the highest order. But we were not going to be pushed around."

The Canadian ambassador to the U.S. at the time, Charles Ritchie, agrees with Diefenbaker's "plot" accusation. "The Norstad thing did not happen in a vacuum," he said in his diary. "This was another American turn of the screw to bring down the Conservative Government."

But Dean Rusk denies there was any Machiavellian scheming behind the NATO commander's comments: "We gave Norstad no instructions on this." Indeed, what Norstad was saying was little more than what Canadian military officials and Defence Minister Harkness himself had been saying for months. "He carefully looked up what I'd said," says Harkness, "and, in effect, repeated it."

The day after Norstad's visit, Diefenbaker called Sévigny to his office and accused him of being part of an American plot. "All this was engineered by Kennedy," he fumed.

"If you were not prime minister, I'd say you were crazy," responded Sévigny.

"What do you mean, calling your prime minister crazy?" demanded Diefenbaker.

Sévigny threw up his hands and stomped out of the office.

Surprised at Diefenbaker's fury at his comments, which had been conveyed to him, Norstad told a Washington reporter five days after his Ottawa visit, "Why should not Canada fulfil its nuclear role? If Canada does not do it, then some other country will have to do it. This does not sound Canadian." One day after that comment, General John Gerhart, the NORAD commander, was visiting the Bomarc base at North Bay, Ontario, and was quoted as saying the lack of nuclear warheads for the Bomarcs was "a chink in the North American polar shield." He later said his words were misconstrued, but the reports further undermined Diefenbaker's political support. On the day Norstad was in Ottawa, a Gallup Poll had shown a decline in popularity of his government; another poll had shown a swing towards support for Canadian acquisition of nuclear arms. All this, said Diefenbaker, "revealed that the campaign against me was gaining ground."

While Norstad was setting off his political rockets in Ottawa,

Mike Pearson was preparing to reverse his previous opposition to Canadian nuclear warhead acquisition. Although he, like Diefenbaker, had indicated support for nuclear weapons for Canadian forces in 1958, by August 1960 he was telling the House of Commons, "In my view we should get out of the whole . . . Bomarc operation. . . . Let us withdraw from that direct form of continental defence. . . . Canada should categorically reject the proposition that her NATO forces should be equipped with nuclear weapons of any kind." Six months later, in another speech, Pearson had demanded Canadian renunciation of nuclear weapons and abandonment of the Bomarcs and interceptors for North American defence. Harkness had accused him of "neutralism." The New York *Daily News* had editorialized, "We'd suggest that a Royal Commission, including some psychiatrists, be set up to find out what ails Pearson." Even as late as midwinter 1962, Pearson felt Canada should not acquire nuclear warheads, believing, as Diefenbaker and Green had proclaimed, that such a move would "weaken our advocacy" of disarmament.

But now he felt Canada had committed itself to NATO and to the Americans on acquiring nuclear weapons, and he was planning to say publicly that this commitment had to be fulfilled, especially after the frightening brinksmanship of the Cuban Missile Crisis. He was also contemplating one reservation: that after accepting the nuclear weapons as promised, Ottawa should open negotiations with Washington to talk about a future non-nuclear role for Canada. In other words, get in the nuclear water and then try to get out. But Jack Pickersgill, a key Pearson adviser, wrote to him on January 3, the day Norstad was in Ottawa, urging him to speak out on nuclear acquisition "simply and decisively and without any qualifications about trying to get out of it." Pickersgill also noted that "as a practical politician," he wanted the support of the armed forces, "without which we cannot win an election." He estimated a quarter-million votes were at stake.

As a founding father of NATO, Pearson worried that Canadian influence in the alliance would shrink perilously if Canada failed to live up to its commitments. He took a transcript of Norstad's news conference with him, along with memos from

Pickersgill, Paul Hellyer, and military writer John Gellner, on a week-long trip to New York in January. Among other things, he was attending a New York meeting of the Council on World Tensions, of which he was executive chairman. In New York, he talked with UN Secretary General U Thant for half an hour. He had also arranged to see his old friend Adlai Stevenson, the U.S. ambassador to the UN, but there is conflicting evidence as to whether he actually met Stevenson. His key adviser Walter Gordon believed he did, and that he discussed the warhead question with Stevenson. Pearson said he cancelled the appointment, probably out of fear that a conversation with the American diplomat might lay him open to taunts from Diefenbaker about getting instructions on the warhead issue from the Americans.

He spent much of his New York visit scribbling out a draft speech on the issue at a desk in his room at the Sheraton-East Hotel, although he also took time out to see five Broadway plays. Six drafts later, and with a final polish at the Park Plaza Hotel in Toronto, Pearson had his speech, which he delivered on Saturday, January 12, to the York-Scarborough Liberal Association.

"As a Canadian, I am ashamed if we accept commitments and then refuse to discharge them," he told the Liberal luncheon meeting. "In acting thus we deceive ourselves, we let our armed forces down and betray our allies." The government, he said, "should end at once its evasion of responsibility by discharging the commitments it has already accepted for Canada. It can only do this by accepting nuclear warheads for those defensive tactical weapons which cannot effectively be used without them but which we have agreed to use."

He spoke of a joint agreement with the U.S., in which "a U.S. finger would be on the trigger, but a Canadian finger would be on the safety catch." He made reference to the possibility of a new role for Canada's defence forces later on, but his central theme was acceptance of the warheads and fulfilment of the commitments. He knew that he was aggravating the split within the Tory ranks, and he knew, too, that the public opinion polls showed a majority supporting warhead acquisition; later he told historian Denis Smith, "That was when I really became a politician."

Reacting to Pearson's statement, Washington was euphoric; Harkness was delighted; and Diefenbaker was contemptuous.

"I thought that ended it," Harkness says. "I believed that this would enable the matter to be settled. I thought now that the Liberals were not opposing warhead acquisition, we could go ahead. This would make it easier for Diefenbaker to say yes." As soon as he heard of Pearson's speech, the defence minister went to Diefenbaker and told him, "Now we can proceed."

To his astonishment, the prime minister replied, "Oh no. No. If they're not opposing it any more, then we can't do it. . . . Now we must oppose it."

Diefenbaker condemned Pearson's switch, saying, "The day the strike takes place, eighteen million people in North America will die in the first two hours, four million of them in Canada. Mr. Pearson shouldn't play politics with four million dead Canadians." Diefenbaker linked the Pearson switch to Kennedy; he later charged, "President Kennedy had achieved his dearest Canadian wish. It was a partnership complete. The Liberals under Pearson had progressed . . . to embracing the United States position on arming with nuclear weapons the Bomarcs and, no doubt, yielding to United States demands for storage of all manner of nuclear devices in Canada."

Agriculture Minister Alvin Hamilton told reporters the Pearson switch was "a pure example of Pearson's willingness to accept the leadership of the United States on any vital matter."

Diefenbaker was convinced that Pearson's speech proved a Kennedy–Pearson conspiracy to overthrow him. In a television interview, Diefenbaker stated his belief with stark simplicity: "Mr. Pearson went to New York. He went there. He saw the Americans in Washington. He came back and he made the speech." Dean Rusk, however, says Pearson was never in touch with any U.S. official on the matter.

Diefenbaker and his Conservative loyalists loudly taunted Pearson in the House of Commons and elsewhere with accusations of "American toady" and "Yankee-lover," and some suggested Pearson should give back his 1956 Nobel Peace Prize. Not all Conservatives took the Diefenbaker line, however. A sizeable number were concerned that the prime minister was on the wrong side of the argument. "This will deal us a devastating blow," prominent Toronto Tory Eddie Goodman told colleagues. Bunny Pound, who had just listened to a vitriolic anti-American rant by the prime minister, told Goodman, "He must come to his senses about the United States."

"She was visibly upset about criticizing her revered boss," Goodman says. Diefenbaker had drafted what Goodman calls "an incredible anti-American tirade" for a forthcoming speech, and Goodman told him, "You're prime minister. You can't do that." In the end, Diefenbaker did not use the draft. However, he was unswayed by Goodman's arguments on nuclear weapons and felt the Pearson switch was a political boon for the Conservatives.

Criticism of Pearson came from others, too, including NDP leader Tommy Douglas, who charged that Liberal policies were being "made in the United States." More damaging to Pearson, however, were the resignations of a number of party veterans and the criticism from a couple of Quebeckers whom Pearson had desperately wanted to run for the Liberals in the next election. Both now refused to run because of his nuclear switch. Pierre Trudeau poured scorn on Pearson's nuclear turnaround and shared Diefenbaker's suspicion that it was all part of an American plot. He called Pearson the "unfrocked priest of peace." Jean Marchand said he could not join the Liberals because of his own vigorous anti-nuclear stand.

Even some of Pearson's strongest supporters were aghast at his volte-face. "It was very upsetting to me," said Walter Gordon, who would later be Pearson's finance minister. Tom Kent, a senior Pearson adviser, said he was "appalled" by the policy change. He later said, "I think politically it was an issue on which he lost more than he gained."

But Liberal tactical wizard Keith Davey says Pearson's nuclear turnaround gained him votes and editorial support. "More important than the issue was the fact that he had taken a position in contrast to Diefenbaker's waffling and waffling," says Davey.

Diefenbaker publicly lambasted Pearson at the Progressive Conservatives' annual meeting in Ottawa in mid-January. He talked of Pearson's "recklessness with principle" and noted, "Every time Mr. Pearson goes across the line he has a new policy." He echoed his own new rationale for delaying any decision on warhead acquisition by saying, "Today all over the world – the Free World – there is uncertainty in the field of defence." He spoke of changes in NATO strategy as a result of the Nassau conference and of the change in the Soviet threat as bombers gave way to missiles.

The Ottawa meeting, however, further exposed a widening split within the party over Diefenbaker's vacillation on the nuclear issue. Party vice-president George Hogan, who had been Diefenbaker's campaign tour manager for his past three successful campaigns, was especially concerned about Diefenbaker's anti-Americanism. Hogan's speech in early November 1962 still angered the prime minister, and it had encouraged anti-Diefenbaker forces within the party. Prompted by the efforts of Hogan and other Tories, a large number of proposed resolutions came in from Conservative constituency associations across the country. Much to Diefenbaker's chagrin, the Young Progressive Conservatives approved a resolution "to adopt within the framework of the existing alliances, a nuclear role." The Alberta Conservative leader also backed a nuclear role.

"People expressed their beliefs that a strong continental defence required mutual trust and confidence between Canada and the United States, and that we were dangerously weakening this crucial relationship," says Eddie Goodman, who was chairman of the party policy and resolutions committee at the time. "The issue now was whether we would or would not live up to our commitments to our most important ally. Most Canadians simply did not want to go back on their word to a friend."

Goodman also scoffed at Diefenbaker and Green's idea that "nuclear virginity" was beneficial for Canadian disarmament efforts. "I like getting laid, you know," he says. "I've never believed in virginity in any way, shape, or form, and I didn't see anything wrong politically or I don't see anything evil in nuclear arms. . . . The fact that they were nuclear warheads on Canadian soil, it didn't bother me one tittle."

Goodman found Harkness was enthusiastic about a pronuclear resolution at the full party conference. "It might give me the support I need to persuade the prime minister to live up to our commitment to the Americans," he told Goodman.

Goodman prepared a draft resolution based on what had come in from the constituency associations; he felt he had the support of two-thirds of the cabinet for it. It commended

Diefenbaker and Green for their efforts on disarmament and then called for fulfilment of Canada's commitment to the U.S. to accept nuclear warheads. When he heard of the draft, Diefenbaker hit the roof, stung as he already was by the Young Conservatives' resolution. "The resolution on the Bomarc warheads is not to go to the meeting!" he ordered Goodman. The Toronto lawyer was instructed to meet Howard Green and work out language more attuned to Diefenbaker's attitude. "We are making great progress in our disarmament talks and I would not want anything to happen this weekend that would interfere with that," Green told Goodman. "We need more time."

Finally Green and Goodman agreed to a resolution proposing that if a disarmament agreement were not reached by the superpowers by December 1963, then Canada would accept nuclear weapons, providing those under NORAD were jointly controlled. Diefenbaker was enraged and threatened to resign. "In my opinion," says Goodman, "he was against nuclear arms on the basis of political expediency, not because he had any deep-set conviction about nuclear arms."

On the Friday night, January 18, Diefenbaker made an impassioned speech, pleading with convention delegates not to tie the government's hands on acquisition of nuclear weapons. "Do not bind us," he said. "This is no time for the declaration of great principles on matters that are in the process of change. . . . It is all well to say we should take definitive action. It is easy to sit in the bleachers and play a successful game. The man who has the responsibility for office sits in solitary loneliness in his room and in his soul." The prime minister's oratory won over the delegates. Instead of approving the nuclear resolution, they agreed by a two-to-one margin to simply forward it to the government for its "consideration and decision." Even the head of the Young Conservatives said their earlier resolution had been approved by only a small number of their members and did not represent the majority.

Harkness was now ready to make an all-out drive for the warheads. At a long and bitter cabinet meeting at 24 Sussex on Sunday, the defence minister insisted the nuclear issue had to be resolved. Equally adamant, Diefenbaker insisted on delaying any decision until after the next election.

"Do that, and I quit," said Harkness.

In Washington, Kennedy and Rusk were fully aware of the dissension tearing at the vitals of the Diefenbaker government; they quietly hoped it might force Diefenbaker into making a final nuclear decision. But John Diefenbaker was not their main preoccupation in January 1963; Charles de Gaulle was. Like Diefenbaker, de Gaulle used anger as an instrument of authority (some in Washington had called Diefenbaker "a pocket de Gaulle"), and now de Gaulle's anger erupted majestically.

In a mid-January news conference de Gaulle brutally struck down two pillars of Kennedy's foreign policy: he signalled that France would veto British membership in the European Common Market; and he rejected a co-ordinated Western nuclear policy, saying France had to have its own nuclear deterrence because France could not totally rely on U.S. nuclear arms to defend Europe. He also pointed to the Kennedy–Macmillan agreement on a multilateral, seaborne nuclear force as an "Anglo-Saxon Nassau conspiracy," relegating France to "second place" in developing global defence policies.

"What can you do with a man like that?" Kennedy muttered to the American ambassador to France, much as he had ruefully commented earlier on John Diefenbaker.

Even in the turmoil of his own political crisis, Diefenbaker gloated at de Gaulle's momentous slap in Kennedy's face. He felt it vindicated his own long and noisy opposition to British membership in the Common Market and his hesitancy to accept American nuclear weapons. Besides, he enjoyed the public spectacle of Kennedy's embarrassment and the fact that both he and de Gaulle were using Nassau as a rationale to resist Kennedy's defence design. Nassau, the prime minister later said, "had proved to de Gaulle that Britain was in fact turning its back on Europe in favour of the United States' conception of an Atlantic community dominated from Washington." Kennedy had given de Gaulle "a final proof when he secured Britain's agreement to end the Skybolt missile program and become part of a new American-controlled defence strategy."

In his comments at this time, Diefenbaker portrayed himself as an intimate of Kennedy and Macmillan at Nassau, suggesting

Canada's influence was high in world councils even though he was simultanously denouncing Kennedy. "I think that Canada is at the cock-crowing of her greatness," he told a media black-tie dinner in Ottawa.

Diefenbaker had little time for self-satisfied musing, however, as he faced a fractious cabinet, an uneasy party, and a riotous Parliament. He was, in fact, heading into the most dramatic fortnight of his life.

The House of Commons resumed sitting on Monday afternoon, January 21, the day after the Conservative convention ended, and Diefenbaker immediately offered his interpretation of the Nassau Agreement. He stated that Nassau put emphasis on increasing conventional military strength as against nuclear weaponry.

Harkness violently disagreed with this interpretation of Nassau and yet again demanded a cabinet showdown on the nuclear issue.

While the Diefenbaker cabinet was teetering on the brink of collapse over the nuclear issue, the Americans were approaching complete exasperation with Diefenbaker's decision-making paralysis, which was leaving a gap in North American defence. On Tuesday, January 22, the State Department told Canadian diplomats in Washington that Defense Secretary McNamara was refusing to meet again to discuss the issue with Canadian cabinet officials. McNamara simply felt it would be a waste of time. Basil Robinson reported from the embassy in Washington the American feeling that "they can afford to wait a little longer in the expectation that another election in Canada will result in a better prospect of a solution palatable to the United States."

However much Diefenbaker's domination of his cabinet may have diminished, it was not extinguished, and on the same Tuesday, he yet again manoeuvred more delay on the nuclear decision. He proposed striking a cabinet committee to find an answer, and Harkness reluctantly agreed. That afternoon and evening and the next day, the committee members – Harkness, Green, Gordon Churchill, and Donald Fleming as chairman – met ten times to examine documents and records of cabinet decisions dating back to 1957, some earlier. Green argued Canada had never made a commitment to accept nuclear weapons, but with the documentary evidence before him, he acquiesced. "There was no question acquisition had been approved of at several times," Harkness says. "Howard very reluctantly agreed that we had committed ourselves." But the Diefenbaker defence minister thinks that while Green would have accepted warheads in Europe, he likely would have resigned before accepting them on Canadian soil for NORAD.

Knowing Diefenbaker's extreme sensitivity, the cabinet committee prepared a one-page report saying that Canada had committed itself to a NATO nuclear role, although Nassau placed that role "in some doubt," and that there was need for a clarification from the forthcoming May meeting of NATO, which would be in Ottawa. On NORAD, the cabinet committee said negotiations with the Americans should continue "with a view to reaching an agreement."

The report was unanimous, although Harkness had wanted something stronger. Fleming had written it out in longhand, and the ministers had initialled it. Most other cabinet members agreed with the report. But Diefenbaker was furious. "I won't be forced into taking a position on the matter," Harkness recalls Diefenbaker shouting. In a verbal toe-to-toe confrontation with the prime minister, Harkness again threatened to resign. They calmed down enough to agree the report would go to the full cabinet the next day, Thursday, January 24. The stained-glass doors of the Cabinet Room on the second floor of the East Block swung open repeatedly on Thursday with the comings and goings of ministers at two cabinet meetings. At the first one, the prime minister said he could not accept the terms of the report from the Fleming group, and he pleaded with his colleagues not to break up the government on this issue, then left early. "He wasn't present, but the majority of cabinet was definitely in favour of going ahead," Harkness recalls. "They knew the weapons weren't effective without nuclear warheads."

The cabinet approved the committee recommendation, and Fleming left to give the prime minister the news over lunch. To Fleming's surprise, Diefenbaker again said no, and at the second cabinet meeting of the day, in the late afternoon, Harkness again threatened to resign. Later, meeting Diefenbaker in his hideaway office behind the Speaker's chair, Harkness loudly reiterated his threat. The prime minister's special assistant, Dick

Thrasher, who was sitting outside the office, worried as he heard ear-splitting shouts thundering through the closed door for fifteen minutes, culminating in Harkness saying, "Well, I'm going to resign!" However, he was persuaded to hold off until Diefenbaker made a major speech the next day in the House of Commons on defence policy. But Harkness still grumbles, twenty-seven years later, "There was no logic whatever in his position other than delay. He had such an overinflated ego. You were not only opposing him, but opposing God."

With bitterness in Washington and chaos in Ottawa, a sour debate got under way in the House on the nuclear question. Social Credit spokesman Robert Thompson lashed into "the pathetic spectacle" of Green as "the apostle of disarmament" and Harkness "telling us we need nuclear weapons and all the while the Prime Minister . . . sits in between remaining evasive and uncommitted." NDP leader Tommy Douglas attacked both the indecision of the government and the pro-nuclear stance of Pearson. Earlier, Pearson had called the government defence policy "a fog of silence penetrated occasionally by a Ministerial platitude," and now he reiterated his new support for nuclear warhead acquisition on the grounds of Canada's commitment to NATO and the U.S. "How we manage our relationships with our neighbour," he told the House, "is one of the most important aspects . . . of our foreign policy. . . . We do not prove our Canadianism . . . but only our immaturity when we confuse the defence of Canada's rights with emotional breast-beating." Howard Green, however, remained unmoved by Pearson. Condemning the Americans, Green said, "When you are the biggest fellow in the schoolyard, it is quite a temptation to shove everybody else around."

On Friday, January 25, Diefenbaker rose in the House to deliver his promised nuclear statement, a two-hour masterpiece of obfuscation filled with illusions, delusions, and confusions. "One of the most baffling and controversial speeches to be found in the parliamentary record," says historian Peyton Lyon. Affirming Harkness's position that Canada had committed itself to accepting nuclear arms, Diefenbaker said that in December 1957, "We undertook to equip our squadrons assigned to NATO for a strike reconnaissance role, which role would include the mission of delivering nuclear weapons. No one was under any misunderstanding in that connection." He added, "Canada does not, has not and will not renege on her responsibilities." The prime minister noted the forthcoming May NATO meeting in Ottawa and said he would seek "clarification" of Canada's NATO role at that meeting; he would then "make a decision, a consistent decision, first to maintain our undertakings and second, to execute, if that be the view, the maintenance of our collective defence."

The prime minister revealed the secret talks with the Americans about nuclear warheads for the Bomarcs and interceptors for North American defence. "We shall continue our negotiations," he said. "They have been going on quite forcibly for two months or more." He added, "If nuclear weapons are required we shall not accept them unless we have joint control," something the Americans had been willing to agree to for years. Diefenbaker also said the Soviet bomber threat was diminishing, which signalled a declining need for Bomarcs and interceptors. He spoke of a change in strategy in Western defence plans from nuclear to conventional weaponry. "I was in Nassau," the prime minister said, as he offered his version of what went on between Kennedy and Macmillan and what their agreement meant. It meant, he said, more conventional forces and a multilateral nuclear force. "That," he said, "is a tremendous step – a change in the philosophy of defence."

When the prime minister finished, Harkness followed him into the government lobby, shook hands with him, and said, "Thank you very much." "I thought that at that point, Diefenbaker had surrendered, shall I say," he now says. "In a rather concealed way, he had put in his speech just what our cabinet committee had recommended and which he'd earlier rejected. I was very pleased. I thought I'd won my point."

However, Diefenbaker had pleased Howard Green, too. After noting the Canadian nuclear commitments and the negotiations with Washington, he had spoken of Canada's commitment to disarmament. "We shall not, so long as we are pursuing the ways of disarmament, allow the extension of the nuclear family into Canada," he told Parliament.

"It was," said Donald Fleming, "without exception the most equivocal" House of Commons speech he'd ever heard. "An undigestible stew" was the later verdict of Basil Robinson, who, as the Canadian minister in Washington, began hearing rumbles immediately from his State Department contacts.

The U.S. ambassador to Canada, the short-tempered Walton Butterworth, thought the speech was a diplomatic atrocity and demanded Washington make a formal response at once. Privately, U.S. embassy officials began telling Canadian reporters that Diefenbaker was seriously damaging NATO with misinterpretations of the Macmillan–Kennedy Nassau meeting and by his vacillation on nuclear warheads.

As he read the newspapers and watched the television accounts of Diefenbaker's address, Harkness was also angry. He thought the reporters had got it all wrong, as their news stories took the line that the prime minister had rejected a nuclear role for Canada. "The headlines were completely inaccurate," says Harkness. "I wanted to set the record straight and I believed an agreement [with the Americans] could be arrived at in the near future."

On Sunday, January 27, after a late breakfast, Harkness began writing a press release on his interpretation of what Diefenbaker had said. On Monday morning at nine-thirty, the defence minister took the extraordinary step of issuing the release as a "clarification" of the prime minister's address. "I was surprised and disappointed by the interpretation put on the Prime Minister's speech," his statement said. It repeated several paragraphs of the prime minister's address and said, "Those paragraphs state a definite policy for the acquisition of nuclear arms on these terms: First, our obligations to equip certain weapons systems with nuclear arms are reiterated, together with the determination to honour those obligations. . . . Second . . . should NATO reaffirm for Canada a role involving nuclear weapons, Canada will equip her NATO forces to discharge her obligations. Third, so far as NORAD is concerned, Canada has been negotiating with the United States for the past two to three months in order that nuclear warheads will be made available for our two squadrons of Bomarcs and for the F-101 interceptor squadrons. These negotiations will be continued in order to reach a satisfactory agreement. I believe such an agreement can be arrived at in the near future." He added,

"Headlines that the nuclear weapons carriers we have secured are to be scrapped and nuclear arms decisions avoided are completely incorrect."

Harkness sent a copy of the release to the prime minister; at eleven o'clock Diefenbaker called Harkness to come to his office. When they met, a frothing Diefenbaker let out a cry of anguish at the "clarification." "He was ranting and raving about it," says Harkness. "What are you doing?" he shouted at the defence minister. "This is terrible. . . . You had no right to make such a statement. You have put me in an impossible situation. You've ruined everything! You've ruined everything! Why did you do it?"

Harkness attempted to explain, but Diefenbaker shouted, "I won't argue with you any more," and the conversation ended. "It was a very unpleasant five minutes," Harkness recalls.

Harkness had no regrets. "I did it deliberately," he says. "I hoped it would force a final decision by the prime minister." But the Tuesday-morning cabinet meeting ended inconclusively when Diefenbaker left before it was over, and on Wednesday morning, January 30, another cabinet meeting saw Diefenbaker again rejecting Harkness's demand to fulfil the commitment to nuclear weapons, and Harkness again threatened his resignation. In fact, he left the cabinet meeting, went back to his office, and dictated a letter of resignation. Several cabinet colleagues came to see him at noon, however, and persuaded him to wait a little longer.

If there were sparks in Ottawa over Diefenbaker's speech, there were flames in Washington. Ambassador Butterworth's call for a quick American response to Diefenbaker had won fast approval among senior State Department and Pentagon officials, who had hurtled from logic to emotion in their fury at Diefenbaker. On Saturday, January 26, Willis Armstrong and his colleagues talked about the need to respond to Diefenbaker's House of Commons speech. Armstrong was the senior State Department official with direct operational responsibility for Canada, and he orchestrated the American reaction among officials of the State Department, the Pentagon, and the White House. On Monday they began a series of meetings in Armstrong's office, and after heated discussion, they decided on an extraordinary public rebuke of the prime minister rather than an ambassadorial protest or the traditional private diplomatic note of protest. It was a measure of their rage. "We felt we just had to say something public," says Armstrong. "Diefenbaker had made an erroneous statement on a major, important subject. Our own policy had been improperly described. Unless we issued a public statement, we would never catch up. You just couldn't let it pass. Besides, we'd had experience with Diefenbaker with formal notes. They kept getting lost somehow in Ottawa, if Ottawa didn't like them.

"And we were tired of the fuzz from Diefenbaker that surrounded the whole issue. We'd been getting it for months. We hoped it would force Diefenbaker to get off his duff and decide."

Butterworth, who had been in Ottawa for only two months, demanded a hellfire-and-brimstone response. "We decided we had to set the record straight," he said. "There was too much at stake. We decided to do it that way because Canadian statements had not come in polite notes through channels, but on the floor of the House. If you want to play rough, then we'll play rough, too."

On Monday and Tuesday, Charles Ritchie and his minister, Basil Robinson, were informally warned that a public reaction was under consideration at high U.S. levels. "It was clear they weren't going to take it lying down," Robinson remembers. Robinson and Ritchie cautioned their State Department contacts against any public slap at the prime minister, but, as Robinson has written, "our approach received a polite hearing, but had no chance of survival against the wave of indignation which Diefenbaker's speech had unleashed."

Washington was embittered at Diefenbaker's indecision on nuclear warheads for North American defence, but it was his interpretation of Nassau that sent the Americans over the brink. "Diefenbaker portrayed himself as a confidant of Kennedy and Macmillan, and he had grossly misrepresented the U.S. position," says Rufus Smith, who was the U.S. counsellor for political affairs in Ottawa at the time. "He had to be set straight. His words could have been misinterpreted by other NATO allies."

The Americans felt Diefenbaker's speech implied some secret Kennedy–Macmillan agreement profoundly changing NATO nuclear strategy without any consultation with other NATO members. De Gaulle had referred to "the Anglo-Saxon Nassau conspiracy," and already worried queries had come in from Germany, Italy, and other NATO capitals asking for clarification. Rusk says this was "very damaging" and "insufferable" for the Americans. "We were besieged," one U.S. official said, with queries at the State Department, the Pentagon, and the Atomic Energy Commission. "We needed to reassure our European allies quickly."

The Americans were also infuriated at Diefenbaker's revelation of the secret Canada–U.S. talks on nuclear warheads for the NORAD Bomarcs and interceptors, especially after the prime minister had explicitly warned that any leak about the talks would result in an immediate breaking-off by Canada.

Butterworth cabled suggestions for the statement to the State Department and sent Rufus Smith to Washington to help draft the document. With Armstrong chairing, half a dozen officials from State, the White House, and the Pentagon met in his office through the early part of the week, shaping the rebuke to the Canadian prime minister. The more they examined Diefenbaker's speech, the angrier they got. "Now, where the hell did he get that idea?" Armstrong exploded at one point.

As they drafted and redrafted the statement, they were aware of the almost unheard-of public indignity they were planning. "For God's sake, it was like tossing a match into dry hay," admits Rufus Smith.

Armstrong agrees they knew it would be explosive. "We were in effect saying that the prime minister of a neighbouring country is lying in his teeth, and that's not a normal or easy thing to do," he says. "But we were exasperated with Diefenbaker. Reasonable conversation had gotten nowhere. All you got was another plate of fudge."

Smith remembers one official asking, "Are we really calling the prime minister a liar?" They were, and, they felt, with good reason. The officials shuttled between Armstrong's office and their own offices in State, the Pentagon, and the White House, checking the drafts with their superiors to be certain everyone agreed on the precise wording. They knew there was a possibility that a public rebuke to Diefenbaker might boomerang against the man they really wanted as prime minister, Mike

Pearson. They knew he might be labelled a "little Sir Echo" of Washington.

As the officials sat in his office, Armstrong reminded them that the State Department had issued a correction to something Diefenbaker had said earlier about NATO and the prime minister, he said, had later thanked them for it. "There was no problem then," Armstrong said. "Diefenbaker just said, 'Thank you very much. I was wrong.'" This time, however, they knew they were handling a "correction" with far greater explosive potential.

By Wednesday morning, they had finished the draft of the press release. It was sent on for polishing by Under-Secretary of State George McGhee and then final State Department approval by George Ball, who was the acting secretary of state since Rusk was away. Throughout the drafting of the release, Ball had been kept fully briefed on what was being done. He was contemptuous of Diefenbaker, angered at Diefenbaker's delay in fulfilling the commitment to nuclear warheads, but most of all, Ball was furious at what he felt was the prime minister's gross distortion of the Nassau talks for domestic political purposes. Ball had been at Nassau and was the architect of the Kennedy–Macmillan agreement; he felt personally affronted by Diefenbaker's interpretation of it. "I was slightly amused by Diefenbaker," Ball says unsmilingly. "It was a charade what Diefenbaker was doing, political shenanigans."

Nor was Ball admired by Diefenbaker, who felt the American was a "pushy" and "arrogant" Kennedy acolyte. In fact, however, Ball had been a campaign manager for Adlai Stevenson before Kennedy named him to the State Department. He was a blunt-speaking lawyer with a wide knowledge of Canada and Canadian issues. Aside from being a significant architect and ardent advocate of Kennedy's foreign policy, he was a friend of Mike Pearson ("A very engaging personality," Ball says) and a committed continentalist. Ball urged Canada–U.S. free trade, later noting, "The result will inevitably be substantial economic integration which will require for its full realization a progressively expanding area of common political decision." Ball rejected Diefenbaker's nationalism, saying, "Canada, I have long believed, is fighting a rearguard action against the inevitable."

With that thinking, Ball was easily convinced of the wisdom

and necessity of publicly excoriating the prime minister, and he gave quick approval to the press release. But such a major attack on an ostensibly friendly prime minister of a neighbouring country demanded President Kennedy's approval as well.

Late Wednesday afternoon, Ball telephoned McGeorge Bundy at the White House to ask the national security adviser to get Kennedy's okay. Like almost all the others around Kennedy, Bundy was a product of the eastern establishment. He had been the youngest dean at Harvard, where he headed the Arts and Sciences faculty, before he joined Kennedy's White House – in short, he had all the credentials Diefenbaker disliked.

Ball told Bundy, "Time is of the essence." "He felt we ought to have it out by the end of the day," Bundy says.

Kennedy was not immediately available at the time – he'd started his day with an 8:45 A.M. coffee reception for Democratic senators and had hurtled from meeting to meeting after that. He was to wind up with a 9:45 P.M. speech to a B'nai B'rith Anti-Defamation League dinner. Throughout the day, however, his preoccupation had been de Gaulle's formal veto the day before of British membership in the Common Market. But both Bundy and Ball knew of Kennedy's anger at Diefenbaker's statements and his bitter distaste for the man himself. "He was sore as hell at Diefenbaker," Ball says.

Feeling the time pressure from Ball, and convinced it was the right thing to do, Bundy remembers, "I thought the president would agree with it, so I told Ball, 'Go ahead.'" The action, after all, fitted in with Kennedy's interview at the beginning of the year, when he spoke of taking a stronger NATO leadership role even if he had to risk "offending sensitive allies." And Ball remembers that "a lot of things Bundy did, he didn't clear with Kennedy. It speeded up the process and got us into trouble only a couple of times."

This was one of those times. Bundy's "Go ahead" was to cause the sharpest Canada–U.S. confrontation since the War of 1812.

With White House approval, Ball quickly notified his colleagues. Phone calls went out to Butterworth in Ottawa (Rufus Smith had flown back a couple of days before) and to the

Canadian embassy. Canadian reporters were also telephoned and told by State Department public relations officer Jim Bishop, "We've got something interesting. It's about the nuclear warhead stuff. At a quarter after six."

As he spoke, Willis Armstrong read over the release one more time:

January 30, 1963
PRESS RELEASE
UNITED STATES AND CANADIAN
NEGOTIATIONS REGARDING NUCLEAR WEAPONS

The Department has received a number of inquiries concerning the disclosure during a recent debate in the Canadian House of Commons regarding negotiations over the past two or three months between the United States and Canadian Governments relating to nuclear weapons for Canadian armed forces.

In 1958 the Canadian Government decided to adopt the Bomarc-B weapons systems. Accordingly two Bomarc-B squadrons were deployed to Canada where they would serve the double purpose of protecting Montreal and Toronto as well as the U.S. deterrent force. The Bomarc-B was not designed to carry any conventional warhead. The matter of making available a nuclear warhead for it and for other nuclear-capable weapons systems acquired by Canada has been the subject of inconclusive discussions between the two Governments. The installation of the two Bomarc-B batteries in Canada without nuclear warheads was completed in 1962.

In addition to the Bomarc-B, a similar problem exists with respect to the modern supersonic jet interceptor with which the RCAF has been provided. Without nuclear air defense warheads, they operate at far less than their full potential effectiveness.

Shortly after the Cuban crisis in October 1962, the Canadian Government proposed confidential discussions concerning circumstances under which there might be provision of nuclear weapons for Canadian armed forces in Canada and Europe. These discussions have been exploratory in nature;

the Canadian Government has not as yet proposed any arrangement sufficiently practical to contribute effectively to North American defense.

The discussions between the two Governments have also involved possible arrangements for the provision of nuclear weapons for Canadian NATO forces in Europe, similar to the arrangements which the United States has made with many of our NATO allies.

During the debate in the House of Commons various references were made to recent discussions at Nassau. The agreements made at Nassau have been fully published. They raise no question of the appropriateness of nuclear weapons for Canadian forces in fulfilling their NATO or NORAD obligations.

Reference was also made in the debate to the need of NATO for increased conventional forces. A flexible and balanced defense requires increased conventional forces, but conventional forces are not an alternative to effective NATO or NORAD defense arrangements using nuclear-capable weapons systems. NORAD is designed to defend the North American continent against air attack. The Soviet bomber fleet will remain at least throughout this decade a significant element in the Soviet strike force. An effective continental defense against this common threat is necessary.

The provision of nuclear weapons to Canadian forces would not involve an expansion of independent nuclear capability, or an increase in the "nuclear club". As in the case of other allies, custody of U.S. nuclear weapons would remain with the U.S. Joint control fully consistent with national sovereignty can be worked out to cover the use of such weapons by Canadian forces.

At quarter past five, Basil Robinson received a phone call from the State Department to go over to Armstrong's office immediately. With a foreboding sense of alarm, he arrived at quarter to six, and Armstrong, an old friend, brusquely handed him the 450-word press release. "It was a very crisp meeting," Robinson recalls. Armstrong, "in a stiffly businesslike manner," Robinson says, told him the statement was being released in half an hour's time. Robinson scanned the release with rising alarm and indignation. "This is going to raise hell," Robinson said. "I'm not surprised," answered Armstrong.

For fifteen frosty minutes they argued about the substance and tone of the American statement. Robinson, having worked closely with Diefenbaker and knowing what an explosive emotional reaction the prime minister would have to the statement, was shaken. Armstrong said the Kennedy administration knew there would be concern and controversy in Canada.

"I got increasingly irritated at it all," Robinson says. "The way it was being done. . . . I felt amazed and indignant . . . but there was no point in arguing." He rushed back to the embassy just as reporters were gathering in State Department spokesman Lincoln White's conference room. The dozen or so reporters were greeted by the normally jovial "Linc" White, who looked glum; he was unusually quiet and muttered about the press releases still coming off the mimeograph machines. Finally they arrived and White emphasized that this was a full State Department release, not a statement by any individual official. That meant it had the full backing of the U.S. government. He read it very slowly before handing it out and refused all questions. The reporters were stunned as they heard it, hardly believing their ears at such a blunt attack on the leader of a friendly neighbouring nation. Since White offered no more details, reporters scrambled back to their offices to write stories and phone contacts about the astonishing public repudiation of the Canadian prime minister.

Equally thunderstruck was Ambassador Ritchie, whose first reaction was that it "was an absolute outrage, the most blatant, heavy-handed, intolerable piece of bullying. And who the hell do they think they are?" He felt it was a "horrendous miscalculation" by the Americans, who, he believed, "welcomed this opportunity to injure the government of Mr. Diefenbaker." Like Robinson, Ritchie didn't quarrel so much with the substance of the U.S. attack; it was the "heavy-handed and overbearing" way they did it that infuriated him. While reporters were still writing their stories, Ritchie was on the phone to Ottawa and packing to fly to the Canadian capital. He had been recalled as a diplomatic protest, the first time in the history of Canada–U.S. relations that that had occurred.

Reviewing the release twenty-seven years later, Armstrong

says, "It had a deliberate, clear, plain tone. I think that it reads pretty well, although we recognized there would be some downside damage to Canada–U.S. relations. But I slept well every night. I had a perfectly clear conscience."

Butterworth didn't worry about any "downside." "Very useful," he cabled the State Department a few days later. "Highly beneficial in advancing U.S. interests by introducing realism into a government which has made anti-Americanism and indecision practically its entire stock in trade."

John Diefenbaker was stunned by the release. It was "like a bombshell," an aide said. He also couldn't believe his good luck. The State Department had given him, he thought, the gift of re-election. The prime minister was in Toronto that evening, delivering a speech to a black-tie dinner of a thousand members of the North Toronto chapter of the Association of Professional Engineers of Ontario. When he arrived from Ottawa, a furious Gordon Churchill called to read him the State Department release.

Just before Diefenbaker began his speech, reporters asked him, "Have you heard about the statement from Washington?"

"No. No . . . what is this?" he asked them. An aide took a copy of the statement to him in a small room, where he waited before speaking, but he didn't have much chance to study it as his hosts gathered about him. In his speech, he told the meeting of the qualities needed for political leaders ("courage, patience, and a sense of humour") and he warned the engineers, "No one knows what the future may bring." What it had brought him, he believed, as he read the State Department release on his plane back to Ottawa that night, was a sure-fire election issue. As his hero Sir John A. Macdonald had done so successfully, he would campaign against what Sir John called "the wretched Americans."

Donald Fleming sat facing Diefenbaker on the plane back to Ottawa, and they discussed the Washington statement. "We've got our issue now!" exulted Diefenbaker. "We can call our general election now!"

"No, John, you can't do that!" Fleming argued heatedly. It would be, he said, "an irresponsible and divisive issue."

"No, we've got our issue now," Diefenbaker repeated.

Fleming was aghast at the idea of a campaign based on anti-Americanism. "To me," he later said, "it was utterly un-thinkable. [It] could do profound and lasting mischief."

Bunny Pound remembers Diefenbaker's excitement at the press release. "We've got them," he said. "Everything's going to be okay." When he got to Ottawa that night, he told reporters at the airport, "No comment"; he went home, had something to eat, and went to bed a happy man.

The next day Charles Ritchie flew to Ottawa from Washington. His recall was meant as a slap in the face to the Kennedy administration. He later said, "I had hopes of repairing the damage . . . [finding] some way to paper over the crisis and get the U.S. to apologize. . . . But I was so naive when I saw the Prime Minister. I was a virgin in a whore house. The last thing they wanted was to paper over the cracks."

Ritchie went to Diefenbaker's East Block office with Howard Green and listened as the prime minister bitterly attacked the U.S. ambassador, Walton Butterworth. "It was quickly clear to me," Ritchie says, "that my little suggestions were not what they wanted to hear." Looking at Diefenbaker and Green in the prime minister's office, Ritchie thought of them as "two old men, old cronies, old scarred soldiers of political battles."

"A pretty brazen interference," Green said. He believed the release was a deliberate attempt to destroy the Diefenbaker government.

The cabinet met that morning. Harkness remembers Diefenbaker's gleeful defiance of Kennedy: "He immediately proposed that we should dissolve right away and go to the country on an anti-U.S. stand. . . . He kept on pounding at that. . . . He was convinced he could win an election on an anti-U.S. appeal and this, to him, was all that mattered."

Harkness argued that an anti-American campaign would "do terrible damage to the economy of the country, weaken the NATO alliance, and endanger the defence of Canada and the continent as a whole. . . . None of these arguments seemed to worry him in the slightest."

At this point, Diefenbaker was aflame with his obsessive anger at Kennedy. Ellen Fairclough was shaken at the intensity of the prime minister's anger. "He was frothing at the mouth," she says. "He was so mad. Oh, he was furious, just furious!" But he listened to Harkness, Fleming, George Hees, and other cabinet ministers, and reluctantly put off his plan to call an immediate election on an anti-Kennedy, anti-American platform.

The galleries were jammed when the House of Commons met that Thursday afternoon at two-thirty; the parliamentary halls echoed with thumping desks, rhetorical spleen, and cries of "Shame!" as MPs from all sides of the House denounced the Americans. Quivering with outrage, the prime minister thundered, "This action by the Department of State of the United States is unprecedented – and I weigh my words when I said that it constitutes an unwarranted intrusion in Canadian affairs. . . . [Canada] will not be pushed around or accept external domination or interference in making its decisions. Canada is determined to remain a firm ally, but that does not mean she should be a satellite." Reflecting on the State Department action, Diefenbaker later told a television interviewer, "President Kennedy was going to obliterate us. I dared to say to him that Canada's policies would be made in Canada by Canadians."

One of the Social Credit party leaders, MP Robert Thompson, warned Diefenbaker that an election "carrying anti-American overtones would be a tragedy for Canada." And then he added, mystifyingly, "The United States is our friend whether we like it or not." Even Diefenbaker guffawed and slapped his desk at that.

But the prime minister was venomous in his thrusts at Pearson, saying the State Department press release "bears a striking resemblance to the statements made here last Friday by the Leader of the Opposition." Pearson was further stung when he rose to speak, as cries were heard of "Go ahead, Yankee" and "You want to dance with Uncle Sam." Diefenbaker himself interrupted Pearson's comments to shout, "When are you going back for further instructions?" and "Are you speaking for yourself?" "A cheap and false insinuation," snapped Pearson. For his part, Pearson endorsed the substance of the State Department release, but condemned the manner of Washington's protest as "inappropriate." Pearson also quoted Macmillan's denial of Diefenbaker's statement that the Nassau Agreement had affected Western defence policy.

NDP leader Tommy Douglas was almost as angry as Diefenbaker, and he told the House, "I think the Government of the United States should know from this Parliament that they are not dealing with Guatemala . . . nor are they dealing with Cuba."

NDP backbencher Douglas Fisher told reporters, "It is an insult to me as a Canadian. I see the next election between Diefenbaker and Kennedy, and Kennedy's going to lose." Liberal warhorse Jack Pickersgill agreed when he read the State Department release. "We thought we were sunk," he says.

Even Harkness was appalled at the State Department release. While he agreed with the substance of it, he felt the public rebuke of Diefenbaker "was a very stupid thing to do. They undermined me. . . . I think they did themselves a great deal of damage. All they had done was to make things much worse."

Bill Lee, who had laboured so vigorously to undermine Diefenbaker's position on warhead acquisition, was equally unhappy with the State Department action. "We could have done without it," he says. "They didn't realize how well we were doing."

All this was music to Diefenbaker's ears, and he now felt he had an effective political reason to further delay an answer to Kennedy on nuclear warheads and that he could, in effect, run against Kennedy and win an election. He could even tie in Pearson as Kennedy's "lap dog."

But not all Tories agreed with his assessment. Dalton Camp strongly supported Diefenbaker on the nuclear issue with the Americans but warned that he "could not win against Kennedy in Canada."

The Americans were staggered by the intensity of the Canadian reaction, and none more so than President John F. Kennedy. "What the fuck have you done!" friends quoted him as saying when he first heard of the State Department release. He did not disagree with what was said, but he thought it monumentally stupid in political terms to say it publicly. He knew the State Department had given Diefenbaker a sack full of political hand grenades that not only could be used to stir up anti-Americanism but could also destroy the election chances of his friend Mike Pearson. He knew, too, that he would be blamed for it personally.

Kennedy immediately sought to distance himself from the press release. He went to extraordinary lengths to be certain that influential journalists portrayed him as angry about the release and having no part whatever in its preparation. He talked to his friend the widely read columnist Joseph Alsop, telling him he was "furious"; he assumed that Alsop would write about his anger and affirm that Kennedy had not been involved. Alsop did exactly that, saying the State Department was guilty of "yielding to the human – all too human – temptation to show up Prime Minister Diefenbaker who clearly deserved it [but] . . . yielding to this temptation only made a bad business worse."

New York *Times* correspondent Max Frankel was also made aware of Kennedy's reaction; in a CBC radio commentary he said, "President Kennedy blew his top in anger when the crisis burst upon him."

But Kennedy's most important conversation was with another friend,.a man with whom Kennedy discussed Canadian–American affairs more than any other: Canadian journalist Max Freedman, who wrote for the Winnipeg *Free Press* and the Manchester *Guardian*. Freedman had been a confidant of Kennedy since his early days in the U.S. Senate – he'd had breakfast with him on the morning Kennedy announced for the presidency on January 2, 1960, and they had discussed what Kennedy would say in his announcement and do in his political strategy. Indeed, Freedman was one of several credited with originating the phrase "the New Frontier." Walt Rostow was given credit by Kennedy for suggesting it, but Rostow says Freedman wrote a draft of the inaugural address for Kennedy in which he was the first to use the phrase.

Freedman had escorted Jackie Kennedy to the theatre, was a regular diner with the Kennedys at the White House in their upstairs private quarters, and often talked long into the night with the president about everything from summit politics and John Diefenbaker to baseball, about which he had an encyclopedic knowledge and eloquent enthusiasm. His not infrequent anger at an umpire was expressed not by the usual "Kill the ump" shout but by cries of "You clodpole," "You dunderpate," "You lummox," or, on occasion, "You Tom Noddy!"

Freedman, pudgy with slick black hair, grew up in Winnipeg. He had been an aide to Prime Minister Mackenzie King, was a great admirer of Lester Pearson, and loathed John Diefenbaker. His brother, Sam Freedman, became the chief justice of the Manitoba Supreme Court. He never went to university because his family couldn't afford it, but he read every word of Burke and Macaulay and was unquestionably the most scholarly member of the Washington press corps. He referred to himself as "a graduate of the University of Manitoba Library."

"I wouldn't change my office for a reserved seat in Heaven," he once said, and no wonder, with his unmatchable contacts at the White House. He relished his entrée and influence at the White House and nurtured a middleman role for himself between Kennedy and Pearson. Freedman's friendship with the Kennedys was no secret, but few people realized at the time how close and intense the relationship was.

Kennedy not only admired Freedman's sweeping knowledge and sparkling conversation but valued his insightful advice. "We admired Max's mind, his wit, and his eloquence," says Ted Sorensen, who adds that Freedman discussed policy issues with him and McGeorge Bundy as well as with the president. Kennedy discussed with Freedman Diefenbaker's visit to Washington in February 1961 and later had lengthy conversations with the correspondent about his presidential trip to Ottawa in May of that year. Freedman advised Kennedy on the diplomatic aftermath of the Bay of Pigs fiasco, and later in the summer he helped write the president's television address during the Berlin Crisis. He was a behind-the-scenes adviser during the Cuban Missile Crisis as well as the Congo Crisis. He also sent a steady stream of his speeches and articles to Kennedy.

When Freedman got married on June 28, 1962, in New Hampshire, to the wealthy widow of a Washington editor, Kennedy sent him a joshing telegram saying, "Heartiest congratulations on your marriage. We shall look forward to reading about this event in your New Hampshire affiliate, the Manchester *Union Leader*" – a vociferously anti-Kennedy New Hampshire newspaper.

With Freedman, Kennedy let down his hair and sought guidance in the private informality he could not have with Dean

Rusk and other officials. Indeed, he talked much more often with Freedman than he did either with his own ambassadors to Canada or the Canadian ambassadors to Washington. The intense, egocentric, and somewhat shy journalist passed information and advice from the White House to Ambassador Ritchie, with whom he had weekly lunches, and he was in touch with Pearson from time to time, both on his own and transmitting messages between Pearson and Kennedy.

With Freedman's rapier wit and Kennedy's brutal profanity, Diefenbaker's name and character were frequently on the White House guillotine. Freedman, with Kennedy's nodding agreement, would describe Diefenbaker as "perpetually truculent" or as "a pouting, erratic problem child" and characterize him as "a small boy with a chip on his shoulder who asserts his strength by snarling at grown men." Diefenbaker made Canada an international "laughing stock," he said.

"President Kennedy," Freedman reported shortly after the State Department release, "in the face of undeserved and unprecedented challenges by Diefenbaker, has never once wavered in his steadfast conviction that the repeated tantrums in Ottawa must not be suffered to impair cooperation with Canada. In short, the real story is the exact opposite of the one which Diefenbaker has put into circulation. . . . As one who is familiar with the whole record, I wish to testify that the publication of this record would forever shatter Diefenbaker's standing as a public figure." Freedman felt the Diefenbaker government had brought Canadian–American relations to the lowest point in history by a series of "catastrophic blunders."

In this new crisis over the State Department press release, the president turned to Freedman for advice. "Kennedy talked to Freedman. It was understood that was what had detached Kennedy from the release. He began to walk away from it. He immediately distanced himself," says Willis Armstrong.

Kennedy not only took advice from Freedman, but also, as he did frequently, sought to use the Canadian as a messenger. Kennedy asked him to phone the Canadian embassy to say the president "had no part" in the State Department press release. Kennedy also used Freedman's columns as a way of getting his thoughts out through friendly journalists, assuring him of supportive news reports. Kennedy told Freedman, as he had told Alsop, that he had not been aware of the State Department press release before it was issued and that he was outraged at the tactic, which, he knew, was bound to damage Pearson. Within hours of talking to Kennedy, both Alsop and Freedman were not only writing stories, but telling colleagues of Kennedy's anger, and so the story spread.

But the president took more direct action that Thursday morning after the press release had been issued with George Ball and McGeorge Bundy. Like two abashed scholboys going to the principal's office for a misdemeanour, Ball and Bundy entered the White House Oval Office to see a thunderous president. "We knew he thought we'd screwed up," says Bundy. "I certainly didn't anticipate what would happen."

"God damn you!" the president exploded. "Bundy, I know you don't know a goddam thing about politics, but George here knows a lot about it and should know better. George, how could you have done something as stupid as that?"

"Well, I thought we were right," Ball responded.

Kennedy said he knew the statement was right on substance but it was idiotic in style and timing. "Why in hell did you do it?" said Kennedy.

"He gave me absolute hell. . . . I've seldom seen him so angry," says Ball. "In no uncertain terms, it was clear I had made a mistake by not clearing the statement directly with him. I accepted the blame because I knew I was wrong. But the substance of our complaint was right."

For twenty minutes, Kennedy lambasted his two aides. "But after a while," recalls Ball, "he cooled off and became his jaunty self again."

Presidential aide and historian Arthur Schlesinger recalls some "bitter kidding" of Bundy around the White House for his "single-handed destruction of Canadian–American relations." As Bundy himself admits, Canadian policy questions were "not my happy hunting ground." A couple of years later, in a memo to President Lyndon Johnson on Canada–U.S. relations, Bundy made a light-hearted reference to the State Department press release: "I myself have been sensitive to the need for being extra polite to Canadians ever since George Ball and I knocked over the Diefenbaker Government by one incautious press release."

Ironically, a couple of hours after dressing down Ball and Bundy, Kennedy found himself at a White House ceremony presenting the American Heart Association "Heart of the Year" award to General Norstad, whose press conference four weeks earlier had set off the most recent series of incidents. That night, Basil Robinson hosted a long-planned dinner party attended by some of the same American officials who had just castigated the prime minister, including Willis Armstrong. "It was difficult," Robinson wrote his parents, "because some of the people there were actors in the drama, but it came out well enough."

McGeorge Bundy re-emphasized to Canadian embassy officials that Kennedy did not know of the press release in advance; Bundy said he had "goofed . . . a case of stupidity and the stupidity was mine." But he was not too upset, telling Ritchie that he had "never spent a sleepless night about it."

Kennedy's special counsel and longest-serving aide, Ted Sorensen, says that while Kennedy was unaware of the release before it was issued, the president "did not like and did not respect Diefenbaker and had no desire to see him continue in office. . . . Diefenbaker and his government not only refused to fulfill their commitments on the location of nuclear warheads on Canadian soil, but . . . consistently misrepresented both their position and that of the United States."

Ritchie characterized the press release as "in the Boston Irish style of politics." "Kennedy," Ritchie now says, "was an Irish street fighter with a layer of sophistication on top. It was the layer on top that mostly irritated Diefenbaker."

"JFK decided that I must be KO'd," Diefenbaker later told a television interviewer. "Never before in history, certainly not since 1898, had the American government interfered as directly as it did. It came out with the attack."

It was all a Kennedy coup d'état conspiracy, he believed, to get rid of him and install Pearson as prime minister. He was reinforced in that belief by the ardent and repeated comments of his special assistant Burt Richardson and Howard Green. They felt sure Pearson had made a deal with Kennedy that in exchange for Pearson's switch on nuclear warheads, Kennedy would help destroy Diefenbaker. If Diefenbaker had known of the Freedman–Pearson–Kennedy relationship, he would have been even louder in his conspiracy accusations. But as it was, he felt surrounded by traitors. He added together the Norstad statement, Pearson's nuclear policy reversal, the State Department release, the pressures from the RCAF and the Pentagon, the growing media antipathy, his own cabinet crisis, and the party's unease – and concluded that Kennedy was a Machiavellian monster pulling all these strings to oust him. "They're trying to destroy me!" he shrieked at colleagues.

Health Minister J.W. Monteith agreed, as did Immigration Minister R.A. Bell, who said later, "My gut reaction is that Kennedy had decided that the government has got to go and that Kennedy treated Canadians like a parish in some backwoods place in Manitoba. I certainly wouldn't put it past Kennedy just to say, 'Get rid of these bastards, get them out of there.' The most cold-blooded individual I ever met in my life."

Today many Canadian officials remain convinced that Kennedy knew about the release beforehand and that its objective was to get rid of Diefenbaker. "It was as deliberate an attempt as ever made to bring down a foreign government," says Ed Ritchie, former under-secretary of state for external affairs. "Kennedy must have known in advance and the game plan was to hold to the story that he didn't know. You can't prove it, but it's a cover-up that worked."

Even Pierre Trudeau accepted the theory of Kennedy intrigue. In an article a few weeks after the release, he linked, as did Diefenbaker, Norstad's Ottawa trip, Pearson's nuclear switch, and the State Department statement as all part of a political scheme to oust Diefenbaker. "But how do you think politics works?" he wrote. "Do you think that General Norstad . . . came to Ottawa as a tourist? . . . Do you think it was by chance that Mr. Pearson . . . was able to quote the authority of General Norstad? Do you think it was inadvertent that on January 30 the State Department gave a statement to journalists reinforcing Mr. Pearson's claims and crudely accusing Mr. Diefenbaker of lying? You think it was by chance that this press release provided the Leader of the Opposition with the arguments he used abundantly . . . ? You believe that it was coincidence . . . ? But why do you think that the United States should treat Canada differently from Guatemala when reason of state requires it and circumstances permit?"

Some in the American media believed that, too. Scripps-Howard columnist Richard Starnes wrote, "Adroit statecraft by the American State Department brought down the bumbling crypto anti-Yankee government of John Diefenbaker. . . . The American intervention was coldly calculated to do precisely what it did – and it was a brilliant success."

Dean Rusk, however, bitterly denies any such scheming. "If anybody suggests that the CIA was given a mission to go up there and destabilize the Diefenbaker government, that's non-sense," he says. George Ball today laughingly dismisses the idea that he or Kennedy was trying to overthrow Diefenbaker: "I didn't know I had the power. . . . I wish I'd thought of it. I would like to have seen him out, but that wasn't the objective."

"Quite unintentional," says Bundy. "It was never intended that it would bring the government down. The conspiracy theory is all baloney."

"Did we try to knock him over?" asks Willis Armstrong. "No, we didn't. No, we just thought that it might solve the problem, or at least he would fish or cut bait."

Weighing the evidence of the participants leads to the con-clusion that Kennedy, in fact, did not deliberately use the press release to "knock him over," but that his White House and State Department colleagues knew that he profoundly wished to see the end of John Diefenbaker, and they felt sure he would endorse the release.

Rusk, who had had nothing to do with the preparation of the press release, was alarmed by the accusations of conspiracy spilling out of Ottawa. Prompted by Kennedy himself, he sought to minimize the damage at his eleven o'clock news conference on Friday, February 1. Kennedy had telephoned Rusk the day before to make sure that Rusk would make it clear that he, Kennedy, had had no part in the State Department release.

In as close as he came to an apology, the secretary of state said, "We regret it if any words of ours have been so phrased as to give offence, but the need to make some clarifying statement arose from a situation not of our making." But then Rusk went on to defend the release. "Without notice to us – and we understand how this can happen in the heat of debate," he said, "there was a disclosure then of confidential exchanges between our two governments and a number of arguments were put forward by various speakers, which appeared to offer new interpretations of the policies of the United States. . . . It became clear that we should have to give some account of our own views. . . . I believe the facts of the position as we understand them were fairly set out."

"A further intrusion into Canadian public debate," Diefenbaker responded. "Mere words. . . . We do not need any assistance from the State Department. Canada is not in the New Frontier of the United States."

The U.S. Congress now got into the controversy, ordering Rusk to appear on Monday at a hearing of the Canadian Affairs Subcommittee of the Senate Foreign Relations Committee. Subcommittee chairman Senator George Aiken, a seventy-year-old Vermont liberal Republican long interested in Canadian affairs, said, "It is difficult to understand why it was seen fit to express official displeasure with Canada by a public rebuke. . . . The administration has mishandled this matter."

Arthur Krock, a New York *Times* columnist and long-time Kennedy family friend, put Aiken's distress in tougher language. He called the press release "one of the most ham-handed, ill-conceived and undiplomatic . . . in the record of American diplomacy." The Washington *Post* was equally caustic, calling the release "impolitic and undiplomatic, but worst of all, it was foolish." "Thoughtless," said columnist Walter Lippmann.

Basil Robinson feared the worst from the prime minister. "Now he was able to charge the Kennedy Administration with an 'unwarranted intrusion' into Canadian affairs," Robinson noted. "He would exploit this for all it was worth."

In Ottawa, at two cabinet meetings on Friday, Harkness, with bravery bordering on foolhardiness, again sought to get Diefenbaker's agreement to revive negotiations with the Americans on the nuclear warheads, which had sputtered into inactivity after the American rejection of Diefenbaker's "missing part" proposal. The prime minister would have none of it, however, and reiterated his demand for an immediate anti-

American election. He could not get a majority of cabinet to support him, and Harkness edged closer to a public break with Diefenbaker. Harkness's nerves began to fray; Ellen Fairclough remembers, "He popped little pills in his mouth all the time. His nerves were all shot." His colleagues persuaded him to hang on a while longer, and another cabinet meeting was scheduled for Saturday.

As the days passed after the jolt of Washington's public rebuke, the solid Canadian front against the Americans began to crumble. Almost everyone agreed the State Department tactics had been deplorable, but by the weekend, attention began to focus increasingly on the substance of the American complaint against Diefenbaker. His indecision on the nuclear issue, the accusation that he was failing to live up to commitments to NATO and Washington, and a widespread admiration for John Kennedy all led to evaporating public support for Diefenbaker, and a cabinet that was on the verge of self-destruction. "There is no question that the [State Department] action harmed the Diefenbaker Government and helped to weaken it immeasurably on the eve of its defeat," influential Conservative Senator Grattan O'Leary later wrote.

Ambassador Butterworth cabled Washington that Diefenbaker's anti-Americanism was not working. Quoting newspaper editorials, interviews, and business community comments, he said there was growing sympathy for the United States on the nuclear issue. By Saturday he was telling the State Department that Canadian public reaction had toned down "after first shock to a predominantly positive attitude." "Initial resentment at United States 'intrusion,' as was expected, widespread but by no means universal," he cabled the State Department. "Strong swing now clearly appearing in direction. . . . This overridingly important matter had to be brought into open and United States had long been patient and forebearing. Man on street interviews carried by press and radio reflect strong sympathy for United States position. . . . Major political cartoonists concentrating their ridicule on Prime Minister Diefenbaker."

In a memo to the president, Don Wilson, director of the U.S. Information Agency, said, "Our people in Ottawa expect Canadian opinion to continue to be more and more favorable toward U.S. point of view."

Friday night and Saturday in Ottawa, pro- and anti-Diefenbaker cabinet members furtively conferred in small groups, jockeying for a showdown. Some wanted an immediate election on the issue of American interference, others plotted to overthrow the prime minister. At both the Friday and Saturday cabinet meetings, Diefenbaker pushed his idea of calling an election on the anti-American issue. He demanded a yes or no answer from each member. "He was convinced he could win an election on an anti-U.S. appeal," Harkness says. "This, to him, was all that mattered. His dislike of Kennedy was quite a factor. He had become more and more anti-American."

Harkness was amused at Diefenbaker's intensifying anti-Americanism because, he says, "If anyone should have been anti-American, it was me." His great-great-grandfather was killed by the rebelling Americans in the Battle of Yorktown, his relatives fled north to Canada after the American Revolution, and his great-grandfather was killed by the Americans in the War of 1812.

Starting at nine on Saturday morning, Diefenbaker took the cabinet through a lengthy process of dealing with minor appointments before getting to the question of an immediate election call. There were vociferous objections around the cabinet table and several threats of resignation if an anti-U.S. campaign were launched. R.A. Bell recalled there was general support for Diefenbaker personally, but a sense that "he bloody well better pick up his socks and stop emoting." He didn't stop, however, and before the cabinet meeting ended at twelve-thirty, Bell said there was "another hell of a blow-up" as the prime minister grabbed his papers and rushed out "in one of his unbelievable displays of hysterical temperament." The whole question of the election was put off until another meeting of cabinet ministers, to be held on Sunday at 24 Sussex Drive.

Saturday night, this maelstrom of intrigue and high drama swirled into, of all places, the annual Parliamentary Press Gallery dinner. Gallery dinners are evenings of highly alcoholic, off-the-record high jinks; reporters perform skits lampooning the politicians, and the governor general, the prime minister, and other political leaders make valiant attempts at humorous speeches. This night, Diefenbaker was in a sombre mood. He declined to speak and was outraged at one musical skit that made fun of his normal hand-trembling and head-shaking as well as his feud with Harkness. Reporters sang that the prime minister was suffering from "Harkness's disease." "Tasteless and offensive" was Diefenbaker's later comment; he had not been wearing his hearing aid that night and believed the reporters had sung "Parkinson's disease." He also resented reportorial ridicule of his role in Nassau. "I had been marked for demolition. . . . They sang and acted out my physical and mental sufferings." Diefenbaker left the dinner early in a rage, escorted out by *Globe and Mail* reporter Walter Gray. Gray later told his editors that the prime minister was literally frothing at the mouth in anger. "He stood very close to me and shouted," Gray said. "I could feel the spittle on my face."

"With the gallery dinner tensions and the cabinet blowing apart, and all the resignation and election speculation, Ottawa seemed like it was just going to explode that weekend," says Keith Davey, Liberal Party national director at the time.

Diefenbaker had little sleep that Saturday night and was awakened between two and three in the morning by a phone call from a friend, reporting that Harkness, who also had been at the gallery dinner, had been well fuelled by alcohol as the evening wore on and was threatening to resign. Harkness denies the story and says after the dinner he took Air Marshal Frank Miller up to his office, told him he was going to resign if Diefenbaker did not accept nuclear weaponry, and then left for home at eleven-thirty. Miller, Harkness says, agreed that he had no alternative. At 24 Sussex, Diefenbaker drifted back into a troubled sleep as he thought over the evening and considered the next day's cabinet confrontation, scheduled for nine o'clock in the blue-walled dining room downstairs.

As Green, Harkness, Fleming, Sévigny, Hamilton, and the other cabinet ministers stamped their shoes and shed their coats on arriving in the bitter cold and swirling snow of Sunday morning, they knew this would be a watershed cabinet meeting. Diefenbaker knew that he was facing a cabinet revolt, that there would be an attempt to force him to resign, and that Harkness was on the verge of resignation. "They were planning mutiny," Howard Green said later. "They were planning or plotting a revolution."

As they sat down at the table, sipping orange juice, tea, or coffee, most of them tired and cranky since the gallery dinner had ended only a few hours earlier, the unseen presence of John Kennedy hovered over the dining room. Diefenbaker still lusted for an election over Kennedy's interference in Canadian affairs, and Harkness, even at this impossibly late date, still hoped he might pressure the prime minister to make a nuclear warhead deal with Kennedy. He didn't have a hope, however, because, among other things, Diefenbaker felt that Harkness had become, as he later said, "the puppet of the military mind." Still, Harkness thought he had a chance: "Diefenbaker was very concerned at the cabinet breaking up. If I resigned a whole lot more would resign. And I still thought there was a fair chance. The final decision was to be made that Sunday."

The meeting, however, was almost at once plunged into a convulsive shouting match. Diefenbaker reiterated his desire to hold an immediate election on the basis of "intolerable" American interference in Canadian policy on the nuclear warhead issue. George Hees, minister of trade and commerce, demanded a clear-cut decision on nuclear warhead acquisition but was shouted down by anti-nuclear, anti-American cabinet voices. Tempers flared as Diefenbaker referred to "a nest of traitors" within his cabinet. Harkness, flushed with anger and speaking in cold, biting terms, said Diefenbaker had lost the confidence of the nation and a large part of the party. "Prime Minister," he said, "the Canadian people, have lost confidence in you, the party has lost confidence in you, the cabinet has lost confidence in you. It's time you went."

There was silence for a few electric moments around the dining room table. Diefenbaker uttered a couple of sentences ignoring Harkness, then suddenly smashed his fist on the table and jumped to his feet. Harkness is "a traitor," the prime minister snapped, his face reddening in fury, and at that point "all hell broke loose," Pierre Sévigny says.

Alvin Hamilton was the loudest with "army language" denunciation of Harkness. "You son of a bitch!" he screamed. "You open, unashamed shit! After being in cabinet all this time, you've betrayed your prime minister." Broadening his attack to other anti-Diefenbaker cabinet ministers, Hamilton shouted, "You're a bunch of treacherous bastards. No prime minister ever had to deal with so many sons of bitches." Remembering with a sheepish grin, Hamilton now says, "Well, yeah, I blew my top."

"Alvin was ready for a fistfight," says Sévigny.

Now Diefenbaker was pounding the table, shaking in rage, and shouting in torment, "Who supports me and who doesn't? Stand up those who do!"

Howard Green, who was sitting beside Diefenbaker, shouted "Treachery . . . betrayal!" Donald Fleming, sitting on the other side of Diefenbaker, and Bell both shouted questions, unsure in the general chaos whether standing up as Diefenbaker demanded meant supporting him or dissolution.

Less than half stood and the rest sat, including Fleming and Bell, who were still trying to determine what they were voting for or against. "All right. All right," Diefenbaker said. "I'll go to the governor general. I'll resign."

"He stormed towards the door, saying he was going to Government House to submit his resignation," Bell later said. "He said he would resign by six o'clock that day. He then turned around and came back and, looking at Fleming, said, 'I'm designating my successor. It's you, Don. . . . You'll be prime minister by six o'clock.'"

Gordon Churchill shook his fist in Fleming's face and shouted, "Count me out! I wouldn't follow you, you little bastard Fleming! I wouldn't follow you anywhere." Harkness, on the other hand, says he would have supported Fleming as prime minister.

As Diefenbaker left the room, the cabinet ministers saw Olive coming up to him and saying, "Calm down, dear. Calm down. Calm down." Sévigny felt Diefenbaker was on the verge of physical collapse. "[He] was indeed giving every indication of being a very tired and possibly a very sick man," Sévigny says. "His face was pale and his nervous tics – the shaking of the head, the twitching of the lips, and the inability to keep the hands in a still position – were now more apparent than ever before."

Green, Hamilton, and three or four Diefenbaker loyalists walked to the door with Diefenbaker, saying they would resign, too, if the prime minister did. They went into the library next door to the dining room with the prime minister. Three or four of those remaining in the dining room went to the library to persuade the cabinet ministers to return. "It became a mob scene in the library with insults hurled and people shouting and pushing," said Bell. "It was just unbelievable that mature men who had the responsibility for the government of this country were conducting themselves like a bunch of school children." Meanwhile in the dining room, Fleming, fed up with the chaos, told Ellen Fairclough and several others, "I'm sorry. I'm going to church," whereupon he left the house, returning an hour and a half later to find the arguments still going on.

Finally Green, Hamilton, Churchill, and their colleagues were persuaded to come back into the dining room to continue the meeting and a tremulous and ashen Green took over as chairman of what had to be the wildest cabinet meeting in the history of Canada. After about an hour and a half, the pro-Diefenbaker forces had the upper hand. "There's no use fiddling any longer," Harkness said. "This is the end. I'll write out my resignation."

"Let him go," said Hamilton. "He was never anything but a drag on the party anyway." Nobody else offered to resign. "A failure in human courage," says Harkness, who had a reputation as a loner but had expected others would quit with him. As he rose from the table to leave, a now calm Howard Green made a speech paying tribute to his adversary. Harkness shook hands with a few of the ministers and left the room.

After more heated discussion, the ministers slowly calmed down and agreed they should support Diefenbaker. But they did not want an immediate election and said there should be an early meeting between Diefenbaker and Kennedy to settle the warhead issue. Bell drafted a document that spoke of full support for Diefenbaker, seeking "by every means to avoid defeat" in the House of Commons and saying "immediate consideration should be given by the Prime Minister and the Cabinet to an early meeting between the Prime Minister and the President of the United States to discuss an early settlement of all outstanding issues on defence policy." After further discussion, the cabinet ministers decided to leave out the reference to Kennedy, to avoid upsetting Diefenbaker.

With the document in hand, Green and Fleming left the room to bring back Diefenbaker, who was with Olive and his golden Labrador retriever, Happy, in the far corner of the living room, having a lunch of tea and sandwiches. To their amazement the prime minister was in "wonderful spirits." "I've had a good lunch," he said.

"He accepted the memorandum, with thanks," Bell said. It was clear when the prime minister came back to the table that he still longed for an immediate election because, he said, "The Americans are out to destroy me." He saw that a majority of cabinet opposed the idea, however, and the meeting broke up in the early afternoon with the cabinet members again expressing loyalty to the prime minister. It had been, as Bell said later, "the most fantastic meeting of ministers I'm sure that there's ever been in the whole history of Canada."

A short time later, at quarter to six, a messenger arrived at 24 Sussex with Harkness's resignation. "For over two years you have been aware," he wrote, "that I believed nuclear warheads should be supplied to the four weapons systems we have acquired. . . . It has become obvious during the last few days that your views and mine as to the course we should pursue for the acquisition of nuclear weapons for our armed forces are not capable of reconciliation."

Not since the 1944 Conscription Crisis had a cabinet minister resigned on a matter of principle. Although with Harkness's resignation, Green had finally won his anti-warhead battle, at least temporarily, he hadn't been sure of winning until then. "I never knew which side Diefenbaker was going to come down on, but he did come down on mine eventually," Green later said. In his letter of response to Harkness's resignation, Diefenbaker wrote, "I am at a loss to understand your suggestion . . . that your views and mine are not in agreement."

The plotting against Diefenbaker was not over for the day, however. Later that Sunday, the prime minister was visited by cabinet minister and Toronto businessman Wallace McCutcheon, who proposed that Diefenbaker resign and become chief justice of the Supreme Court, replacing Patrick Kerwin, who had died the previous day. McCutcheon suggested that George Nowlan, the finance minister, become prime minister. At nine o'clock Sunday night, George Hees and Davie Fulton came back to 24 Sussex. Diefenbaker recalled Fulton saying, as they sat in the library, that he should resign as prime minister "for the good of the party. We'll make you chief justice of Canada."

Diefenbaker rejected both overtures. "I would not agree to anything of the kind under any circumstances," he said.

"Hees came out and told me, 'We've offered him the chief judgeship of the land; he won't even take that,'" recalls Bunny Pound, who was at 24 Sussex all through what she describes as "that most awful, awful day." She remembers Diefenbaker telling her, "They're never going to get rid of me." And she adds, "He would never give in." She recalls being almost in tears with all the tension, and Gordon Churchill patting her on the back, saying, "It's not as bad as it seems."

Dick Thrasher worried about the intolerable pressures on Diefenbaker and urged him to resign for his own sake. "You don't have to put up with all this crap," Thrasher told him. But Diefenbaker refused. "I've got to stand for Canada," he said.

While Diefenbaker spent Sunday with the chaos of his cabinet, in Washington Dean Rusk spent the day preparing for his Monday grilling by the Senate subcommittee. Even though he had not been a participant in the preparation and release of the now infamous press statement, Rusk felt that, as secretary of state, he had to take full responsibility for it. This stance won him undying respect from his senior staff, who contrasted his action to Kennedy's. "Kennedy ran away from it; Rusk did not," says Willis Armstrong.

Republican senators said the Kennedy administration had deliberately issued the release to embarrass Diefenbaker and should have used diplomatic channels instead of going public. Occasionally stroking his shiny bald head nervously as he testified before the subcommittee, Rusk said a private diplomatic note would have been ineffective because Diefenbaker's parliamentary speech had publicly "misrepresented" the American views. It was necessary, Rusk said, to reassure Western allies that basic NATO defence strategy had not changed as the Canadian prime minister had claimed.

In discussing Diefenbaker's idea for "missing part" storage in the U.S., Rusk said the U.S. government had to condemn it because it was "a fraud." He said the Pentagon "could not figure out any way" to get the missing part installed in time, and besides, he said, there was "the chance of an actual nuclear explosion in the process of putting pieces into the weapons . . . under conditions of great urgency."

At the end of the Senate subcommittee hearing, the chairman, Senator Aiken, concluded that, while he agreed with the substance of the U.S. complaint against Diefenbaker, he thought the best policy would be for both countries to stay out of each other's domestic affairs.

After strongly defending the Kennedy administration press release for more than a quarter of a century, Rusk now admits it was wrong. "My impression is now that it was a mistake," he says. "Butterworth could have said it, or Ball could have had a press conference. There were various informal ways of getting the idea across. It was a mistake to release it in that form. There were other ways that were better than that.

"It was," Rusk concludes, "a very unusual thing to challenge the veracity of a head of a foreign state."

"Well," Rusk's under-secretary, George Ball, says today with a smile, "it seemed like a good idea at the time."

In Ottawa that Monday, it was the coldest day of the year; it was 19 below, Fahrenheit, and the nation's capital was drenched with political tension. At two-thirty, a raucous House of Commons met amid rumours of a cabinet collapse, a prime ministerial resignation, and an immediate election. The scene was reminiscent of the government-destroying Pipeline Debate seven years earlier, which eventually brought Diefenbaker to power.

Douglas Harkness rose to explain his resignation, saying his views and the prime minister's on nuclear arms were "irreconcilable." Harkness says almost up until the moment he resigned, Diefenbaker kept saying he'd get the nuclear weaponry "but then he'd say, 'This isn't the time.'" Now, Harkness says, he realizes the State Department press release had turned Diefenbaker "from delay to 'No.' He told me, 'I'm not going to let the State Department tell me what to do.'"

Amid the parliamentary commotion, opposition leader Pearson introduced a non-confidence motion, charging a lack of government leadership; if passed, it would defeat the government and mean an election. "I had enough of a political nose not only to smell their defeat, but our electoral triumph," Pearson later said.

In spite of his eagerness to go into an election, the prime minister wanted to do it on his own terms, and he was confident he could win the vote in the House of Commons. "The central question," he later said, "[was] whether Canadian policies would be made in Canada by Canadians or by the United States. . . . The Kennedy Government . . . had committed itself to aiding and abetting the Liberal Party in its attempt to throw out my government."

That Monday evening, Diefenbaker went home to dinner with his old friend David Walker, whom he had just made a senator. Diefenbaker had offered him the post of lieutenant-governor of Ontario, but Walker preferred the Senate. They talked about "the plot" against Diefenbaker, and the prime minister asked Walker, "The plot goes back for months. What shall I do?"

"You tell them to go to hell," Walker replied. He felt McCutcheon was the orchestrator of the plot to replace Diefenbaker with George Nowlan. He also thought Hees and Fulton harboured prime ministerial ambitions. Diefenbaker seemed somehow to thrive on the political excitement, and Walker remembers him eating two main courses and two desserts at an early dinner. The prime minister decided not to go back to the night sitting of the House, but to go to bed early after his tumultuous and nearly sleepless weekend.

On Tuesday, all eyes were on the House of Commons and the impending vote that would decide whether the Diefenbaker government would survive. In Washington, the State Department, the Pentagon, and the White House paused in the avalanche of world events crossing their desks to watch what was happening in Ottawa. "The president," said White House press secretary Pierre Salinger, "is keeping in close touch with the Canadian situation."

Ambassador Ritchie was now back in Washington and in close touch, too. Diefenbaker had wanted him to stay away from Washington for five or six weeks as a demonstration of Canadian anger at the Kennedy administration, but Ritchie persuaded the prime minister that his recall was not really

worrying the Americans. "Kennedy probably didn't even notice," Ritchie says. But that Tuesday, as he awaited the House
of Commons vote, Ritchie pondered his own future in a sombre
mood. He confided to his diary, "I have presided over this
Embassy during a time of collapse in Canadian–American
relations. Some must surely say that I might have done something to prevent the deterioriation. My grandfather put an
inscription on his second wife's tombstone: 'She did what she
could.' Hardly flattering to the lady. I suppose that might be
the verdict on my efforts. If there is to be a change, won't the
new government say to themselves, 'Let us start with a new
man in Washington'? Then what becomes of old Ritchie?
Banishment to our mission in Berne?"

At eight o'clock that bitterly cold Tuesday morning, George
Hees had been at the prime minister's front door, again asking
him to resign immediately and accept the appointment of chief
justice of the Supreme Court. Diefenbaker told him to "go to
hell." Throughout the morning, pressure built on Diefenbaker
to quit, and Diefenbaker fell back into a black mood. David
Walker, who had returned to Toronto the previous night, took
the 7:10 A.M. plane back to Ottawa at Diefenbaker's request.
He went straight to 24 Sussex, where he found Olive in a red
housecoat and Diefenbaker in tears. "I can't carry on with
traitors in our midst," he said. "I'm resigning."

"Like hell you are," said Walker. "Tell the sons of bitches to
go to hell." Walker remembers his support being reinforced by
Howard Green, who told Diefenbaker, in uncharacteristically
profane language, "Don't give in to those bird-brained bastards."

Throughout Ottawa's corridors of power there was talk of a
CBC-TV network resignation broadcast that night. The governor general cancelled a planned trip to Toronto so he would be
immediately available to accept any resignation. But by the
afternoon, the Diefenbaker supporters were gaining strength
and, thanks to efforts by Alvin Hamilton and Gordon Churchill, the Conservative MPs cheered when Diefenbaker arrived
in the House of Commons government lobby at two-thirty.
George Hees was warned by a Diefenbaker supporter, "When
Diefenbaker speaks this afternoon, you'd better bang your desk
at every opportunity or I'll break your arm!" R.A. Bell got a

similar warning from what he called "Western broncos" as he was entering the House. "One of them said he was going to knock my goddam block off, and he got his fists up, and I got out of his road as fast as I could." As the prime minister's loyalists cheered, however, the Social Credit and NDP, although both strongly anti-nuclear, had decided to support the Liberal non-confidence motion. "The issue didn't count," said the NDP's David Lewis. "It was a carcass; it wasn't a government."

In the House, Diefenbaker pleaded for support, especially to the Social Credit Party and particularly the Quebec members, who had hitherto backed the Conservatives. He spoke of how in the last century non-French Montreal merchants had wanted Canada to join the United States. "I believe," he said, "in the maintenance in spirit and in fact of Canada's identity, with the right to determine her own policy without extramural assistance in determining that policy."

Diefenbaker also brought out the ghost of Sir John A. Macdonald as he referred to the State Department press release, saying, "I cannot accept the fear of those who believe we must be subservient in order to be a good ally of any country in the world. Macdonald fought this battle." The prime minister accused Kennedy of moving in for the kill because of his political vulnerability. "It is obviously true that had we not been a minority government in 1963, President Kennedy would never have dared to intervene in Canadian politics," he later said.

Just before eight-thirty, Tory supporters hoisted Diefenbaker onto a table just off the floor of the House and serenaded him with "For He's a Jolly Good Fellow."

"The die, however, had been cast," Diefenbaker later said. "The 'fix' was in and I knew it." Half an hour after being serenaded, Diefenbaker was defeated in the House, 142 to 111, and that meant a spring election.

There was now intense pressure for Diefenbaker to resign as Tory leader. The *Globe and Mail* editorialized, "If Mr. Diefenbaker continues in the leadership, he will do the Party irreparable harm and perhaps destroy it as a national force."

"Diefenbaker was quickly becoming incoherent and more and more abusive," says Sévigny. "It became quite intolerable."

More and more party officials were lining up against him, but Diefenbaker clung to his party leadership by adroitly switching the times of a caucus meeting and a cabinet session the next day. Knowing he had more support among the MPs than in the cabinet, he met the caucus first. Amid shouts of "Shame," "Traitor," "Quitter," "Floorflusher," and "Georgie Porgie Judas," a teary George Hees spoke for nearly an hour, emotionally denouncing Diefenbaker's plan for an anti-American election campaign and warning of American trade retaliation. He also urged a nuclear deal with the United States. In the end, Hees was shouted down, and he said he would resign. Grattan O'Leary spoke eloquently on behalf of unity and Diefenbaker, as did others. After his own highly emotional threat to resign, Diefenbaker emerged with his leadership intact. "He'd always be saying, 'I'm going to quit. I'm going to quit,'" says Dick Thrasher. "But I don't think he ever was going to quit. It was more of an invitation: 'Support me.'"

The cabinet meeting later that afternoon was anti-climactic, with Diefenbaker, now with the backing of his MPs, in full charge. He told his colleagues that he would be solely responsible for defence policy statements in the election campaign. He said his approach would be "pro-Canadian," not "anti-American," but he recalled that both Sir John A. Macdonald and Sir Robert Borden had won elections on anti-American platforms.

In Ottawa the next day, Hees resigned as trade minister, saying he couldn't accept Diefenbaker's anti-Americanism. "I consider that our present defence policy does not either fulfill our international commitments or provide for the security of our country," Hees told the prime minister. "I have also stated clearly that I consider the present attitude of the government cannot but lead to a deterioration of our relations with the United States." Politically, Hees's resignation was more damaging than Harkness's. J.W. Monteith said later, "From a public standpoint, George Hees was the one that cooked us that election."

Associate Defence Minister Pierre Sévigny resigned, too. He also warned Diefenbaker against anti-Americanism. He said he was not "prepared to lend myself to a wholly unwarranted attack upon the government of a friend and ally who has expressed an honest and sincere apology for any embarrassment caused us by recent events. Any so-called pro-Canadian policy based on this event can only be interpreted as anti-Americanism and manufactured electoral propaganda. Action of this sort will be ruinous for Canada economically and could seriously impair the unity of the free world in matters of defence."

However, Sévigny quickly regretted his resignation. "I'm sorry I did it," he says. "I lost all my power and my influence when I resigned as a minister. I had no input any more." In the election, he lost his seat and was forever after out of politics.

Other cabinet ministers indicated they would resign if the prime minister campaigned on an anti-American platform. Immigration Minister Bell drafted a letter to Diefenbaker threatening to resign and saying, "An election campaign based directly or indirectly on antagonism to the United States of America would be intolerable to me." He didn't send the letter to Diefenbaker, but read it to him instead. His warning was rebuffed by the prime minister, however, who said, "I'll fight any sort of damned election that I like." Bell ran anyway and lost.

The prime minister was more accommodating to George Nowlan, who told the Halifax *Herald* that he had warned Diefenbaker that he too would quit immediately if the prime minister began an anti-U.S. campaign. "However, I am satisfied now that there is not going to be one," said Nowlan. "I am staying in the cabinet." Nowlan won by the narrowest margin of his career.

Donald Fleming decided not to join Diefenbaker in the forthcoming election, although his reasons were personal, not policy differences. Davie Fulton didn't run, either, moving into the political desert of British Columbia Conservative politics. Harkness was approached by the Liberals to run for them in Alberta. "He was a good man and we wanted him," says Keith Davey. "It was a feeler," Harkness says. "It was suggested I might be the minister of agriculture. But I wouldn't consider it." He ran as a Conservative and won, but it was years before Diefenbaker would speak to him again. "If we met in an elevator, he'd look at the ceiling," Harkness says. "If we'd pass in the corridor, he wouldn't say hello."

Intentionally or not, the Kennedy administration's press release had been the catalyst that led to the overthrow of the government of John Diefenbaker. It had encouraged the so-called "plotters" within the Conservative party in sowing anti-Diefenbaker dissent, and it had galvanized the opposition parties into a united rejection of Diefenbaker's minority government by publicly exposing Diefenbaker's indecisive leadership. "When Pearson made his switch . . . and when the U.S. openly supported the Liberal position, the fate of the Government was sealed," says a Tory MP of the time, Jack Horner. The State Department press release had been, in effect, the instrument of an unintended coup d'état.

Defeated in the House of Commons, deserted by key supporters and cabinet ministers, John Diefenbaker stood virtually alone in his battle to win vindication and re-election in the vote that was now set for Monday, April 8, 1963. As he wrote to his brother Elmer in Saskatoon, "It seems that life is just one problem after another."

Chapter Eight

LAST HURRAH

"It's me against the Americans, fighting for the little guy," boasted sixty-seven-year-old John Diefenbaker as he began his lonely crusade to retain the prime ministership in the April 8, 1963, election.

Diefenbaker didn't have a ghost of a chance, ran the conventional wisdom. The Liberals and almost all the media commentators felt he was filled with inflammable gas, staggering towards self-immolation and self-destruction. In his diary, Diefenbaker intimate David Walker wrote that it would be "a rout for the Tory Party and perhaps destruction for all time."

"When we started out, we were reeling from blows, self-inflicted blows," says Dalton Camp, the Tory campaign director that year. The Liberals went into the race leading the Conservatives in the public opinion polls, forty-seven per cent to thirty-two per cent, and they were brimming over with confidence, sure of sweeping Diefenbaker into political oblivion. Pearson thought the Liberals could parade in with 175 seats, an overwhelming majority. "No question, we expected to win a good majority," says Keith Davey, Liberal party national director at the time.

Entrapped by desertions and insurrections within his own party, blasted by the rich and the élite, Diefenbaker himself felt, as he later admitted, "Defeat was in the air." It was going to be, said J. W. Monteith, "a pretty gruesome campaign."

Diefenbaker's strategy was essentially issue-less; instead the old warrior went clanking forth in a campaign of moral outrage against "them." His targets were the Americans, the élite, the media, the big-city sophisticates, and the Bay Street power brokers. His was the politics of revenge as he proclaimed, "I've been derided. I've been condemned. It seems everybody is against me but the people." The political pros and those in the know giggled as he dripped with messianic self-pity and nine-teenth-century platform histrionics, brandishing the polemics of paranoia.

"Never have the wealthy and the clever been so united as they were in their joint attack on Mr. Diefenbaker," philosopher George Grant later wrote. "The full power of the Canadian ruling class, the American Government and the military were brought against him."

Most of the nation's newspapers were against the angry old lion, and so were most Ottawa reporters. R.A. Bell claimed most of the press gallery had been against Diefenbaker since 1959 when he invited them for tea at 24 Sussex and served only tea.

Truth is usually the first casualty in both war and politics, and in the prime minister's 1963 campaign truth became as fragile as a snowflake in May. "He was regarded as a liar," says Arch MacKenzie, former Canadian Press Ottawa bureau chief, not-ing the prime minister's frequent embellishment of such things as his connection to Khrushchev's shoe-banging at the UN. "He was like a man in a fortress. He was capable of being paranoid in the best of times."

"He had been the darling of the press in 1957," Diefen-baker's special assistant Dick Thrasher says. "He had been God in 1958. People fought to reach out to touch him then. Now, his world seemed to be falling apart around him."

But as the campaign got under way, he threw off his despair of late January and early February, the dark pouches under his eyes began to disappear, and he came alive again, like a crusad-ing defence attorney with the country as his courtroom. "The campaign had a galvanizing effect on him," Dalton Camp says. "He was horrible in 1962 because he didn't understand the issue. He was not comfortable and didn't know how to handle it. But he was a counter-puncher, you know, and in 1963 there was nothing to lose. He knew what to do. . . . The campaign gave him adrenalin. He always needed that."

He loved politics but anguished in governing. So now he was suddenly rejuvenated, back on the hustings, whistle-stopping his way across the country; he was leaving behind what he did worst, managing the nation, and taking up what he did best, attacking his enemies: "They who smear. They who vilify. They who condemn and they who menace you," he said. Always identifying himself with his nationalist hero, he said, "In 1886 they attacked Macdonald with the same kind of vilification." Tory stalwart Grattan O'Leary later wrote: "His glands required the excitement of being strapped to a plank while the giant buzz saw screamed nearer and nearer."

Diefenbaker sought to win not on issues, but by a psychic bonding with his fellow Canadians, especially those in the small towns and villages and on the farms. "There was no question," he later said, "that everyone was against me but the people and that unless I could find a way to get the message across, I would be lost. . . . I had to wage a one-man, whirlwind campaign." With his repeated cries of "I'm for the little man" and "They can't push me around," he sounded a demagogic drum roll of defiance against what he perceived to be the forces of darkness allied against him. Sympathy poured out to him in small-town Canada for his valiant defence of the nation against the Americans and for his dedication. At one point he said that when he ended his political career, he would get a pension of only $2,900 a year, although in fact he knew that arrangements had been made by party supporters to ensure him a comfortable financial future.

Although his "vision" of Canada had faded since 1957 and 1958, Diefenbaker's evangelical fervour could still bring tears and cheers on the prairies and in the Maritimes, where there was a ready willingness to credit the allegations that Diefenbaker was being "done in" by "them" in Ontario, Quebec, and Washington. "He was a past master at portraying himself as being a victim," says Pierre Sévigny.

Always at his side, encouraging, advising, and sustaining him, was Olive Diefenbaker, who laughed at every joke she had heard a thousand times and applauded at every speech. She looked over at Bunny Pound at one stop in the campaign and hissed sharply, "Bunny, you're not applauding!"

Emulating his hero Harry Truman, Diefenbaker campaigned by train, spoke at station stops, and mainstreeted small towns. He visited hundreds of barber shops, Chinese restaurants, cigar stores, and bus stops, shaking hands, slapping backs, and remembering names. Resounding with apocalyptic resentment, he attacked "the great interests against me. . . . They ridiculed, they reviled, they lampooned. Every form of vituperation that can be used has been used against me."

His flaming-eyed nationalism led the Toronto *Star* to compare him editorially to "some alcoholic patriot in a tavern." The *Globe and Mail* said disagreement with the United States "is no excuse for Canadians to act like witless and hysterical fools," while the Montreal *Star* warned Diefenbaker and his supporters against behaving "like the outraged citizens of some banana republic."

But for all the criticism, Diefenbaker's style was working. His revivalist exuberance and platform theatrics contrasted dramatically with Mike Pearson's bow-tied, lisping greyness. It was Diefenbaker the fighter against Pearson the mandarin. The fat public opinion poll lead that Pearson took into the campaign began to shrink (by April he had fallen from forty-seven per cent to forty-two), and most of the blame landed on his image.

Pearson's handlers tried to make him into a decisive, shirt-sleeved, down-to-earth Canadian, but they never quite succeeded. "A dangerously large and influential body of opinion holds that Mr. Pearson is really not interested in domestic affairs and, as a consequence, is not now and is never likely to become a genuinely effective leader," said one of his public relations consultants in a report made the previous year to campaign officials.

At times, Pearson would get exasperated with the efforts to reshape his public image and to make his speech-making more forceful. "Oh, for heaven's sake!" he would cry. "I don't want to hear any more," he told his press aide, Richard O'Hagan. "I'm just going to make my own speech in the way I want."

In a letter to his son Geoffrey, Pearson bemoaned modern campaigning. "Political appeals – on the strict partisan level – have now – with mass media – been reduced – if they are to be successful – to an 18th century illiterate simplicity. I don't like it – but there it is." A Liberal colleague of Pearson's, J.J. Greene, sympathized with his leader. "People were trying to make him a Kennedy when that wasn't his bag," Green said.

In person, Pearson exuded boyish charm, but on a platform or television screen he came across as impersonal and unsure. If Diefenbaker had known Pearson had suffered an emotional breakdown during World War I, as historian John English has revealed in his recent biography of Pearson, the Conservative leader would have had an opportunity to exploit this political vulnerability. He may not have taken it, however, because of his own and perhaps not dissimilar vulnerability. Diefenbaker had been injured in a training accident in a trench in England during World War I and was shipped home. Although he loved to tell stories of his past, he rarely spoke of his wartime injury; only once in their more than a quarter-century relationship did he mention to Bunny Pound that his bad back was caused by an injury "overseas." Some say a trench-digging tool struck him in a bloody accident, while others, including Alvin Hamilton, say a trench fell in on top of him. Whatever the cause of the accident, Hamilton says, he had been "trapped like a rat" and had developed an irrational fear that lasted all his life. "He was even frightened of driving a car," says Hamilton. "His fear of rejection was also something terrible. It all went back to his physical fear in the war."

Walter Gordon, Pearson's campaign manager, said Pearson's lisp bothered people, and his bow tie gave him a wimpish image. "They just didn't like the bow tie," Gordon later said. "They thought it was effeminate or they thought it reminded them he had been a diplomat or some damn thing. . . . They don't like people who are too sophisticated." Pearson's political team also emphasized his nickname of "Mike" over what was felt to be the less politically attractive "Lester." He got the nickname in World War I from his Royal Air Force squadron commander, who felt "Lester" was too sissified for a pilot-trainee.

Kennedy's pollster Louis Harris was brought back for the campaign and his message again was: "Emphasize the Liberal team." Harris was expensive for the Liberals, with his five hundred poll-takers, high phone bills, and travel back and forth to New York. "Paid plenty," says Keith Davey. "Paid through the nose!" But Harris was worth it, for his advice and polling sharpened the Liberal efforts; in any event, the party could afford it because it was well financed and well organized as it went into the campaign. The Liberals had just about everything going for them, but the problem was the leader. "We were worried," Harris says. "Support for Pearson was soft in some areas. Pearson was not a jugular politician like Diefenbaker. Now, Diefenbaker had that sense. He was a terrific politician."

What Diefenbaker did so well and Pearson did so poorly was not only political theatrics, but taking a few themes and repeating and refining them in every speech at every stop. Harris would develop a theme such as picking up Kennedy's campaign motto of "Get the country moving again," but Pearson would resist repeating it endlessly. "Well, I've said that," he would tell Harris. "I'm bored with it."

"Yes, but you've got to say it over and over, again and again," Harris would reply, with little result. "There was too much Adlai Stevenson in Pearson," Harris says. "He wasn't as bad as Stevenson, but close, with his dislike for new techniques and his preoccupation with international affairs. The people wanted to hear the bread-and-butter gut issues."

Harris lectured Pearson on how Kennedy had succeeded, saying, "Kennedy had no qualms about concentrating on these mundane issues, no qualms at all, and you shouldn't either." But Pearson resisted being transformed into a tough-talking, domestic-issue politician. "Most Canadians, I think," he later said, "wanted me to continue to wear the mantle of international statesmanship."

Pearson's single greatest fear in the campaign was John Kennedy and what he might do. Pearson was petrified that his White House friend might do or say something good about him, which Diefenbaker would leap to exploit. The worst moment for Pearson came in Edmonton, at a Legion meeting, the third and last engagement of a long campaign night. A phone call came in for Pearson about nine o'clock. When he arrived, the meeting chairman whispered to him that there was "an urgent call" for him from the White House. The janitor had taken the call. Richard O'Hagan, Pearson's press aide, called back to find it was Max Freedman, calling after a late private dinner with Kennedy. He insisted on talking to Pearson only, so O'Hagan passed the message to his boss. Mystified and alarmed, knowing what Diefenbaker might do with such information, Pearson followed the janitor to a basement office. Nervously, he picked up the phone. They spoke for fifteen minutes, with Freedman enjoying his role as middleman between Kennedy and Pearson, passing on the highlights of his conversation with the president that night and some of Kennedy's suggestions. "For God's sake, tell the president not to say anything," Pearson said. "I don't want any help from him. This would be awful."

"Pearson was appalled at the call," O'Hagan remembers. "He felt Max was a little indiscreet to make the call to a public place. It took some doing to keep the call under wraps."

"This was a narrow escape," Pearson later said, "since I knew there were people abroad in this land who would . . . insist that it was a deep dark American plot to take over the country via Pearson and the Liberals. To my relief, it never was reported; the janitor said nothing about the call."

The same message to "not say anything" went to Kennedy from both Lou Harris and Walter Gordon. "Keep your cotton-pickin' hands off the phone to Pearson!" Harris told the president shortly after the campaign began. Meeting him in the Oval Office, Harris complained about the State Department press release, saying, "The release was horrendous for Pearson. If this is the best you can offer in support of Mike Pearson, for Christ's sake, call your dogs off."

"Precisely," the president responded.

"And for God's sake, keep quiet about Pearson no matter what you're feeling," Harris added.

"You don't have to tell me things like that," Kennedy said.

But in one unguarded moment, Kennedy did say something favourable about "my friend" Pearson, and he was immediately jumped on by Gordon. When Harris told Gordon he saw Kennedy from time to time, Gordon said, "Tell the silly bastard to keep his mouth shut! I thought he was a pro. He's not even an amateur."

A few months later when Gordon had become finance minister and was introduced to Kennedy at a White House reception, Kennedy said, "I think I know you."

"I'm afraid you've heard of me," said Gordon, nervously

jiggling his large martini goblet. "Did Lou Harris give you a message?"

"Yes," said Kennedy.

"I hope he expurgated it," Gordon said smiling.

"No," said Kennedy. "I got it straight and of course you were right. I never should have said a word."

Kennedy issued instructions that no U.S. official should say anything about Canada, Diefenbaker, Pearson, or warheads during the Canadian election campaign. McGeorge Bundy phoned Ambassador Ritchie to tell him of the Kennedy gag order and Ritchie, in turn, advised Howard Green. "Kennedy made it very clear," says McGeorge Bundy, "that nobody was to talk about Canada." The great fear at the White House, he says, was that Pearson could be damaged by any American official saying anything.

If Kennedy and his colleagues around the White House were aware of the need to be cautious in their public comments, there was no doubt that to a man, from Kennedy on down, they wanted Diefenbaker out of office. Kennedy, says historian and aide Arthur Schlesinger, "did not like and did not respect Diefenbaker and had no desire to see him continue in office."

"Kennedy liked Pearson because he was bright, humorous, and a liberal," says Keith Davey. "Kennedy was a great believer in the quality of individuals," Bundy says. "Pearson was a man of evident quality. Temperamentally similar to Kennedy. Clear, easy, open. A highly civilized politician."

"I admired Mike Pearson," says George Ball. "He was a nice, decent fellow. He was much like Adlai Stevenson."

"We simply preferred Pearson," Dean Rusk says. "He was a founder of the UN, of NATO, was ambassador to Washington." Rusk remembers that early in his State Department career, there was a crisis in Berlin; when he asked for guidance from the secretary of state, George Marshall, Marshall told him, "Talk to Mike Pearson about it and see what he thinks."

In spite of his instructions to others, however, Kennedy himself kept talking to friends and officials about Pearson. "We had a lot of trouble with him," says Willis Armstrong, who kept getting White House calls to his State Department office on the election. "He wanted to intervene and make sure Pearson got elected. It was very evident the president was uptight about the possibility that Pearson might not win."

Armstrong says Kennedy never actually talked to Pearson personally during the campaign, but he tried several times. "He kept chasing Pearson around Canada by phone," Armstrong says. "He could have been a terrible embarrassment to Pearson. But when Kennedy wanted something, he charged." Not being able to talk to Pearson directly, Kennedy used Max Freedman as a messenger for advice and offers of help. One unsigned memorandum to the president in the White House files is indicative of Freedman's role.

"Max Freedman called:

"Re: Diefenbach's [sic] statements.

"Said he talked with Mike Pearson, who was very grateful for your offer, but Max felt that Pearson did not feel that anything would be gained by doing anything about the statements at this time. He said that the reaction in Canada has not been as bad as the papers have said here. Therefore, unless more is heard of this matter he will perhaps not do anything about it."

Another Canadian with influence in the Kennedy administration was the British Columbia journalist Bruce Hutchison, who journeyed regularly to Washington. Several of Hutchison's old and close friends happened to be working at the senior levels of the White House, the State Department, and other critical areas of the American establishment. On his visits to the American capital, Hutchison would sometimes stay at the home of Bill Bundy, a senior State Department official and a brother of McGeorge Bundy, with whom Hutchison was also very friendly. He was also close to George Ball. "Saw a lot of him," Ball says. Along with Freedman, Hutchison burnished Pearson's already glowing reputation in Washington.

Hutchison wrote to McGeorge Bundy as the election campaign got into full swing, saying the president should not worry about any lasting damage from the State Department press release. "I can assure you, despite all signs to the contrary that [Canadians] have not taken leave of their senses and I would hope the President understands this fact," Hutchison wrote in a "Dear Bundy" letter.

Bundy replied less then a week later, saying, "Dear

Bruce. . . . I agree that the way it was said was a mistake. I also take great courage from your conclusion, which we share, that our relations are not undone by one 'slip of manners'. I only wish the American writers understood this point as well as you do, but I am sure you will be able to do some good when you are down here – above and beyond the necessary task of educating those of us who are trying to avoid further slips."

Hutchison sent Bundy an article in which he said the "final disintegration" of the Diefenbaker government "was caused solely by an attempt to quarrel with the United States. . . . The first lesson of these events, therefore, is that no anti-American government can live long in Canada. . . . As practical politics, anti-Americanism is dead."

One former Diefenbaker cabinet minister, Donald Fleming, worried about the anti-U.S. flavour of the prime minister's campaign and wrote to his old friend, U.S. Treasury Secretary Douglas Dillon, saying Canada–U.S. harmony "is one of the most important facts in the world today." Dillon passed his letter on to Kennedy to demonstrate that there were others in the Conservative party less hot-headed than Diefenbaker. "Apparently he felt that he could not campaign for re-election under the Diefenbaker program and saw no alternative but to leave public life," Dillon wrote Kennedy.

Kennedy was still concerned about the political impact of the State Department release, however, and hoping fervently for Pearson's election. He told an aide, "I suppose if this works out and Pearson is elected, those guys over at the State Department will think they were right all along."

Rusk watched the campaign closely. He warned the Canadian government against any "misrepresentation" of U.S. policy by Diefenbaker during the election campaign. He told Ritchie the administration "wanted to feel free to clarify its position if it was misrepresented," Basil Robinson recalls. The warning was never passed to Diefenbaker.

Diefenbaker said later, "No one will really ever understand the tremendous force of American propaganda as it was mobilized by the Liberal Party. . . . President Kennedy asked, demanded, that I be removed." Diefenbaker claimed Kennedy spent "one million dollars" to defeat him. He wanted to assault Kennedy head-on from the campaign platform, but pressure from his colleagues restrained him. "The problem was to keep him from launching an attack on Kennedy. He couldn't win that," says Dalton Camp.

Despite Kennedy's admonition to keep quiet about anything Canadian, the Americans kept inadvertently providing Diefenbaker with campaign ammunition. *Newsweek* magazine, whose Washington editor was Kennedy's close friend Ben Bradlee, made a martyr of Diefenbaker with a venomous cover story attacking the Canadian prime minister. It was headed: "CANADA'S DIEFENBAKER, DECLINE AND FALL." "Britain's Prime Minister Harold Macmillan can hardly bear the sight of him and President Kennedy dislikes him cordially," the magazine said. It quoted a British Conservative member of Parliament as saying, "It would be too flattering to dismiss him just as a superficial fellow. He's really much dimmer than that." The unflattering front cover picture showed a pouting, defiant Diefenbaker. *Newsweek* said, "He has run the country like a tantrum-prone country judge. . . . Diefenbaker in full oratorical flight is a sight not soon to be forgotten; . . . the Indian rubber features twist and contort in grotesque and gargoyle-like grimaces; beneath the electric gray V of the hairline, the eyebrows beat up and down like bat's wings; the agate blue eyes blaze forth cold fire."

Keith Davey, who first saw the *Newsweek* cover portrait of Diefenbaker in the Château Laurier newsstand when he came out of a Liberal meeting, says, "It was a mean, impossible picture."

Dalton Camp called Diefenbaker at 24 Sussex Drive as soon as he saw the magazine. "It's a scarifying piece," said Camp.

"One of my better pictures?" enquired Diefenbaker lightly. "What's it say?" The prime minister insisted Camp read the whole article to him, from time to time interjecting to tell his wife about it. "Olive, did you hear that!" he would say, repeating to Camp, "Read it all, read it all." At the end he asked Camp, "What are you going to do about it?"

"I'm going to mail it out to everybody on the party list," said Camp.

"Good. You do that," replied Diefenbaker, already relishing the political benefit he could get from more evidence that Washington was out to get him. A short time later, Diefenbaker got a one-page letter of sympathy from Richard Nixon, who noted his own problems with the media and deplored the vilification of the Canadian prime minister in a U.S. magazine.

Diefenbaker said Kennedy had encouraged Bradlee in the story; he probably was right that Bradlee had discussed it with the president. "The *Newsweek* article was all part of a plan to destroy me," Diefenbaker told a Charlottetown campaign audience. He referred to the article repeatedly in his campaign speeches, generating sympathy for himself.

Pearson almost gave Diefenbaker another advantage when he considered endorsing Canadian membership in the Organization of American States. He planned to announce he favoured OAS membership in a Victoria speech, but was talked out of it at the last minute by his old friend Bruce Hutchison. "Okay, I'll skip it," he said. In light of President Kennedy's earlier "pushing" of Canada to join OAS, a Pearson endorsement would have given Diefenbaker another chance to charge that Pearson was a Kennedy "puppet." In any event, Max Freedman had advised from Washington that the Latin American nations were uneasy about Canadian membership after Canada's hesitant behaviour during the Cuban Missile Crisis.

Diefenbaker found some political ammunition, however, in a relatively innocuous report on foreign aid submitted to President Kennedy by an American committee chaired by General Lucius Clay. The prime minister cited it as another example of American interference in Canadian affairs. Among its recommendations was, "Canada to raise the volume of aid." A year before, another report by U.S. foreign aid director Frank Coffin had criticized Canada for contributing only 0.21 per cent of GNP to aid Third World nations, compared with the United States or the United Kingdom, which gave nearly three times that percentage. Diefenbaker, remembering he had rejected a Kennedy "push" on foreign aid at their Ottawa meeting, snapped back at the latest American effort. "I'm not here to take any lectures from anybody on what Canada has done to assistance programs," he told a Kelowna, British Columbia, election rally. In Pincher Creek, Alberta, with what an aide had earlier described as "the power of his glower," Diefenbaker said, "Let that be clear . . . we don't need any lessons on what Canada should do."

Howard Green took up the criticism of the U.S., charging that the Americans were "spying" on him. Before the campaign began, he told Rufus Smith, who was the U.S. minister to Canada at the time, that he had seen Smith in the diplomatic gallery in the House of Commons, acting suspiciously. "I saw you up there today taking notes and watching what was going on," he told Smith when they met later at a reception. Green felt the CIA was watching him, too. Smith had written to the U.S. consuls across Canada to keep themselves fully aware of the issues that arose in the election campaign and especially those that affected the United States. Chuck Kisseljak of the U.S. embassy (in whose basement recreation room Ambassador Livingston Merchant had briefed Canadian reporters in what Diefenbaker had characterized as a "treasonous" effort to undermine him) was assigned as the embassy link to the Liberal party during the campaign, Willis Armstrong says. "But it was purely normal information-gathering," he adds.

Richard King, the U.S. vice-consul in Vancouver, attended two Howard Green rallies and also asked the Conservative party for texts of Green's speeches. This was acutely suspicious behaviour, Green thought, and he told a reporter, "I don't like the idea of the U.S. State Department following us around." At a coffee party in Cranbrook, British Columbia, Green complained of an American being present who did not explain who he was. "I don't know whether he was a CIA agent or not, but he certainly was a most peculiar visitor at a coffee party," Green said.

Alvin Hamilton accused "the Kennedy gang down there" of actively trying to defeat Diefenbaker. "Consul generals of the United States were all informed by somebody, it was their duty as American citizens in Canada to do everything they could to defeat Diefenbaker," he said. American companies raised money for Pearson, he said, "because they thought he was pro-American and we were supposed to be anti-American."

Dean Rusk laughingly dismisses any such American intervention in the Canadian election. "I can't imagine that the United States has the slightest capacity to tell the people of Canada how to vote," he says. "People across the border don't let us campaign about who's going to be elected."

Prime Minister Diefenbaker, however, believed he had proof

of U.S. intervention. He received a copy of a letter supposedly written to Pearson by American Ambassador Butterworth, congratulating Pearson on his switch in nuclear warhead policy. On U.S. embassy letterhead, it began: "Dear Mike. . . . We appreciated your statement which indicated that the points of view expressed by the Liberal Party and my Government are identical. As the result of your address, no other Canadian politician on record has gained as many devoted friends in my country as you have. . . . It will be quite evident to the elector- ate that the policy of the Conservatives is narrow-minded and that they are unfit to continue governing the country. . . . I would like to discuss with you how we could be useful to you in the future."

The copy of the letter Diefenbaker received was postmarked Acton, England, and had been given to former Conservative leader George Drew, who had become the Canadian high commissioner in London. Drew called an old friend in Ottawa, Conservative Senator and Ottawa *Journal* president Grattan O'Leary, saying, "I have a hot document here." The president of the CBC, Alphonse Ouimet, happened to be visiting Drew's office at the time, and the high commissioner gave the letter in a sealed envelope to Ouimet to take back to Canada. Ouimet did not know what was in it. O'Leary telephoned Dalton Camp, who dispatched an aide to Montreal to get the letter from Ouimet as soon as he landed. "It was 'hot cargo,'" says Camp, and he sent it over to Diefenbaker immediately. O'Leary and Diefenbaker met in the prime minister's private railway car in Toronto to discuss it a few days later. "This has got to be published," Diefenbaker told him. "You have got to publish this."

"No, we can't publish it," said O'Leary, who didn't like the look of it and believed the letter was "a complete forgery." "My God, it was libellous as hell," he said later.

Diefenbaker, disgruntled, stuffed the letter back into his pocket, unconvinced by O'Leary's argument. Camp, who was aboard the train as it chugged through southwestern Ontario, was also convinced the letter was a fake. "We all knew it was a forgery," he says. "We all said, 'Don't use it!'" Diefenbaker, however, insisted on trying to get it published, so he talked with Senator Allister Grosart about it. Grosart, the former national director of the party, left the train and went to Toronto to see Winnipeg *Tribune* publisher Ross Munro, who was in Toronto at a publishers' meeting. Munro was instinctively doubtful about the letter's authenticity and called Butterworth in Ottawa. Butterworth exploded with indignation and said it was "a complete forgery."

Diefenbaker's campaign took him next to British Columbia. Undeterred, he showed the letter to Howard Green and urged Green to return to Ottawa at once to confront Butterworth with the letter. Green would not do it. Diefenbaker then suggested that Green "secure samples of Butterworth's signature so that a comparison could be made." Green again refused because, he said, it "would arouse suspicion."

Diefenbaker was fuming at this second rebuff in his effort to use what he called "the Butterfingers affair." When he discussed the letter with Bunny Pound at the Empress Hotel in Victoria she told him, "It's a forgery. Rockcliffe is spelled wrong."

Diefenbaker angrily left her and went on to Winnipeg, where he pursued the matter with his new defence minister, Gordon Churchill. Like Diefenbaker, Churchill disliked Butterworth, calling him "an ugly American type." The prime minister asked Churchill to "investigate" and try to get it published.

Eventually, in the dying days of the campaign, the letter finally was published in a small Manitoba newspaper and picked up by the wire services. It never had much impact, however. Even so, Butterworth was outraged and called Pearson to urge him to deny the story. Butterworth also called the State Department, demanding a public denial by the U.S. government. "The State Department told him to calm down," recalls Rufus Smith, "and Butterworth was angry at them."

A few months later an RCMP investigation found that neither of the two typewriters in Butterworth's office had been used for the letter and that the paper and envelope were English in origin. The RCMP concluded that it was a forgery. Diefenbaker believed ever after, however, that the letter was real. "I have since concluded," he later said, "that it was a true copy and that not using it constituted a major political error."

One American document that was genuine, however, surfaced during the election campaign – the Rostow memorandum the president had lost in Ottawa that had urged Kennedy to "push" Diefenbaker on a number of issues, including OAS and foreign aid. It had remained secret for two years, lying in Diefenbaker's "vault." But in the heat of the campaign, Diefenbaker's aides privately told reporters of the document's existence, hoping it would win him sympathy votes. They suggested the prime minister might release the text of the memo. The Ottawa *Citizen* front-page lead story by Southam reporter Charles Lynch proclaimed, "SECRET PAPER DISCLOSES U.S. PRESSURING CANADA." Diefenbaker at first denied the existence of the memo. "I don't know where that story came from. . . . I have to repudiate it," he said in Kelowna. But his aides continued to talk about it, and Diefenbaker himself had repeatedly referred to it privately. "It was an open secret," says Camp. "He kept saying, 'One of these days, I'm going to tell the Canadian people about it.'"

In Ottawa, the handful of officials who were aware of the secret memo shuddered at the prospect of the prime minister using the document in the political arena. In Washington, officials remembered Diefenbaker's threat a year earlier to Livingston Merchant that he might use the memo to demonstrate how Kennedy was pressuring Canada. Kennedy was furious at the public revelation of the memo; five days after the story broke, he told his friend Ben Bradlee that it was at the root of all Canada–U.S. problems. After a private White House dinner one night, Kennedy told Bradlee it was a "blockbuster" story, which he would tell him if Diefenbaker lost the election. Asked what he would do if Diefenbaker did not lose, Kennedy said, "Well, then we'll just have to live with him."

The memo story became more intriguing when gossip circulated among the press that Kennedy had scribbled in the margin of the memo, referring to Diefenbaker as an "SOB." It quickly became known as "the SOB memo." The president could not remember writing anything on it, although he often scrawled indecipherable notes in the margins of memos.

Kennedy wanted to be sure his side of the story got out, now that the memo's existence had been revealed in Ottawa, and he showed Bradlee a report to the president on the incident, labelled "Eyes Only, Secret." He told Bradlee, "At the time, I didn't think Diefenbaker was a son of a bitch. I thought he was a prick."

Kennedy also talked to a senior Washington *Post* reporter and to Hugh Sidey, *Time* magazine White House correspondent. Kennedy barked at Sidey that he didn't write "SOB" on the memo. "That's untrue," he said. "I'm not that stupid. . . . And besides, at the time, I didn't know him so well. . . . Now I want you to get this damn thing about Diefenbaker correct. I've been in this damn business long enough to know better than that. . . . Some day – it can't be told now – but some day," Kennedy told Sidey, "you'll know just all the difficulties we've had in dealing with this man."

Those who have seen the memo, including Basil Robinson, say there was no "SOB" in the margin. That part of the story had begun after Lynch's article appeared. Montreal *Star* Washington reporter Peter Trueman wrote that he had been told there was a scrawled critical comment about Diefenbaker in Kennedy's handwriting on the memo. His story caused a sensation. Kennedy talked to Freedman, and Freedman dropped into Trueman's office; reflecting Kennedy's own anger, he snapped, "That story is wrong. It's a fabrication."

Kennedy himself ordered his press secretary, Pierre Salinger, to call Trueman to deny the story. In a memo to the president, Salinger said, "Mr. Trueman said, however, that the phrase 'S.O.B.' was supplied to a Montreal *Star* reporter as the missing phrase by an aide to Prime Minister Diefenbaker at a rally in Ontario, Canada last night."

Trueman disputes the Salinger memo, saying that he had in fact heard about the "SOB" from a source in Washington. He had written it into his story, but the Montreal *Star* editors took it out. "They weren't going to put such a naughty phrase in the paper," Trueman says.

Kennedy directed Salinger to warn Rostow about the fuss in case he were chased by reporters. Salinger finally located Rostow at the Royal Military College in Kingston, where he was giving a lecture. "Where are you?" said Salinger. "Well, I'm in Canada giving a lecture." "Oh my God," said Salinger. "We ought to smuggle you out!"

As it turned out, Rostow escaped the media, and Diefenbaker, still being pressed by many supporters to curb his anti-American rhetoric, decided not to use the Kennedy memorandum in his campaign, so it faded as an election issue.

The prime minister's defensive nationalism intensified, however, as the campaign progressed. "We are a power, not a puppet," he said at one stop. "We make our policies in Canada, not generated by pressures or visits across the border," he said at another. "I want Canada to be in control of Canadian soil," he cried at yet another stop. "Keep Canada Canadian," he demanded. "A Canadian I was born, a Canadian I will die." His cry was a twentieth-century echo of Sir John A. Macdonald's nineteenth-century pledge "A British subject I was born, a British subject I will die." Diefenbaker's speeches reverberated with Macdonald's 1891 anti-U.S. campaign oratory. A Kennedy aide, reviewing the campaign, said Diefenbaker's speeches were filled with "snide comments, insinuations, innuendoes and other anti-U.S. overtones." Kennedy told Max Freedman the Diefenbaker campaign was "contemptible."

But it had worked for Macdonald in 1891, and Diefenbaker was convinced it would work for him in 1963. Agriculture Minister Alvin Hamilton cheered on his "Chief" with his own brand of defiance against the Americans. "I say to my friends across the border," Hamilton told a Montreal meeting, "'Don't push us around, chum.'" He complained, "They don't even know we're a sovereign country up here. They think we're a Guatemala or something." This not only riled the U.S. State Department, it angered Guatemala, whose consul general in Montreal strongly protested the remark as a slur on Guatemala's independence.

On another occasion during the campaign, Hamilton raved with resentment at Kennedy's pushing Canada to accept nuclear warheads for its interceptors, Bomarcs, and Honest Johns. "Ye gods," he said. "Where were the Americans in 1914 when Canadians were dying in Europe in defence of freedom, and where were the Americans in 1939, 1940, and 1941 when we were dying?" Although discredited by the political sophisticates as a "boob and a rube" and, at best, "a lovable hayseed," Hamilton was by far the most effective political supporter for Diefenbaker in the campaign, with his record of selling wheat to China, pushing wheat prices up from $1.60 to $2.19 a bushel, and tripling net farm income. As well, he had a reputation for speaking his mind. "His colleagues used to say

Alvin Hamilton doesn't speak, he just froths at the mouth,"
said R.A. Bell. "He was sort of a ham," says David Walker. But
behind his nickel cigars and reputation as a "poor man's
Diefenbaker," Hamilton was a shrewd politician. "Alvin was a
tower of strength," says Bunny Pound. "Alvin was one of the
few people who would be honest with the prime minister."
Although he recognized his mentor's warts, Hamilton to this
day maintains, "Diefenbaker was the only hope for little guys
getting anything."

Diefenbaker resented what he believed was Kennedy's ma-
nipulation of NORAD officials to oppose him during the election
campaign. He blamed the White House for orchestrating the
visits to NORAD headquarters of various groups from Toronto,
Montreal, and elsewhere during the campaign; he charged the
Canadians were being "propagandized" by Air Marshal
Slemon, the deputy commander of NORAD. Under questioning
by the visiting groups, Slemon would strongly insist that nuclear warheads were absolutely necessary for North American
defence. Most visitors came away from Colorado Springs convinced that he was right and Diefenbaker was wrong on the
issue.

There was no doubt the senior NORAD officers were bitterly
opposed to Diefenbaker. The NORAD commander, General
John Gerhart, told reporters in San Diego in early March that
Canada's Bomarcs were ineffective without nuclear warheads.
Two weeks later NORAD headquarters issued a news release
responding to a Diefenbaker campaign speech in Halifax, where
he had said Bomarcs could be refitted to use conventional
warheads. NORAD replied that a conversion of the Canadian
Bomarc-B missiles to conventional warheads would cost an
extra $30 million, take three years, and, in the end, be "vastly
inferior" to using the nuclear warheads for which the Bomarcs
had originally been designed. Thus, NORAD said, it had no
interest in developing conventional warheads for the Bomarcs.

The RCAF's head of public relations, Wing Commander Bill
Lee, also publicly denounced Diefenbaker's contention about
Bomarc conventional warheads, telling reporters, "It's an ab-
solute lie." When called onto the carpet by Defence Minister
Gordon Churchill, Lee said he was simply telling the truth, and

he was backed by the air force chief of staff, Air Marshal Hugh Campbell. Churchill just shrugged his shoulders and urged Lee to be more prudent.

Most U.S. congressmen kept quiet during the campaign, but a few, like Pennsylvania Democrat Dan Flood, could not resist taking shots at Diefenbaker. "I don't like the Diefenbaker government," he said, "because that government doesn't pull its weight in hemispheric defence." Oregon Senator Wayne Morse bitterly attacked the Diefenbaker government, saying that Canadians should be warned "the U.S. can no longer afford to furnish the protection of our military strength while they decline, for domestic political reasons or any other, to fulfill their obligations to us."

The Washington atmosphere remained decidedly uncomfortable for Canadian officials throughout the campaign, so much so that Canadian Ambassador Ritchie declined to go to the annual Gridiron Club Dinner, similar to the Ottawa Parliamentary Press Gallery dinner, "in case someone made an unflattering reference to Diefenbaker and created a further incident."

Pentagon officials made a serious blunder near the end of the campaign when, in simple ignorance of the issues of the Canadian election and Kennedy's own "keep quiet" directive, they approved release of secret testimony by Defense Secretary Robert McNamara. In one brief exchange with members of the House Appropriations Subcommittee, McNamara had inadvertently given Diefenbaker some blockbuster campaign ammunition.

The efficiency-obsessed McNamara was asked by the congressmen whether the Bomarc missiles were not too costly, producing too little defensive effectiveness. That struck a chord in McNamara, who had been responsible for the cancellation of the Skybolt missile on grounds of inefficiency. He defended Bomarc, but only half-heartedly, saying that the missiles and bases had been expensive to build but were already in place, and their operating costs were low.

"At the very least," he told the congressmen, "they would cause the Soviets to target missiles against them and thereby increase their missile requirements or draw missiles onto these Bomarc targets that would otherwise be available for other targets." When one congressman said the Bomarcs had turned out to be "very expensive targets," McNamara replied, "They did, I agree with you fully." The suggestion that the Bomarc bases were nothing more than "targets" to attract Soviet missiles played right into Diefenbaker's hands.

Kennedy exploded when he heard of the release of the testimony and ordered the Pentagon to issue a "clarification." Within hours, the Pentagon said McNamara was referring to U.S., not Canadian, Bomarc bases; the Canadian bases were less vulnerable to attack because they were better dispersed. But the clarification never caught up with McNamara's comments.

"Happy days are here again," Diefenbaker told reporters after he saw the transcript of the testimony. "This is what I've been saying all along," he added. "McNamara's really put the skids under Pearson. This is a knock-out blow."

Dalton Camp also could not believe his luck. "Some of us thought it was was a trap because it was just too good to be true," he says. "And it came just as Diefenbaker began running out of gas. We made good use of it."

Speaking that night in Kingston, the prime minister said, "The Liberal party would have us put nuclear warheads on something that's hardly worth scrapping. What's it for? To attract the fire of the intercontinental missiles. North Bay – knocked out. La Macaza – knocked out. Never, never, never, never has there been a revelation equal to this. The whole bottom fell out of the Liberal program today. The Liberal policy is to make Canada a decoy for intercontinental missiles. . . . I told you the Bomarcs were no defence for Canada."

For the rest of the campaign, he went about the country crying, "Decoys, decoys, decoys! A decoy duck in a nuclear war!" He told a Winnipeg audience, "We don't intend to use Canada as a dumping ground for nuclear warheads." He said there was a Liberal–Pentagon partnership to turn Canada into "a nuclear dump," and at one point he said the Pentagon wanted to make Canada "a burnt sacrifice" in nuclear war.

What was remarkable was that it was Diefenbaker who, five years earlier, had leapt at the Bomarcs as a replacement for the ill-fated Arrow interceptor, which he had cancelled. Now he was attacking his own idea, but in the convoluted emotionalism of the 1963 campaign, the lapse in logic escaped his recognition.

Pearson was furious and the Americans enraged. "I've heard a lot of drivel in this campaign," Pearson said, "but I've never heard of anything so drivellish."

Kennedy and the State Department were indignant at the way Diefenbaker had used the McNamara testimony, but equally, they were mortified at having yet again handed Diefenbaker more political hand grenades. Kennedy sent a sharp rebuking memo to McNamara about his testimony. He said, "It might be worthwhile to bring to the attention of those who read (and censored) your testimony on the Bomarc in Canada, that their failure to catch the political significance has strengthened Diefenbaker's hand considerably and increased our difficulties. It would seem to me that every word in those sentences flashed a red light. They should be on the alert for our political, as well as military, security."

The Americans were angry, too, that Diefenbaker was using in his campaign speeches secret military information on the weapons carried by the U.S. North American defence interceptors. The Pentagon was incensed when the prime minister breached security by revealing in a campaign stop in Prince Albert that there were 1,200 U.S. interceptors defending North America, but that only half of them carried nuclear warheads. Although he did not deny making the statement, Diefenbaker angrily rejected the Pentagon accusation, saying, "I don't at any time reveal classified information and I have always followed that practice. However there have been statements made outside Canada which indicate the same regard for classified information does not apply."

From platform to platform and street corner to street corner across Canada, Diefenbaker fulminated against American pressures and nuclear warheads. He said the threat from Soviet bombers was over; therefore the usefulness of the Bomarcs was also at an end. He said that accepting nuclear warheads would make Canada a member of the nuclear club. He denied charges that Canada was not living up to its NATO and NORAD commitments. Condemning the Bomarc bases, Diefenbaker later said, "The two in Canada would protect no one. They were worthless so far as Toronto is concerned, Hamilton and so on. One might have been useful as far as Montreal was concerned, but their design and purpose was to protect the United States and assure that its striking power would not be undermined by bomber attack." In that comment, Diefenbaker was right, for the prime purpose of NORAD, the Bomarcs, and the interceptors was to protect the Strategic Air Command bomber force, not Canadian cities. Long after the campaign, Diefenbaker's emotions still ran high on this issue. "It was too dangerous to accept nuclear weapons when no longer would they be any defence against intercontinental missiles," he said. "I stood against what would have been the first example of proliferation and had we not stood, no one can say what would have happened in the two wars between Egypt and Syria and the little state of Israel had it been possible for any of them to have used Canada as an example and had available one or two nuclear bombs."

Impossible as it may seem, even while the prime minister's emotional anti-nuclear, anti-American campaign rolled on, his government was, in fact, still negotiating with the Americans over acquisition of nuclear warheads. In late February, Charles Ritchie saw Rusk for half an hour and, among other things, raised the question of continuing the warhead discussions. Two weeks later, Rusk said negotiations for the warheads were "continuing intermittently and we expect those discussions will go forward."

The talks were going forward in secret at senior civil servant level during February and March. Canadian officials were still trying to get the U.S. to agree to store nuclear warheads for Canadian Bomarcs and interceptors at U.S. border points. The Americans kept saying no, but they patiently went through the motions until the last weeks of the campaign, when both sides agreed to wait until the election decided the fate of Diefenbaker and the warheads.

Diefenbaker's defence minister, Gordon Churchill, privately urged the prime minister to reconsider his position on nuclear warheads, but Diefenbaker refused. Churchill wondered if the real reason for the refusal was that Diefenbaker did not want to appear to be giving in to Kennedy. Throughout the campaign Diefenbaker denied – despite his earlier statements in the House – there had ever been a promise to the U.S. to accept nuclear warheads. "We did not undertake at any time such a commitment," he said.

"I think," said Harkness, "by some process of self-hypnosis, he had persuaded himself that he never had been in favour of getting nuclear weapons. How he ever managed that I don't know. . . . It was a matter of self-hypnosis, megalomania, and being really out of touch with what the real political currents in the country were."

Diefenbaker had been given plenty of warning that his anti-Americanism could backfire. But he was unrepentant and later mused on whether he had been too muted in his onslaught against the United States. "In the light of history I wonder whether I went far enough in pointing out what was happening," he said. "But my difficulty was that I had this group of individuals in the Conservative party who suddenly became devoted pro-American. . . . They said we mustn't do anything that could be interpreted as anti-American." Any softening of his assault on the United States was barely discernible, however.

For all Diefenbaker's concentration on the Americans and nuclear warheads, the public opinion polls showed Canadians remained concerned primarily about unemployment, which a March Gallup poll rated as Canada's number one problem; thirty-four per cent of voters were primarily concerned about unemployment, only eleven per cent about nuclear arms. The public also was confused by Diefenbaker's position: a Samuel Lubell poll late in the campaign found about as many people thought Diefenbaker was for nuclear warheads in Canada as thought he was against them. On the nuclear issue itself, a poll by the Canadian Institute of Public Opinion in March 1963 showed fifty-seven per cent in favour of accepting nuclear warheads.

But even with all the power of most of the media and the Establishment against him, the polls showed throughout the campaign that Diefenbaker was more popular personally than Mike Pearson. This was a key reason why Lou Harris and other Pearson aides urged the Liberal leader not to attack Diefenbaker personally but to attack the Conservative party, and to spend more time on the issues of jobs, pensions, and the economy, and much less time on defence policies.

Harris, Gordon, and Davey recognized the validity of such a strategy because they had seen that direct attacks on Diefenbaker earlier in the campaign had made him more popular, not less. Concern about Pearson's campaign style showed up on McGeorge Bundy's White House desk in a copy of a letter written by the treasurer of the Liberal party in Ontario to a New York friend, who had sent it to Bundy. "Every time Pearson speaks," the Liberal official said, "he gives votes to Conservatives."

In the heat of a campaign, Diefenbaker had a remarkably casual attitude towards reality, which drove Pearson around the bend. "These statements went far beyond the normal exaggeration expected," Pearson said as a justification for some of the Liberals' campaign tactics. The party put out colouring books ridiculing Diefenbaker and followed him early in the campaign with a "Truth Squad," trying to use facts to refute his claims and defuse the impact of his passion. But the colouring books, the "Truth Squad," and the *Newsweek* article all generated more support, not less, for an underdog prime minister, who effectively turned the ridicule into sympathy. The Liberals "seemed to mistake our country for the United States," Diefenbaker later wrote. "And their Madison Avenue techniques came a cropper."

In spite of all his censure of the Americans in the campaign, he envisioned himself wearing the mantle of Abraham Lincoln and Franklin Roosevelt, whom he frequently quoted on substance, and he campaigned like Harry Truman and William Jennings Bryan, whom he quoted on style. His confidence grew, and as the race neared its end, he said, "My main political asset is that I know what Canadians are thinking."

Whatever the personal strains, Diefenbaker seemed reborn by the campaign while Pearson became "irritable and nervous," in Walter Gordon's words. "Mike was fed up with campaigning. . . . He had been so sure the election was in the bag," Gordon said. Still Pearson, with gritty determination, defied his nature and slam-banged across the country in the last two weeks of the campaign. But towards the end, Gordon feared it was a lot closer than originally forecast, and he worried that Diefenbaker's formidable and ferocious campaign might cost Pearson his majority victory.

Just before election day, a lengthy memorandum was prepared for President Kennedy on the Canadian election. It included a remarkably accurate forecast of the results, almost dead on in most provinces, with the exception of the Prairies. The White House bias, however, was evident. "There has been a great contrast," the memo advised Kennedy, "between the campaign tactics of Diefenbaker who has concentrated almost entirely on an emotional approach, and those of Pearson who has tried to appeal to logic. Diefenbaker, realizing that he is fighting for his political life, has been frantic. As a former trial lawyer who loved fights before juries, he is a practiced actor and a highly skilled campaign operator. . . . His main pitch this time has been as the lonely defender and friend of the average Canadian and the little man. . . .

"Pearson on the other hand, has conducted an energetic and responsible campaign based essentially on an appeal to fact and reason . . . [but] he has not been able to fire public imagination. . . . He has courageously stood up for acquisition of nuclear weapons."

After all the explosive rhetoric, the campaign bitterness, the clawing at Washington, the hostile sparks of the election were finally over. "Let us decide," said the prime minister at the end of his last whistle-stop tour, "that Canada's future will be determined by Canadians in Canada. That is the issue."

With that, Prime Minister John Diefenbaker went back to his political roots to await the results in Prince Albert, so like all the small towns where he was loved. Mike Pearson went back to Ottawa, the nation's capital, where he was respected.

Monday, April 8, 1963, dawned with icy rain whipping Prince Albert and snowflakes blanketing Ottawa. Diefenbaker was in his old-fashioned railway car on the CNR tracks. Pearson was at the Château Laurier hotel. Kennedy was at the White House. Diefenbaker spent the day telling political anecdotes and joking with reporters ("As Prince Albert goes, so goes the nation"). He walked through deep mud to the small home of a popcorn and peanut vendor, where he voted in the morning; then, smartly dressed in his blue tie and black Homburg, he strolled through a light drizzle along the Prince Albert main street, visiting, among other places, the P.O. Café, to talk to Maw Jong, the owner, about a new cocktail bar being installed. Pearson voted in the morning in Ottawa, bantered with reporters, visited his office, and spent the afternoon at his Stornoway residence. Kennedy spent the sunny afternoon with Max Freedman at the baseball stadium in Washington, where he threw out the first pitch at the opening game of the season for the Washington Senators and the Baltimore Orioles.

Nearly eight million Canadian voters went to the polls across the country after the nastiest, most personal campaign of the century. After the polls closed, Pearson sat in an armchair in his hotel room, watching the results on television and on clattering teletypes and taking phone calls from Keith Davey; Diefenbaker, still wearing his coat and vest, sat in a litter of paper in his old railway car, watching television and getting results on a direct phone line from Ottawa. Kennedy was having a small informal dinner with friends at the White House and watching Gregory Peck and Anne Bancroft win the Best Actor and Best Actress Academy Awards on television. Throughout the night, he was also getting reports on the Canadian election.

By 9:00 P.M., when the election broadcasts hit the Manitoba border, Pearson seemed headed for a majority government. But there, he was stopped cold. As results tumbled in from Manitoba, Saskatchewan, and Alberta, a Diefenbaker resurgence was under way. Pearson won only three seats in the Prairie provinces; Westerners remembered Diefenbaker and Alvin Hamilton selling their wheat to China and remembered, too, all the eastern ridicule of Saskatchewan's hero. A vote for Diefenbaker, they felt, was a punch in the nose to those eastern snobs who had plagued the west ever since their arrogant railways had pushed through the prairies at the end of the last century. In defiant salute to John Diefenbaker, his Prince Albert riding gave him the biggest majority of his political career: 14,451 votes.

Pearson fell four seats short of the majority he so badly wanted. The results were 129 seats for the Liberals, 95 for the Conservatives, 24 for Social Credit, and 17 for the NDP.

Diefenbaker had entered the campaign as an old bull heading into the slaughterhouse. Even within the Conservative party, forecasts were in the 40-to-60-seat range. Alone, unyielding and messianic, he had confounded the experts. With tenacity and mawkish sentimentality, Diefenbaker denied Pearson what had seemed a certain majority just two months earlier and gave the Kennedy administration the scare of its life. "I gave the best that was in me," Diefenbaker told reporters late election night. "I followed the course that was right." In a phone call to an old friend in Duck Lake, Saskatchewan, after the election, Diefenbaker talked nostalgically of going to Ottawa more than two decades earlier. "I went down there," he said, "to see what I could do for the common people, and the big people finished me – the most powerful interests."

"Diefenbaker was such a remarkable campaigner," says Keith Davey. "An absolutely fantastic campaigner. It's a measure of the old bugger's talent that he single-handedly stopped us from getting a majority. He had enormous appeal to older people, to lower-income people, to the less well informed. Let's face it, he was a charismatic character."

Even Pierre Sévigny, who had resigned from Diefenbaker's cabinet over anti-Americanism and the nuclear warheads issue, admired the political skills of his leader. "He had a phenomenal gift for the spoken word," Sévigny says. "He could be hypnotic. As long as he was on the platform he was happy. The greatest parliamentarian I ever saw. He was a combination of Jesus Christ, de Gaulle, and Churchill."

Diefenbaker lost the prime ministership in the big cities in Ontario and Quebec, but he won small-town and rural Canada, especially in the west. His defeat demonstrated a hesitant triumph of rationality over emotion, but he won the hearts of his fellow citizens, even his adversaries, for his defiant fighting spirit, if not for his policies. He was a masterful pragmatist and opportunist, Canada's greatest political actor of the century, done in, in the end, by the battles within himself of his insecurities, his suspicions, and his indecisiveness.

"He had an inferiority complex that big," says Ellen Fairclough, spreading her hands far apart. "That was his basic problem. His indecisiveness stemmed from that."

Diefenbaker was a man bespattered with political warts, the most improvisational prime minister we have ever had. Yet he left an indelible stamp on Canadian politics, for he understood the raw emotions of the country in a way that Pearson never did. He was Elmer Gantry; he was Clarence Darrow. He was also the embodiment of all the historical Canadian suspicions of the United States, and with his 1963 defeat, Canada's old-fashioned, Sir John A. Macdonald nationalism died too.

Conservative philosopher George Grant said in only a slight overstatement that Diefenbaker's defeat was "the last gasp of Canadian nationalism . . . the strident swan song of that hope." Grant blamed it on Kennedy: "The actions of the Kennedy Administration were directed toward removing an unreliable government in Ottawa. . . . Diefenbaker and Green must have seemed too suspicious of American motives to be allowed to remain in office."

"Diefenbaker was really defeated by Kennedy," says veteran Southam columnist Charles Lynch. Social Credit leader Réal Caouette echoed that conclusion. "What happened?" he asked. "I'll tell you. . . . It was the United States who did this to us. It was all those big financiers, those sharks who turned this campaign into a fight between the United States and Canada, and the Canadians got the short end of it."

Even in France that was the view. The headline in *Paris-Presse* translated as "Canada has voted American." Writing in *Cité Libre*, Pierre Trudeau said Diefenbaker was beaten by "les Hipsters" around Kennedy. Diefenbaker himself remained unshakeably certain that Kennedy had provided the money, expertise, and publicity to bring him down.

An argument can be made, however, that Diefenbaker destroyed himself by his managerial incompetence, perennial suspicions, and historical ghosts. "He was the most inadequate of Canadian Prime Ministers since Mackenzie Bowell," says historian W.L. Morton.

That was a sentiment echoed in the White House in conversations between Max Freedman and John Kennedy. After talking with Kennedy about Diefenbaker's defeat, Freedman wrote, "He can be left to the doubtful consolations of his conscience, the most eccentric and underworked instrument in the history of government." After another conversation with Kennedy, Freedman said, "The Kennedy Administration now finds itself dealing with a Canadian Government which it can trust."

"Heartiest congratulations," cabled Kennedy to Pearson. "The early establishment of close relations [is] a matter of great importance to me."

In newspapers across the United States, Pearson was hailed as a giant-killer, with adulation pouring out of the editorial pages of the New York *Times*, the Washington *Post*, the *Wall Street Journal*, *Time*, and hundreds of American newspapers and newsmagazines. Every paper in New York City made his election victory a front-page story; all but one made it the lead. "In Mr. Pearson," said the New York *Times*, "Canada has a man of the highest international stature, admired and trusted by the United States more than any Canadian statesman of modern times."

The ham-handed American efforts to undermine Diefenbaker had been messy but, in the end, effective. Once over the shock of the State Department press release calling the prime minister a liar, the rich and the educated had accepted the inescapable logic of the Washington position and felt embarrassed by Diefenbaker's delays in the Cuban Missile Crisis and his failure to live up to NATO and NORAD commitments. Above all that, to most Canadians, John Kennedy was a hero. A Gallup poll taken shortly before the election showed that fifty-four per cent of Canadians believed the prestige of the United States had increased in the past year, a substantial rise since the beginning of the Kennedy presidency. In a Toronto *Star* poll giving readers their choice between Kennedy and Diefenbaker, readers overwhelmingly chose Kennedy. In his polling for the Liberals, Lou Harris regularly put in a question on Kennedy's popularity. "Kennedy always had a ninety-per-cent approval rating or better," Keith Davey says.

Even Diefenbaker ally Grattan O'Leary conceded that Diefenbaker's assault on Kennedy had not worked. "Certainly it was hard for most Canadians, including Conservative M.P.'s," he later wrote, "to buy the picture of John Kennedy presented by Diefenbaker. That this most literate and articulate of Presidents could be the monster Diefenbaker painted him surpassed the powers of imagination."

Letters and gifts for Kennedy from Canadians poured into the White House during his presidency. The Fredericton Board of Trade sent an eight-pound salmon, a shillelagh was sent to him from E.C. Holub of Lethbridge, a rabbit's foot from Frank Bradly of Frankfort, Ontario, some hand-knit socks from Sadie Hallelt of Montreal, and a flood of other small gifts from Canadians, ranging from religious medals to toys for the Kennedy children. Each well-wisher was carefully thanked by the

White House staff. McGill University put on a musical comedy with a theme song to the tune of "O Canada," entitled "O Kennedy We Stand On Guard For Thee"; it was a sell-out. Thousands of letters to Kennedy tumbled into the White House; from right-wing journalist Lubor Zink, Brandon, Manitoba; from the pupils of Grade 7A in a Saskatoon school; from hundreds who signed "A Friend," "A Canadian," "A Canadian Family." Douglas Markham of Victoria tried to sell the president a musical jewellery box; Kennedy's secretary Evelyn Lincoln wrote back to say, "Although he very much appreciates your thoughtful interest, he does not wish to purchase it. . . . He hopes that you will soon be able to find work."

With all the admiration if not adulation from Canadians, Kennedy felt he had a strong base of support in Canada. After the election, Washington's joy was unconcealed, especially at the White House. "A happy ending," remembers McGeorge Bundy, reflecting on his approval of the State Department press release and his dressing-down by the president. On the day after the election, Bundy's staff scrawled on a big blackboard in the White House Situation Room, "You can stay, Mac!" Ambassador Butterworth quoted Kennedy as saying in reference to the press release, "Those fellows in the State Department were right, and they kept their nerve."

Bundy sent a memorandum to all members of the Kennedy cabinet saying, "The advent of a new government in Canada has naturally stirred nearly all branches of the government to new hope that progress can be made in effective negotiations with this most important neighbor on all sorts of problems. It is the President's wish that these negotiations should be most carefully coordinated under his personal direction through the Department of State."

Butterworth wrote to columnist Walter Lippmann, an American journalistic icon and old friend, saluting Pearson's victory as "so significant." He said, "The outcome holds salutary lessons which will not be overlooked by future aspirants to political office in Canada."

When Lou Harris gave the president a report on the election, Kennedy jokingly told him, "Well, I guess you lucked out with my friend Pearson."

Like the rest of Washington, Charles Ritchie greeted the

results with relief. "I must at once write to Howard Green [who had been defeated in his riding] to express my respect for him and my gratitude for his steady support," Ritchie wrote in his diary. "I shall not be writing to Diefenbaker. I consider his disappearance a deliverance, there should be prayers of thanksgiving in the churches."

For Bunny Pound, who had been Diefenbaker's devoted secretary since his 1952 election, it had been an agonizing campaign. "He'd lost his vision, that feeling of what he could do for the country." Looking back, Pierre Sévigny says, "In the end, the job was too big for him. It was a nation run by an immensely colourful man, but an immensely erratic man." Shaking his head in wonder, Alvin Hamilton says, "He had this desperation to be looked on as a saviour of his people who had done something big for his countrymen."

Dick Thrasher, who had been Diefenbaker's special assistant for a year and a half, had run in the election in his home area of Windsor, Ontario, and had been narrowly beaten by Liberal Eugene Whelan. A short time later, Diefenbaker named him national director of the Conservative party. "After it was all over, and as time went by," he says, "I think he was happier as leader of the opposition. In that job, he could be cross-examining again, instead of defending all the time, as he had to do as prime minister. I never saw any light-heartedness in him until he became leader of the opposition."

During the election campaign, Pearson had said one of his first priorities was to repair Canada–U.S. relations. Kennedy enthusiastically endorsed that repair project and invited Pearson to visit him at his Cape Cod retreat in Hyannis Port. The new prime minister, who turned sixty-six the day after he was sworn in, thought it would be more "politically sound" to visit Harold Macmillan in London first. He flew to London for relaxed, friendly conversations with Macmillan and his cabinet; Pearson knew personally half the members of the British cabinet and had first met Macmillan in 1923 as a student at Oxford. Like Kennedy, Macmillan was relieved to have his old friend Pearson at the helm in Ottawa instead of John Diefenbaker, who had been so much against Macmillan's dream of British membership in the Common Market and who Macmillan felt was devoid of sophistication and intellectual weight. He shared the sentiment of the Washington *Post* London correspondent, who wrote when Diefenbaker had been defeated in the House of Commons, "Fewer tears were shed over the fall of Canadian Prime Minister John Diefenbaker than over the upset of any major Commonwealth political figure since Oliver Cromwell. . . . Officials here have complained privately of [his] pious humbuggery."

There was a very different British attitude towards the new Canadian prime minister. After five easy days of becoming reacquainted with people in his favourite of all cities, London, Pearson flew back to Ottawa and on to Hyannis Port.

Chapter Nine

PLAY BALL!

"The honeymoon was on and everything that had been sour was sweet," says Charles Ritchie, reflecting on the two-day Hyannis Port meeting of Pearson and Kennedy. Americans and Canadians alike felt the glow. "There was a sense of relief that Pearson was back," says Dean Rusk. "He was an old friend. We were relieved that Diefenbaker was being replaced. Pearson had a self-confidence that Diefenbaker lacked."

Pearson, who had worked in Chicago as a young man, simply liked Americans, as he liked most outgoing people, although he still retained the view he had expressed as a University of Toronto lecturer in 1924 when he wrote that the Americans were "the greatest ballyhooers in history."

A stiff sea breeze was blowing when Pearson helicoptered into a chilly Hyannis Port, and he noted a limp, half-masted Red Ensign drooping from a flagpole, having been torn loose by the wind. The prime minister was quickly escorted to Kennedy's big, rambling white-painted frame house, with its spectacular view of the ocean. Before going inside they paused for pictures and chatted with reporters on a flagstone terrace. One reporter said, "It looks like you brought your Canadian weather with you."

"It's miserable here and it was miserable in Ottawa, too," Pearson smilingly replied, thereby insulting two cities for their weather. Kennedy laughed and said, "It takes years of diplomatic training to make a statement like that."

They immediately sat down to a lunch of Kennedy's favourite food, clam chowder and poached flounder. Looking about the dining room table, an impishly grinning Pearson cheerily chatted with old friends among the assembled American and Canadian diplomats.

Kennedy was in a joshing, inquisitive mood, shaking his head in wonderment at John Diefenbaker and asking mischievously if the State Department press release had been "helpful" to Pearson. "It probably cost me fifty seats," said Pearson.

"Kennedy gulped and changed the subject," says Ed Ritchie, who attended the meeting. Pearson was needling the president when he said the release had cost him that dearly, but it certainly did cost Pearson at least half a dozen seats in close races – the difference between minority and majority government. The State Department statement had brought Diefenbaker back to life from a condition of severe political decay. It was the Washington weapon that disintegrated his cabinet and led to his defeat in the House of Commons; but once Diefenbaker was back on the election warpath, the release became something else: a precious, vote-getting gift for Diefenbaker in rural and small-town Canada. He exploited it effectively to validate his claim of victimization by the interfering Americans. That was exactly what Kennedy had feared. "There's no doubt the State Department release was a gift to the Conservatives," says Richard O'Hagan, Pearson's press secretary at the time. "Arguably, it cost Pearson his majority." Without it, however, Diefenbaker might well have survived the crisis of late January and early February and avoided the election altogether. Thus it was truly a mixed blessing for Pearson.

Kennedy also wanted to know about the alleged "SOB" notation on the "lost memo" with which Diefenbaker had threatened him. The president wanted to know if somebody had written "SOB" on it, adding that he could not remember doing so himself. Pearson remarked that Basil Robinson, who was taking notes of the Hyannis Port conversations, had been working with Diefenbaker at the time, and he turned to him for the answer. Robinson confirmed to the president that there had been no "SOB" in the margin. Kennedy was relieved. The memo later provided a jocular moment during a party with reporters at Hyannis Port. Pearson had written out on a piece of paper several points he wanted to make in talking to the reporters, and as he handed it to Richard O'Hagan, it fell to the floor. Pearson picked it up and Kennedy joked, "You've got to watch those pieces of paper."

Pearson replied, "Just a second while I make a note in the margin here. . . . I just happened to find this on the floor."

One reporter at the party suggested that when Kennedy came to Ottawa to see Pearson he should plant another tree, and Kennedy produced a mock groan. State Department officials and Washington reporters said they had never seen Kennedy so relaxed with a foreign leader.

But Kennedy remained angry at Diefenbaker's threat to use the memo. When Charles Ritchie introduced him at Hyannis Port to Montreal *Star* reporter Peter Trueman, whose story had carried the reference to the marginal note, Trueman says, "He stared at me glassy-eyed and smartly moved away." Pearson wrote in his notes after his Hyannis Port meeting, "The President remains deeply disturbed by the action of the Canadian Prime Minister in keeping this document."

Kennedy enjoyed Pearson's bantering humour and the gift Pearson had brought with him from Ottawa, a specially made rocking chair. Both Pearson and Kennedy tried it out at one point as they shared baseball reminiscences. Pearson, who had been given a lifetime pass to Yankee Stadium even though he was a National League devotee, had played semi-pro baseball with the Maple Leafs of Guelph, Ontario. He had an encyclopedic knowledge of baseball lore that astonished both Kennedy and a canny old Boston Irishman named Dave Powers, who had been a Kennedy friend and aide since Kennedy first ran for Congress in 1946. Powers and Pearson tried to outdo each other as they hauled out baseball arcana. Powers remembered a game in Detroit where a pitcher had thrown a no-hitter, but lost the game. Powers and Kennedy were stunned when Pearson said the pitcher had been pulled in the seventh inning, having allowed no hits, and was replaced by reliever Ken MacKenzie, who let in the winning run in the tenth. It happened that MacKenzie was from Manitoulin Island, in Pearson's constituency, and Pearson had helped him get into professional baseball.

Laughing at the incredulous Powers, Kennedy nodded at Pearson and said, "He'll do!" Pearson, in fact, was more of a sports fanatic than Kennedy and had been a star at the University of Toronto and Oxford in football, hockey, and lacrosse as well as baseball.

"A grand man!" says Powers. "But I got him back, though. I asked who had the most home runs next to Babe Ruth's sixty before Roger Maris got his sixty-one in 1961. He thought maybe Jimmy Foxx or Hank Greenberg with fifty-eight. But it was Ruth with fifty-nine. He claimed I'd tricked him.

"It was great for Jack to have a man who was so easy to work with," says Powers. "They sat around the fire there swapping stories."

One thing Pearson would not do with Kennedy, though, was accept the president's invitation to go sailing in the rough waters of Nantucket Sound. Pearson said his stomach could not take it. "Touch football, baseball, basketball, tiddly-winks, or anything else, but don't take me on the water," Pearson moaned.

Their personal talks were relaxed and intimate, but their business discussions, lasting a total of ten hours (about twice as much time as Kennedy and Diefenbaker had spent in serious conversation over more than two years), were brisk, detailed, and fruitful, as they broke the logjam of Canada–U.S. issues that had been piling up because of the Kennedy–Diefenbaker feud. Pearson said it was "a stimulating experience to be exposed to the charm of Kennedy's personality and the toughness and clarity of his mind." With Kennedy in a rocking chair and Pearson in a big easy chair, they sat by a crackling fireplace off to the side of the room, ranging over a laundry list of items. Their discussions included the Columbia River Treaty, oil, lumber, fishing, East–West relations, Southeast Asia, defence production-sharing, and Canada–U.S. defence issues. Diefenbaker's long battle with Washington over nuclear warheads was quickly ended as Pearson agreed to take them in Canada under a joint-control "two-key" arrangement with the U.S., and for Canadian NATO forces in Europe. The agreement in principle was revealed informally at the end of the Hyannis Port meeting. "Within days of my assumption of office," the new external affairs minister, Paul Martin Sr., says, "Walt Butterworth, the

American Ambassador to Canada, told me that President Kennedy wanted to conclude early agreements authorizing the joint control of nuclear weapons deployed with the Canadian Armed Forces."

Details of the formal agreement were finally announced on August 16, 1963. It provided nuclear warheads to the Bomarcs and Voodoo interceptors in NORAD and to the CF-104 Starfighters and Honest John artillery rockets of our European NATO forces. Canada also later agreed to accept for storage in Canada air-to-air nuclear missiles for U.S. interceptors based in Canada and under NORAD command. As a gesture to Pearson's political sensitivities, Kennedy decided the only announcement of the deal would come from Ottawa. "We have to let them pick the time from the point of view of their politics," McGeorge Bundy advised press secretary Pierre Salinger.

Pearson made the formal announcement when Parliament was in its summer recess, and there was no significant public outcry. The first Bomarc warheads were delivered to La Macaza, Quebec, on New Year's Eve, 1963, which, in a historical irony, was the anniversary of the 1775 assault on Quebec City by U.S. revolutionary forces under General Richard Montgomery. The Bomarcs at La Macaza and North Bay were declared operational on January 16, 1964. They were there until the last one was phased out in July 1984.

"This decision in no way makes Canada a member of the nuclear club," said Paul Martin at the time. Indeed, a nuclear test ban treaty was reached with Moscow in early August, outlawing tests in the atmosphere, in outer space, and under water. Diefenbaker and Howard Green had warned for years that Canadian acceptance of warheads could jeopardize disarmament negotiations, but in the end, the agreement in principle at Hyannis Port in May had no impact whatsoever on those talks.

A more difficult issue for Pearson and Kennedy was the recent violence among dockworkers on the Great Lakes. The Canadian head of the Seafarers International Union, Hal Banks, an American, had been accused by the Canadian government of directing widespread terrorism and corruption. Pearson wanted Kennedy to put pressure on the U.S. parent union to have the SIU clean up its act in Canada. As they walked alone around the grounds of the Hyannis Port compound, Pearson asked, "What can you do about the dockworkers?" "Mike," said Kennedy, "I don't know what I'm going to do about those fuckers!" Being a Methodist preacher's son, Pearson was aghast, as he often was, at Kennedy's salty language, but he appreciated the president's help. When he got back to Washington, Kennedy discussed the problem with Willis Armstrong of the State Department, who describes one not especially successful presidential effort.

"Get me George Meany [president of the AFL-CIO]," Kennedy barked into the telephone in his Oval Office, as Armstrong sat off to the side.

"There was a long pause as the president waited with the phone in his hand," Armstrong recalls. Then the president said, "Oh. I see." He looked ruefully over at Armstrong and said, "Meany says he's busy. He'll call me back."

Meany did call back, and the president pressured him into trying to resolve the SIU problem. He also enlisted the help of his labour secretary, Willard Wirtz, who exerted his own pressure and travelled to Ottawa to pursue the matter with Canadian officials. When one difficult hurdle was surmounted, thanks to the efforts of the U.S. Labor Department, Kennedy phoned James J. Reynolds, an assistant secretary, and told him, "Jim, I just want you to know that I think you did a great thing yesterday, and I want you to know I appreciate it."

It was not the kind of follow-through Kennedy would ever have done for John Diefenbaker. But he did it again for Pearson in the summer, when a U.S. tax was imposed on the sale of foreign securities in the U.S. The tax would have hurt Canada, and Finance Minister Walter Gordon became concerned. He called Treasury Secretary Douglas Dillon in Washington, who, in turn, called Kennedy about the possibility of an exemption for Canada from the impact of the law. "The president," says Assistant Treasury Secretary James Reed, "was anxious to have our relationship improved with the Canadians." The result was an exemption for Canada.

As Pearson left the Kennedy compound, the president insisted on walking with him down to the beach, where the presidential helicopter was waiting to take Pearson back to the

Boston airport. It had begun to rain, and Pearson urged the coat-less Kennedy to go back. "No," Kennedy said. "I want to give you something when we get to the helicopter."

When they got to the end of the driveway, Kennedy stopped at a flagpole and lowered the presidential flag that was flown whenever the president was in residence. It was pelting rain by now, but Kennedy carefully rolled up the flag and gave it to Pearson as a symbol of their friendship. Later in the summer Pearson asked the White House if he could display the flag in his home constituency of Algoma East. "The President said 'Yes,'" was the response in a scribbled note from Kennedy's secretary, Evelyn Lincoln.

Observing the startling difference between the Kennedy–Pearson meeting and those of Kennedy and Diefenbaker, Charles Ritchie says the Hyannis Port talks were "tinged with euphoria." "The atmosphere was that of clearing skies after a storm – the clouds of suspicion covering Canada–U.S. relations had parted, the sunshine of friendship shone," Ritchie wrote in his diary. "There was also an undercurrent of complicity be-tween them as though they had both escaped – like schoolboys on a holiday – from under the shadow of an insupportedly tiresome and irrational Third Party and were now free, within limits, to crack jokes at the expense of the Absent One. Indeed, it was mutual relief at the departure of Mr. Diefenbaker from power which gave added savour to the encounter between them."

Assistant Secretary of State for European Affairs William Tyler, who was at the Hyannis Port meeting, says, "There was no doubt that the President was very much as his ease with Prime Minister Pearson, and . . . felt very much reassured by the conversations they had." Altogether, the Pearson–Kennedy meeting was, wrote Walter Lippmann, "a good scrubbing and a cool shower after a muddy brawl."

"The Hyannis Port meeting augurs well and seems to have got us back into a framework of rational cooperation toward shared goals," U.S. Ambassador Walton Butterworth wrote, in a somewhat smug letter to his old friend Lippmann. "The important thing to grasp is that our recent differences were over fundamentals. That is why facing up to them was so very serious and why the Pearson victory in the April 8 election was so significant. . . . I have been reassured that the average Canadian voter responded to sober appeals to reason and was unmoved by neurotic demagoguery."

As the cleansing process proceeded in Canada–U.S. relations, there were nevertheless some cautious warnings about all the euphoria. "We have made a new start," Ritchie wrote in his diary. "It remains to be seen whether the sweetness and light last."

The new start included making a deal on air routes, in response to Canada's desire to have landing rights at more U.S. cities. Kennedy suggested his old friend J.K. Galbraith look into it, and Pearson heartily agreed. "We'll both appoint him as representing each country since he's from Canada and lives in the States," Galbraith remembers Pearson saying. Within a few months, Galbraith had completed his task and new air routes were arranged.

Free trade between Canada and the U.S., a pet project of Under-Secretary of State George Ball, was also considered in the State Department. Ball says he tried to interest Kennedy in the idea, but during the Diefenbaker period the best Ball got from Kennedy was an apathetic "Uh-huh," and a comment that it was "academic." Ball, a free trade enthusiast, says it involves greater political intimacy between Canada and the U.S., but he rejects the notion of absorption. "We would have a hell of a time absorbing Canada in the United States even if Canadians wanted it," he says. "I don't know that it would get through the Congress."

But the State Department abandoned the idea of proposing free trade because of political sensitivity in Canada. "Even a hint that the United States is thinking of a far reaching agreement with Canada relating to trade," said a State Department memorandum, "might revitalize the old spectre within some Canadian circles of the integration of Canada into the United States with its concomitant submersion of Canadian nationality. . . . It would be politically very dangerous to mention this matter and . . . any initiation in this direction must originate in fact with the Canadians." It eventually did, but a quarter-century later.

Meanwhile, there were still seemingly unresolvable disputes over fish, which had gone on for a hundred years; questions of trade in oil, lead, zinc, and lumber; and disagreements over tariffs and taxes. As the months went by, Pearson, pushed by the economic nationalism of Walter Gordon, was accused in the American press of being "anti-American," "xenophobic," and "a protectionist nationalist."

The two leaders had differences, too, over Vietnam. At Hyannis Port, the president had asked Pearson for his advice. "I'd get out," the new prime minister advised. Kennedy snorted in response, "Any damn fool knows that. The question is, how?" In his self-deprecating style, Pearson enjoyed recounting that byplay with the president as an example of the easy relationship between the two men. Later there was a much more bombastic outburst by an American president when Pearson spoke out in a speech at Philadelphia, urging a cessation of American bombing of North Vietnam. Kennedy's successor, Lyndon Johnson, exploded at the speech when they met the next day for lunch at Camp David. "Lester, you pissed on my rug!" exclaimed Johnson in an extraordinary, non-stop, fist-waving, expletive-filled harangue. Later, when Charles Ritchie was given a farewell dinner on leaving Washington, LBJ again sounded off about Canada. After referring to the retiring West German ambassador, who was also at the dinner, Johnson looked intently at Ritchie and said, "The Germans are good solid friends of the United States. And the Canadians are very, very clever. First of all they come down into my back yard and tell me how to run the Vietnam war, and then they screw us over the Auto Pact."

Both Pearson and Ritchie took the presidential rebukes with diplomatic aplomb, but one wonders how John Diefenbaker would have responded.

Later still, President Richard Nixon, in conversations with colleagues, referred to the Canadian prime minister as "that asshole Trudeau." Pierre Trudeau did not get along with Ronald Reagan, whom he disdained as an intellectual lightweight.

But with all the momentary presidential–prime ministerial eruptions and confrontations both before and after Kennedy and Diefenbaker, nothing equalled the lasting and deep-rooted personal hatred and contempt between the thirty-fifth president and the thirteenth prime minister. Never before or since have Canadian–American relations sunk to such a low level.

Who was to blame? Certainly Diefenbaker was, with his

visceral, ancient fears of the grasping Americans and his obsessive detestation of the Kennedy style. And certainly Kennedy was, with his arrogance and contempt at what he considered Diefenbaker's old-fashioned humbuggery, and his failure of patience in dealing with the nationalistic demons and domestic political motives driving the Canadian prime minister. They were fated to clash.

Did it matter? Clearly, it did. "Sure," says McGeorge Bundy. "After the election the great sunlight arrived."

"Some Canadians find it very difficult to live next door to a giant," Dean Rusk says. "Pearson was able to be wholly independent. He didn't fret about U.S. power, was not at all inhibited. But it bothered Diefenbaker a great deal. There was always a sense of tension with Diefenbaker."

"Personal relationships at the top certainly play a significant role," says George Ball. "They put a personal overlay on issues."

"Of course relations at the top are extremely important," says J.K. Galbraith. "Look at the results of close relations between Churchill and Roosevelt, or Roosevelt and Mackenzie King. It's bad if you have a prickly relationship, as between Diefenbaker and Kennedy. But Pearson and Kennedy – now they were compatible, were very much alike."

Even while the two at the top rumbled at each other in the Diefenbaker–Kennedy era, some senior mandarins in Ottawa and Washington sought to carry on as harmoniously as possible. "We were still friends with our counterparts," says the State Department Canadian expert, Rufus Smith. "We still tried to get things done. But it was sometimes difficult." There were "wasted opportunities" because of the Kennedy–Diefenbaker feud, Donald Fleming said.

Willis Armstrong echoes that sentiment and says, "We talked about how we could get things done without the president and prime minister knowing about it."

The efforts of the bureaucrats were a moderating influence, which surmounted some of the brutal hostility between Diefenbaker and Kennedy, but they made a difference only at the margins. Little progress was made on the central Canada–U.S. problems.

One of President Kennedy's last projects before his assassination was an effort to streamline the handling of Canada–U.S.

relations, so that he could put his own stamp on that aspect of foreign policy. William Brubeck was named as the White House staff officer for Canadian affairs; all reports and negotiations with Canada were to flow through him. A memorandum from McGeorge Bundy to the cabinet on November 11, 1963, said, "All aspects of Canadian–American relations are of intense interest and concern to the President himself. . . . The President desires that the White House be fully informed of all significant negotiations or plans for negotiation with the Government of Canada."

Coping with a hulking neighbour ten times our size who is eating away at Canadian sovereignty is the age-old challenge for Canadian prime ministers. "It's a family relationship between Canadians and Americans," says Ritchie. "So cosy one moment and so rough the next." Pierre Trudeau once told a Washington audience, "Living next to you is in some ways like sleeping with an elephant. No matter how friendly and even-tempered the beast, one is affected by every twitch and grunt."

Years after the Diefenbaker era, McGeorge Bundy reflected on Canada–U.S. relations, saying, "We have found Canadians good people to bargain with. They lack the insecurity which so often breeds misunderstanding and deception. Indeed, that is precisely why Diefenbaker was exceptional. It was our failure to understand how exceptional he was that led us to overreact. The fact that he was exceptional also led the Canadian democratic process in the end to disown him."

"We never took Canadian affairs very seriously because there was never any sense of menace from Canada," says George Ball. But throughout history, Canadians have always felt "a sense of menace" from the United States, whether it was the threat of invasion in the 1800s or the threat of economic and cultural domination in the last half of the twentieth century. With our anxiety about whether we can sustain a separate identity north of the Forty-ninth Parallel, we have, through history, nourished our nationalism on sometimes virulent and sometimes subconscious anti-Americanism.

In his book *Sunshine Sketches of a Little Town*, Stephen Leacock wrote about a member of Parliament, John Henry Bagshaw, who was campaigning for re-election: "Anyone who has heard Bagshaw knows what an impressive speaker he is, and on this night when he spoke with the quiet dignity of a man old in years and anxious only to serve his country, he almost surpassed himself. . . .

"'I am an old man now, gentlemen,' Bagshaw said, 'and the time must soon come when I must take my way towards that goal from which no traveller returns.'

"There was a deep hush when Bagshaw said this. It was understood to imply that he thought of going to the United States."

Mordecai Richler put it more bluntly in his novel *Solomon Gursky Was Here*, saying, "Most of us are still huddled tight to the border, looking into the candy store window, scared by the Americans on one side and the bush on the other."

The yin and yang of Canadian emotions about the United States – our envy and our fear – puzzles Americans. They feel "You're just like us!" but they are painfully uninformed about things Canadian. John Kennedy liked us, but did not know us. He could not understand what was behind John Diefenbaker's belief that moral fresh air flowed across Canada. Dean Acheson, in a quote from Wordsworth, once labelled Canada the "stern daughter of the voice of God."

Even some Canadians question our frequently self-proclaimed moral superiority. "We cling to this as the white trash cling to segregation," Robert Fulford wrote years ago in the Toronto *Star*. "Heaven help us if it ever vanishes and we must see ourselves naked." It was a comment quoted mischievously from time to time by Dean Acheson. But, in truth, we Canadians retreat to the self-deluding comfort of that safe haven of "moral superiority" as part of our defensive protestation of our separate identity from the United States. It was something Kennedy never understood.

When diplomacy was overwhelmed by venom in the Kennedy–Diefenbaker years, the prime minister used public bluster as his weapon and the president used private excoriation. A few years later, former ambassadors Arnold Heeney and Livingston Merchant, who had lived through the hell of their leaders' rancour, presented a report to the two governments called "The Principles of Partnership." In urging establishment and use of a continuing consultative mechanism between the two governments, they wrote, "It is in the abiding interest of both countries that whenever possible, divergent views between the two governments should be expressed and if possible resolved, in private through diplomatic channels."

Predictably, there were Canadian cries that this meant Canada would be a "lap dog" and "a lackey," while the American response was one of yawning indifference. Even so, progress was made in the Pearson years to establish and use consultative mechanisms, ranging from a revival of regular joint cabinet committee meetings to a direct phone line between the president and the prime minister. But that didn't solve everything. "Consultation," says Charles Ritchie, "was not really understood by the Americans. They told us and we were supposed to toe the line. . . . It's what we pay for being so intimate. When Canada differs with the United States, American officials are more hurt and surprised and irritated by us than by a foreigner."

For Canada, the challenge is the delicate balance between co-operation and absorption. The United States is our national obsession. As Mike Pearson once wrote, "We like to think of ourselves as strong and free and are worried that we may have gone merely from the colonial frying pan into the continental fire."

"Canada is not an institution which can be taken for granted, a state that follows whatever the United States does regardless of whether it's beneficial to Canada," said John Diefenbaker. "That's the stand I took. That was regarded as anti-American."

Before he became president, John F. Kennedy told an audience at the University of New Brunswick, in 1957: "In the final analysis, the elimination of those various tensions and misunderstandings on both sides of the border cannot depend upon any treaty or mechanical formula or ancient statute, but must rely upon the wisdom, understanding and ability of the leaders and officials of our two nations, upon the thought and effort they are willing to give to clearing up those misunderstandings. It will require in both Canadian and American political leaders . . . patience, tact and foresight – dedicated responsible men who can look beyond the problems of the next election to see the problems of the next generation."

In their relationship, neither Diefenbaker nor Kennedy could do that. And we all lost because of their failure.

Epilogue

On November 22, 1963, John Diefenbaker was having lunch with five friends in the far corner of the parliamentary restaurant in Ottawa when Bunny Pound rushed to the table and said, "Kennedy's been shot. He's dead."

"Ohhh . . . ," said Diefenbaker, turning pale. "That could have been me." With a stricken look on his face, he jumped up from the table and walked quickly to his office. He shut his door and stayed there for half an hour. "Get Tommy," he said, wanting his colleague Tommy Van Dusen to write something for him to say in the House of Commons. "Diefenbaker disliked the man but he was awed by the office of the presidency," Pound says.

"A tribune of freedom has gone," the former prime minister told the House of Commons that afternoon. "Whatever the disagreement, to me he stood as the embodiment of freedom not only in his own country, but throughout the world. Canadians, yes free men everywhere, will bow their heads in sorrow. . . . Free men everywhere mourn. Mankind can ill afford to lose this man at this hour."

Diefenbaker would quickly revive his belief in Kennedy's satanic behaviour, however, blaming him in the years to come with increasing ferocity for his defeat as prime minister.

Kennedy's friend and Diefenbaker's unseen nemesis, Max Freedman, would write of Kennedy's death, "He will be remembered as the man who broke the furrows and walked always to the far horizons."

After his defeat by Pearson in 1963, Diefenbaker held Pearson to another minority government in the 1965 election. But he finally was overthrown as party leader in 1967, mostly by the same people who had opposed him inside the party over his battles with John Kennedy.

His last years were empty ones, especially after the death of his wife Olive in 1976. "Olive was the only thing he had left," Bunny Pound recalls. "When she died, there was nothing – no friends, no colleagues. He was a lonely old man. It was the saddest thing you ever saw, for those who knew him in his prime. . . . Nothing mattered but politics. He had nothing, no interest but politics." Towards the end, Pound would call people, asking them to have lunch with the former prime minister.

John Kennedy used to say, "In politics, you have no friends, only allies." In the end, John Diefenbaker had no close friends and no allies – but, ironically, he had millions of admirers, who remembered his "vision" of 1957 and 1958. He died on August 16, 1979. A master dramatist to the end, he had planned every detail of his elaborate funeral himself, including the train journey that took his body from Ottawa to Saskatoon for burial.

Sources

Much of the information in the text comes from personal interviews with the author, the author's own contemporary notes, articles, and broadcasts, oral history tapes and transcripts, and archival papers. Documents such as speeches, drafts, memos, letters, notes, datebooks, telephone logs, and clippings were available in the widely scattered collections listed below. The Library of Congress in Washington and the Metropolitan Toronto Reference Library were thorough and helpful sources of published information. Hansard and the Congressional Record as well as newspaper and magazine articles and broadcasts were also invaluable sources of background information.

Primary Sources

Personal interviews by author:
   Willis Armstrong (Washington)
   George Ball (Princeton, N.J.)
   McGeorge Bundy (New York, N.Y.)
   Dalton Camp (Ottawa)
   Gilbert Champagne (Hull, Que.)
   Keith Davey (Toronto)
   Ellen Fairclough (Hamilton, Ont.)
   J.K. Galbraith (Boston)
   Gowan Guest (Vancouver)
   Alvin Hamilton (Manotic, Ont.)
   Douglas Harkness, (Calgary)
   Lou Harris (New York)
   George Ignatieff (Toronto)
   Bill Lee (Ottawa)
   Charles Lynch (Ottawa)
   Ross Munro (Toronto)

Richard O'Hagan (Toronto)
Jack Pickersgill (Ottawa)
Bunny Pound (Ottawa)
David Powers (Boston)
Basil Robinson (Ottawa)
Charles Ritchie (Ottawa)
Edgar Ritchie (Ottawa)
W. Walt Rostow (Austin, Tex.)
Dean Rusk (Athens, Ga.)
Pierre Sévigny (Montreal)
Rufus Smith (Washington)
Ted Sorensen (New York)
Richard Thrasher (Windsor, Ont.)
Peter Trueman (Kingston, Ont.)
Tommy Van Dusen (Ottawa)
David Walker (Toronto)

Diefenbaker Library (Saskatoon, Sask.):
John G. Diefenbaker Papers
Oral History Transcripts and Tapes: John Dafoe, Alvin Hamilton, Marcel Lambert, Arch MacKenzie, Bunny Pound, Norman Ward.

John F. Kennedy Library (Boston, Mass.):
Audio-Visual Archives
National Security Files
Presidential Papers
White House Central Files
White House Social Files
Oral History Transcripts and Tapes: Dean Acheson, George Aiken, Charles Bohlen, Henry Brandon, McGeorge Bundy, Sir Alec Douglas-Home, Myer Feldman, Orville Freeman, Averell Harriman, Luther Hodges, Robert Kennedy, Foy Kohler, Peter Lisagor, Robert McNamara, Livingston Merchant, Myer Rashish, Teno Roncalio, Walt Rostow, Charles Roberts, Dean Rusk, Arthur Schlesinger, Hugh Sidey, Theodore Sorensen, William Tyler.

Seeley G. Mudd Library (Princeton University, Princeton, N.J.)
John Foster Dulles Papers
Livingston Merchant Papers

National Archives of Canada (Ottawa)
  Cabinet Summaries and Documents, 1957, 1958, 1959
  Gordon Churchill Papers
  Department of Defence Records
  John G. Diefenbaker Papers
  Donald Fleming Papers
  Howard Green Papers
  Douglas Harkness Papers
  Photography Records
  Oral History Transcripts and Tapes: William Bundy, Gordon Churchill, Keith Davey, Davie Fulton, Howard Green, Allister Grosart, Alvin Hamilton, Douglas Harkness, Averell Harriman, George Hees, Charles Ritchie, Dean Rusk, David Walker.

Province of Manitoba Archives (Winnipeg)
  Samuel Freedman Papers

United Nations Archives
U.S. Senate Foreign Relations Committee
U.S. State Department Archives

York University Archives (Toronto)
  Oral History Transcripts and Tapes: R.A. Bell, Ellen Fairclough, Eddie Goodman, Howard Green, Douglas Harkness, J.W. Monteith, George Pearkes, David Walker.

Secondary Sources

Acheson, Dean. *Grapes from Thorns.* New York: Norton, 1972.

Allen, Ralph. *Ordeal by Fire: Canada, 1910-1945.* Toronto: Doubleday, 1961.

Bailey, Douglas L., and Stanley Tupper. *One Continent – Two Voices: The Future of Canada/US Relations.* Toronto: Clarke Irwin, 1967.

Ball, George W. *The Discipline of Power.* Boston: Little, Brown, 1968.

Barber, Joseph. *Good Fences Make Good Neighbours: Why the United States Provokes Canadians.* Toronto: McClelland & Stewart, 1958.

Bothwell, Robert. *Pearson: His Life and World.* Toronto: McGraw-Hill Ryerson, 1978.

Bothwell, Robert, and William Kilbourn. *C.D. Howe: A Biography.* Toronto: McClelland & Stewart, 1979.

Bradlee, Benjamin C. *Conversations with Kennedy.* New York: Norton, 1975.

Brebner, John Bartlett. *North Atlantic Triangle: The Interplay of Canada.* Toronto: McClelland & Stewart, 1966.

Brock, Jeffry V. *The Thunder and the Sunshine.* Vol. 2: *With Many Voices.* Toronto: McClelland & Stewart, 1987.

Brown, Robert Craig. *Robert Laird Borden: A Biography.* Toronto: Macmillan, 1975.

Brown, Robert Craig, and J.M.S. Careless. *The Canadians: 1867-1967.* Toronto: Macmillan, 1967.

Bundy, McGeorge. *Danger and Survival: Choices About the Bomb in the First Fifty Years.* New York and Toronto: Random House, 1988.

Camp, Dalton. *Gentlemen, Players and Politicians.* Toronto: McClelland & Stewart, 1970.

Careless, J.M.S. *Brown of The Globe.* 2 vols. Toronto: Macmillan, 1959-63.

Clark, Gerald. *Canada: The Uneasy Neighbor.* Toronto: McClelland & Stewart, 1965.

Conant, Melvin. *The Long Polar Watch: Canada and the Defense of North America.* New York: Harper, 1962.

Conrad, Margaret. *George Nowlan: Maritime Conservative in National Politics.* Toronto: University of Toronto Press, 1986.

Corbett, E.A. *Sidney Earle Smith.* Toronto: University of Toronto Press, 1961.

Cox, David. *Canada and NORAD, 1958-1978: A Cautionary Retrospective.* Aurora Papers 1. Ottawa: Canadian Centre for Arms Control and Disarmament, 1985.

Creighton, Donald. *Canada's First Century: 1867-1967.* Toronto: Macmillan, 1970.

— . *The Forked Road: Canada 1939-1957.* Toronto: McClelland & Stewart, 1976.

— . *John A. Macdonald.* 2 vols. Toronto: Macmillan, 1952-55.

— . *The Road to Confederation: The Emergence of Canada, 1863-1867.* Toronto: Macmillan, 1964.

Davey, Keith. *The Rainmaker: A Passion for Politics.* Toronto: Stoddart, 1986.

Diefenbaker, John G. *One Canada: The Memoirs of the Right Honourable John G. Diefenbaker.* 3 vols. Toronto: Macmillan, 1975-77.

Doyle, Richard J. *Hurly Burly.* Toronto: Macmillan, 1989.

Eayrs, James G. *Northern Approaches: Canada and the Search for Peace.* Toronto: Macmillan, 1961.

Edmonds, J. Duncan, and Lansing Lamont. *Friends So Different.* Ottawa: University of Ottawa Press, 1989.

English, John. *Shadow of Heaven: The Life of Lester Pearson.* Toronto: Lester & Orpen Dennys, 1989.

Fleming, Donald M. *So Very Near: The Political Memoirs of the Honourable Donald M. Fleming.* 2 vols. Toronto: McClelland & Stewart, 1985.

German, Tony. *The Sea Is At Our Gates.* Toronto: McClelland & Stewart, 1990.

Ghent, Jocelyn Maynard. "Canada, the United States, and the Cuban Missile Crisis." *Pacific Historical Review* (May 1979).

— . "Did He Fall or Was He Pushed: The Kennedy Administration and the Collapse of the Diefenbaker Government." *International History Review* (April 1979).

Goodman, Eddie. *Life of the Party: The Memoirs of Eddie Goodman.* Toronto: Key Porter, 1988.

Goodwin, Doris Kearns. *The Fitzgeralds and the Kennedys: An American Saga.* New York: Simon & Schuster, 1987.

Gordon, Walter L. *A Political Memoir.* Toronto: McClelland & Stewart, 1977.

Grafftey, Heward. *Lessons from the Past: From Dief to Mulroney.* Montreal: Eden Press, 1987.

Granatstein, J.L. *A Man of Influence: Norman A. Robertson and Canadian Statecraft, 1929-1968.* Ottawa: Deneau, 1981.

— . *Canada 1957-1967: The Years of Uncertainty and Innovation.* Toronto: McClelland & Stewart, 1986.

— . *Canada's War: The Politics of the Mackenzie King Government, 1939-1945.* Toronto: Oxford University Press, 1975.

— . *The Ottawa Men: The Civil Service Mandarins, 1935-1957.* Toronto: Oxford University Press: 1982.

Grant, George. *Lament for a Nation: The Defeat of Canadian Nationalism.* Toronto: McClelland & Stewart, 1970.

Harris, Stephen J. *Canadian Brass: The Making of a Professional*

Army. Toronto: University of Toronto Press, 1988.

Heeney, Arnold. *The Things That Are Caesar's: The Memoirs of a Canadian Public Servant.* Toronto: University of Toronto Press, 1972.

Hilliker, John F. "The Politicians and the 'Pearsonalities.'" Canadian Historical Association *Historical Papers* (1984).

Hogan, George. *The Conservative in Canada.* Toronto: McClelland & Stewart, 1963.

Holt, Simma. *The Other Mrs. Diefenbaker: A Biography of Edna May Brower.* Toronto: Doubleday, 1982.

Horne, Alistair. *Harold Macmillan.* New York and Toronto: Viking Penguin, 1989.

Horner, Jack. *My Own Brand.* Edmonton: Hurtig, 1980.

Hughes, Emmet John. *The Ordeal of Power: A Political Memoir of the Eisenhower Years.* New York: Atheneum, 1963.

Hutchison, Bruce. *The Far Side of the Street.* Toronto: Macmillan, 1976.

— . *The Struggle for the Border.* Toronto: Longmans, Green, 1955.

Ignatieff, George. *The Making of a Peacemonger.* Toronto: University of Toronto Press, 1985.

Jockel, Joseph T. *No Boundaries Upstairs: Canada, the United States, and the Origins of North American Air Defence, 1945-1958.* Vancouver: University of British Columbia Press, 1987.

Johnston, James. *The Party's Over.* Don Mills, Ont.: Longman Canada, 1971.

Keate, Stuart. *Paper Boy.* Toronto: Clarke Irwin, 1980.

Kennedy, John F. *The Strategy of Peace.* New York: Harper, 1960.

Kennedy, Robert F. *Robert Kennedy in His Own Words: The Unpublished Recollections of the Kennedy Years.* New York: Bantam, 1988.

— . *Thirteen Days: A Memoir of the Cuban Missile Crisis.* New York: Norton, 1968.

Kent, Tom. *A Public Purpose: An Experience of Liberal Opposition and Canadian Government.* Kingston: McGill-Queen's University Press, 1988.

LaMarsh, Judy. *Memoirs of a Bird in a Gilded Cage.* Toronto: McClelland & Stewart, 1969.

Lasky, Victor. *JFK: The Man and the Myth.* New York: Macmillan, 1963.

Lincoln, Evelyn. *My Twelve Years with John F. Kennedy.* New York: D. McKay Co., 1965.

Lloyd, Trevor. *Canada in World Affairs: 1957-59.* Toronto: Oxford University Press, 1968.

Lower, A.R.M. *Colony to Nation.* Toronto: Longmans Green, 1946.

Lynch, Charles. *The Lynch Mob.* Toronto: Key Porter, 1988.

— . *You Can't Print That! Memoirs of a Political Voyeur.* Edmonton: Hurtig, 1983.

Lyon, Peter. *Eisenhower: Portrait of the Hero.* Boston: Little, Brown, 1974.

Lyon, V. Peyton. *Canada in World Affairs: 1961-63.* Toronto: Oxford University Press, 1968.

Macmillan, Harold. *At the End of the Day: 1961-63.* London: Macmillan, 1973.

Martin, Lawrence. *The Presidents and the Prime Ministers.* Toronto: Doubleday, 1982.

Martin, Paul, Sr. *A Very Public Life.* 2 vols. Ottawa: Deneau, 1983-85.

Martin, Ralph. *A Hero for Our Time.* New York: Macmillan, 1983.

McCall-Newman, Christina. *Grits: An Intimate Portrait of the Liberal Party.* Toronto: Macmillan, 1982.

McInnis, Edgar W. *The Atlantic Triangle and the Cold War.* Toronto: University of Toronto Press, 1959.

McIntosh, David. *Ottawa Unbuttoned.* Toronto: Stoddart, 1987.

McLin, Jon B. *Canada's Changing Defense Policy 1957-63.* Baltimore: Johns Hopkins Press, 1967.

Merchant, Livingston. *Neighbors Taken for Granted: Canada and the United States.* New York: Praeger, 1966.

Minifie, James M. *Open at the Top: Reflections on U.S.-Canada Relations.* Toronto: McClelland & Stewart, 1964.

— . *Peacemaker or Powder-Monkey: Canada's Role in a Revolutionary World.* Toronto: McClelland & Stewart, 1960.

Mosley, Leonard. *Dulles.* New York: Dial, 1978.

Nash, Knowlton. *History on the Run: The Trenchcoat Memoirs of a Foreign Correspondent.* Toronto: McClelland & Stewart, 1984.

Newman, Peter. *The Distemper of Our Times.* Toronto: McClelland & Stewart, 1968.

— . *Renegade in Power: The Diefenbaker Years.* Toronto: McClelland & Stewart, 1963.

Nicholson, Patrick. *Vision and Indecision: Diefenbaker and Pearson.* Don Mills, Ont.: Longmans Canada, 1968.

Nolan, Brian. *King's War.* Toronto: Random House, 1988.

O'Leary, Grattan. *Recollections of People, Press, and Politics.* Toronto: Macmillan, 1977.

O'Sullivan, Sean. *Both My Houses.* Toronto: Key Porter, 1986.

Pearson, Lester B. *Diplomacy in a Nuclear Age.* Toronto: S.J. Reginald Saunders, 1959.

— . *Mike: The Memoirs of the Right Hon. Lester B. Pearson.* 3 vols. Toronto: University of Toronto Press, 1972-75.

— . *Words and Occasions.* Toronto: University of Toronto Press, 1970.

Pickersgill, J.W. *The Mackenzie King Record.* 4 vols. Toronto: University of Toronto Press, 1960-70.

Preston, Richard A. *Canada in World Affairs: 1959-61.* Toronto: Oxford University Press, 1965.

— . *The Defence of the Undefended Border: Planning for War in North America, 1867-1939.* Montreal: McGill-Queen's University Press, 1977.

Redekop, John. *The Star Spangled Beaver.* Toronto: P. Martin Associates, 1971.

Reford, Robert W. *Canada and Three Crises.* [Ottawa]: Canadian Institute of International Affairs, 1968.

Regenstreif, Peter. *The Diefenbaker Interlude.* Toronto: Longmans Canada, 1965.

Ritchie, Charles. *Diplomatic Passport.* Toronto: Macmillan, 1981.

— . *Storm Signals.* Toronto: Macmillan, 1983.

Robinson, Basil. *Diefenbaker's World: A Populist in Foreign Affairs.* Toronto: University of Toronto Press, 1989.

Salinger, Pierre. *With Kennedy.* Garden City, NY: Doubleday, 1966.

Schlesinger, Arthur M. *A Thousand Days.* Boston: Houghton Mifflin, 1965.

— . *Robert Kennedy and His Times.* Boston: Houghton Mifflin, 1978.

Schull, Joseph. *Laurier: The First Canadian*. Toronto: Macmillan, 1965.

Sévigny, Pierre. *This Game of Politics*. Toronto: McClelland & Stewart, 1965.

Sidey, Hugh. *John F. Kennedy: A Reporter's Inside Story*. New York: Atheneum, 1964.

Smith, Denis. *Gentle Patriot: A Political Biography of Walter Gordon*. Edmonton: Hurtig, 1973.

Smith, I. Norman. *The Journal Men*. Toronto: McClelland & Stewart, 1974.

Sorensen, Ted. *Kennedy*. New York: Harper & Row, 1965.

Stewart, Walter. *As They See Us*. Toronto: McClelland & Stewart, 1977.

Stursberg, Peter. *Diefenbaker: Leadership Gained, 1956-62*. Toronto: University of Toronto Press, 1975.

— . *Diefenbaker: Leadership Lost, 1962-67*. Toronto: University of Toronto Press, 1976.

— . *Lester Pearson and the American Dilemma*. Toronto: Doubleday, 1980.

— . *Lester Pearson and the Dream of Unity*. Toronto: Doubleday, 1978.

Taylor, Charles. *Six Journeys: A Canadian Pattern*. Toronto: Anansi, 1977.

Thomson, Dale. *Alexander Mackenzie: Clear Grit*. Toronto: Macmillan, 1960.

— . *Louis St. Laurent: Canadian*. Toronto: Macmillan, 1967.

Truman, Margaret, ed. *Where the Buck Stops: The Personal and Private Writings of Harry S. Truman*. New York: Warner Books, 1989.

Van Dusen, Tommy. *The Chief*. New York: McGraw-Hill, 1968.

Walker, David. *Fun Along the Way*. Toronto: Robertson Press, 1989.

Warnock, John. *Partner to Behemoth*. Toronto: New Press, 1970.

White, Theodore H. *The Making of the President, 1960*. New York: Atheneum, 1961.

Winks, Robin W. *Canada and the United States*. Baltimore: Johns Hopkins, 1960.

Index

CBS

C B S